BACK to the BEACH

A Brian Wilson
and The Beach Boys Reader

Edited by Kingsley Abbott

Helter
Skelter

Publishing

This revised and updated edition published 2003 by Helter Skelter Publishing
First edition published 1997 by Helter Skelter Publishing
4 Denmark Street,
London WC2H 8LL

Typeset by Caroline Walker
Cover design by Chris Wilson

A CIP record for this book is available from the British Library.

ISBN 1-900924-46-3

Every effort has been made to contact the copyright holders of the articles in this book, but one or two were unreachable. The publishers would be grateful if the writers concerned would contact Helter Skelter Publishing.

Printed in England by The Bath Press, Bath.

For Elaine, Rosie and Luke.

Also dedicated to the memory of Timothy White

Contents

Part One: Their Hearts Were Full of Spring

The Golden Years of the California Sound. The Beach Boys moved from the simple joys of Surf Music to the maturity and complexity of Pet Sounds *and the aborted* Smile *album.*

Part Two: Surf's Up

In the seventies, attempts were made to re-define the band, and Brian Wilson's role within it. Previous excesses had caused Brian's withdrawal and subsequent "problem years"; and Dennis Wilson, seen by many as the Spirit of the group, died.

Part Three: Hang On To Your Ego

With the Beach Boys in danger of becoming the Endless Summer cliché, the eighties saw the re-emergence of Brian Wilson from his own legend and tribulations. Whilst the group seem happy to stay in California, Brian has a new agenda which may yet encompass a much greater landscape …

Part Four: Goin' On

It is time to look back over the group's story from some different and interesting perspectives, and to consider the amazing re-emergence of Brian Wilson that has seen live activity that fans never dreamed possible. Maybe the story isn't over yet...

Appendices: A Casual Look

Permissions

Foreword by Brian Wilson

It's my pleasure to write a foreword to *Back to the Beach: A Brian Wilson and The Beach Boys Reader*

The press in the UK has always treated me with much respect and honor. They always had the most interesting questions to ask. The whole thing that goes on there—people wanting to know what we were up to-well, it touches my heart. It really does.

English fans are the very best. I don't know why! When I visited a bunch of them at a London fan convention in 1988, they were shocked to see me and they were all really nice. I have always felt overwhelming love from them. England has been very good to me and the Boys. I get warm feelings—nostalgic feelings—when I'm there. It feels like a second home somehow.

Enjoy the book. And remember it was always our intention that our music would give you a bellyful of love.

Love and Mercy,

Brian Wilson
July 1997
Beverly Hills, California

Editor's Introduction

I remember it as if it was yesterday. It was a midweek evening in September or October 1962, and I was sitting on my grandmother's bed, turning the radio dial. I was explaining to her how you had to really fine tune to pick up Radio Luxembourg, and how even then it would fade a lot. That evening I was quite successful, and reception was good.

All of a sudden "Surfin' Safari" came racing from the speaker, and it was my own personal "What is that?" moment. All those bright, young sounding vocals: there was just so much going on in that record! And perhaps more importantly, in London at that time, it was totally unlike anything else around. Had I been born in the States, perhaps I might have been more aware of the R'n'B and Doo Wop vocal group influences that had converged in this Beach Boys single, but in England the sound was brand new, and it went to my heart like nothing else had done before. Here, I suspect, is part of the reason that the British press and fans have always shown such great interest, respect and honour to the band: the Beach Boys' sound arrived on our shores so fully formed and without known precedents that its impact would never abate.

In his foreword to this book, Brian Wilson talks warmly of the reciprocal love between the band and their British fans, and anyone who was at the 1988 Beach Boys "Stomp" Convention, at which Brian was the surprise guest, will give testament to that feeling. *Q* magazine described the moment when a curtain was drawn back to reveal a smiling Brian at the piano thus: "A stunned silence, broken only by the collective sound of jaws hitting the floor, then the whole place, as one, is on its feet, applauding and applauding and applauding".

Back to the Beach contains many of the most important articles on The Beach Boys, some written contemporaneously, and others written as retrospective overviews of particular events of Beach Boys history. Many have been specially written, or adapted, for this publication. My guiding light in selecting the articles was simple: to build a picture of the band insofar as it relates to the growth of their music, so that any future students of 20th century music could find at least some answers to the question "How did Brian Wilson and The Beach Boys make such wonderful music?" It should be borne in mind, that this book is not a biography, it is a companion to the band's music, and accordingly, personal aspects of the story that do not impinge directly on the development of the music have been omitted. Such elements have been dealt with more than adequately elsewhere.

That the recordings of Brian Wilson and The Beach Boys are of prime importance to the history of twentieth century popular music is beyond question. Along with The Beatles they are the true innovators of the post-war era. Their voices and their vocal arrangements gave them an instantly recognisable identity, which blended with Brian Wilson's songs and studio mastery to set the standard for others to try and match. It should also be remembered that while The Beatles had George Martin as their producer to help them through the intricate arrangements, multi-tracking and studio trickery, of *Revolver* and *Sgt Pepper*; on "Good Vibrations", *Pet Sounds* and the the Beach Boys' other ground-breaking recordings, it was Brian who was the producer-arranger: he alone translated the music he heard in his head into harmonies, strings, and horn sections.

There is undoubtedly a British, and personal, perspective in the selection of material for this book. The media in Britain recognised the value of The Beach Boys early on, and have maintained this high view of them throughout the years; indeed recent polls in *The Sunday Times* and *Mojo* magazine both voted *Pet Sounds* the greatest album ever made, and a recent *Mojo* poll of musicians and producers nominated "Good Vibrations" as the best ever single. *Pet Sounds* and the surrounding sessions, not surprisingly, are well represented in this collection. There is also plenty of material about the legendary unreleased album *Smile*, and the solo work of Brian Wilson in particular. That there are very few articles on the pre-*Pet Sounds* era in this book is because at that time there just wasn't any serious rock criticism from which to now draw. When the Beach Boys cut their early records, there were no serious rock magazines on either side of the atlantic.

All the pieces included in *Back to the Beach* are presented chronologically according to the period of Beach Boys history that they discuss, rather than the time when they were written or first published. As this project grew and grew, we discovered against our will, we had far too much material to cram into a book of a size that would be manageable and economically viable. We were extremely sad to have to omit certain articles previously planned for inclusion, and to these writers we send our greetings, thanks and apologies. Interspersed amongst the main pieces, you will also find excerpts from British reviews of a selection of the singles and albums as they were originally issued.

Finally, *Back to the Beach* was conceived both as a book to read through from cover to cover, and also as something to pick up and dip into repeatedly over a number of years. Hopefully, when in ten years time, you buy a copy of *Pet Sounds* on mini-digital floppy disc or the finally released and remastered *Smile* box set you will still find insight and commentary in this book that will add to your understanding and appreciation of the timeless music of Brian Wilson and the Beach Boys.

The reaction of everyone that replied to my enquiries has been tremendous, and I hope that at least a little of their enthusiasm comes through in the book. My thanks go to all the writers whose work is included here: Neal Umphred, Peter Doggett, Nick Kent, Jules Siegal, Tom Nolan, Shelly Benoit, David Fenton, John Tobler, Richard Williams, Timothy White, Jerry McCulley, Bill Holdship, Melodye Dorst and Dominic Priore. Very special thanks go to Stephen McParland, who was originally responsible for turning me from a passive fan into an active one, and to David Leaf, whose input and help with this book has been invaluable. Special thanks also go to Marilyn Wilson and Steve Kalinich who came on board through the efforts of Daniel Rutherford. Thanks go to Andrew Doe for the "Dramatis Personae" which we were at one stage planning as a separate mini-production. And to all the kind and helpful people who have helped, either directly or indirectly along the way, my thanks are due to Evelyn Bernal at *Rolling Stone*, Mike O'Connell, Lauri Klobas, Max Bell, Jeff Tamarkin, Tony Asher, David James, Steven Dunn, Paul Shakespeare, Charlie Brennan, Mike Grant, Roy Gudge, Nick Guy, Vivien Kemp, Chris and Pip White, Phil Wilcock, Stuart Talbot, John Francis, Peter Whitfield, Patrick Curran, John Purdue, Sean

Macreavy, Mark Service, David Toop, John Reed, Pete Frame, Goran Tannfelt, Ingemar Gustavsson, Elliot Kendall, Andy Paley, Luke Abbott, Stephen Lumb, Mike Wheeler and friends, Alan and Stephanie Franks, Mick Patrick and Keith Beach. As always at this point there is a nagging doubt that I will have forgotten someone, so I beg forgiveness if I have. Thanks are perhaps due from all of us to Sean Body of Helter Skelter Bookshop and Publishing for the idea of the book, having the courage to entrust the project to someone he hardly knew, and believing in it all the way.

Finally, of course, all of this counts for nothing, but for the work across 35 years of Carl Wilson, Dennis Wilson, Mike Love, Alan Jardine, Bruce Johnston and all those involved in keeping the good ship 'Beach Boys' afloat for all these years...

And to Brian Wilson goes our thanks, love and respect.

Kingsley Abbott
August 1997

Reaction to the first printing of *Back To The Beach* in 1997 from the press and fellow fans was literally heartening, as publication came very shortly after a quad by-bass operation that I had that Autumn. The reviews showed that the book had been received in the way that I had intended – like a 'cut-and-come-again' cake – with goodies to return to over time. After the first and a second print had sold out, Helter Skelter decided that a third printing should include updates and extensions to the story in an extra 32 pages. Given this opportunity, I wanted to add certain aspects that I felt were slightly lacking in the first edition as well as accounting for the tremendous resurgence of interest in Brian since 2000. For the former, I have added a wide perspective from Carl, a more specific one from Van Dyke Parks, and spoken afresh to Bruce Johnston and Tony Asher. My thanks go to all the writers and interviewees, and especially to Sean Body at Helter Skelter for allowing me the luxury to indulge myself further.

Kingsley Abbott
June 2002

PART ONE

Their Hearts Were Full Of Spring

The Beach Boys: The Capitol Years
by David Leaf

*The key relationship in the early years of The Beach Boys career was that with Capitol Records. The first piece in this book takes a critical look at that relationship, and illustrates how it played a key part in Brian's breakdown and subsequent withdrawal from the music business. This piece was written in 1992 for the Capitol Records 50th Anniversary in-house book. David Leaf is a television writer and producer ("You Can't Do That: The Making of A Hard Day's Night"; "The Unknown Marx Brothers"). His writings on the Beach Boys include his much sought after biography (*The Beach Boys And The California Myth*) and liner notes for Capitol Records' re-issues of their Beach Boys catalogue.*

Spring 1962, in Hawthorne, California, an obscure working class town just about a dozen miles with the top down from the Capitol tower, lived a 19-year-old adult child who was poised on the cusp of immortality.

One day soon he would create a body of work so commercially and artistically valuable that, with his family, he would simultaneously solidify rock's importance in the market place, confirm its validity as an artform, and challenge and overturn the conventions that governed artists in the music business. That boy, drawing on a creative well as deep as the nearby Pacific, would, between 1962 and 1968, embellish, embrace, and conceive musical innovations that would forever change both the creative record-making process and the record company-artist relationship.

However, before that was going to happen, that young musician, who grew up loving not only rock and pop but Gershwin too, had to get a record deal, had to find a way to get his music out. He may have been deaf in one ear, but there was this sound in his head and he had a feeling it was something he should share with the world.

Fortunately, his father also sensed the boy had something. He wasn't quite sure how to sell it, but he was going to give it his best shot. So quickly, let's set the scene. Imagine this burly, ambitious, pipe-smoking man who storms into record companies with a demo tape. On it were his son's first songs ... exuberant tunes about surfing and hot rod ("Surfin' Safari", "409") and a plaintive love ballad ("Surfer Girl").

His boys – The Beach Boys – had scored a hit with their first record, a crude curiosity called "Surfin'", released in 1961 on a tiny Californian label, Candix Records. It reached the top 10 locally, No. 75 Nationally. Then, the record disappeared. Sunk. Without a trace. Like a surfer hit in the head by his board.

But this man is determined to get a major label deal for his kids. He understands enough about the record business to know that only a major label can get you a follow-up hit. Remember, it's the era when one-hit wonders were the rule, not the exception. Nobody yet knew that the Beach Boys were destined to break all the rules.

So he makes the rounds. He's rejected at Dot (Wink Martindale loved it but his boss was certain "surf" was a fad that had crested). Decca said no, too. Liberty, as well, thought the Beach Boys were not worth a contract.

But Murry Wilson was nothing if not persistent. Russ Regan, who had signed the group to Candix and had come up with their name, advises Murry to try Nick (Nik) Venet at Capitol. Regan knew that Venet, who was only 21, had youthful ears, that the Beach Boys might appeal to him. So in the spring of 1962, Murry goes to Capitol and plays the tape for Venet, who immediately falls in love with the group's sound and songs. And Murry leaves that day with a deal. Just like that, the Beach Boys – brothers Brian, Dennis, and Carl Wilson, their first cousin Mike Love and David Marks (in 1963 to be permanently replaced by returning founding member Al Jardine) – became Capitol recording artists.

Brian Wilson and the Beach Boys' tenure at Capitol Records from 1962-1969 was one of the most successful in the history of the company and the music business. More than just hits, though, Beach Boys records meant quality. The up-tempo numbers featured supercharged backing tracks ("Surfin' U.S.A.", "Be True To Your School"), incredible vocal gymnastics ("Help Me Rhonda", "Do You Wanna Dance") and the best white rock 'n' roll around ("Fun, Fun, Fun", "I Get Around"). The ballads, where Brian's heart still shines through, are masterpieces of heavenly harmonies ("Surfer Girl", "Girls On The Beach"), and soaring falsetto ("The Warmth Of The Sun", "Don't Worry Baby").

One after another, those now-familiar songs – the intricate instrumental arrangements, the complex harmonies – emerged almost full-blown from inside Brian's head. With the help of the Beach Boys and a lot of talented session musicians, Brian turned those feelings into incredible records.

It seemed like each Beach Boys release showcased a new idea (the strange stops of "Wendy", the extraordinary harmonies of "When I Grow Up", the majestic, symphonic opening to "California Girls", the unique breaks in "The Little Girl I Once Knew", the track dropping out on "Sloop John B", the shifting tempos of "Wouldn't It Be Nice", the orchestral magnificence of "Here Today" and "I'm Waiting For The Day") which all lead up to what Brian called his pocket symphony "Good Vibrations", a landmark single which managed to somehow sum up everything that had gone before and yet present it all in a brand new way.

Besides all the smash singles, just about every album was loaded with great stuff, too, like "Spirit of America" or "Don't Back Down"; songs that might have been hits for other groups had to fight to stand out on the Beach Boys' LPs. There were the classic "B" sides ("She Knows Me Too Well", "Let Him Run Wild"), accapella reveries ("And Your Dream Comes True" and the wordless "Our Prayer"), complex instrumentals ("Let's Go Away For A While", "Diamond Head"), wonderful vocal workouts ("You're So Good To Me"), neglected latter day treasures ("Wonderful", "Darlin'", "Passing By" and "Time To Get Alone") and even the cover versions ("Hushabye", "Why Do Fools Fall In Love") – all with something special to say.

Brian's best compositions were hook-filled melodies seemingly plucked from the heavens, featuring jazz-influenced chords, changes and modulations, many of which were new to rock, some having never been heard anywhere before. When those sounds were combined with candid, autobiographical lyrics ("In My Room", "Please Let Me Wonder", The *Pet Sounds* album [especially "I Know There's An Answer", and "I Just Wasn't Made For These Times"], "I Went To Sleep", "Busy

Doin' Nothin'"), the songs became nothing less than Brian Wilson's soul on vinyl. Maybe more than anything, the depth of those honest feelings accounts for the timeless appeal of the Beach Boys records.

Yet during the sixties, for all their commercial and creative success, the Beach Boys – thanks or no thanks to Murry Wilson – were never really welcome at Capitol.

What caused the friction? Probably the bottom line was just the way the record business was run in the early '60s. When the Beach Boys signed with Capitol, it was standard procedure for the record company to control every aspect of their artists' music, what Venet would later term "the major label syndrome". In those days, staff A&R men signed singers and vocal groups, chose songs, hired musicians and arrangers and produced the company's artists in company studios. These A&R men oversaw everything from promotion to cover art, from unions to budgets. There was no such thing as a producer's royalty. The staff A&R men were on a salary; they produced the records. That's the way it was, and it was a system that worked.

Like most of the major companies in 1962, Capitol concentrated on producing classy pop music for an adult audience. When Murry took on the Tower, there was a lot of resistance at first; after all, Brian and the Beach Boys were just boys. But by the group's third LP, *Surfer Girl*, Brian had what he wanted, the freedom to take the music he had in his head and put it on record, with no company personnel hovering nearby to break the mood or second-guess his creative decisions.

The Beach Boys thus became the first self-contained, self-produced group in rock; the first to decide which songs they would record; the first to write the vast majority of their own material and to own their own publishing. The Beach Boys were also the first major label rock group to move out of the company's in-house recording studios. Even the Beatles always recorded at EMI's studios.

There would be other "firsts". In 1966, Brian would become the first artist from a group to release a solo single (the heartbreaking "Caroline No") and the Beach Boys would be the first group to get their own custom label, Brother Records, which was designed (but never used) as an outlet for Brian's more exotic experiments.

As the Beach Boys' and Capitol's history tells us, however, none of it came easy, and the battle scars are still there today. Basically, as Venet would later observe, Brian Wilson was five years ahead of his time in the business. When the Beach Boys came along, accepted practice was to get as much product from a group as the market could stand, get it out there as quickly as possible and as soon as the public's taste had changed, get rid of the group.

Steve Douglas, an artist and producer probably best-known for his sax playing, is unique in Beach Boys history in that not only did he play on most of their best records, but in 1965, he moved to the Tower as a label executive. Douglas says that by the time he was working at Capitol as head of singles A&R, the company's position toward the Beach Boys had solidified into a pragmatic one – "As long as you're selling records, you can do what you want".

In '64 and '65, The Beach Boys' sales were second only to the Beatles at Capitol. (Douglas remembers a meeting where it was discussed that the two groups provided 56% of the company's revenue). Still, as Douglas recalls, there was always "an attitude that rock 'n' roll is a passing thing; Capitol was a pop label … Al Martino … Nancy Wilson … The Lettermen".

It was this antipathy for rock that in part fueled Capitol's desire to milk the Beach Boys for new records, because there was always a sense that the ride would end soon. Like most of the industry, they didn't yet realise that it was a permanent wave. Additionally, as Douglas explains, "there was always pressure on them to come up with stuff" and "Brian … a sweet, innocent kind of guy, no sense of business acumen or slickness" would do his best to meet the demand for product.

Murry, on the other hand, was, by all accounts, overzealous in his fights with Capitol, but it was often necessary, or so the late disc-jockey and lyricist Roger ("Don't Worry Baby") Christian insisted. "If it weren't for Murry in the early days, pushing, the royalties wouldn't have been what they were. Murry fought hard to get things straight."

Considering how important the Beach Boys were to Capitol's bottom line, Christian felt the label never treated Brian with proper respect. According to Christian, Capitol showed little interest in or sensitivity to Brian's value or his growing artistic achievement, be it the day Brian was made to feel unwelcome at a company party for another artist on the label or the time the Beach Boys recorded "The Lord's Prayer" and Capitol was unenthusiastic about the results. Christian: "That crushed Brian because that was a work of art. No matter how great his accomplishments were, he'd pick up the negative vibes and retreat." As Brian himself told journalist and publicist Earl Leaf in the mid-60s, "I just want to adjust to the music industry as much as possible."

He made quite an adjustment. Between 1962 and 1969, the Beach Boys provided Capitol with a staggering 13 studio LPs, and that doesn't include *Party*, *Concert*, *Christmas*, *Stack-O-Tracks* and hits compilations. Considering the personalities involved, it's remarkable that so much great music was made and released.

From the moment in August 1962 that the Beach Boys' Capitol debut 45, "Surfin' Safari", entered the *Billboard* charts until their final and appropriately titled single, the gorgeous and underrated "Breakaway", fell off the Hot 100 exactly seven years later, the Beach Boys had 34 chart records, 26 top 40 hits, 12 top ten singles and three No. 1's.

From 1963's *Surfer Girl* album through 1965's *Summer Days...* LP, Beach Boys albums struck gold with almost monotonous regularity. Then the changing currents of popular music proved too treacherous for the group. In the face of the Beatles' *Rubber Soul*, Brian went introspective. The next album was to be very personal and spiritual, his favorite sounds. Unfortunately, Brian's new music was ahead of both the Beach Boys' still-stuck-in-the-sand image and Capitol's executives.

As Brian began his experiments in the fall of '65, Capitol was demanding new Beach Boys product (Douglas: "There was further pressure when they heard the weirdness of *Pet Sounds*"). Brian was forced to interrupt the creative flow to record *Beach Boys Party!* That was just about the last time Brian succumbed to Capitol's needs. For at least this next album, Brian was determined to take his time and get it right.

The result was *Pet Sounds*, a record that unbelievably, given its exalted status today, Capitol didn't want, primarily because they didn't know how to sell it to the group's predominantly male audiences.

Ironically, at the same time Capitol and American Beach Boys fans were distancing themselves from the new music, rock critics, English fans, and musicians like Paul McCartney, were declaring that Brian was a genius. In a 1990 interview, McCartney not only acknowledged that *Pet Sounds* was his primary influence during the creation of *Sgt Pepper*, but said "I've often played *Pet Sounds* and cried… it may be going overboard to say it's the classic of the century, but to me, it certainly is a total classic record that is unbeatable in many ways."

But in 1966, there was not much enthusiasm for *Pet Sounds* in the Tower, and the label quickly assembled the first of the highly successful Beach Boys' greatest hits albums.

It's almost impossible to imagine anything like that happening today. Artists who achieve the kind of stature that Brian Wilson had earned by 1966 are nurtured, not constantly pressured. If Stevie Wonder or Michael Jackson or even Guns 'N' Roses want to take three years between albums, "That's ok", the execs say, "They're the artists. Whatever they want". But it was Brian who took the shots, who earned for other artists the right not only to record what they wanted but to record at their own pace. If nothing else, the one lesson Brian learned from his final Capitol days was how *not* to record.

The demand from Capitol for more commercial product, not spiritual gems like "God Only Knows" (which, in '66, McCartney called the greatest song ever written) was a source of significant disagreement, both between the group and the label and within the group itself. And as Brian embarked on the recording of "Good Vibrations" and the late, lamented and still-unreleased *Smile* LP, the group's internal relationship and the one with Capitol started to sour.

In the midst of all this thickening bad blood, there was one final improbable triumph: "Good Vibrations", a record that in length, style, subject, and mood changed the way producers and musicians viewed the record-making craft. It soared to the top of the charts in the late fall of '66, and became the Beach Boys' first million-selling single. With the promise of *Smile* on the horizon, The Beach Boys, if you read the rock press of the day, and as incredible as it may seem today, were creatively hurtling past the Beatles. Brian just needed some time and space. He didn't get it.

In part trying to get a more equitable deal, and in part searching for a way to make sure that Brian's heartfelt art wouldn't be rushed or perfunctorily released as had happened with *Pet Sounds*, the Beach Boys sued Capitol. While the goal was to bring Capitol to the bargaining table, the ultimate, unexpected result was something close to suicide.

Just when it seemed that the group and the label had reached an accomodation, two events made all the squabbling irrelevant. In May of 1967, Brian put *Smile* aside. And then on June 1, the Beatles released *Sgt. Pepper's…*, usurping the artistic and technological claims that *Smile* mythologists had assumed would accrue to Brian and the Beach Boys. The production race was over.

Unfortunately, the strain of all the work, the hard-fought victories and occasional defeats had taken their toll on Brian. And while he managed to squeeze out one last single, "Heroes and Villains", he basically quit. After five precedent-setting years, Brian was again first – in 1967, he was the first rock 'n' roll burnout. The demands for new product, the drug use, and the internal and external pressures he could no longer bear or control were too much, so Brian put down the musical reins and saved his life.

The group's moment, too, had passed. From a commercial standpoint, all that remained of their first Capitol era was a fast plunge into obscurity, buffeted by more hits re-issues and a little self-produced Beach Boys nostalgia, "Do It Again", an anomalous hit in riot-plagued 1968.

In the wake of the assasinations of Martin Luther King and Bobby Kennedy and the tumultuous Democratic National Convention in Chicago, listeners wanted to get out of their heads, not into the Beach Boys. Musically, their latest (Brian's favorite … the gentle, peaceful *Friends*) was a plea that fell on deaf ears. Even if Carl Wilson had risked jail by declaring himself a conscientious objector; even if Brian and Dennis were living lives so unusual that no hyperbole could exaggerate their strangeness; even if Mike was meditating right alongside the Beatles – the Beach Boys' image was still striped shirts.

By 1969, when the Beach Boys left Capitol, record companies were bending over backwards to please their artists. Where Murry once had to fight to get Brian a producer *credit*, let alone payment, producer's royalties were becoming commonplace. Five and even six figures signing bonuses were not unheard of.

For Capitol and the Beach Boys, the industrywide changes came too late. Like a good marriage gone bad, there were too many bitter words that couldn't be taken back. And so the Beach Boys left the label. Ironically, the music they left behind was so powerful that five years later, a repackage of hits would yield a No. 1 album, *Endless Summer*, and help turn the Beach Boys finally and forever, into America's band.

Since 1974 and until 1990, Capitol was an inconsistent keeper of the flame. Frequently criticised for their cavalier treatment of the Beach Boys' classic work, the label more than redeemed itself when, to overwhelming critical and popular acclaim, Capitol reissued the group's sixties catalog on CD in 1990. This made the music available to a new generation of fans so they could hear for themselves why composers like Randy Newman consider Brian Wilson's work with the Beach Boys the most important pop music of our time.

© 1992 David Leaf (All Rights Reserved)

Original Reviews Part 1

Surfin' U.S.A.

"More surfing song stuff … it will do for dancing even though you may not have a surf board on which to twist" *Disc and Music Echo*

"…fast moving very teen beat number … Chuck Berry fans won't like it, but plenty of other people will." *Melody Maker*

"…proves you can't keep a good tune down…" *NME*

Shut Down.

"A mechanical item about a teen motor race…" *NME*

"… a jaunty number…it's about a hot rod and is a very polished professional effort…" *Melody Maker*

Fun, Fun, Fun.

"Typical Chuck Berry backing on this pounding beater…" *Record Mirror*

"…white boy group sound … surf or drag music, whatever you like to name it, here again in guitars and group voice … I find it more of a drag than a dragster." *Melody Maker*

I Get Around.

"Falsettos and vibratos and the surf twist rhythm that invariably backs them… another of those songs that glorify speeding… poor material, but a shattering beat and an arresting vocal performance…" *NME*

"I like the harmony…" *Disc and Music Echo*

"… sounds a monotonous trip to me." *Melody Maker*

Understanding The Beach Boys
For The Best In Surf Music
by Stephen J McParland

There must be thousands around the world who still think of The Beach Boys as purely a surf group. Indeed they were that only for a short time in the early sixties. In this short piece their surfing roots are explained and put into the context of the wider eventual story. Stephen McParland is an Australian to whom the rest of the world goes for information about Surf Music, Brian Wilson and the Beach Boys. He has an ever growing list of publications to his credit, all of which are worthy of further investigation by afficianados.

Surf music and the Beach Boys have been synonymous for many years, but in actual fact their product was never really surf music in the true sense of the word.

For many, surf music is epitomised by a high falsetto and bright harmonies, yet when you analyse this form, the only conclusion you can reach is that it is a musical expression ABOUT surfing and its related activities. The Beach Boys actually sang ABOUT surfing, and that is one of the major differences between what people perceive as surf music and what IS surf music.

Surf music in its original form was simply a type of instrumental music that was performed by a number of small combos that usually comprised members who lived in beach side areas. The music was a mixture of various styles and influences, ranging from Johnny & The Hurricanes, Link Wray, Duane Eddy, etc., to ethnic melodies, particularly the Latino and Chicano sounds emanating out of East Los Angeles.

These styles were all absorbed, adapted and modified until slowly but surely an identifiable sound, a true form of folk music, evolved. This sound was christened surf music simply because the majority of the recipients of the music were surfers or beach goers. It became THEIR music.

Much of this early music echoed a relatively strong rhythm and blues sound, often with a saxophone backing, but as a more distinctive guitar style evolved (courtesy of Dick Dale's work with reverb), the saxophone was pushed further to the background until it was virtually discarded.

This musical development was taking place during 1960 and early 1961 and it was this period that also saw the Beach Boys develop as a musical unit. However, being from Hawthorne, about five miles inland from Manhattan Beach, the happenings referred to earlier had little effect on the musical aspirations of those who would soon find themselves in the group – at least at this time.

Once "the sound" had been established and Dick Dale and his group began filling the 3,000 person Rendezvous Ballroom in Balboa to capacity, a young Carl Wilson would occasionally venture the thirty/ forty miles down Route 405 to the peninsula to catch Dick and his Deltones in action. However, being barely fifteen years old and certainly the baby of the group, not much attention was paid to what he had to say, particularly his babbling about "the sound" he had heard down in Balboa.

As far as music was concerned in the Wilson household, only two individuals had any say: Murry the patriarch, and Brian the musical creator and eldest son. Although both were musically worlds (if not galaxies) apart, vocal music and sweet melodies were their dual focus. Vocal music to Brian meant groups such as The Four Freshmen. Surf music, as yet still unchristened (but in existence), offered little in the way of interest.

Brian's first foray into a recording studio (although an earlier session has been mentioned to this author, but not yet verified) during the summer of '61 produced a folk tune about the Rio Grande, complete with four part harmony courtesy of Brian, Al Jardine, Gary Winfrey (a friend of Al) and Keith Lent (a friend of Brian). The studio chosen for this auspicious debut was operated by Hite Morgan, a music business acquaintance of the senior Wilson. Murry had tried unsuccessfully to break into the music business for many years.

While Brian was listening to and memorising the vocal technique of The Four Freshmen and wasting his time cutting folk material, the rumblings heard at nearly every beach side hop were finally beginning to eke their way onto a few local radio stations.

The first of these were "Moon Dawg" by The Gamblers, "Underwater" by The Frogmen, "Church Key" by The Revels and "Mr Moto" by The Belairs.

"Mr Moto" is particularly important because apparently it was a real favourite of Carl's. The young Wilson was then a struggling guitarist, occasionally going for lessons from John Maus (later to emerge as John Walker of The Walker Brothers). At best, Carl was a mediocre guitarist; Al Jardine was vaguely adequate on stand up bass; Brian was a reasonably accomplished pianist, Dennis was not much into music and cousin Mike appeared to spend most of his time worried about his receding hairline, unable to come to grips with the saxophone that hung like an albatross around his neck. By the late summer of '61 this was The Beach Boys, as yet unnamed and without a recording contract or a definite musical direction.

Like most Southern California teenagers, the beach was a familiar place to the Wilsons and their friends, but other activities usually took preference and so the beach and related activities remained an occasional adventure, rather than a constant challenge. After all, they were from Hawthorne!

However, of all the fledgling "group" members, Dennis was at least intrigued, and whenever he had access to some wheels he tried his hand at the sport of surfboard riding. Dennis was usually the first to try anything; usually because it was new and new was exciting. So enamoured was he by his attempts to master both board and waves, his constant prattling soon developed into a song that ultimately bore the combined credit of Brian Wilson and Mike Love.

At this point it should be stressed that Dennis was no surfer. He simply indulged in the sport more as a fad than as a lifestyle.

With a song to their credit and some money left by their parents, who had taken a few weeks vacation in Mexico, the Wilson brothers combo booked some time at Keen Recording Studios in Beverly Hills during early October, and committed the song "Surfin'" to tape. Those present on this auspicious occasion were Brian, Al, Mike and Carl. Interestingly, Dennis, whose idea it was to record a song ABOUT surfing failed to appear at the prearranged date.

The song, backed with a recording of "Luau", (by the same personnel) eventually surfaced as a single on the small Candix record label in early December 1962, coinciding with the release of The Original Surfer Stomp (on Del-Fi Records) by future Beach Boy Bruce Johnston.

By this time the term surf music had been established, particularly with the release in September of "Let's Go Trippin'" by Dick Dale, the first recognisable surf music hit.

Yet the Beach Boys' recording of "Surfin'" was NOT surf music. It possessed none of the elements that were then identifiable with the musical genre. All it had was the word surf in the title and lyrics. Instead, it was a musical story ABOUT the surfing experience, like someone recounting their past vacation. Its musical roots lay in a style of popular music performed and recorded by fellow Californians … Jan & Dean.

The "bop, bop, dit, dits" in "Surfin'" were taken straight from Jan & Dean's 1959 hit for Dore Records "Baby Talk". Even "Luau" written by Bruce Morgan (and later recorded by popular surf band Dave Myers and The Surf Tones as "Laguna Limbo Luau", included on the various artists' longplayer *Surf's Up At Banzai Pipeline* issued as Northridge 101 in early 1963) bore none of the hallmarks of surf music. It was simply a case of the A side getting the exposure at a time when interest was being focused on anything SURF. Nonetheless it was THE first vocal recording ABOUT the surfing experience.

The single received considerable local airplay, ultimately peaking nationally at #75, and early in the new year another session was booked to produce a follow up. This time Dennis tagged along and a total of four tunes were waxed: three vocals "Judy", "Surfer Girl" and "Surfin' Safari" and one instrumental, the short "Karate" (aka "Beach Boy Stomp").

Again there was no effort made to inject authentic surf music sounds into the vocal sides although there was a half hearted attempt made on "Karate". This ultimately proved that the group's knowledge and understanding of the genre was basic at least.

By the time of these early February recordings, the group (now dubbed the Beach Boys) were attempting to get their live act together, performing at a variety of local hops. Their repertoire at this stage basically comprised standard rock and roll tunes with of course their one hit thrown in. Instrumentally they barely held their act together, which certainly did not endear them to their teenage audience, most of whom were used to more experienced and adept instrumental and R&B combos.

At this point a certain amount of animosity began to develop amongst the more beach side teenage groups who viewed the Beach Boys as exploiters rather than extollers.

"How could they sing ABOUT a way of life they had not or were not experiencing?"

This situation persisted for some time, but for the majority of America and the world, The Beach Boys ruled while the real protagonists and exponents of surf music were mostly lost in the shuffle. Even Dick Dale struggled for national acceptance, something that Brian and his fellow group members had more than their share of.

However, although the Beach Boys and surf music never really found any common ground, their interpretation of the musical genre provided a universal appreciation. As a result, they did in effect "give" it to the world, but the "it" had undergone such immense and irretrievable changes that "it" was no longer surf music; "it" was now surf SONGS and the flood gates were well and truly opened.

NOTE:

"Mr Moto" actually became a Beach Boys' early concert staple, being one of the few instrumentals that Carl Wilson could handle reasonably well.

There is in existence a poorly recorded tape of The Beach Boys performing the tune live in Oxnard, California on July 14, 1962. The short tape begins with about fifteen seconds of the group wailing on "Mr Moto". Although nothing exceptional, it does show that the group had a rudimentary grasp of the musical genre of surf music

The remainder of the tape is taken up with an interview between Brian and local KXOR radio personality Nelson Eddy.

Original Reviews Part 2

When I Grow up (To Be A Man).
"A soft surf feeling … the distinctive tones are there but gentler … Brian Wilson takes the falsetto part of which there's a great deal …" *Melody Maker*

"Brian Wilson wrote the number in one of his 'I want to be alone' sessions." *Disc and Music Echo*

Dance, Dance, Dance.
"…fantastic to dance to, as it should be… definitely one for my two friends who insist on surfing down Oxford Street every Friday night on their 'Jan and Dean' boards." *Disc and Music Echo*

Help Me Rhonda.
"Another class song from Brian …[with the] usual harmonic bits and pieces…nice guitar going on behind… not their briskest performance… Brian wrote the flip too, a rather draggy ballad ("Kiss Me Baby")…" *Record Mirror*

"I'm sorry to say The Beach Boys have turned up with a rather dull offering…I still have no idea who or what Rhonda may be, but this doesn't sound half as interestingly recorded as usual which is probably the main fault…it goes on and on too." *Disc and Music Echo*

California Girls.
"A weird introduction and some first class vocal and instrumental work – but will it mean anything here? I'm inclined to doubt. It's not a particularly strong song." *Disc and Music Echo*

"The surfing sound is slower, ponderous almost, and doesn't have the usual strident falsetto bits." *Record Mirror*

"The Beach Boys continually produce good records. 'California Girls' is no exception." *Melody Maker*

The Little Girl I Once Knew.
"The overall effect is not as catchy as 'California Girls'" *Melody Maker*

"…the number is far from the boys' best…" *NME*

"there are super surfy tambourine noises and a great organ and 'bowowo' voices." *Disc and Music Echo*

Barbara Ann.
"The Beach Boys do up the bop bop oldie and sound slightly dated." Disc and *Music Echo*

Surfing U.S.A. **album.**

"Rock is the basic ingredient.... nice vocal harmony... songs which combine tunefulness with beat..." *Melody Maker*

"...if you like excellent pop, this is for you... tremendous surfing music that swings in really great style" *Record Mail*

"...one of the best surf discs of all time... Noble Surfer seems a bit sick." *Record Mirror*

Shut Down Vol 2. **album.**

"If this is Vol 2, whatever happened to Vol 1?... the tracks are printed twice on the sleeve, once on the front and once on the back, but to get the correct playing order you have to look on the label!" *Record Mirror*

"America's only real challenge to the 'British Invasion' show themselves to be a competent and compelling group... a group of all American boys eager to have fun ... the accent is now placed more upon 'hot rods' and 'drag strips'..." *Record Mail*

"... this set has some distinct connections with the surf suds, but mostly it's straight beat... I don't rate it more than a highly commercial LP ideal for parties." *Melody Maker*

Little Deuce Coupe **album.**

"This set has been issued in the States for some time, but it doesn't sound dated..." *Record Mirror*

"...various songs about cars and motor racing, dragsters and burn ups...it doesn't matter if they're singing about surfing adventures, or their current road and track winners... simply because the Beach Boys are the greatest...Just listen you'll get the message – I did!" *Record Mail*

All Summer Long **album.**

"With their surfing and high pitched harmony sounds they have become extremely distinctive... there are some kooky lyrics... [one] unusual track is just a collection of phrases and jokes made by the boys while recording... 'Carl's Big Chance' is an instrumental and shows how well Carl Wilson can play his guitar..." *Record Mail*

"The Beach Boys are an acquired taste which I don't have, but at least they produce some solid 'beatful' sounds." *NME*

Beach Boys Party **album.**

"The atmosphere of a beach rave up..." *Melody Maker*

"... too late to have a party? Not on your life, not with these lads around on disc... an album worth a celebration..." *NME*

"...some of the impromptu laughs and 'I forgot the words!' make humorous listening, but it's not a novelty the British market will plump for..." *Disc and Music Echo*

"...not, however, as good as usual Beach Boys' records." *Record Mirror*

Let's Go Away For Awhile
The Continuing Saga of Brian Wilson's *Pet Sounds*
By Neal Umphred

Pet Sounds is hailed by almost anyone with more than a passing interest in the band, as The Beach Boys' best album, and indeed, in many quarters it is still considered to be the best rock album of all time. However, since its initial release, as this previously unpublished article documents, the album has never fared as well in the commercial market-place, as its critical standing would suggest. This piece also leads us up to the release of the Pet Sounds Sessions *boxed set, which is due for release at approximately the same time as this book.*

Neal Umphred is the author of several price guides for record collectors, notably Goldmine's Price Guide To Collectible Record Albums *and* Goldmine's Rock'n Roll 45RPM Record Price Guide. *Over the past decade, he has also written several articles on Brian Wilson, The Beach Boys, and related topics for publications such as* Goldmine, DISCoveries, *and* Pulse!. *Sections of this article originally appeared in the fifth edition of the above mentioned LP price guide and in the January 1997 issue of* Live! Music Review. *Mr Umphred wishes to extend his thanks to Steve Andrews and Neal Skok, without whose suggestions (the former) and arguments (the latter) he says this would be a lesser piece, indeed!*

The phrases "long awaited" and "much anticipated" have rather subjective meanings: for instance, in the world of collecting bootlegs, a board recording from Springsteen's or U2's current tour may be long awaited by fans, but the wait may only be a matter of weeks or, at most, months. Anticipatory fans of countless acts wait for similar unauthorised concert recordings on a daily basis, whether by such hoary monoliths as the Stones and Zep or any contemporary band that has devoted followers. Dylan's followers had to wait almost a decade for an official release of 1967's influential "basement tapes," only to be highly disappointed when it arrived in 1975. What each of the above has in common is that the fans are expecting recordings *never intended for them to hear*. But fans of Brian Wilson and The Beach Boys have been waiting for the debut of a stereo version of one of rock music's most highly regarded, legitimately released albums more than thirty years after its mono debut!

This situation was to have been rectified in 1996 with the release of the second boxed set devoted to The Beach Boys: *Pet Sounds Sessions: A 30th Anniversary Collection* was to have been four CDs devoted to one LP, almost all of the material previously unreleased, including the first stereo mix of the album. Capitol had already released *Good Vibrations: Thirty Years of The Beach Boys*, a boxed set of five compact discs (CDP 0777 7 81294 2 8) in 1993. This excellent overview of the group's career, compiled by David Leaf, Mark Linnett, and Andy Paley, was warmly received by fans and reviewers alike, comfortably outselling the company's admittedly modest expectations. Several outtakes from *Pet Sounds* were included, notably the original version of "God Only Knows."

Pet Sounds Sessions was to have included a 60 page booklet annotated by Leaf that included the following astute observation:

"In the 1960s, the Beach Boys created a body of work so commercially and artistically valuable that their records would simultaneously solidify rock's importance in the marketplace, confirm its validity as an art form, and challenge and overturn the conventions that governed artists in the music business." (This, along with other quotes in this article, was taken from the original manuscript to the unpublished booklets intended to accompany the as yet unreleased *Pet Sounds Sessions*.) The majority of the evidence to support the second part of such a claim – confirm its validity as an art form – comes from a two year period in the group's history that began in mid '65 and ended in the first half of 1967 and revolves around one released album, *Pet Sounds* (Capitol T-2458)

Leaf's statement expresses an opinion that should, at this point in time, be unimpeachable. But, in the less than formal atmosphere of rock & roll historians, this elevated observation of the group is often taken to represent the type of sentiments that one expects from the egoistic fanboys that seem to dominate the field's debates. That a claque of ageing observers, many of them writers, continues to champion an album entering its fourth decade should surprise few: through the years, *Pet Sounds* has consistently made the upper echelons of various best of rock surveys, usually taken from polls among just such professionals. But, in a rather amazing tribute, the staff of writers and reviewers from England's *Mojo* magazine, many of them born years after its initial release, voted *Pet Sounds* as the #1 Rock album of all time in a 1995 survey!

Pet Sounds was issued at the early stages of what I have coined the "Golden Age of Rock With A Capital R", more or less 1966 through 1972. These were the years in which the effects of expanded consciousness led creative types to explore the manifold possibilities of the expanding wonders of the recording studio, all in search of the perfect "concept album". In a year filled with important albums – *Aftermath, Blonde on Blonde, Buffalo Springfield, East-West, Face To Face, Fifth Dimension, Freak Out, Fresh Stream, Revolver, Sunshine Superman,* and *Over Under Sideways Down* come immediately to mind – *Pet Sounds* may have been both the best and the most influential. It was also one of the first pop productions created with the belief that the music would still be listened to and enjoyed generations later.

Following the creation of *Pet Sounds*, Brian Wilson embarked on a series of projects that began – and, in hindsight, culminated – with the release in October 1966 of one of the truly wondrous singles in Rock's brief history, "Good Vibrations", Wilson's visionary work was carried through the next year with the trauma of what was to have been one of rock's greatest albums, *Smile*, only to end with the denouement that was *Smiley Smile* in September 1967. But, before going any further, perhaps a bit of background is in order…

You Are Invited To A Beach Boys' Party!

God, did I hate The Beach Boys! Way back in early 1966, when "Barbara Ann" was riding its wave of popularity to the crest of the charts, I summarily dismissed the group's every effort by referring to them as the "balls-less-wonders". For me, then a wise-ass, fourteen year old know-it-all, they could do no right. And, like most AM radio-oriented record buyers, while I knew more about John, Paul, George & Ringo than I cared to acknowledge, I hadn't a clue as to who Brian Wilson was. Then came "Sloop John B", the first release by the wimps to showcase their new, more "manly" (ho ho) sound. And I liked it! When my brother received *Pet Sounds* in the mail as the Capitol Record Club's selection of the month, he traded it to me 'cause I liked the hit. But, I've digressed before I've even started!

Pet Sounds, the eleventh album from Capitol Records' West Coast wunderkind, The Beach Boys, broke barriers for pop and rock, both as music and as recordings. It was lushly impressionistic in a Gershwinian (sic) mode, with melodies that recalled the Romantic beauty of Schubert, and introspective, questing lyrics that matched the mood of the sounds. And, while it still rocked, no one was about to accuse them of having nicked any of Chuck Berry's licks here. "Surfin U.S.A." and "Fun, Fun, Fun" had given way to "I Know There's An Answer and "I Just Wasn't Made For These Times." Yet, considering that the album was by America's most popular group, at the height of their success, and that it boasted a huge international hit, *Pet Sounds* had an uphill battle for survival from the start.

Even before the completion of the sessions, those involved in creating the music realised that this album represented a *very* different approach to record-making from a group with a *very* established sound and image. The vehemently negative response of at least one member in the group to this new music was the real beginning of the now legendary internecine squabbling that has plagued The Beach Boys through the rest of their checkered history. And Capitol, upon hearing this dramatically different album from one of their two biggest breadwinners (The Beatles had bumped them out of the company's top spot in 1964), did their damndest to undermine the album's success.

The group's previous album, *Summer Days (And Summer Nights!!)*, while transitional, gave no real cause for alarm. Certain tracks did predict the achievements of the immediate future, such as the complex instrumental backing track to "Salt Lake City", and the texture and arrangement of "Let Him Run Wild," a true harbinger of things to come. But these were comfortably cushioned by reminders of an era almost over, notably "Amusement Parks U.S.A.", which is a more sophisticated telling of the events that took place in the song "County Fair", from the group's first album of 1965, and a cover of The Crystals' "Then I Kissed Him" (lyrically adapted for the male members to sing as "Then I Kissed Her"). It also contained the by now de rigeur filler, including "And Your Dreams Come True", an obvious nod to The Four Freshmen, and "I'm Bugged At My Old Man," which was insightfully [frighteningly?] funny, if blatantly sophomoric.

Actually, there was an album recorded and released between *Summer Days* and *Pet Sounds*, one from which the aforementioned "Barbara Ann" was culled: *Beach Boys Party!* was a stop gap to fill the void left by Brian's growing involvement with *Pet Sounds*. Recorded in September of 1965, it can be seen as Brian's attempts to deal with the demands of a seemingly insatiable market that required new "product" on a regular basis, usually three LPs per annum. Brian took the concept of the "live" album – a good many of which were heavily doctored after the fact in the studio – one better by recording a simulated party in the studio and then over dubbing ad-libbed "party" sounds. The effect is charmingly accurate: the record is smooth, unforced, and essentially acoustic, the line-up consisting of strummed guitars, some often hilarious bongos and near a cappela vocals. And noise – never forget the noise: laughing gals, arguing guys, pouring drinks, and munched chips.

While detractors have long derided it as a motley collection of moldie oldies performed in a slipshod manner, there is a real sense of iconoclasm in the selection of material and the performances each is rendered. While several party songs receive obvious treatment, interspersed are some rather serious songs that receive the same type of interpretation. These included a hilarious pseudo-folkie arrangement of "You've Got To Hide Your Love Away", a real folk protest in "The Times They Are A Changin'". And, should anyone think that the group was taking cheap shots at their competition, they included hilarious send ups of "I Get Around" and "Little Deuce Coupe" that forever alter the listener's interpretation of the originals!

For many casual fans, the only thing they heard from this slab of joy was the monster hit single, "Barbara Ann", which, in 1966, was interpreted as a regressive move, coming as it did in the beginning of Rock's self conscious period. What we were not aware of was that the single was an edited version of the LP track, which goes on into a coda that hammers home the humour of the whole album. (And that it was released as a single without the group's consent, of which more later.)

What *Party!* accomplished, in essence, was to reduce all of rock & roll, from its loftiest heights (Lennon and Dylan) to its more sublime moments – the versions of "Devoted To You" and "There's No Other (Like My Baby)" are as close to "straight" as the album gets, and they are prefaced by, and punctuated with, raucous tidbits – to party music, sing along stuff. Or, in kinder, gentler words, *Party!* celebrated all rock & roll as joyous noise! If groups devoted to rhythm & blues could claim, "After all, it's really all about dancing, isn't it?" why shouldn't The Beach Boys just say that "It's really all about having fun, isn't it?"

That all of this succeeds may strike some as silly; to others it is both a wonderful farce and an artistic statement. Easily dismissed by jaded ears, this album is a succinct summation of Brian's ability to pull off anything in the studio his heart desired. A masterful recording that is both hilarious in its complete lack of pomposity and demythologising in its approach to rock & roll, this could be considered amongst his greatest achievements. In the December 1967 issue of *Crawdaddy*, Paul Williams, the grandad of rock journalism as personal and intelligent writing, noted *Beach Boys Party!* is an excellent album containing excellent music that is easy to relate to! And that's why the fans dug it. And that's the real reason people buy records-not because they're dupes, but because they like the music, and the better it is the more they like it as long as they are still able to relate to what's good about it." And that's also why people bought the group's next album, when they could find it for sale. . .

More of A Brian Wilson Album

Pet Sounds was almost exclusively the vision of Brian Wilson. In fact, he has referred to it as "My first solo album. [It was] a chance to step outside the group and shine." The core of the album was a cycle of ten interrelated songs that dealt with the transition from the innocence of first love to the self conscious reflection of experience. As for Brian's vision, he claimed that, with this album, The Beach Boys "were trying to capture spiritual love that couldn't be found anywhere else in the world. We figured we had that love." This statement, inclusive as it is, seems to have been made in a moment of generosity, as hindsight indicates that love – and I am not referring to familial affection – was one element that was lacking in the group's chemistry.

Brian wrote the music and worked closely with lyricist Tony Asher, a former songwriter who had turned to writing jingles for an advertising agency. The two had struck up a brief acquaintance; one that had left quite an impression on the head Beach Boy. When invited to contribute his skills to Wilson's latest endeavour, Asher proved more than up to the task. That he was able to work with Wilson on one of Rock's most important albums and then all but disappear from the scene is one of the genre's more interesting sidebars.

The songs these two men composed did not fit any mold with which anyone was familiar let alone comfortable. In the booklet accompanying *The Beach Boys: The Capitol Years* (World Records of Great Britain, 1980), collector Peter Reum wrote, "[*Pet Sounds*] was not teenage good time music... its songs bared a kaleidoscope of emotions which a typical adolescent would rather not think about... The arrangements of the album's songs are orchestral, but in a Rock sense. A variety of instruments appear in context to accentuate shades of feeling which are never overbearing, but are turbulent."

Two things are immediately apparent when listening: the use of such uncommon (for Rock) instrumentation as flutes, accordions, strings, and exotic percussion, and the recurring phrases and themes running through the music and arrangements. This gives the album a cohesiveness, a conceptual unity in musical texture as well as in lyrical content, that have led many to dub it Rock's first true "concept album." In fact, it sounds as if all of the songs were conceived and recorded as a piece and then, cut into pieces and allowed to fall where they may, creating a collage of internal references and allusions.

For the actual recording of these songs, Brian arranged and produced every session, using the creme de la creme of Los Angeles session musicians in lieu of the five touring Beach Boys, then busy conquering Japan. This included, but was not limited to, Al DeLory and Don Randi, piano; Carol Kaye, Fender bass; and Lyle Ritz, string bass; Al Casey, Glen Campbell, Jerry Cole, Barney Kessel, Bill Pitman, Ray Pohlman, and Billy Strange on guitars; Larry Knechtel, organ; Steve Douglas, Plas Johnson, and Jay Migliori on saxophones; Frank Capp and Julius Wechter, percussionists; and de facto leader of the pack, drummer Hal Blaine. He also hired members of local symphonic orchestras to record live with the pop people. To the astonishment of those who participated in the sessions, Wilson taught the older, more experienced musicians – pop and serious alike – how to "unlearn" their musical predispositions so that the parts they played fitted the aural schemata that filled his head.

Wilson also sang all of the vocals, from the complex leads to over-dubbing his parts countless times to achieve the dense, choir-like backing. [Ed: It should be pointed out that whilst Wilson sang all the lead and guide vocals, the eventual released album does indeed feature all the Beach Boys vocals.] "I did most of the singing because I thought, in a way, I wanted people to know it was more of a Brian Wilson album than a Beach Boys album." The result was an album of wondrous music that dealt with such secular topics as sexual longing and teen angst but in a soulful, spiritual, tone. Brian has often stated the desire to create a "white soul music" that addressed love in all of its forms, including caritas, the spiritual love for God.

In *The Nearest Faraway Place*, Timothy White wrote that the album contains "Songs of longing, songs of anticipation, songs of anxiety, and songs of regret and in between are instrumentals that describe without words the ineffable transitions behind the other tracks' distressed emotional states. Yet what shines brightest behind, within and above the peal of Brian's exquisite material is the presence of the thing not named: 'An unanswerable belief in the enduring power of one's better self'." Despite these weighty intentions and the bravura display of multifaceted virtuosity, the album still sounded like fun!

Regardless of its merits, *Pet Sounds* was problematic for virtually everyone involved on any level, professional and personal. The creatively competitive Wilson justifiably viewed it as ground breaking, a challenge to all the other major movers in the heady pop music scene of the mid 60s. The capitalistically competitive executives at Capitol just as correctly saw it as risk taking by their California clients, a group that had proven themselves a veritable gold mine.

As for the precedents shattered by *Pet Sounds* and Capitol's response, it has been recited so often that the company had no problem accepting the "daring-do" of The Beatles but fought the progressive elements of the Beach Boys music – which was certainly true during the *Smile* sessions – that it has become virtual litany among fans and historians that such was always the case. Actually, a careful review of the chronology of events and the inferences gleaned from a bit of hindsight render this point more than a little moot. While The Beatles' music had grown appreciably over the previous three years, it had evolved gradually, record by record. And, once again benefiting by the obviousness of hindsight, the music appeared to have evolved very logically.

A Whole Album of Good Stuff

It is true that the release of The Beatles' *Rubber Soul* in December 1965 did blow more than a few minds, Brian's included. He dubbed it "a whole album with good stuff" and has long credited it as the inspiration for *Pet Sounds* (despite the fact that *Pet Sounds* had been planned and songs written and recorded before Brian had even heard *Rubber Soul*). The "good stuff" refers to the fact that all of the tracks on *Rubber Soul* were of the quality of a single, an accomplishment that no Beach Boys album had come close to. And, not only was it good stuff, but there was an ambience to the album that, gestalt-like, seemed far greater than the sum of its parts.

This was partially due to the acoustic nature of the tracks that found their way onto the Capitol version of the album, of which there were twelve, versus the Parlophone version, of which there were fourteen, only ten of them in common. (But that's another story.) It was also due to the mystically moody, introspective sounds, which were attributed by insiders to the pungent presence of a certain proscribed ant circulating within The Beatles small circle of friends. Still, the music on *Rubber Soul* was predicted by the songs on the second side of their previous album, *Help!*

Of course, we Yanks did not get to hear many of these new songs in 1965: to the rest of the world, Parlophone issued *Help!* as The Beatles fifth album with the seven songs from the film of the same name on the first side and seven new, more ambitious, tracks on side two. Here in the States, Capitol issued it as a soundtrack, combining the seven film songs with incidental music from the movie by George Martin's studio orchestra. This left seven new tracks for Capitol do with as it saw fit. While the rest of the world received the new tracks as a whole in August 1965, in America, the fourteen songs were spread out over four LPs (*Beatles VI*, *Help!*, *Rubber Soul*, and *Yesterday & Today*) covering a twelve month period (June 1965 through June 1966).

The two songs that veered most from the Fabs' beat based repertoire were the almost acoustically folk based, "I've Just Seen A Face and "It's Only Love", both of which appeared on Capitol's restructured version of *Rubber Soul*. Consequently, this made the transition from *Help!* to *Rubber Soul* appear far more dramatic for Stateside fans than it really was, although only Capitol knew that. This contributed mightily to the perception of astonishing stylistic leaps in the early Beatles' albums, passed down as gospel by unquestioning rockwriters and the enduring memories of 'facts' by fans. And while this opinion is more than justified by the procession of LPs issued by Parlophone, it is not true of those issued by Capitol.

The first truly "far out" sounds from the Fab Four were the psychedelic excursions of John Lennon and the overtly Indian influences on George Harrison's compositions being prepared for *Revolver*, an album that would follow in *Pet Sounds'* wake in August 1966. And even the threatening edge of experimentalism on *Revolver* was softened by the release of *Yesterday & Today* the previous June, which previewed three of the aforementioned Lennon tracks – "I'm Only Sleeping", "And Your Bird Can Sing", and "Dr. Robert" – alongside the first American appearance of the four leftovers from the Parlophone version of *Rubber Soul*. Needless to say, this was done against Lennon's will, which, in tandem with Capitol's "butchering" of their catalog up to that point in time, was an indication that their corporate arrogance was not reserved for specific clients.

Thus, with *Pet Sounds'* release in the early summer of 1966, there was, in fact, precious little precedent for Capitol to be anything but uncomfortable with the plainly progressive sounds from a group they associated with deuce coupes, girls on the beach, and the warmth of the sun. Which, while not exonerating the company for its conservative, or, one might be nasty and say squeamish, lack of foresight, nonetheless does explain their apparent lack of desire to, as they say in the biz, "get behind" the strange new album. While it is evident that company policy makers were taken aback by *Pet Sounds*, Brian had provided warning signals with a quartet of almost avant garde singles, all released by Capitol in 1965 and '66 ...

To Watch A Sweet Thing Die

In the latter part of 1964, Brian had announced that he could no longer write, arrange, and produce Beach Boys records and hit the road with the group. Los Angeles studio guitarist Glen Campbell was hired as Brian's stage replacement. He fitted in perfectly with the group's image, being tall, lean, blonde, handsome and could play bass as well as guitar, and sing the high parts. He wisely declined a permanent position as the sixth Beach Boy, after which the group latched onto the services of Bruce Johnston to fill that role. Glen already had a solo career (independent of the healthy salary he drew from playing on countless other artists' records), although his eight previous singles for Capitol, primarily country & western standards such as "Too Late To Worry, Too Blue To Cry", "Long Black Limousine", and "Tomorrow Never Comes", had gone nowhere.

In return for his yeomanly duty in an emergency situation, Brian dug up a song from the previous year and took Campbell into the studio in April of 1965. "Guess I'm Dumb", featuring a melody that owes a nod to "Don't Worry, Baby", was a minor gem. Campbell's singing displays the supple clarity and strength of his best pop sides (yet to come) and is so accurately patterned after Brian that this track can be dropped on almost any Beach Boys collection and none but the true fan would know it wasn't a group recording! Backing vocals were provided by Brian along with the ubiquitous Honeys; strings and horns were used spartanly and tastefully incorporated into the arrangement. Aside from the necessary production credit, the single's label proudly proclaimed "Arranged and conducted by Brian Wilson", surely a sign that Capitol expected some name recognition, and, from it, both spins and sales. Released in June '65, "Guess I'm Dumb" failed to chart.

That "Guess I'm Dumb", both as a song and as a completed, conceptualized recording, heralded the extraordinary accomplishments to come in 1966 is impossible to ignore. That this predates much of *Summer Days (And Summer Nights!!)* shows that Brian was capable of a subtlety and sophistication at which his Beach Boys recordings only hinted. That he chose a non-member for his first steps towards his masterwork shows wisdom coupled with caution. Of all of Brian's outside productions, this may be the one that most obviously justifies the collector's avid interest in vinyl spelunking.

Aficionados could make an argument that the sessions for *Pet Sounds* began in October of 1965 with the waxing of "The Little Girl I Once Knew". It was issued as The Beach Boys' new single (Capitol 5540) during the latter weeks of the year. According to legend, it failed to reach the top of the charts because of the reluctance of jocks and programmers to play a single with several moments of "dead space" in its decidedly daring arrangement and production. This ignores the fact that the track, while an excellent pop/rock construction, was probably the group's least "commercial" single thus far. Its stop and go arrangement interrupts any sense of melody, rhythm, or beat (i.e., not only can't you dance to it, it's difficult just to sing along) and the song's "hook" is the same stop and go arrangement that made it difficult to program!

Another aspect of this single's supposed failure that has been all but overlooked is the fact that just as it was entering the upper portion of the charts, Capitol released a new Beach Boys single, "Barbara Ann", on December 20! This was done against all common sense and against previous practice, which called for waiting patiently for the group's current hit to ascend and then begin its descent before releasing their next single. It was also done without consulting the group; Brian had never intended any part of the *Party!* album to be issued as a single. With this infectious "new" single competing for oh so valuable air play, many radio stations simply stopped playing the "old" single and added "Barbara Ann" to their rotation. Two weeks after peaking, "Little Girl I Once Knew" was off the charts while the new one was shooting to the top.

The fact that "Little Girl I Once Knew" just reached the Top 20 probably says more about the group's positive standing as hit makers with DJs than it does about the negative opinions of radio personnel. Had it soared to the top of the charts, it could have filled the role of hit single for the album. That it fitted the theme and sounds of the album so comfortably must surely be a sign that it was at least considered for a spot on the album. As David Leaf has aptly noted in the *Good Vibrations* notes, "In retrospect, "The Little Girl I Once Knew" was to *Pet Sounds* what "Penny Lane/Strawberry Fields" would be to *Sgt. Pepper*. This hints at the fact that The Beatles greatest double sided 45 was forced out by a record company, EMI/Parlophone in this case, anxious for new product, despite the fact that both sides were intended for *Sgt. Pepper*.

The third of these singles, "Caroline, No", was a brief, plaintive farewell to a love lost. In Brian's words, the song is a story about how, once you've fucked up … with a chick, there's no way to get it back. At the same time, just as with many of Dylan's vitriolic lyrics aimed at some un-named lover, one can just as easily read this as the singer reflecting on his own self, his growth and its accompanying losses. At Brian's insistence, "Caroline, No" was issued in March, not as the new Beach Boys single, but under his own name (Capitol 5610). While Brian Wilson has achieved a type of fame in 1996 that makes him a welcome guest on major talk shows and fodder for national tabloids, in 1966 his stature outside of the group was less certain. "Caroline, No" received adequate play initially and some sales. While it is a lovely recording and worthy of attention, it was not a natural "hit" single and petered out quickly, just grazing the Top 40. There has been long running speculation that had it been a hit, Brian may have opted to release *Pet Sounds* as a solo album.

Brian's first and only solo single of the 60s was followed in a matter of weeks (despite its lower catalog number, Capitol 5602) by "Sloop John B." which surfed into the Top 5. As stated earlier, this was the first release to showcase The Beach Boys' new sound, which jumped out at listeners in early 1966. With the lead sung by Brian in a relaxed register, the harmonies, while still full, seemed positively subdued compared to former singles. The cause was the reigning in of the [perceived] wimpy tendencies in the group's singing, taming such instantly identifiable trademarks as Mike Love's adenoidal voicings and Brian's swooping falsetto. The fact that the song was an accepted folk standard instead of another of their patented teen fantasies also lent a degree of now necessary credibility with the increasingly hip circles of musicians, artists, journalists, and sundry scene makers dominating the international pop scene.

The basic track had been recorded on July 12, 1965, but the 12 string was overdubbed, courtesy of Billy Strange, along with the vocals, on December 22. Thus, while the track itself predates *Pet Sounds* by several months, the vocals were added at the beginning of the LP sessions. Both it and "Caroline, No" found their way onto *Pet Sounds*. While the former was an essential part of the album's concept, Capitol insisted on the inclusion of the latter as a sales vehicle, even though the song played no part in the song cycle. Brian obliged and found a spot for it as the last song on the first side, neatly reversing the then common practice of kicking off an album with the big hit as the first song on the first side. To add further distance, it was segregated, at least lyrically, from the rest of the album's songs by an instrumental track. Although these last three 45s had been chart hits, Capitol did not see any commercial potential in selecting a single from the similar sounding tracks on the album…

Poo Pooed By The Big Boys

Of course there were potential hits. Brian argued for the issuance of "God Only Knows", only to be poo pooed by those who believed they knew better than the man who had already provided the company with eighteen Top 40 hits in four years. After EMI called the label's hand by releasing it as a single in England, where it soared to the top of the charts, Capitol acquiesced and issued it in the States in July, but as the B side to the more upbeat "Wouldn't It Be Nice", the group found their "new" single uncharacteristically (for the 60s) released months after the album. The fact that the single was a double sided hit (Top 10 and Top 40, respectively) certainly vindicated Brian's projections; had it been issued a month before *Pet Sounds*, it might have helped the album spend more than a brief respite in the Top 10.

The sessions for the album commenced on November 1, 1965, with the recording of "Trombone Dixie", a track that was not used on the record, and was completed in March.

Aside from the obvious theme of the lyrics in the cycle of ten songs, several other themes run through these songs. A sense of karmic displacement in both time and place is evident. Examples include "in the kind of world where we belong" (from "Wouldn't It Be Nice"), and I know perfectly well I'm not where I should be" (from "You Still Believe In Me"), and "I keep looking for a place to fit in" (from "I Just Wasn't Made For These Times"). The titles of several songs also allude to this, the most obvious being "Let's Go Away For Awhile", "That's Not Me", and "Wouldn't It Be Nice," which implies that it is not nice now.

A second thematic undercurrent is the need for the singer to identify his "self" through communion with another, loved one. This is stated when the singer claims "I'm waiting for the day when you can love again" (from "I'm Waiting For The Day"), and "I could try to be big in the eyes of the world, [but] what matters to me is what I could be to just one girl" (from "That's Not Me"). One line alone, "God only knows what I'd be without you" (from "God Only Knows") sums up this theme neatly.

The recording of another song not used on the album was begun on February 18. "Good Vibrations", originally written by Brian and Tony but later graced with new lyrics from Mike Love was set aside and continuously reworked, eventually finding its way onto AM radio waves in the fall of 1966 as the group's final single before the debacle that would be *Smile*. It stands thirty years later as one of the towering achievements of the heady 60s. And although Brian's experiences with LSD had tended to turn him inward up to this point in his life, the psychedelic effervescence of this track is all but unstoppable. "Good Vibrations" topped the charts, turning the pop music world upside down, establishing The Beach Boys as a world class Rock With A Capital R group and earning Brian Wilson a reputation as a genius. Appropriately, it is often cited as the #1 Rock single of all time.

For a brief while, "Good Vibrations was considered for *Pet Sounds*. Heard as the album's coda, it would have brought the songs primary theme, that of love found and lost and wisdom achieved through pain, around full circle. Its presence would have given the album a cyclical motif, replacing the yearning resignation of "Caroline, No" with renewed expectancy. It would also have left the listener aware that, when one is receptive, good vibrations and excitations (sic) are available everywhere, "on the wind that lifts her perfume through the air", and anytime, especially "in the morning when the day is new". In hindsight, one must assume that it was fortunate that "Good Vibrations" was held for later release...

A Town Full of Heroes And Villains

July of 1966 also saw the decision makers in Los Angeles release the previously unannounced *Best of The Beach Boys*, a compilation of singles and LP sides whose selection was without rhyme or reason and assembled without the cooperation of the group. Its release within two months of *Pet Sounds* has long remained a damning indictment against the company, at least in the eyes of fans. Admittedly, several of the group's albums in the past had been issued almost concurrently: *Surfer Girl* and *Little Deuce Coupe* were issued only weeks apart in October '63, but aesthetically, as two sides of a coin; *Beach Boys' Christmas Album* and *Beach Boys Concert* were released within days of each other in October '64, although both of these were highly specialised product and not part of the group's studio catalog.

In both of these instances, the LPs were conceived and issued with the full cooperation of Brian and the group. The average lapse in time between the group's LPs was approximately four months. The real problem began when Capitol started meeting reorders for *Pet Sounds* by substituting copies of the new hits package. Many retailers found themselves in the position of being unable to stock a Top 10 album at the height of its demand! While *Best of The Beach Boys* received heavy promotion, *Pet Sounds*, with 200,000 copies sold domestically, was placed in the commercially awkward but historically interesting position of achieving collectable, cult like status at the very time it should have been a well stocked item in every store in the country! The reluctance of Capitol to back Brian and the boys was yet another insult to the band. These slights, along with other business shenanigans, caused an irreparable tear in their relationship.

Of course, Capitol can – and has – claimed this was coincidental: *Best of The Beach Boys* was already planned, they say, and issued because they felt that *Pet Sounds* had run its course. It was an unspoken rule of thumb in the '60s that a "best of" retrospective generally indicated that the company believed that the artist had seen the last of their hits and that such a set was issued to capitalize on the waning interest still present. One year later, in July of 1967, Capitol released a second, unannounced *Best of The Beach Boys, Volume 2*, this time one week after the release of the group's long awaited new single, "Heroes And Villains". With these two situations added to the surprise release of "Barbara Ann", which torpedoed "The Little Girl I Once Knew", coincidence as an excuse holds little water.

Neither of these explanations are particularly complimentary towards the executives at Sunset and Vine. While on this subject, it is worth noting that, to this day, no one at Capitol has ever publicly acknowledged that any of this occurred anywhere but in the fertile [fevered?] imaginations of the group members and thousands of their fans, including more than a few investigative rockwriters. In *Heroes And Villains*, probably the best-selling book on The Beach Boys and the first "true story of The Beach Boys", author Steven Gaines actually spends very little space discussing the music and recordings of the group. He did devote an eight page section (pages 142-149 in the cloth edition) on *Pet Sounds*. His research turned up a series of "facts" and quotes that, when read as a whole, only add to the confusion.

For example, he notes that "Statistically, *Pet Sounds* didn't do too badly – it spent a total of thirty-nine weeks on the charts, peaking at number 11 (sic) *only five weeks* after its release, with *well over half a million units sold*." In the very next paragraph, he quotes Al Couri, head of Capitol promotion, as saying "[*Pet Sounds*] was probably ahead of its time and yet it didn't sell. *The retail activity was not as good as previous Beach Boys albums.*" Gaines then remarks, "Only eight weeks after the release of Brian's precious *Pet Sounds* LP, Capitol released *Best of The Beach Boys*, which *quickly* went gold". [Emphasis added in all three quotes. NU] Of course, conflicting remarks concerning this project are not exclusive to Capitol; reread this article and pay attention to some of Brian Wilson's claims.

Now, prior to 1974, to qualify for an RIAA Gold Record Award, an LP had to have sold $1,000,000 at the manufacturer's wholesale price which was based on one third of the album's listed retail price. This was approximately 550,000 copies sold in the United States. By the end of 1966, eight Beach Boys albums had gone gold (only *Surfin' Safari*, *Beach Boys Christmas Album*, and *Beach Boys Party!* had failed to sell the requisite number of copies) with the length of time between release and RIAA certification being at least six months for all but one title. The average wait was more than eighteen months; three albums took almost three years each! The above cited *Best Of The Beach Boys* took nine months to quickly go gold. Therefore, if Gaines' statistics are accurate, it would seem that *Pet Sounds* was doing just fine for a Beach Boys album of the time, which is, of course, far better than we have ever been led to believe.

Finally, I realise that this article gives the reader little, if any, sense of what this music means to me as an individual, so I'll end it with a very personal anecdote: Not a week before completing this, I had my sleep disturbed by a nightmare, one that I have since found is all too familiar with parents. In the dream I was made aware of the death of my eight year old daughter, Amanda, and I was powerless to do anything but weep uncontrollably. Needless to say, this jolted me to consciousness – it was just past 3:00 AM – where I found myself shaking, near tears. So, I did what any sane person would do in such a situation, at such a time: I got up, found my stereo bootleg of *Pet Sounds* (which I keep beneath my pillow), put it on, and listened, peacefully. . .

Landmark Albums: Pet Sounds
by David Leaf

A shorter version of this piece appeared in the July 1997 issue of Musician *magazine for a cover story on the 10 greatest rock productions of all time. The full version appears here. This is the second piece in this collection by David Leaf.*

The release of *Pet Sounds* was "Independence Day" for rock 'n' roll. From that 1966 May day on, the "rules" of record making vanished; producers and groups were now free to try anything. Sir Paul McCartney calls *Pet Sounds* the primary influence on the Beatles circa 1966-67. Beatles' producer Sir George Martin acknowledges an enormous debt – "*Pepper* was an attempt to equal *Pet Sounds*." If for no other reason than how it inspired the Beatles, *Pet Sounds* is a landmark record.

But, of course, there is much more – the breathtaking beauty and classical nature of the compositions, the sophistication of the jazz influenced instrumental arrangements, the power and purity of the church like vocals are, in broad strokes, what make *Pet Sounds* such a stunning musical accomplishment. Part symphony ("Let's Go Away For Awhile" and "Here Today"), part California rhapsody ("Caroline, No"), part pop rock ("Wouldn't It Be Nice") and part prayer ("God Only Knows"), Pet Sounds was Brian Wilson's heart on vinyl. Each song expressed a mood, an emotion, Brian's most intimate feelings ("That's Not Me"), dreams ("I'm Waiting For The Day"), desires ("Don't Talk") and fears ("You Still Believe In Me" and "I Just Wasn't Made For These Times"). Very simply, *Pet Sounds* was autobiography-the gospel of Brian. Its bone-honest musical expression of an artist's soul, combined with the revelational sense of the lyrics (by Tony Asher, et al), gives *Pet Sounds* its profound and timeless nature.

Pet Sounds is, in a way, a culmination of the romantic recording art ... in a sense, the final peak of one kind of studio expression and the beginning of another. Unlike any other pop music of its time, *Pet Sounds* wasn't a record made by a 4 or 5 piece rock band playing songs; it was a rock orchestra with the composer, Brian, as conductor. Certainly the way Brian produced the backing tracks, literally arranging and rearranging his compositions "live," on the spot, was an artform in itself. Of course, before a session began, he had a strong sense of what he wanted, but once in the studio, he remained spontaneous, ready to change if he heard something better. And while he was clearly in charge and gave the musicians the parts they were to play, he was always open to their improving the arrangement. For example, on the tracking session of "God Only Knows", the staccato bridge was born from a suggestion by piano player Don Randi. There was no "pride of authorship" or ego involved. The musicians and Brian were a team, in search of fresh sounds, and all that mattered was making a recording that felt right. Feeling was paramount.

Brian's desire to impart his emotions to the listener was what drove him, and Brian relied on his own musical curiosity to keep each track interesting. In a way, even his impatience made the record more interesting, because before the listener could get bored, before *Brian* could get bored, something would happen in the track or in the vocals that would delight the ear. A subtle key change or a shifting tempo, a surprising burst of strings or a harmony shower were but a few of the musical tricks he treated us with.

His ability to combine instruments to create layers and textures and new sounds while simultaneously maintaining their clarity was miraculous, and Brian also evoked feelings in the listener with unfamiliar sounds. His use of the theremin on "I Just Wasn't Made For These Times", the English horn on "I'm Waiting For The Day", bass harmonica on "I Know There's An Answer" and unusual percussion (e.g. upside down, empty plastic bottles on "Caroline, No") brought new sounds to contemporary music. Brian would use both a stand-up and electric bass, a piano and an organ and multiple guitars, and through the musical lines he would have them play, create other new vibrations. He would open a recording like "God Only Knows" with a French horn figure and resolve it at the end with a vocal part; each track is filled with similar epiphanies. But what makes it all work, what makes it so special, is that he never called attention to what he was doing; everything felt natural and the overall effect was pleasing to the ear.

Brian's understanding of recording dynamics and use of microphone technique was also unparalleled. Nowadays, engineers spend hours carefully placing microphones to record individual instruments that will allow the producer to mix them at a later time. Brian did it live, and he didn't labor over where a microphone was in the room. He would balance the recording as the track was being played by having the players move closer or further away from the mike at key moments. That you could see. But there was something else, something indescribable about how he recorded, something inexplicable – he could just throw up a microphone and get sounds from it that nobody else could.

Of course, there is so much more. We haven't even begun to talk about the vocal work or his string and horn arrangements. Nobody else put all those skills together as Brian did. Alone among his contemporaries and almost all his disciples, Brian was the composer, the arranger, the producer and, on over half of *Pet Sounds*, the lead vocalist. The auteur.

Brian: "From a technical point of view, I'm proud of the combination of instruments I used and the echo, because it made the instruments 'swim' a bit. Also, I thought the vocal arrangements were an achievement in 'choir boy' sounds. To me, what is most innovative about *Pet Sounds* are the orchestrations. I moved into bigger instrumentations; it made it different because it was a fuller sound. I wanted people to hear Beach Boy music more sweetly than in the past. After *Pet Sounds*, albums became more creative, used more creative bass lines. I think it was also innovative because of the songs and my voice. It taught people how to sing sweeter. My voice sounded sweet and innocent; it was to bring love to people like a mother or father would bring to a baby." To Brian, the record is a landmark because "it represents a spiritual aspect that is very rare in the business. It brought a special kind of spiritual love to people. And people loved it."

Long a fan of Spector's "Wall of Sound", Brian set out instead to create a "Wave of Love" that would roll over the listener. Indeed, the depth and power of his love is still a strongly felt tonic over 30 years later.

From Brian's point of view, *Pet Sounds* was what he calls an "industrial success". He's right; it forever changed the way records would be made. So in terms of it being worthy of inclusion on a list of landmark productions, there is little doubt. Recording in mono and using the limited palette of usually only 4 (and no more than 8) tracks, Wilson, in essence, laid down the last word in record production that to this day is a holy grail for legions of record makers trying to achieve what he did. Countless artists and producers have been influenced by Brian and many have tried to "get" his sound. It's impossible.

They tell a "story" from the mid 1960s, of producers booking the same studio that Brian worked in, hiring the same musicians and still not getting the sound. So the word went out that Brian was using some "magic box"…that without this "magic box", you couldn't get the sound.

That was true, because the "magic box" was inside Brian's head. It was the way he heard music in his head, the way he felt it and the way he realized that vision which gave his work such heartbreaking depth. It's why his 1966 creations *Pet Sounds* and "Good Vibrations" (which was begun during *Pet Sounds*) continue to amaze and inspire, proving yet again that timeless art has little to do with cutting edge technology. It's all about one thing – an artist's heart.

Out of Tune Prettiness:
Pet Sounds 1966 album review
by Norman Jopling

The arrival of the Pet Sounds *album proved difficult for fans and reviewers alike – it was such a step away from their traditional happy summer sound. This review shows how one critic reacted in an almost hostile fashion.*

Pet Sounds has been the most widely heralded long play pop album for some time, the subject of much praise and no criticism. If anyone is vaguely interested here is an UNBIASED in-depth review...

"Wouldn't it Be Nice" starts off prettily and develops into a complicated ponderous beat number...[it] slows down half way...[the] lyric is pleasant...[but this is] not exceptional Beach Boys...

"You Still Believe in Me" [is] slightly off tune...[it has] a delicate backing which thank heavens doesn't interfere with the complicated but smoothflowing vocal harmonies...

"That's Not Me" [is a] quizzical sort of beat ballad...[with a] self-obsessed sort of lyric which is clever without being in the least appealing...Spectorish at times...

"Don't Talk (Put Your Head on My Shoulder)" [has a] ponderous church organ...[and a] hymnal sound...with a tremendous atmosphere...of late night, very tired sitting on the rug at your girl's place...

"I'm Waiting For The Day" [features] shotgun drums...strings and organ, but used completely differently to the last track...it suddenly develops into a thumpy heartbeating noise, which is the introduction for Brian Wilson to throw in everything including the proverbial kitchen sink, and presumably the washing up water...

"Let's Go Away For A While" [is a] romantic instrumental which suggests the beating of the waves against something or other...[and is] full of that out of tune prettiness that so typifies the LP...

"Sloop John B" needs no description...

"God Only Knows" [has] a rollicking salvationist flavour but isn't going to convert anyone (??!!?-Ed.)...[it's a] simple medium tempo number...perhaps one of the best on the LP...Whoever writes the lyrics of the Beach Boys tunes (almost certainly Brian) has a poetical and astute insight into romance...

"I Know There's An Answer". [This] bell like item...starts off Ronette-ishly... [has a] strong hymnal flavour,...the backing dominates the vocal...[until it's] tambourines galore at the end...

"Here Today" [is] probably the corniest song on the LP...[but] it would still be quite advanced for anyone else...the backing sounds change suddenly and one is left with the feeling that this track is a kind of condensed showcase of all the backing sounds that anyone could cram into a few minutes. Not too good at all...

"I Just Wasn't Made For These Times" [is a] nostalgic ballad...[with] sympathetic lyrics and a clever sense of development... It's somehow depressing which was probably the intention...

"Pet Sounds" [is] a sombre little tune…[with] fast backing but slower musical lead… [but] quite imaginative…

"Caroline No" [is] very sad and very romantic…Brian's singing is excellent..[it has] a good deal of continuity, which is more than can be said for some other tracks on the LP…unfortunately, the addition of sound effects (bells, dogs, express train) ruins an atmosphere which must have taken some amount of time and trouble to create…Beach Boys fans won't thank them for that kind of musical development…

The album is very clever and every track seems to have been planned and prepared individually. The overall sound is similar throughout which is good, and interest isn't lost…the only real complaint is that nothing has been left to the listener's imagination. Every track is terribly complicated and cluttered up with vocals and backings galore, and even Beach Boys fans must like some simple and uncomplicated forms of music from their idols.

It will probably make their present fans like them even more, but it's doubtful whether it will make them any new ones.

Note: Main title added by ed. for this edition.

Remember The Zoo? The *Pet Sounds* Sessions
by Dwight Cavanagh

Dwight Cavanagh is a New Zealander best known for his book The Smile File, *which meticulously documents all of the known sessions for that mythical recording project. Here is a concise version for the* Pet Sounds *sessions, which originally appeared in* Beach Boys Australia *magazine.*

1966 was the year of change for the Beach Boys and more importantly Brian Wilson. While still popular, the days of fun in the sun surf music were rapidly becoming passe as far as the eldest Wilson brother was concerned. The Beatles were setting new standards for every new release and as Brian would later note of *Rubber Soul*, "I saw that every cut was very artistically interesting and stimulating." The production race had begun and Brian was determined to see his new concept to fruition.

In an effort to alleviate the pressure from Capitol to supply more product, Brian used a stopgap album titled *The Beach Boys' Party!* which discretely pointed towards the future, while simultaneously looking back at the early years. Though simple and fun, the album was an incredible put-on that very few people caught sight of. Using the studio as an instrument, the atmosphere of a party was created using overdubs and sound effects. However, the record was light and entertaining, lacking the "real" soul Brian wanted in the music.

Such intense endeavours pursued by Brian could not simply be recorded overnight and such efforts would have to be given enormous time and attention in order to work. Brian Wilson, a perfectionist, would need the time borrowed by *Party!* in order to create his new work *Remember The Zoo*. A full year ahead of the Beatles' *Sgt. Pepper's* album, *Zoo* would look back at childhood and the subsequent loss of innocence.

Over several months, recordings were held for the album of which none were actually discarded; only changed lyrically (sans "Trombone Dixie"). Released May 16, 1966, *Zoo* finally emerged as the album *Pet Sounds* and stood alone in originality and progressiveness. Many have argued that while the set is the finest work of The Beach Boys, the album marked the beginning of the end for the band.

While reaching #10, better than *Shutdown Vol.2*, the transition was not comfortable for the traditional flock of fans. It was too arty and too new.

On the other hand, musical artists of 1966 were astounded by the production revolution pioneered by the recording. Britain in particular welcomed the set with open arms and proclaimed Brian Wilson as a musical genius.

Pet Sounds marked the pinnacle of The Beach Boys' career, separating them from the other surf/ hot rod bands of the time. Indeed *Pet Sounds* is as distant from the sounds of summer as one could get, bar the incredible harmonies.

The album never went gold, but the positive repercussions were felt among the rock community. A standard was set from which there could be no turning back and for a short time, Brian led the new pathway to "glory".

The Pet Sounds Sessions 1965 -1966

JULY 12 – "Sloop John B"
Track recorded from 12am to 3am with a total of 13 musicians featuring:
Hal Blaine: Contractor and drums, Charles D.Britz: Engineer, Frank Capp: Percussion, Alvin W.Casey: Guitar, Alfred V.Delory: Sax, James R.Horn: Sax, Carol Kaye: Bass, Steve Kriesman: Sax and session leader, Jerry Kolbrak: Guitar, Jay Migliori: Clarinet, Jack Nimitz: Sax, Lyle Ritz: Guitar, William E.Strange: Guitar. STUDIO: Western Recorders, MASTER #53999, TIME: 3:06

NOVEMBER – "Trombone Dixie"
The CD issue of *Pet Sounds* featured this track which is only known to have been recorded during November, 1965.

NOVEMBER 17 – "Pet Sounds"
According to the CD liner notes, the finished track was taken from this session. A session card indicates another date for the recording of this song. STUDIO: Western Recorders.

DECEMBER 22 – "Sloop John B"
Beach Boys vocals recorded to the July 12 instrumental track. MASTER #53999

JANUARY 18 – "Let's Go Away For Awhile"
Instruments recorded only. STUDIO: Western. MASTER #55557

JANUARY 22 – "Wouldn't It Be Nice"
Instrumental track recorded. STUDIO: Gold Star. MASTER #55558

JANUARY 24 – "You Still Believe In Me"
Instrumental track and vocals recorded with Hal Blaine and Nick Pelico (percussion). STUDIO: Western. MASTER #55314

JANUARY 31 – "Caroline, No"
Backing track (featuring Hal Blaine on plastic water bottle) and vocals recorded. STUDIO: Western. MASTER #55536

FEBRUARY 9 – "Hang On To Your Ego"
Instrumental track and vocals recorded. STUDIO: Western.

FEBRUARY 14 – "I Just Wasn't Made For These Times"
Instrumental track recorded featuring Hal Blaine and Glen Campbell. STUDIO: Gold Star. MASTER #55598

FEBRUARY 15 – "That's Not Me"
Instrumental track and group vocals recorded. STUDIO: Western. MASTER #55591

FEBRUARY 18 – "Good Vibrations"
First session for the song and a Capitol memo lists the song as a preliminary track for the upcoming album *Pet Sounds*. STUDIO: Gold Star

MARCH – "I Know There's An Answer"
New vocals recorded for the song "Hang On To Your Ego".

MARCH 6 – "I'm Waiting For The Day"
Instrumental track recorded. STUDIO: Western. MASTER #55865

MARCH 9 – "God Only Knows"

According to CD liner notes the instrumental was recorded on this date. STUDIO: Western. MASTER # 55849

MARCH 10 – "God Only Knows"
AFM session date for the track recorded and basic vocals added (according to the CD liner notes) with a total of 19 musicians featuring:
Hal Blaine: Drums, Jay Migliori: Sax, Leonard Hartman: Sax, M.R.Pohlman: Bass, Lyle Ritz: Bass, Carl L.Fortina: Accordion, Frank Marucco: Accordion, Leonard Malarsky: Violin, Sidney Sharp: Violin, Darrel Terwilliger: Violin, Jesse Ehrlich: Cellos, Lawrence W. Knetchel: Keyboard, Carol Kaye: Bass, William Earnest Green: Sax/ Flute, Charles Britz: Engineer. STUDIO: Western. MASTER #55849. TIME: 2:30
"Here Today" – Music track recorded. STUDIO: Sunset Sound
"I'm Waiting For The Day" – Vocals recorded.
"Wouldn't It Be Nice" – Vocals recorded.
"I Just Wasn't Made For These Times" – Vocals recorded.

MARCH 11 – "Pet Sounds"
Track recorded with a total of 12 musicians featuring: Frank Capp: Percussion, Alvin W.Casey: Guitar, Michael W.Deasy: Guitar, Lawrence W.Knetchel: Keyboard, Gail Martin: Trombone, Nicholas Louis Martinis: Drums, Jay Migliori: Sax, Jack Nimitz: Sax, M.R.Pohlman: Bass, Don Randi: Organ, Lyle Ritz: Guitar, Ernie Tack: Baritone Horn, STUDIO: Sunset Sound Recorders. MASTER: #55848. TIME: 2:40

APRIL 3 – "Don't Talk (Put Your Head On My Shoulder)"
Instrumental track recorded featuring Al Delory on keyboard. Brian also added the final vocals. MASTER #55597.

APRIL 9 – "Good Vibrations"
Second known session for the track. STUDIO: Gold Star

APRIL 11 – "God Only Knows". Final vocals added.
"Wouldn't It Be Nice" – Final vocals added.

APRIL 13 – "I Just Wasn't Made For These Times"
Final vocals recorded.

Chart Action

Originally released on May 16, 1966 as US Capitol T-2458. The album charted on May 28, 1966 and reached #10 on the *Billboard* Charts.
    In the United Kingdom the album charted on July 7, 1966 and reached #2.

"Sloop John B"
Originally released March 23, 1966 (Capitol 5602) and charted on April 2, 1966 reaching #3 on the *Billboard* Charts and #5 on the *Cashbox* Charts.
In England, the single charted on July 8, 1966 and reached #2.
In Australia the single was originally released as a double A side with "You're So Good To Me" in April 1966. The single charted on April 20 1960 at #40 and reached #14 staying on the charts for 10 weeks.

"God Only Knows"
Originally released as the B side to "Wouldn't it Be Nice" on August 1, 1966 (Capitol 5706) and charted August 13, 1966 reaching #39 on the *Billboard* Charts and #38 on the *Cashbox* charts.

In the United Kingdom, the song charted August 6, 1966 and reached #2.

In Australia, the B side was released in August 1966, and charted August 24, 1966 at #39 reached #2 and stayed on the charts for 17 weeks.

"Wouldn't It Be Nice"

Originally, released August 1, 1966 backed with "God Only Knows". The single charted on August 13, 1960 and reached #8 on the *Billboard* Charts and #7 on the *Cashbox* Charts.

In Australia, the single was released August 1966, entered the charts on August 24, 1966 at #39 reaching #2 and staying on the charts for 17 weeks.

"Caroline No"

Originally released as a Brian Wilson solo single March 7, 1966, charting March 19, 1966 and reaching #32 on the *Billboard* Charts.

Official Release Curios

Ever since the late 1980's, a plethora of previously unheard music has reached the eager ears of fans worldwide. Surprisingly some of the rarest material has been officially released, providing extremely high quality reproductions of *Pet Sounds*.

As an album, *Pet Sounds* is still found in stores as a remastered CD that also includes the tracks "Trombone Dixie", "Hang On To Your Ego" and backing vocals for "Don't Talk"

A minor fault in the editing of these tracks to the end of the original album has seen the last bark of Banana (Brian's dog at the time) being lost: the album has three barks, the CD only has two.

The Japanese CD of the album with no bonus tracks features the album in its entirety.

Featured at the end of "Hang On To Your Ego" is a control room snippet that features Brian saying, "hey Chuck, is it possible we can bring a horse in here without...if we don't screw anything up?" Chuck Britz can be heard answering, "I beg your pardon?"

The Capitol Box set of 1993 contains the most interesting segments from the album sessions with "Hang On To Your Ego" (or Libido as Brian jokes). Studio chatter reveals Brian mentioning the World Peace phrase and one can hear how the track developed into the familiar "I Know There's An Answer".

Following this is the session for "God Only Knows" where the musicians suggest to Brian that staccato playing on the bridge would sound better than what was originally intended. It seems that Brian converses with Murry Wilson as he can be heard asking "Right Dad?". Given that Murry was present for the second "Help Me, Rhonda" session, it is reasonable to suggest that he was present for certain *Pet Sounds* tracking sessions. Also featured is a version with Brian's scratch vocals and then a mix of the song with an acappella ending. Another inclusion is an alternate mix of "Hang On To Your Ego". On the bonus disc, "Wouldn't it Be Nice" is featured as left channel vocals/right channel music.

The August 1968 album *Stack O' Tracks* (Capitol DKAO 2893) featured several *Pet Sounds* instrumental tracks: "Wouldn't it Be Nice", "God Only Knows", "Sloop John B" and "Here Today". The CD reissue presented the mixes in stereo.

Made In USA, a 1986 compilation, had an alternate vocal mix of "Wouldn't it Be Nice" and the original single mix (sans train and dogs) of "Caroline, No."

The Vestron Video *The Beach Boys: An American Band* features rough mixes of "Wouldn't It Be Nice", "That's Not Me", "I Just Wasn't Made For These Times" and a very different orchestral hit featured on "Here Today". Unfortunately, these tracks were cut short and in some cases spoken over.

Unofficial Release Curios

Recently there has been a huge influx of rough takes and studio sessions of *Pet Sounds*. Thankfully, most of this material is "new" and thus supplements the official material available.

"Wouldn't It Be Nice"
One of the oldest circulating tapes with an early Brian only vocal similar to that found on the Vestron video. This version features Brian slating the take as "21 please!" and concluding with the tape ending abruptly rather than fading out.
The session tape of the song is available of the few takes prior to the culled take 21, which is mainly false starts.
A further rough mix has Brian singing the opening verse couplets in reverse order, while another almost finished mix cuts abruptly just before the middle section vocals which are barely audible.

"You Still Believe In Me" (Aka "In My Childhood")
The session tapes begin with Brian directing Hal Blaine and then runs through the chatter of Brian and Tony Asher striking the piano strings. Chuck Britz advises Brian to turn a microphone away from them to eliminate phasing problems. Brian tinkers "You've Lost That Lovin' Feelin'" and then numerous takes of the intro to the song are recorded. Brian indicates the time at 7:30 and asks how long into the night they can record thanks to their repeated false starts.
Notably, he also mentions the title "You Still Believe in Me", suggesting that the plucked intro was recorded well after the actual backing track, which itself is noted by Brian as the "childhood song" in the session for the track
The tracking session (takes 6 through to 23) of the entire song features Brian comically mimicking the horn sound and generally guiding the musicians. Marilyn is heard in the control room along with Chuck Britz. Suspected session players are Hal Blaine, Nick Pelico and Al DeLory among others. A rough edited version of the song is heard with "You Still Believe in Me" lyrics.
A further tape features unsweetened and unmixed doubled vocals by Brian of the song sans the intro.
In the above session, Brian clearly asks for a loud count off as the vocal is from the top.

"Don't Talk (Put Your Head On My Shoulder)"
A session tape exists that features takes 1 and the slate only for take 2. Brian is heard directing Al Delory, and commenting on trouble with the "five bar break". Frank Capp and Chuck Britz were also apparently in the studio.
Two further rough mixes of the song are available with Brian laying down his lead vocal and then again doubling them on the second take.

"I'm Waiting For The Day"
An instrumental track exists of take 14 of the song.

An alternate mix of the track features Mike Love singing the verses in a style very unorthodox to his regular nasal singing. The vocal is treated with delay which is not evident on the final version. Brian sings the verses which appear to be the vocals kept on the released track.

It appears that Brian decided in the last moment (typical behaviour in years to come) to change the composition of the song.

"I Just Wasn't Made For These Times"

A session tape is available of takes 1 through to 6 with Brian directing Glen Campbell and Hal Blaine.

Mention is made to Glen about using his vox, probably suggesting either fuzz (aka distortion) or compression for the guitar.

A rough mix of the track is also available featuring Brian's vocals and a psychedelic ending.

The Religious Conversion of Brian Wilson: Goodbye Surfing, Hello God
There is something strange and new in the sound of the Beach Boys and it's coming out of what used to be the squarest head in pop music
by Jules Siegal

This article was one of the earliest to recognise, and attempt to explain, Brian Wilson's prodigious talent. Siegel was present at some of the Smile *sessions and used his observations to good effect. First published in the October 1967 issue of* Cheetah *magazine, it also appeared in* Record *by Jules Siegal in 1972. It is from this early piece that stem many of the best known quotes about Brian.*

It was just another day of greatness at Gold Star Recording Studios on Santa Monica Boulevard in Hollywood. In the morning four long-haired kids had knocked out two hours of sound for a record plugger who was trying to curry favor with a disk jockey friend of theirs in San Jose. Nobody knew it at the moment, but out of that two hours there were about three minutes that would hit the top of the charts in a few weeks, and the record plugger, the disk jockey and the kids would all be hailed as geniuses, but geniuses with a very small g.

Now, however, in the very same studio a Genius with a very large capital G was going to produce a hit. There was no doubt it would be a hit because this Genius was Brian Wilson. In four years of recording for Capitol Records, he and his group, the Beach Boys, had made surfing music a national craze, sold 16 million singles and earned gold records for 10 of their 12 albums.

Not only was Brian going to produce a hit, but also, one gathered, he was going to show everybody in the music business exactly where it was at; and where it was at, it appeared, was that Brian Wilson was not merely a Genius – which is to say a steady commercial success – but rather, with Bob Dylan and John Lennon, a GENIUS – which is to us, steady commercial success and hip besides.

Until now, though, there were not too many hip people who would have considered Brian Wilson and the Beach Boys hip, even though he had produced one very hip record, "Good Vibrations", which had sold more than a million copies, and a super-hip album, *Pet Sounds*, which didn't do to well at all-by previous Beach Boys sales standards. Among the hip people he was still on trial, and the question discussed earnestly among the recognized authorities on what is and what is not hip, was whether or not Brian Wilson was hip, semi-hip or square.

But walking into the control room with the answers to all questions such as this was Brian Wilson himself, wearing a competition-stripe surfer's T-shirt, tight white duck pants, pale green bowling shoes and a red plastic toy fireman's helmet.

Everybody was wearing identical red plastic toy fireman's helmets. Brian's cousin and production assistant, Steve Korthoff was wearing one; his wife, Marilyn, and her sister, Diane Rovell – Brian's secretary – were also wearing them,

and so was a once-dignified writer from *The Saturday Evening Post* who had been
following Brian around for two months trying to figure out whether or not this 24-
year-old oversized tribute to Southern California, who carried some 250 pounds of
baby fat on a 6-foot-4-inch frame, was a genius, Genius or GENIUS, hip, semi-hip
or square – concepts the writer himself was just learning to handle.

Out in the studio, the musicians for the session were unpacking their instruments. In sport shirts and slacks, they looked like insurance salesmen and used-car
dealers, except for one blonde female percussionist who might have been stamped
out by a special machine that supplied plastic mannequin housewives for detergent
commercials.

Controlled, a little bored after twenty years or so of nicely paid anonymity,
these were the professionals of the popular music business, hired guns who did
their job expertly and efficiently and then went home to the suburbs. If you wanted swing, they gave you swing. A little movie-track lushness? Fine, here comes
movie-track lushness. Now it's rock-and-roll? Perfect rock-and-roll, down the
chute.

"Steve," Brian called out, "where are the rest of those fire hats? I want everybody to wear fire hats. We've really got to get into this thing." Out to the Rolls
Royce went Steve and within a few minutes all of the musicians were wearing fire
hats, silly grins beginning to crack their professional dignity.

"All right, let's go," said Brian. Then, using a variety of techniques ranging
from vocal demonstration to actually playing the instruments, he taught each musician his part. A gigantic fire howled out of the massive studio speakers in a pounding crush of pictorial music that summoned up visions of roaring, windstorm
flames, falling timbers, mournful sirens and sweating firemen, building into a peak
and crackling off into fading embers as a single drum turned into a collapsing wall
and the fire engine cellos dissolved and disappeared.

"When did he write this?" asked an astonished pop music producer who had
wandered into the studio. "This is really fantastic! Man, this is unbelievable! How
long has he been working on it?"

"About an hour," answered one of Brian's friends.

"I don't believe it. I just can't believe what I'm hearing,"said the producer and
fell into a stone glazed silence as the fire music began again.

For the next three hours, Brian Wilson recorded and rerecorded, take after take,
changing the sound balance, adding echo, experimenting with a sound effects
track of a real fire.

"Let me hear that again." "Drums, I think you're a little slow in that last part.
Let's get right on it." "That was really good. Now, one more time, the whole
thing." "All right, let me hear the cellos alone." "Great. Really great. Now let's do
it!"

With 23 takes on tape and the entire operation responding to his touch like the
black knobs on the control boards, sweat glistening down his long, reddish hair
onto his freckled face, the control room littered with dead cigarette butts, Chicken
Delight boxes, crumpled napkins, Coke bottles and all the accumulated trash of the
physical end of the creative process, Brian stood at the board as the four speakers
blasted the music into the room. For the 24th time, the drum crashed and the sound
effects crackle faded and stopped.

"Thank you," said Brian, into the control room mike. "Let me hear that back." Feet shifting, his body still, eyes closed, head moving seal-like to his music, he stood under the speakers and listened. "Let me hear that one more time."

Again the fire roared. "Everybody come out and listen to this," Brian said to the musicians. They came into the control room and listened to what they had made.

"What do you think?" Brian asked.

"It's incredible. Incredible!" whispered one of the musicians, a man in his fifties, wearing a Hawaiian shirt, iridescent trousers and pointed black Italian shoes. "Absolutely incredible."

"Yeah," said Brian on the way home, an acetate trial copy or "dub" of the tape in his hands, the red plastic fire helmet still on his head. "Yeah, I'm going to call this 'Mrs O'Leary's Fire' and I think it might just scare a whole lot of people."

As it turns out, however, Brian Wilson's magic fire music is not going to scare anybody-because nobody other than the few people who heard it in the studio will ever get to listen to it. A few days after the record was finished, a building across the street from the studio burned down and, according to Brian, there was also an unusually large number of fires in Los Angeles. Afraid that his music might in fact turn out to be magic fire music, Wilson destroyed the master.

"I don't have to do a big scary fire like that," he later said. "I can do a candle and it's still fire. That would have been a really bad vibration to let out on the world, that Chicago fire. The next one is going to be a candle."

A person who thinks of himself as understanding would probably interpret this episode as an example of perhaps too excessive artistic perfectionism. One with psychiatric inclinations would hear all this stuff about someone who actually believed music could cause fires, and start using words such as neurosis and maybe even psychosis. A true student of spoken hip, however, would say hang-up, which covers all of the above.

As far as Brian's pretensions toward hipness are concerned, no label could do him worse harm. In the hip world, there is a widespread idea that really hip people don't have hang-ups, which gives rise to the unspoken rule (unspoken because there is also the widespread idea that really hip people don't make any rules) that no one who wants to be thought of as hip ever reveals his hang ups, except maybe to his guru, and in the strictest of privacy.

In any case, whatever his talent, Brian Wilson's attempt to win a hip following and reputation foundered for many months in an obsessive cycle of creation and destruction that threatened not only his career and his future but also his marriage, his friendships, his relationship with the Beach Boys and, some of his closest friends worried, his mind.

For a boy who used to be known in adolescence as a lover of sweets, the whole thing must have begun to taste very sour; yet, this particular phase of Brian's drive toward whatever his goal of supreme success might be began on a rising tide that at first looked as if it would carry him and the Beach Boys beyond the Beatles, who had started just about the same time they did, into the number one position in the international pop music fame and power competition.

"About a year ago I had what I consider a very religious experience," Wilson told Los Angeles writer Tom Nolan in 1966. "I took LSD, a full dose of LSD, and later, another time, I took a smaller dose. And I learned a lot of things, like patience, understanding. I can't teach you or tell you what I learned from taking it, but I consider it a very religious experience."

A short time after his LSD experience, Wilson began work on the record that was to establish him right along with the Beatles as one of the most important innovators in modern popular music. It was called "Good Vibrations", and it took more than six months, 90 hours of tape and 11 complete versions before a 3 minute 35 second final master tape satisfied him. Among the instruments on "Good Vibrations" was an electronic device called a theramin, which had its debut in the soundtrack of the movie Spellbound, back in the '40s. To some people, "Good Vibrations" was considerably crazier than Gregory Peck had been in the movie, but to others, Brian Wilson's new record, along with his somewhat earlier LP release, *Pet Sounds*, marked the beginning of a new era in pop music.

"THEY'VE FOUND THE NEW SOUND AT LAST" shrieked the headline over a London *Sunday Express* review as "Good Vibrations" hit the English charts at number six and leaped to number one the following week. Within a few weeks, the Beach Boys had pushed the Beatles out of first place in England's *New Musical Express*' annual poll. In America, "Good Vibrations" sold nearly 400,000 copies in four days before reaching number one several weeks later and earning a gold record within another month when it hit the one million sale mark.

It was an arrival, certainly, but in America, where there is none of the Beach Boys California mystique that adds a special touch of romance to their records and appearances in Europe and England, the news had not yet really reached all of the people whose opinion can turn popularity into fashionability. With the exception of a professor of show business (right, professor of show business; in California such a thing is not considered unusual) who turned up one night to interview Brian, and a few young writers (such as The Village Voice's Richard Goldstein, Paul Williams of *Crawdaddy*, and Lawrence Dietz of *New York Magazine*) not too many opinion makers were prepared to accept the Beach Boys into the mainstream of the culture industry.

"Listen man," said San Francisco music antic Ralph Gleason who had only recently graduated from jazz into Bob Dylan and was apparently not yet ready for any more violent twists, "I recognize the LA hype when I hear it. I know all about the Beach Boys and I think I liked them better before, if only for sociological reasons, if you understand what I mean."

"As for the Beach Boys," an editor of the *Post* chided his writer, who had filed the world's longest Western Union telegram of a story filled with unrelieved hero worship of Brian Wilson, "I want you to understand that as an individual you can feel that Brian Wilson is the greatest musician of our time, and maybe the greatest human being, but as a reporter you have got to maintain your objectivity."

"They want me to put him down," the writer complained. "That's their idea of objectivity – the put down."

"It has to do with this idea that it's not hip to be sincere," he continued, "and they really want to be hip. What they don't understand is that last year hip was sardonic – camp, they called it. This year hip is sincere.

"When somebody as corny as Brian Wilson starts singing right out front about God and I start writing it – very sincerely, you understand – it puts them very up tight. I think it's because it reminds them of all those terribly sincere hymns and sermons they used to have to listen to in church when they were kids in Iowa or

Ohio. Who knows? Maybe they're right. I mean, who needs all this goddamn intense sincerity all the time?"

What all this meant, of course, was that everybody agreed that Brian Wilson and the Beach Boys were still too square. It would take more than "Good Vibrations" and *Pet Sounds* to erase three and a half years of "Little Deuce Coupe" – a lot more if you counted in those J. C. Penney style custom tailored, kandy striped sport shirts they insisted on wearing on stage.

Brian, however, had not yet heard the news, it appeared, and was steadily going about the business of trying to become hip. The Beach Boys, who have toured without him ever since he broke down during one particularly wearing trip, were now in England and Europe, phoning back daily reports of enthusiastic fan hysteria-screaming little girls tearing at their flesh, wild press conferences, private chats with the Rolling Stones. Washed in the heat of a kind of attention they had never received in the United States even at the height of their commercial success, three Beach Boys – Brian's brothers, Dennis and Carl, and his cousin, Mike Love – walked into a London Rolls Royce showroom and bought four Phantom VII limousines, one for each of them and a fourth for Brian. Al Jardine and Bruce Johnston, the Beach Boys who are not corporate members of the Beach Boys Enterprises, sent their best regards and bought themselves some new clothing.

"I think this London thing has really helped," said Brian with satisfaction after he had made the color selection on his $32,000 toy – a ducal burgundy lacquered status symbol ordinarily reserved for heads of state. "That's just what the boys needed, a little attention to jack up their confidence." Then, learning that he wouldn't be able to have his new car for three months, he went out and bought an interim Rolls Royce for $20,000 from Mamas and Papas producer, Lou Adler, taking possession of the automobile just in time to meet his group at the airport as they returned home.

"It's a great environment for conducting business," he explained as his friend and former road manager, Terry Sachen, hastily pressed into service as interim chauffeur for the interim Rolls Royce, informally uniformed in his usual fringed deerskins and moccasins, drove the car through Hollywood to one of Brian's favorite eating places, the Pioneer Chicken drive-in on Sunset Boulevard.

"This car is really out of sight," said Brian, filling up on fried shrimp in the basket. "Next time we go up to Capitol, I'm going to drive up in my Rolls Royce limo. You've got to do those things with a little style. It's not just an ordinary visit that way – it's an arrival, right? Wow! That's really great – an arrival, in my limo. It'll blow their minds!"

Whether or not the interim Rolls Royce actually ever, blew the minds of the hard nosed executives who run Capitol Records is something to speculate on, but no one in the record industry with a sense of history could have failed to note that this very same limousine had once belonged to John Lennon; and in the closing months of 1966, with the Beach Boys home in Los Angeles, Brian rode the "Good Vibrations" high, driving forward in bursts of enormous energy that seemed destined before long to earn him the throne of the international empire of pop music still ruled by John Lennon and the Beatles.

At the time, it looked as if the Beatles were ready to step down. Their summer concerts in America had been only moderately successful at best, compared to earlier years. There were ten thousand empty seats at Shea Stadium in New York and 11 lonely fans at the airport in Seattle. Mass media, underground press, music industry trade papers and the fan magazines were filled with fears that the Beatles were finished, that the group was breaking up. Lennon was off acting in a movie; McCartney was walking around London alone, said to be carrying a giant torch for his sometime girl friend, Jane Asher; George Harrison was getting deeper and deeper into a mystical Indian thing under the instruction of sitar master Ravi Shankar, and Ringo was collecting material for a Beatles museum.

In Los Angeles, Brian Wilson was riding around in the Rolls Royce that had once belonged to John Lennon, pouring a deluge of new sounds onto miles of stereo tape in three different recording studios booked day and night for him in month solid blocks, holding court nightly at his $240,000 Beverly Hills Babylonian modern home, and, after guests left, sitting at his grand piano until dawn, writing new material.

The work in progress was an album called *Smile*. "I'm writing a teenage symphony to God," Brian told dinner guests on an October evening. He then played for them the collection of black acetate trial records which lay piled on the floor of his red imitation velvet wallpapered bedroom with its leopard print bedspread. In the bathroom, above the wash basin, there was a plastic color picture of Jesus Christ with trick effect eyes that appeared to open and close when you moved your head. Sophisticate newcomers pointed it out to each other and laughed slyly, almost hoping to find a Keane painting among decorations ranging from Lava Lamps to a department store rack of dozens of dolls, each still in its plastic bubble container, the whole display trembling like a space-age Christmas tree to the music flowing out into the living room.

Brian shuffled through the acetates, most of which were unlabeled, identifying each by subtle differences in the patterns of the grooves. He had played them so often he knew the special look of each record the way you know the key to your front door by the shape of its teeth. Most were instrumental tracks, cut while the Beach Boys were in Europe, and for these Brian supplied the vocal in a high sound that seemed to come out of his head rather than his throat as he somehow managed to create complicated four and five part harmonies with only his own voice.

"Rock, rock, Plymouth rock roll over," Brian sang. "Bicycle rider, see what you done done to the church of the restive American Indian… Over and over the crow cries uncover the cornfields. Who ran the Iron Horse?"

"Out in the farmyard the cook is chopping lumber; out in the barnyard the chickens do their number. Bicycle rider see what you done done…" A panorama of American history filled the room as the music shifted from theme to theme; the tinkling harpsichord sounds of the bicycle rider pushed sad Indian sounds across the continent; the Iron Horse pounded across the plains in a wide open rolling rhythm that summoned up visions of the old West; civilized chickens bobbed up and down in a tiny ballet of comic barnyard melody; the inexorable bicycle music, cold and charming as an infinitely talented music box, reappeared and faded away.

Like medieval choirboys, the voices of the Beach Boys pealed out in wordless prayer from the last acetate, thirty seconds of chorale that reached upward to the vaulted stone ceilings of an empty cathedral lit by thousands of tiny candles, melting at last into one small, pure pool that whispered a universal amen in a sigh without words.

Brian's private radio show was finished. In the dining room a candlelit table with a dark blue cloth was set for 10 persons. In the kitchen, Marilyn Wilson was trying to get the meal organized and served, aided and hindered by the chattering suggestions of the guests' wives and girl friends. When everyone was seated and waiting for the food, Brian tapped his knife idly on a white china plate.

"Listen to that," he said. "That's really great!" Everybody listened as Brian played the plate. "Come on, let's get something going here," he ordered. "Michael – do this. David – you do this." A plate and spoon musicale began to develop as each guest played a distinctly different technique, rhythm and melody under Brian's enthusiastic direction.

"That's absolutely unbelievable!" said Brian. "Isn't that unbelievable? That's so unbelievable I'm going to put it on the album. Michael, I want you to get a sound system up here tomorrow and I want everyone to be here tomorrow night. We're going to get this on tape."

Brian Wilson's plate and spoon musicale never did reach the public, but only because he forgot about it. Other sounds equally strange have found their way on to his records. On *Pet Sounds*, for example, on some tracks there is an odd, soft, hollow percussion effect that most musicians assume is some kind of electronically transmuted drum sound – a conga drum played with a stick perhaps, or an Indian tom tom. Actually, it's drummer Hal Blaine playing the bottom of a plastic jug that once contained Sparklettes spring water. And, of course, at the end of the record there is the strangely affecting track of a train roaring through a lonely railroad crossing as a bell clangs and Brian's dogs, Banana, a beagle, and Louie, a dark brown Weimaraner, bark after it.

More significant, perhaps, to those who that night heard the original instrumental tracks for both *Smile* and the Beach Boys new single, "Heroes and Villains", is that entire sequences of extraordinary power and beauty are missing in the finished version of the single, and will undoubtedly be missing as well from *Smile* – victims of Brian's obsessive tinkering and, more importantly, sacrifices to the same strange combination of superstitious fear and God like conviction of his own power he displayed when he destroyed the fire music.

The night of the dining table concerto, it was the God-like confidence Brian must have been feeling as he put his guests on his trip, but the fear was soon to take over. At his house that night, he had assembled a new set of players to introduce into his life game, each of whom was to perform a specific role in the grander game he was playing with the world.

Earlier in the summer, Brian had hired Van Dyke Parks, a super sophisticated young songwriter and composer, to collaborate with him on the lyrics for Smile. With Van Dyke working for him, he had a fighting chance against John Lennon, whose literary skill and Liverpudlian wit had been one of the most important factors in making the Beatles the darling of the hip intelligentsia.

With that flank covered, Brian was ready to deal with some of the other problems of trying to become hip, the most important of which was how was he going to get in touch with some really hip people. In effect, the dinner party at the house was his first hip social event, and the star of the evening, so far as Brian was concerned, was Van Dyke Parks' manager, David Anderle, who showed up with a whole group of very hip people.

Elegant, cool and impossibly cunning, Anderle was an artist who had somehow found himself in the record business as an executive for MGM Records, where he had earned himself a reputation as a genius by purportedly thinking up the million dollar movie-tv-record offer that briefly lured Bob Dylan to MGM from Columbia until everybody had a change of heart and Dylan decided to go back home to Columbia.

Anderle had skipped back and forth between painting and the record business, with mixed results in both. Right now he was doing a little personal management and thinking about painting a lot. His appeal to Brian was simple: everybody recognised David Anderle as one of the hippest people in Los Angeles. In fact, he was something like the mayor of hipness as far as some people were concerned. And not only that, he was a genius. Within six weeks, he was working for the Beach Boys; everything that Brian wanted seemed at last to be in reach.

Like a magic genie, David Anderle produced miracles for him. A new Beach Boys record company was set up, Brother Records, with David Anderle at its head and, simultaneously, the Beach Boys sued Capitol Records in a move to force a renegotiation of their contract with the company.

The house was full of underground press writers; Anderle's friend Michael Vosse was on the Brother Records payroll out scouting TV contracts and performing other odd jobs. Another of Anderle's friends was writing the story on Brian for *The Saturday Evening Post* and a film crew from CBS TV was up at the house filming for a documentary to be narrated by Leonard Bernstein. The Beach Boys were having meetings once or twice a week with teams of experts briefing them on corporate policy, drawing complicated chalk patterns as they described the millions of dollars everyone was going to earn out of all this.

As 1967 opened it seemed as though Brian and the Beach Boys were assured of a new world of success; yet something was going wrong. As the corporate activity reached a peak of intensity, Brian was becoming less and less productive and more and more erratic. *Smile*, which was to have been released for the Christmas season, remained unfinished. "Heroes and Villains", which was virtually complete, remained in the can, as Brian kept working out new little pieces and then scrapping them.

Van Dyke Parks had left and come back and would leave again, tired of being constantly dominated by Brian. Marilyn Wilson was having headaches and Dennis Wilson was leaving his wife. Session after session was canceled. One night a studio full of violinists waited while Brian tried to decide whether or not the vibrations were friendly or hostile. The answer was hostile and the session was canceled, at a cost of some $3,000. Everything seemed to be going wrong. Even the *Post* story fell through.

Brian seemed to be filled with secret fear. one night at the house, it began to surface. Marilyn sat nervously painting her fingernails as Brian stalked up and down, his face tight and his eyes small and red.

"What's the matter, Brian? You're really strung out," a friend asked.

"Yeah, I'm really strung out. Look, I mean I really feel strange. A really strange thing happened to me tonight. Did you see this picture, *Seconds*?"

"No, but I know what it's about; I read the book."

"Look, come into the kitchen; I really have to talk about this." In the kitchen they sat down in the black and white houndstooth check wall-papered dinette area. A striped window shade clashed with the checks and the whole room vibrated like some kind of pop art painting. Ordinarily, Brian wouldn't sit for more than a minute in it, but now he seemed to be unaware of anything except what he wanted to say.

"I walked into that movie," he said in a tense, high pitched voice, "and the first thing that happened was a voice from the screen said 'Hello, Mr. Wilson.' It completely blew my mind. You've got to admit that's pretty spooky, right?"

"Maybe."

"That's not all. Then the whole thing was there. I mean my whole life. Birth and death and rebirth. The whole thing. Even the beach was in it, a whole thing about the beach. It was my whole life right there on the screen."

"It's just a coincidence, man. What are you getting all excited about?"

"Well, what if it isn't a coincidence? What if it's real? You know there's mind gangsters these days. There could be mind gangsters, couldn't there? I mean look at Spector, he could be involved in it, couldn't he? He's going into films. How hard would it be for him to set up something like that?"

"Brian, Phil Spector is not about to make a million dollar movie just to scare you. Come on, stop trying to be so dramatic. "

"All right, all right. I was just a little bit nervous about it," Brian said, after some more back and forth about the possibility that Phil Spector, the record producer, had somehow influenced the making of *Seconds* to disturb Brian Wilson's tranquillity. "I just had to get it out of my system. You can see where something like that could scare someone, can't you?"

They went into Brian's den, a small room papered in psychedelic orange, blue, yellow and red wall fabric with rounded corners. At the end of the room there was a juke box filled with Beach Boy singles and Phil Spector hits. Brian punched a button and Spector's "Be My Baby" began to pour out at top volume.

"Spector has always been a big thing with me, you know. I mean I heard that three and a half years ago and I knew that it was between him and me. I knew exactly where he was at and now I've gone beyond him. You can understand how that movie might get someone upset under those circumstances, can't you?

Brian sat down at his desk and began to draw a little diagram on a piece of printed stationery with his name at the top in the kind of large fat script printers of charitable dinner journals use when the customer asks for a hand lettered look. With a felt tipped pen, Brian drew a close approximation of a growth curve. "Spector started the whole thing," he said, dividing the curve into periods. "He was the first one to use the studio. But I've gone beyond him now. I'm doing the spiritual sound, a white spiritual sound. Religious music. Did you hear the Beatles album? Religious, right? That's the whole movement. That's where I'm going. It's going to scare a lot of people.

"Yeah," Brian said, hitting his fist on the desk with a slap that sent the parakeets in the large cage facing him squalling and whistling. "Yeah," he said and smiled for the first time all evening.

"That's where I'm going and it's going to scare of lot of people when I get there."

As the year drew deeper into winter, Brian's rate of activity grew more and more frantic, but nothing seemed to be accomplished. He tore the house apart and half redecorated it. One section of the living room was filled with a fullsized Arabian tent and the dining room, where the grand piano stood, was filled with sand to a depth of a foot or so and draped with nursery curtains. He had had his windows stained gray and put a sauna bath in the bedroom. He battled with his father and complained that his brothers weren't trying hard enough. He accused Mike Love of making too much money.

One by one, he canceled out the friends he had collected, sometimes for the strangest of reasons. An acquaintance of several months who had become extremely close with Brian showed up at a record session and found a guard barring the door. Michael Vosse came out to explain.

"Hey man, this is really terrible," said Vosse, smiling under a broad brimmed straw hat. "It's not you, it's your chick. Brian says she's a witch and she's messing with his brain so bad by ESP that he can't work. It's like the Spector thing. You know how he is. Say, I'm really sorry." A couple of months later, Vosse was gone. Then, in the late Spring, Anderle left. The game was over.

Several months later, the last move in Brian's attempt to win the hip community was played out. On July 15, the Beach Boys were scheduled to appear at, the Monterey International Pop Music Festival, a kind of summit of rock music with the emphasis on love, flowers and youth. Although Brian was a member of the board of this nonprofit event, the Beach Boys canceled their commitment to perform. The official reason was that their negotiations with Capitol Records were at a crucial stage and they had to get "Heroes and Villains" out right away. The second official reason was that Carl, who had been arrested for refusing to report for induction into the Army (he was later cleared in court), was so upset that he wouldn't be able to sing.

Whatever the merit in these reasons, the real one may have been closer to something another Monterey board member suggested: "Brian was afraid that the hippies from San Francisco would think the Beach Boys were square and boo them."

But maybe Brian was right. "Those candy striped shirts just wouldn't have made it at Monterey, man," said one person who was there.

Whatever the case, at the end of the summer, "Heroes and Villains" was released in sharply edited form and *Smile* was reported to be on its way. In the meantime, however, the Beatles had released *Sergeant Pepper's Lonely Hearts Club Band* and John Lennon was riding about London in a bright yellow Phantom VII Rolls Royce painted with flowers on the sides and his zodiac symbol on the top. In *Life* magazine, Paul McCartney came out openly for LSD and in the Haight Ashbury district of San Francisco George Harrison walked through the streets blessing the hippies. Ringo was still collecting material for a Beatles museum. However good *Smile* might turn out to be, it seemed somehow that once more the Beatles had outdistanced the Beach Boys.

Back during that wonderful period in the fall of 1966 when everybody seemed to be his friend and plans were being laid for Brother Records and all kinds of fine things, Brian had gone on a brief visit to Michigan to hear a Beach Boys concert. The evening of his return, each of his friends and important acquaintances received a call asking everyone to please come to the airport to meet Brian, it was very important. When they gathered at the airport, Brian had a photographer on hand to take a series of group pictures. For a long time, a huge mounted blow up of the best of the photographs hung on the living room wall, with some thirty people staring out – everyone from Van Dyke Parks and David Anderle to Michael Vosse and Terry Sachen. In the foreground was *The Saturday Evening Post* writer looking sourly out at the world.

The picture is no longer on Brian's wall and most of the people in it are no longer his friends. One by one each of them had either stepped out of the picture or been forced out of it. The whole cycle has returned to its beginning. Brian, who started out in Hawthorne, Calif., with his two brothers and a cousin, once more has surrounded himself with relatives. The house in Beverly Hills is empty. Brian and Marilyn are living in their new Spanish Mission estate in BelAir, cheek by jowl with the Mamas and Papas' Cass Elliott.

What remains, of course, is "Heroes and Villains", a record some people think is better than anything the Beatles ever wrote. And there is also a spectacular peak, a song called "Surfs up" that Brian recorded for the first time in December in Columbia Records' Studio A for a CBS TV pop music documentary. Earlier in the evening the film crew had covered a Beach Boys vocal session which had gone very badly. Now, at midnight, the Beach Boys had gone home and Brian was sitting in the back of his car, smoking moodily.

In the dark car, he breathed heavily, his hands in his lap, eyes staring nowhere. "All right," he said at last, "Let's just sit here and see if we can get into something positive, but without any words. Let's just get into something quiet and positive on a nonverbal level." There was a long silence.

"OK, let's go," he said, and then, quickly, he was in the studio rehearsing, spotlighted in the center of the huge dark room, the cameramen moving about him invisibly outside the light.

"Let's do it," he announced, and the tape began to roll. In the control room no one moved. David Oppenheim, the TV producer, fortyish, handsome, usually studiously detached and professional, lay on the floor, hands behind his head, eyes closed. For three minutes and 27 seconds, Wilson played with delicate intensity, speaking moodily through the piano. Then he was finished. Oppenheim, whose last documentary had been a study of Stravinsky, lay motionless.

"That's it," Wilson said as the tape continued to whirl. The mood broke. As if awakening from heavy sleep the people stirred and shook their heads.

"I'd like to hear that," Wilson said. As his music replayed, he sang the lyrics in a high, almost falsetto voice, the cameras on him every second.

"The diamond necklace played the pawn," Wilson sang. *"...A blind class aristocracy, back through the opera glass you see the pit and the pendulum drawn."*

"Columnated ruins domino." His voice reached upward; the piano faltered a set of falling chords.

In a slow series of impressionistic images the song moved to its ending:

"I heard the word, Wonderful thing! A children's song!"

On the last word Brian's voice rose and fell, like the singing in that prayer chorale he had played so many months before.

"That's really special," someone said.

"Special, that's right," said Wilson quietly. "Van Dyke and I really kind of thought we had done something special when we finished that one." He went back into the studio, put on the ear phones and sang the song again for the audience in the control room, for the revolving tape recorder and for the cameras which relentlessly followed as he struggled to make manifest what had only existed as a perfect, incommunicable sound in his head.

At home, as the black acetate dub turned on his bedroom hi-fi set, Wilson tried to explain the words.

"It's a man at a concert," he said. And around him there's the audience, playing their roles, dressed up in fancy clothes, looking through opera glasses, but so far away from the drama, from life – *back through the opera glass you see the pit and the pendulum drawn.*"

"The music begins to take over. *Columnated ruins domino.* Empires, ideas, lives, institutions-everything has to fall, tumbling like dominoes.

"He begins to awaken to the music; sees the pretentiousness of everything, *The music hall a costly bow.* Then even the music is gone. Turned into a trumpeter swan, into what the music really is.

"*Canvas the town and brush the backdrop.* He's off in his vision, on a trip. Reality is gone; he's creating it like a dream. *Dove nested towers.* Europe, a long time ago. *The laughs come hard in Auld Lang Syne.* The poor people in the cellar taverns, trying to make thernselves happy by singing.

"Then there's the parties, the drinking, trying to forget the wars, the battles at sea. *While at port a do or die.* Ships in the harbor, battling it out. A kind of Roman Empire thing.

"*A choke of grief.* At his own sorrow and the emptiness of his life, because he can't even cry for the suffering in the world, for his own suffering.

"And then, hope. *Surf's up!... Come about hard and join the once and often spring you gave.* Go back to the tides, to the beach, to childhood.

"*I heard the word* – of God; *Wonderful thing* – the joy of enlightenment, of seeing God. And what is it? *A childrens's song*! And then there's the song itself; the song of children; the song of the universe rising and falling in wave after wave, the song of God, hiding His love from us, but always letting us find Him again, like a mother singing to her children."

The record was over. Wilson went into the kitchen and squirted Reddi Whip direct from the can into his mouth; made himself a chocolate Great Shake, and ate a couple of candy bars.

"Of course that's a very intellectual explanation," he said. "But maybe sometimes you have to do an intellectual thing. If they don't get the words, they'll get the music, because that's where it's really at, in the music. You can get hung up in words, you know. Maybe they work; I don't know." He fidgeted with a telescope.

"This thing is so bad," he complained. "So Mickey Mouse. It just won't work smoothly. I was really freaked out on astronomy when I was a kid. Baseball too. I guess I went through a lot of phases. A lot of changes, too. But you can really get into things through the stars. And swimming. A lot of swimming. It's physical; really Zen, right? The whole spiritual thing is very physical. Swimming really does it sometimes." He sprawled on the couch and continued in a very small voice.

"So that's what I'm doing. Spiritual music."

"Brian," Marilyn called as she came into the room wearing a quilted bathrobe, "do you want me to get you anything, honey? I'm going to sleep."

"No, Mar," he answered, rising to kiss his wife goodnight. "You go on to bed. I want to work for a while."

"C'mon kids," Marilyn yelled to the dogs as she padded off to bed. "Time for bed. Louie! Banana! Come to bed. Goodnight, Brian. Goodnight, everybody."

Wilson paced. He went to the piano and began to play. His guests moved toward the door. From the piano, his feet shuffling in the sand, he called a perfunctory goodbye and continued to play, a melody beginning to take shape. Outside, the piano spoke from the house. Brian Wilson's guests stood for a moment, listening. As they got into their car, the melancholy piano moaned.

"Here's one that's really outasight from the fantabulous Beach Boys!" screamed a local early morning Top 40 DJ from the car radio on the way home, a little hysterical, as usual, his voice drowning out the sobbing introduction to the song.

"We're sending this one out for Bob and Carol in Pomona. They've been going steady now for six months. Happy six months, kids, and dig! Good Vibrations! The Beach Boys! Outasight!"

Original Reviews Part 3

The reviews in this part and those through to part 8 all cover the Beach Boys albums as they were released. In the first half of the sixties, albums were rarely reviewed in depth, but as the importance of LPs grew with the decade, so pop pages concentrated on them at the expense of singles. The review excerpts have been chosen from the weekly pop press of the day: *NME*, *Record Mirror*, *Melody Maker* and *Sounds*.

Wild Honey / Friends Capitol double album.

"[This double album reissue is] in the grand old tradition of milking every last drop from the Beach Boys catalogue". (The critics were even saying it back then! Ed.)

"The lyrics, Mike Love's, are a vehicle for supporting Brian Wilson's music, something they do remarkably well. After the excesses of Van Dyke Parks these marked a comforting return to normality…"

"*Friends* did nothing to counteract The Beach Boys establishment image and in some ways it is a lousy album, in fact, after *Wild Honey* it's a qualified disaster…"

"Let it be said that, at their worst, *Friends*, the Beach Boys manage to produce songs which would be karma to most other bands. At their best, well, see for yourself at Wembley. Meanwhile watch *Spirit of America* burn up the Yankee chart. It's a compilation [album], of course."

Smile: The Great Lost Album
by Peter Doggett

This is a revised version of an article that originally appeared in Record Collector *magazine as part of their Great Lost Albums series.*

Across the forty-year history of rock music, legends have grown, or in some cases deliberately been constructed, around the records that never were – the great lost albums that were doomed by a combination of fate, loss of artistic nerve, or physical or psychological collapse.

If they'd been released, then the course of rock history might have been… well, better, perhaps, or maybe worse, but undoubtedly different. For some artists, the sacrifice of an almost complete record liberated them from a musical straitjacket; for others, like Brian Wilson and the Beach Boys in the case of *Smile*, the loss is measurable in personal as well as artistic terms. To understand exactly what *Smile* might have been, you have to think yourself back to 1966, when the Beach Boys were not an oldies act touring on fading glory, but arguably the most innovative and ambitious rock group in the world. Or, at least, their creative leader, Brian Wilson was: while he laboured over grandiose projects in the studio, the rest of the band were doing what they've always done, performing their hits in public. And that was part of the problem.

1966 was the year when the Beach Boys toppled the Beatles as the most popular group in the world – a judgement cemented into fact that December, when they triumphed in the *New Musical Express* readers' poll, a result that sent shockwaves around the world .

A year or two earlier, the Beach Boys had been one of the few American acts to survive the onset of Beatlemania. Emerging as spokesmen for the male hedonists of California, with nothing more than surf, speed and sex on their minds, they'd gradually widened their palette. Brian Wilson – devotee in equal doses of Phil Spector, George Gershwin and the Four Freshmen – established himself as one of the most inventive melodists and arrangers in pop.

Capitol Records treated them as fan fodder from the start, whipping Wilson into completing three or four albums a year, and triggering a nervous breakdown in the process. By the end of 1964, Wilson was ensconced in the studio, leaving the rest of the group to tour as his representatives on earth. Freed from the treadmill, he gave his creative talent free rein. At first, he merely gave the accepted boundaries of teen pop a gentle tug, introducing "California Girls" with a mournful, touching instrumental progression that undercut the message of the song, or scoring album tracks like "In The Back of My Mind" as if they were a mini symphony.

By late 1965, Brian was thinking beyond the charts. His next album, *Pet Sounds*, brought the tone poems of 20th century classical music into the pop field for the first time, and tied them to lyrics – mostly written by advertising man Tony Asher – which explored the emotional roller coaster of adult romance. In Britain, *Pet Sounds* was greeted as a masterpiece; musicians as diverse as Paul McCartney and John Cale have described it as pop's finest moment. But in America, where the Beach Boys' pleasure seeking image was set in stone, it failed to match the sales of their earlier releases.

From then on, Wilson was back under the heat – Capitol wanted more teen oriented hits, and various members of the band, notably Mike Love, were suspicious of Wilson's increasingly obsessive work habits. Meanwhile, Brian was blowing his mind – partly on drugs ("I totally fried my brain", he admitted in one of his pathetically revealing interviews a decade later), partly on the artistic and intellectual stimulus of new friends like Van Dyke Parks and David Anderle. They persuaded Brian that being ambitious didn't mean that he was crazy, and encouraged him to follow his whims wherever they took him.

That destination turned out to be "Good Vibrations". Wilson had been toying with the concept, and the title, since the *Pet Sounds* sessions; in February 1966, he began to work on the basic track. Over the next five months, through 90 hours of sessions at four Los Angeles studios, Wilson perfected the single which became a worldwide hit in November, greeted universally as the most breathtaking and adventurous piece of pop music ever released.

"Good Vibrations" set the style for what was to follow, linking together several apparently unrelated musical fragments with stunning self-confidence-and leaving the Beach Boys the puzzle of how to reproduce the complex changes of key and tempo on stage. More than 30 minutes of out takes from the "Good Vibrations" sessions have emerged on official and bootleg releases; they show Brian Wilson in absolute control of sessions, experimenting endlessly with different combinations of instruments, months before the rest of the group were pulled in to add the vocals. Brian himself sang lead on some of these out takes, unveiling lyrics that didn't make the final record; his brother Carl contributed the final lead vocal to the single.

With lyricist Van Dyke Parks as his collaborator, Brian now embarked on what Parks called "an American Gothic trip". Van Dyke dragged Brian away from the familiar territory of romantic love towards a new style of writing, full of elliptical images and verbal free association. "I tried to contribute to the idea that perhaps all music did not have to be for dancing", Parks explained later, though "Good Vibrations" had already drawn complaints from a minority of pop fans who found its sudden switches of tempo unsettling on the discotheque floor.

Another vital ingredient was humour, or at least Brian Wilson's version of it. The Beach Boys had already indulged themselves on album with trite verbal battles like "Cassius Love vs. Sonny Wilson"; now Brian wanted music that would encapsulate the "Universal Smile" he'd found from mind expanding drugs. And so the album in the making, originally titled "Dumb Angel" in an astute piece of self analysis, became *Smile*. As *Rolling Stone* writer Tom Nolan noted in 1971, "Humour was salvation, the Holy Grail, for Brian"; and Wilson's associates remember his ambitious, unrealisable plans around this time for records of water noises, comedy and even a health food album, based around one of the *Smile* tracks, "Vegetables".

That was still a long way off in May 1966, when Wilson and Parks began to assemble the pieces of *Smile*. Remarkably, that was when work commenced on the centre piece of *Smile*, "a three minute musical comedy" in Brian's words called "Heroes And Villains". The song was still being recorded eight months later, long after its proposed release date.

The saga of that single is in many ways a microcosm of the entire *Smile* tragi-comedy. On previous albums, Brian Wilson had conceived each song as a separate entity. With *Smile*, all boundaries were knocked aside, and he crafted two dozen or so fragmentary pieces of music, some conventional, others totally oddball, which he tried to shape into some kind of coherent whole.

The problem was, Brian never quite decided which combination of fragments should make up a particular song. That's why it's never been possible for anyone to reconstitute the complete *Smile*, even though there is around two hours of material circulating among collectors. Around the end of 1966, Capitol were demanding finished cover artwork, which Brian duly provided; for the back of the sleeve, he wrote out by hand a list of a dozen song titles, which were printed up with the note, "see labels for correct playing order".

We have the song titles, then, and a large proportion of the tapes; but how do the two fit together? "Heroes And Villains", for instance, was originally planned to run for seven minutes, across both sides of a single. That complete version has never been released, though the first half was included on the 1991 CD box set. Various archive projects have unveiled additional melodic sections of the song, among them a fragment called "Bicycle Rider" – a theme which was incorporated into "Heroes And Villains" when the group performed the song live in the 1970s. Equally fragmentary is "Barnyard", quoted by many sources as another segment of "Heroes And Villains". The shifts of melody and tempo on the out-takes are so dramatic that virtually anything could have been considered part of that song; in Brian Wilson's mind, virtually anything was.

"Heroes And Villains" was eventually issued in July 1967 – almost two months after the Beatles' *Sgt. Pepper* had sent rock spinning in an entirely new direction. It's no secret that the Beatles intended parts of *Revolver* as a direct response to *Pet Sounds*; the friendly competition between the two groups was so intense that the release of anything like a full bore *Smile* would surely have set the Beatles back for months while they considered a suitable reply.

Beautiful and intriguing, "Heroes And Villains" was nowhere near as commercial as "Good Vibrations"; and just as they had done with *Pet Sounds*, Capitol did their best to overshadow its release by rushing a greatest hits set onto the market.

In September 1967, the Beach Boys finally released their new album-only it wasn't *Smile*, but *Smiley Smile*, which wasn't exactly the same thing. "Good Vibrations" and "Heroes And Villains" were on board, together with new versions of songs originally intended for Smile, like "Vega Tables", "Wind Chimes" and "Wonderful"; but the overall effect was trivial and unfocused, like a hippy's drug den set to music. Compared to the lavish orchestrations of *Pepper*, it didn't stand a chance.

The anti-climax of *Smiley Smile* convinced most onlookers that Smile was more hype than reality. Even the smattering of pro-Wilson press coverage, from insiders like Jules Siegel, cast more doubt on Brian's sanity than anything else. But the myth of this impossibly perfect album grew – particularly as tales spread of a track called "Fire", which Brian had destroyed after a series of conflagrations had affected the area of L.A. around his studio; and after Brian's solo rendition of another *Smile* extract, "Surf's Up", was featured on the U.S. TV show "Inside Pop: The Rock Revolution", complete with appreciative commentary by composer/conductor Leonard Bernstein.

Internal Capitol memos suggest the company were still expecting *Smile* to be released after *Smiley Smile*. A photo booklet was prepared for *Smile* early in 1967; staff were advised not to include it as a bonus with *Smiley Smile*, but to save it for the group's next LP. In the event, *Smile* was completely abandoned, and most of the booklets were destroyed.

The subsequent trickle down release of *Smile* material – "Cabinessence" and "Our Prayer" on the 20/20 album in 1969, "Surf's Up" as the title track of a 1971 album – helped restore the legend. Then in 1972, Carl Wilson announced that *Smile* would be issued later that year, as part of a double set with the group's latest album. *Carl & The Passions* duly appeared, but with *Pet Sounds*, not *Smile*, as its companion.

Almost a decade later, Bruce Johnston told the American magazine *Goldmine* that he was intending to assemble a *Smile* suite for the Beach Boys' upcoming retrospective. "Ten Years of Harmony" followed a few months later, without a hint of a *Smile*.

In the late 80s, Brian Wilson – previously averse to the release of any Smile material, even on *20/20* and *Surf's up* – delighted his supporters by announcing that he was in the process of piecing together the complete album, along with his *Brian Wilson* solo set. Once again, the project foundered. Only with the appearance of the *Smiley Smile / Wild Honey* double CD, and then the Beach Boys' box set, did any quantity of *Smile* material surface legally for the first time.

What went wrong? Back in 1971, Brian tried to explain: "That was because Van Dyke Parks had written lyrics that were all Van Dyke Parks and none of the Beach Boys. The lyrics were so poetic and symbolic they were abstract, we couldn't... oh no, wait, it was, no, really, I remember, this is it, this is why, it didn't come out because, I'd bought a lot of hashish..." and off he rambled into a convoluted and ultimately meaningless anecdote about being stoned.

In all his confusion, Brian had fingered the two main reasons for the non appearance of *Smile*. First, the album was indeed a Brian Wilson/Van Dyke Parks project, not a Beach Boys album, and when certain members of the Beach Boys confronted the pair with what they saw as the meaninglessness of the new songs, Brian didn't have the strength to stand his ground. Then, as on many occasions thereafter, Brian adopted the ostrich position and left the rest of the Beach Boys to deal with the crisis. They concocted the semi-inspired *Smiley Smile* – sessions for which, pointedly, began the day after the release of *Sgt. Pepper* – and then saw themselves through two years of collapsing sales figures by draping the shadow of *Smile* over their next few albums.

Sadly, the drugs played an equally vital role in snuffing out Wilson's creative flame. Brian's massive ingestion of LSD induced first euphoria ("I'm writing a teenage symphony to God", he announced in 1966), then rampant paranoia, followed by some kind of personality collapse – documented in style, if not entirely accurately, in Wilson's "autobiography", *Wouldn't it Be Nice*. After the enormous emotional and physical stress of the *Smile* episode, Wilson was unable to give his all to any recording project for the next two decades. Almost every Beach Boys album had some contribution from Brian, but he remained unable to focus his energies in one coherent direction until he completed his epic solo album, *Brian Wilson*, in 1988.

There was a third, less dramatic reason for the shelving of *Smile*. During late 1966 and early 1967, the Beach Boys were in dispute with Capitol Records over royalty payments and the renewal of their contract. The group eventually decided to form their own Brother Records label, to give themselves total artistic control over their product, and distribute their releases through Capitol. Lost in the dispute was the release of the two part "Heroes And Villains", which Brian had finished by early March 1967. By the time the dispute was settled, four months had passed, and Brian Wilson's will to complete and issue the project had dissipated.

So *Smile* remains a fantasy in the minds of Beach Boys fanatics, and a room full of tape in the Capitol Records archive. Imagine an alternative scenario, however: it's March 1967, the seven minute "Heroes And Villains" has just reached the American Top 10, and *Smile* is just about to reach the stores. Pre-publicity has been enormous; the world is ready for a masterpiece from the group who toppled the Beatles.

Fantasy No. 1 comes from the unofficial Brian Wilson fan club: in their version of the fairy tale, *Smile* astounds the world, alters the course of rock, forces the Beatles to scrap *Sgt. Pepper*, establishes Brian Wilson as a modern day Gershwin, and redirects the sound of California from acid rock to the "American Gothic trip" of the Beach Boys' shifting melodic structures and painstakingly layered harmonies. Brian escapes his drug paranoia, and is presumably awarded the Nobel Prize for Music – a category invented just for him – around 1975. The world lives happily ever after.

I'd love to believe that story too, but somehow I think the world is fiercer than that. On the evidence of what we have, *Smile* would have been a remarkable record, stunningly original, full of daredevil melodies and abstract lyricism that transcended the bounds of the popular song. But it wouldn't have been commercial, in the way that the Doors, or Love, or Jefferson Airplane were. Unless your fantasy insists that the entire Summer of Love – the extension of the Haight Ashbury across the Western world – is abandoned, then it's unlikely that *Smile* would have beaten back the advent of psychedelia from San Francisco, or London.

So Fantasy No. 2 goes like this. *Smile* is greeted with an initial intake of breath, and immediate cult adulation. Devotion to the album is compulsory among hip persons on both sides of the Atlantic. But like *Pet Sounds* in the States, the album fails to find a mass audience. You can't dance to it; you can't even sing along without taking a course in harmony; and letters in the pop papers complain that the Beach Boys should go back to what they do best, and cut another surfing album. Brian Wilson is crushed with disappointment, and the remaining Beach Boys don't even have the salvation of unused *Smile* tracks with which to bolster their subsequent albums. Otherwise, life carries on much as before. It's less romantic that way, but then life is rarely as romantic as fantasy.

Smile A-Z

BARNYARD: This title is given to two entirely different fragments – the first was a vocal refrain which was later reworked for the opening of "With Me Tonight" on "Smiley Smile"; the second emerged alongside "Do You Like Worms" on a bootleg album, and may form part of that track, or "Heroes And Villains".

BICYCLE RIDER: Less than 25 seconds long, this keyboard refrain matches the chorus melody of "Heroes And Villains"; some "Bicycle Rider" lyrics were added to live renditions of that song in the 1970s.

CABIN ESSENCE: As the final track on *20/20*, "Cabinessence" (one word) is one of the highlights of the Beach Boys' catalogue. That recording was obtained by overdubbing existing *Smile* versions of "Cabin Essence" (two words), "Who Ran The Iron Horse" and "Home on The Range", and editing them into one track – in keeping with Brian Wilson's original intention. The original two word title supports the 'Americana' theme of the album, with the song trying (among many other things) to evoke the essence of life in the cabins for the American pioneers. An entire instrumental track of the piece emerged on the box set.

CHILD IS FATHER TO THE MAN: William Wordsworth's poem inspired not only Blood, Sweat & Tears' first album but also this two minute fragment – which opens with a gentle keyboard pattern and a distant French horn, and then merges into a circular vocal refrain. The instrumental track was used as the basis for the "Child is Father To The Man" section added to "Surf's up" for official release in 1971, and then overdubbed with fresh vocals.

DO YOU LIKE WORMS: One of the highlights of the *Smile* tapes is this track, unveiled at last on the band's CD box set. It begins with a ponderous instrumental section, moves into a vocal harmony piece known to fans as "Plymouth Rock", segues into the familiar "Bicycle Rider" tune with additional vocals that sound like an Indian chant, and then returns to "Plymouth Rock" – repeating the same structure but adding a separate "Hawaiian" vocal piece. The reappearance of the "Bicycle Rider" theme merely helps to heighten the symphony feel of the album.

THE ELEMENTS: "The Elements" or "The Elements Suite" apparently exists in its entirety, though it's never been aired in public. There are four basic elements – earth, air, fire and water. Fire would have been represented by "Mrs O'Leary's Cow"; water by "Love To Say Da Da"; but air and earth are more mysterious, although both seem to have been instrumental themes.

FIRE: The common title given to the track officially known as "Mrs O'Leary's Cow".

FRIDAY NIGHT: A variant title for the mysterious "I'm in Great Shape".

GEORGE FELL INTO HIS FRENCH HORN: The title given by bootleggers to the session logged at Capitol as "Talking Horns".

GOOD VIBRATIONS: Besides the hit single, also included on *Smiley Smile*, additional out takes from the lengthy sessions for this song have been included on *Beach Boys Rarities* and the *Smiley Smile / Wild Honey* double CD set. An extended medley of session out takes was included on the box set. Without exception, these working fragments document the taping of the backing track, plus Brian's guide vocals, rather than the layering of the Beach Boys' final harmony parts.

HEROES AND VILLAINS: As explained above, the single *Smiley Smile* version of this song was merely part of the original blueprint; additional fragments were included on an alternate take on *Smiley Smile/Wild Honey*, while further out-takes appear on the box set.

HOLIDAYS: A muted tenor saxophone cries over a piano figure as this instrumental track begins, followed by an uptempo theme which breaks into a fairground motif and hints at the melodies of several other *Smile* tracks, notably "Child is Father To The Man". A pocket symphony in less than three minutes, "Holidays" remains officially unreleased. The instrumental piece included on the first *Smile* bootleg under the name "Holidays" was actually an extract from Miles Davis's "Porgy And Bess" album.

HOME ON THE RANGE: One of the themes incorporated into the *20/20* version of "Cabinessence".

INSPIRATION: Taped on June 2nd 1966, this otherwise unidentified track remains buried in the vaults.

I DON'T KNOW: Me neither; the identity of this track remains unconfirmed, though Dennis Wilson did record a song of this title a decade later – itself still unreleased.

I LOVE TO SAY DA DA: "Cool Cool Water" on *Sunflower* is a fully developed version of the original *Smile* concept, although only the chaotic "flowing river" vocals in the middle of that track actually date from the *Smile* sessions. A full length version recorded during the *Wild Honey* sessions later in 1967 appeared on the box set.

I RAN: Another track yet to surface, unofficially or officially.

MRS O'LEARY'S COW: Like the orchestral session for the Beatles' "A Day in The Life", the recording of this purely instrumental track has become part of rock legend. The intention was to create a track that conjured up the sound of fire: the musicians were presented with firemen's helmets and rubber axes to create the mood, and then began to perform a terrifying, sliding piece of music which evoked the ebb and flow of flames burning out of control, while percussion instruments imitated the crackling of the flames. The session was filmed, and combined with madcap footage of the Beach Boys riding a fire engine; the results can be seen in the video, *The Beach Boys: An American Band*. A couple of versions of the "fire" music remain intact – Brian didn't, as he claimed at the time, destroy the master tapes – but they are only available on bootleg.

THE OLD MASTER PAINTER / YOU ARE MY SUNSHINE: This one minute track combined a Brian Wilson instrumental theme for cello and percussion with a mournful arrangement of the familiar country hit by Tex Davis, which ended with the string section sliding to a stop as if their powerpacks had just run down. Dennis Wilson overdubbed a lead vocal for "You Are My Sunshine" in late November 1966.

PRAYER: A soaring vocal harmony piece – a spiritual tribute to the power of the human voice – this *Smile* track was overdubbed and extended by editing the tape to make up "Our Prayer" on the *20/20* album. The original version appeared on the box set.

SURF'S UP: The pinnacle of the *Smile* writing sessions was this remarkable Wilson/Parks composition, which in turn provided the finest moment on the 1971 album to which it gave its name. Though it was difficult to tell, that recording was salvaged from a mess of fragments-adding a new Carl Wilson vocal to a 1966 backing track of the initial verses, then switching to the recording that Brian Wilson made, solo at the piano, in December 1966. The 1971 cut ended with a revamped

"Child is Father To The Man". The *Smile* cut was worked on intermittently between November 1966 and January 1967, but never completed. A session out take demonstrates the musicians using shakers to evoke the sound of the opening lyric: "a diamond necklace plays the pawn". What we don't have, as yet, is a complete 1966 vocal performance over the finished backing track. Instead, the CD box set featured Brian's 1966 vocal/piano performance.

TALKIN' HORNS: Take a room full of top hornmen; tell them to communicate to each other through their instruments; and the result is a glorious three minute extravaganza that is part Ornette Coleman avant garde, part Disney fantasy, part pure stupidity. This piece, which surely can't have been intended for *Smile*, is otherwise known as "George Fell Into His French Horn", after a line of the saxophone "dialogue" heard during the track.

TONES: The bootleg tape of this track opens with Brian Wilson exalting his instrumentalists to go "all out". The track that follows epitomises the humour of *Smile*, with a xylophone playing a ridiculous solo theme, before a bank of drums, percussive pianos and brass venture into a catchy, irrepressible march tune. Another shorter take exists, with additional woodwind instrumentation taking us closer to the sound of a fairground – before the tape abruptly switches into a few seconds of "Heroes And Villains" vocal riffs, and then fades away.

TUNE X: An alternate title for "Tones".

VEGA TABLES: After "Mrs O'Leary's Cow", the sessions for "Vega Tables" attracted most media attention at the time – simply because Paul McCartney dropped in to chew some carrots and drop some radishes in the mix. The song was re-recorded for *Smiley Smile*, but the original "Vege Tables" (heard finally on the box set) incorporated the vocal chant issued as "Mama Says" on the *Wild Honey* album.

WHO RAN THE IRON HORSE: Another of the themes that constituted "Cabinessence".

WIND CHIMES: Recut for *Smiley Smile*, this tribute to the ethereal music of the air around us was originally recorded in August and October 1966. The original version, which surfaced on the box set, featured a Brian Wilson solo vocal, and none of the bubbly, stoned atmosphere of the July 1967 cut on *Smiley Smile*.

WONDERFUL: on *Smiley Smile*, "Wonderful" – a mysteriously lovely Van Dyke Parks love song – had a lead vocal by Carl Wilson. The *Smile* original, taped in August, October and December 1966, was something else entirely, with Brian's vocal adding another layer of emotion to the piece. It's thankfully available on the box set. A complete backing track for the song is also in circulation .

THE WOODSHOP: One night at Goldstar Studios, Brian Wilson persuaded a team of experienced session musicians to down their violins and attack other pieces of wood-with hammers, nails and saws. The results appeared as a coda to the 1968 recording "Do it Again", but only on the *20/20* LP version.

YOU ARE MY SUNSHINE: See "The Old Master Painter".

YOU'RE WELCOME: An eerie, heavily echoed vocal chant, which had the air of a mantra, "You're Welcome" was a genuine *Smile* outtake, taped on 15th December 1966. Not included in the original handwritten track listing for the LP, it emerged finally as the flipside of "Heroes And Villains".

PART TWO

Surf's Up

The Beach Boys: Tales Of Hawthorne
by Tom Nolan

This piece was originally Part Two of a retrospective in Rolling Stone, *October 28th and November 11th 1971), when rock writing in general was in its infancy. The full feature was certainly the first truly in-depth, intelligent and lengthy article on the band to appear in a national magazine. Part One has been omitted as, while it is an excellent piece and covers all of the key elements and problems of the band up to that point, it would involve retreading a lot of the ground covered by a number of the previous articles in this book. In 1971 it would have cost you 15p to buy each of these issues of* Rolling Stone.

There is a tale, told by an anonymous Beach Boy, about an outrageous instance of Brian Wilson's creative humour. Brian was about 18. The family was preparing to eat dinner. Brian got his father's plate, went into the bathroom, dropped his pants and squeezed a pretty good-sized shit onto it, brought it back and put it on his father's place. The father came in and blew his mind. A turd for dinner. "Who did this?" Carl, sensing impending disaster, started to cry. Brian, though, was laughing. His punishment was to crouch outside with his arms behind his back and eat with the dogs. This story will be denied in the following pages.

Father Murry Wilson and his wife Audree raised their three famous sons in the post World War II stucco community of Hawthorne, Calif. A strict, self made rugged individualist, Murry borrowed on their modest home to start his own business, dealing in heavy machinery. But his real love was music. He wrote songs, sang them to his family and friends, had some published. No hits. Once he wrote English lyrics to the B side of some Gordon MacRae single but says he never got paid for it.

Eventually, in 1960, Murry realized his most promising musical creations were his sons, Brian, Dennis and Carl, and decided to sink heavy machine money and time into producing their first hits and selling the boys to Capitol Records. He managed the group until 1964, when ulcers and arguments forced him to semi-retire and devote most of his energy to publishing his own and Beach Boys music. He continued dabbling with new singing and songwriting talent, including a Beach Boys type group called the Sun Rays, who had two hits, and a songwriting plumber named Eck Kynor, whom Murry discovered while having some pipes repaired in his home. Murry even got an album of his own songs, *The Many Moods of Murry Wilson*, released on Capitol. ("The talented father of the famous Beach Boys presents instrumental interpretations of his and other original compositions.")

But the Beach Boys remain his real management success and, of course, his proudest achievement. Today he lives in the less modest surroundings of Nixonian Whittier, on the other side of Los Angeles County. Yet, as Murry fondly recalls those good fighting show biz times with his boys in the early Sixties, one can still detect a little Hawthorne in the man.

"See, the Beach Boys," explained Murry, "the Wilson Boys, have always heard music in their home. from my writing songs and friends of ours who came over. We were all so poor we'd just sit around singing and on occasion drinking a glass of brew. Not the children, the adults. And then I bought a Hammond electric organ, on time, and we'd play duets, my wife and I. And then Brian would get in the act and sing. All they ever heard was music in their house. And, on occasion, family arguments."

Murry let out a hearty laugh, then got serious again.

"So, you understand, their training has been Americana type music, stuff that our friends would come over and sing; and their cousin, Mike Love, was hearing a lot of music in his home at the same time, and they'd sing. Americana. See, a lot of the public doesn't realize this, but the Beach Boys' style has had a flavor of Americana. Brian's written a lot of his songs about his own life and himself, like 'In My Room'. That was written, you know, about his room. He'd go in there and ponder the worries of the day, an argument with a girlfriend, or the happy times. And then he later on wrote a song called 'I'm Bugged at My Old Man', and he meant it as a put-on, but he meant it.

"It was early 1961 when Mike Love and Al Jardine were coming over to the house and Brian was teaching them songs, with Carl. They sang Four Freshman songs almost like the Four Freshman, except they had a sweeter, younger sound. So, eight months before the record 'Surfin'' of December 8th, 1961, is when the Beach Boys really started.

"Brian taught himself. He's a musical … he thinks in six part harmony, instead of two or three part. He's not only a writer, he's an arranger and he has a concept of harmonies which is uncanny.

"When Brian was eight years old, he sang in a concert, singing one of Mike Love's songs."

A public concert?

"Well, my sister – Mike's mother, Mrs. Love, Emily Love – loved music. She didn't play piano or anything, but she loved music and she gave this concert in my honor as a songwriter. And they featured several of my songs – she even hired a trio, a musical group, to play my songs for this concert."

This was for an audience?

"Yes, it was for school friends and teachers and friends of hers. And Mike Love wrote a song called 'The Old Soldier,' about a soldier that died, you know, in the war? He was only nine and a half when he wrote it. I heard it over at my sister's house, and I thought it was just darling. But I heard it as a hymn, it was a song in hymn form."

Murry started to sing, slowly with great reverence. " 'Da da do da/da da dee da/dee dee da da/da dee do'. See? I went home and composed other lyrics to it 'When Jesus Calls His Soldiers – When Jesus says to follow, I will be there.' It's called 'By His Side.' subtitled, 'When Jesus Calls His Soldiers.'

"So when he was eight years old I bought Brian his first suit with long pants, and he sang both versions of Mike's song at this concert. We taught him both sets of lyrics, Mike's and mine, and he brought the house down.

"So Brian showed early promise. In fact – now this is the truth, you may not believe it – when Brian was born, I was one of those young, frightened fathers, you know? But I just fell in love with him, and in three weeks he cooed back at me, responded. And when he was eleven and a half months – it was just at World War

II – I would carry Brian on my shoulders with his little hands up above, and I would sing, "Do do *do*, do do do," you know, "Caissons Go Marching Along? And he could hum the whole song – 'Do do *do*, do do *do*, do do *do* dee do do *do*.' But he didn't know how to end the last line.

"When he was 11 months old he was very clever and quick. I taught him how to say Mississippi. When most children were saying 'Da-da ma-ma, da-da, ma-ma', he said 'Mi-sez-zip-py,' you know? He's a very smart kid."

The first man manager Murry Wilson ran into at Capitol Records was Producer Nick Venet. Their association, in fact, was a series of run-ins, which Venet has a talent for recounting rather colorfully. Before he gets started, however, Carl Wilson would like to put in this disclaimer:

"I must say Nick Venet is really full of shit. Regarding us. He did an interview with a large magazine, the *Saturday Evening Post*, and he really lied his balls off in it. See, actually, he hardly had nothing to do with the group. He would be in the booth, and he would call the take number, and that was about it. ... Brian didn't want anything to do with Venet.

"The people at Capitol didn't like my dad at all, because he really gave them a hard time. If he thought that something was unfair. A lot of the executives didn't like him at all – which is perfectly understandable, but we were his kids, you know?"

Now, here's the Venet version:

"I don't think the father really knew where his son was at. Murry Wilson once told me that his son was the next Elvis Presley. I said, 'Mr. Wilson, I think Brian might be as big as Presley's sales, but I don't think he wants to be Presley'. He said, 'No, he's doing everything Presley does – but he's doing better.' I said. 'Mr. Wilson, I think Brian's doing a different kind of music which is really Brian Wilson music.' He kind of shook his head, looked at me and walked away.

'I thought at first that the father would be an anchor, but later I found out he had his own theories and he was also a songwriter, in the great style of Albert Crankshaw. Albert Crankshaw died in 1936. People who knew him well called him Mr. Show Business. That was in Cleveland. He wrote three or four songs 'I Want To Go Back To Copenhagen,' 'Mary Sweet Mary Come Back Some.' He also wrote a song called 'Adios, My Buddy, Adios.' Murry wrote in this flavor, and I think Murry wanted to be more involved with the Beach Boys' music. Because in those days you could put one side on the record for the kids and one side for the grown ups – terrific!

"I think Murry wanted to 'elevate' the boys by putting them into 'pretty music,' nice music, terrific music, a rhumba, a foxtrot, a mambo. I think that was an underlying thing in Murry's mind. They had a few fights about music and things. Yeah, I think Murry really fucked up the group for a couple of years. Oh, I'm gonna get sued again ...

"I used to get locked up in the office with the man. I was into all kinds of great things with Les McCann and Lou Rawls, and the next morning I would have to come to work at 9 o'clock after being up all night with great music – and I would walk into that office and there would be Murry Wilson. And that motherfucker would sit there till 5 or 6 o'clock and tell me about his songs and play me his melodies, and I had to listen to him because somewhere in the conversation he would always drop to me what Brian's next record was gonna be. Everyone in the building avoided him but I was stuck with him, 'cause I was the 'producer'.

"The father kept trying to worm his way into a recording deal. Eventually he made one with Capitol. This is a bust, this is hilarious, now that I'm not with Capitol. Capitol made a whole album and released it for that asshole, just so they could satisfy him and so he wouldn't hassle them so much on some of the Beach Boy things. It was the worst fucking album, and Capitol put it out, and they had to advertise it.

"One day I looked out my window and My God! he had cornered the president of Capitol in the parking lot. I was sent down there. They said, 'Get out there and somehow draw his attention.' I had to bump into him and say, 'Oh Murry, I've been looking for you all day. I have some new pictures of the kids I have to show you.' Just to get the motherfucker away from the owner of the company so he'd get something done for the day.

"I think the father did nothing but hinder them, but I think he assumed a lot of credit. If he heard them doing something good, he'd say, 'Right'. And he was about three beats behind Brian. For instance, Brian would say, 'Let's do that again.' He would say, 'Let's do that again.' Got to the point where Brian would say, 'Le ...' and he would say, 'Let's do that again.'

"The old man got to the point where he could see when a cat put his instrument down out there, that he was gonna stop the take. And Brian wouldn't see, say for instance, that the drummer had put his sticks down or waved his arm to stop the take. The father would say, 'Let's stop that take.' And of course, Brian thought for a while, there, the old man knew what he was doing.

"I used to hide under my desk. He used to look in my office to see if I was in there so I ordered a new desk because it had a front on it. The chick downstairs would buzz me: 'Man, here he comes.' I would tuck myself under my desk, 'cause there was no exit but the front door. And he would come in, wouldn't take the secretary's 'he's not in,' would walk into the office; he would look and I wasn't there and he would split. Well, one day he came in and used the fucking phone, man, and I got to tell you, I sat under that desk for five hours. And when I came out I couldn't use my left leg for two days. But I would rather sit under that desk than face that man and his neverending success stories of 1920s melodies.

"I could never get along with the father. He's rather Bomb-Hanoi-ish, but he's a very nice kind of guy."

* * * * *

This album is a first! Because it features Murry Wilson – songwriter!

Until this time, the public has known Murry Wilson only as the father and initial personal manager recording director of the world famous Beach Boys. The man who rocketed them into a phenomenal career.

Now, it's Murry Wilson's turn! You will hear a side of Murry that only his family and close friends are aware of – the songwriter with a flair for melodic structure! And you'll also hear a fantastic mixture of sounds uncommon to most recordings!

Album notes to *The Many Moods of Murry Wilson* Capitol T 2819
File under: Wilson – Instrumental

* * * * *

"Nick is a nice guy," reflected Murry. "He's got a lot of talent, apparently, 'cause he's still around. He may never get rich, but he's made a lot of records.

"I had to get rid of Nick Venet out of the Beach Boys' careers because he was not doing right by them. He was responsible for having the big shot at Capitol, Voyle Gilmore, hear the song, 'Surfin' Safari.' Nick acted real cool. He says 'You come back in an hour and we'll let you know if we want you to be Capitol recording artists'. He didn't act like he was too excited.

"So we walked out of there, and I said, 'Brian, let's make them wait five minutes, you know, let's don't act too eager.' This is the truth. And we got back in an hour and five minutes.

"In the meantime – we found out later – Nick Venet rushed across the tower on the 12th floor, raced across the offices, burst in on Gilmore and says, 'Boss, I've got a double sided smash for Capitol.' And he was right.

"We knew we were good. We told Nick Venet right at the outset we thought 'Surfin' Safari' was the A side. He says, put all the push on '409' and had to turn the damn record over in about three weeks. 'Surfin' Safari' was the song that made them surfing kings, vocally and lyrically, around the United States.

"Actually, the truth is, Nick started out OK. He called me up one day, after I handed him the tapes on 'Surfin' Safari,' and said, 'Now, we can't have two producers. You're over the hill, old man, and I'm young and I know the tempo and I sold $50 million worth of records for Capitol last year, so move over and let me take your sons and make big stars out of them.' That's what he told me in a nice way. And I said, 'OK, well, do a good job with them, Nick, they're your babies.' And I was kinda glad because it was a lot of pressure. You can work with strangers easier than you can your own goddamn kids, you know.

"But the boys refused to have Nick as their producer because he didn't tell the truth to them. He'd say, 'Brian, be here at 2:00; we're going to master out your record,' and then he would do the mastering himself, before Brian got there. What he did was outsmart Brian.

"So Brian came home one day from Capitol very blue, and he broke into tears and said, 'Goddammit, Dad ...'

Murry made some boo hoo noises with his lips. " 'Bub ub ub ub, will you go down and tell Capitol we don't want him anymore, he's changing our sound.' So Dad went down and talked to Voyle Gilmore, the vice president, and I told him right to his face, 'You folks don't know how to produce a rock and roll hit in your studios downstairs.' See, their engineers were used to good music, not rock and roll. We wanted to use Western Recorders. I told him, 'Leave us alone and we'll make hits for you.' He got red in the face. But that's all petty shit, I mean petty crap, sorry.

"We knew we were right. Before the Beach Boys went to Capitol, Capitol was number eight on singles hits. But the year they joined, Capitol went from number eight to number two, you understand?

"As far as I'm concerned about Nick Venet, naturally he probably feels aggrieved because he could have had world fame as their producer. So all the stuff he said about me I discount. I was tough as a manager. I fought Capitol for four and a half months, straight. Finally, Capitol recapitulated and let us record where we wanted to, without the impedence of the, ha ha, Artists' Representative. That'll give Nick a little joggle in his memory.

"The boys were so eager to prove how good they could be as artists- record makers, not artists, they weren't artists till the phonies started telling them they were. At Western Recorders I remember they stood and sang 13 hours straight, 13 hours straight, to get an album out – *Surfin' U.S.A.* Sometimes they were so exhausted, I had to make them mad at me to get the best out of them. So I'd insult their musical integrity, I'd say, 'That's lousy, you guys can do better than that.' I'd make them so damn mad they'd be hitting me over the head practically, but they'd give that extra burst of energy and do it beautifully. The old man outsmarted them without their knowledge, see what I mean? There's more than one way to give love to kids, you know, for their own good.

"I held them down for nine months – you might write this in – I held them down from the big time for nine months. Even after they had two major doublesided hits in the nation, they were too green to go way into the big time and New York and huge concerts. I held them down and took jobs at dances, first, and then we went to different department stores, you know one of their first dates was a dance in Inglewood, California, and they played at Long Beach. Their first major concert was one I produced at the Sacramento Civic. We have a dear feeling for Sacramento.

"You see a manager and a father is like being one of their teachers. The kids hate the teacher's trying to give them knowledge, you know? And till they're grown up and married, they don't realize how nice the teacher was to bang at them, you know, to bang their ears.

"I drove the Beach Boys through the wall. When they were exhausted, I drove them harder, because they asked for it. They said, 'Help us, make us famous, help us record, we need you, Dad.' I wish you'd print this – I was told by a young man, a 22 year old man at William Morris, that the Beach Boys would never make more money than Ruby and the Romantics, who were grossing $3500 for seven days a week. This was after my sons' first double sided hit on Capitol. I got so mad. It was December 17th. I called from my home to key places, and we worked between Christmas Eve and New Year's Eve. We grossed $26,684, write it down – $26,684 for five nights, five concerts. That was in 1962."

* * * * *

"Ever since I was born – or maybe, when I was two-years-old, somebody punched me in the ear."

– Brian Wilson explaining why he is deaf in one ear.

* * * * *

Earl Leaf of Hollywood, the elder teen columnist once hired by the Beach Boys to start a fan sheet, recalled with no little relish certain eccentricities of Mike Love during the group's first European tour.

"Well, maybe you can't say he's eccentric, but he's wild," said Earl, leafing through a pile of glossies he'd shot of the trip. "He was awfully wild and still is, I suppose. I don't mean violence ... girlwise, he'd fuck any ... he was worse ... Dennis was the worst. Dennis was an animal.

"Mike was always getting into some kind of jam. He was stupid. We were in Paris, for instance. We got in a night club … a clip joint actually. I didn't want to go in; I lived in Paris, you know, for a couple of years, I know a clip joint. So we went in, and he got this girl, and she said, 'Yeah, I'll go home with you. I can't go home now. Just hang around. I have to wait till we close at 4 AM.'

"Meanwhile, this guy is pumping him with champagne, about 4,000 francs a bottle. He took one glass out of a bottle and threw the rest away, bring another bottle. Four AM, well, he couldn't find her, she's nowhere around, she split.

"He was just a horse's ass. Same thing happened in Munich. He went and found a girl and started feelin' her up and her pimp came and got a gun and held him until the police came. He spent the night in jail. Same thing happened in London. He gave this girl a whole lot of money to fuck her. She said, 'OK. I'll meet you in 15 minutes. You go down to such and such a street and turn right two blocks and wait for me on the corner.' So he rushes down there and of course she never showed up. He was old enough to know better. Over and over and over again he was taken.

"We were goin' down in a cab from the Hilton to Soho. I said, 'Listen, you guys, don't be a horse's ass. This place is so full of whores and places that are just clip joints. You never get anything out of it.' I can't remember if it was Mike or Dennis said, 'Well, we can afford it. I don't care if we get clipped, we can afford it.' "

Nick Venet had something to add: "If I had listened to the father back then, the Beach Boys would have fired Mike Love on their first tour. The father came roaring into my office one day and asked me to check out the legality and prepare papers. I just said, 'That's terrific. How shall we do this? That's just terrific sir. Do you want me to call him on the phone, or send him a telegram? Or do you want me to push him out a window? Which way do you want me to do this?' He got very serious, he got bugged with me and he said, 'The boy used profanity backstage.'

"Well, shit, my curiosity … you know, what kind of profanity could he have used? It was 'fuck' he had said twice, once before the show, once after the show, both times backstage. Biggest act in the country and he wants to break them up 'cause he used the word fuck!"

Later, Murry indicated he never actually planned to break up the group over Mike. "Nick said that? I probably threatened to do it. I was tough on obscenity. Mike swore under the mike one time at a dance. It slipped. I said, 'Don't you ever pull that again, Mike'. He said, 'Well, it slipped,' and I said, 'Well, don't let it slip again.'

"There was nothing vulgar. I even had their attire – I don't want to go into detail – but even their wearing apparel was purchased so it wouldn't be vulgar. There wasn't any vulgarity on stage. They wore those striped shirts, and they wore pants. But they didn't wear those, you know, those continental type tight things that a lot of the New York boys were coming out with at that time. Elvis, you know? Don't use Elvis; say 'other artists.'

"I worried about things like that. I traveled around with my kids, worrying about them, getting rid of girls with shady characters, on occasion getting rid of girls who were too eager, shall we say, to become acquainted. They had a clean cut American image. Mike was 21, you know, so he was allowed to drink beer. If I caught anyone else drinking beer – once in a while in my home a glass was all right – but on tours, I said, "No Drinking. If I catch any of you guys, you're going to be fined *five hundred dollars*. I was tough on them. Once, I assessed a $300 fine to one of them – I can't say which one – for drinking a cocktail. I never got a dime of it.

"In other words – if you print anything – I love my sons, you understand? And although they were big stars, I never gave up on them. Even to this day, when a son comes off and starts giving me a Hollywood approach, I say, 'What are you doing – coming off phony, Hollywood, baby?' Right down their throat. I kept at them, beating their eardrums because I knew that fame and fortune might distort them."

Brian's not the only Beach Boy who likes to explore the borders of inner space. His cousin Mike Love once fasted for three weeks, taking only water, fruit juice, and a little yogurt. It was an approximation of a regimen, developed by a strict sect of religious Jews. Everything got very amplified during the fast, he became quite sensitive to all positive and negative forces around him. He began to look at things rather metaphorically. The birds in the sky seemed to have a purpose in flying southwesterly, and if he could try a little harder, perhaps he could talk to the birds...

As he protested, "I'm fine, I'm going to Hawaii to mellow out," his brother drove him to a hospital and said, "You'd better check this boy over."

They simply found that he hadn't been eating. Once he started to eat and meditate again, he was out in four or five days. He learned from the fast. He learned not to do it again.

Mike was given equal time to refute Earl Leaf's contention that he had been taken for a ride all over Europe. "It wasn't all over Europe, it was only once, in Germany. I was going to go to this girl's house for a drink. I found her outside with some other fella in a Mercedes. I was pretty drunk. I had on these black gloves. I smashed his window in. The only minor problem was, he had a gun. That was in my wild youth, I don't do that anymore. I never did make a habit of it.

"Earl's a lecherous old man, he's just jealous. Anything Earl Leaf says must be sifted through a sieve. He elaborates in his senility "

Mike wanted a plug given to his little brother Steve who graduated magna cum laude from the University of Southern California in history and Spanish and recently earned his Master's in business administration and works full time for the Beach Boys' management; and a plug to his other little brother Stanley (6'9") who broke all basketball scoring records at the University of Oregon and was signed to the Baltimore Bullets for half a million dollars. He also has a sister who sings and another who plays the harp.

Dennis Wilson, toenails tough like brazil nuts, has been surfing for 13 years. It was Dennis who came out of the water and told Brian what it was like out there. It was Brian who fooled the world.

Dennis was asked if it was true Charles Manson wrote the words of "Never Learn Not to Love," an eerie opus on the *20-20* album with an ominous message: Surrender ... I'm your kind ... Come in, closer, come in, closer, closer.

"That's right, he did."

Why didn't you give him the label credits

"He didn't want that. He wanted money instead. I gave him about a hundred thousand dollars' worth of stuff.

"But I don't think you should put that in your story. I see no reason the story should mention him at all."

Another Beach Boy, an anonymous one, is a little more talkative about it. "Charlie struck me as a very intense and dogmatic hype. I didn't want nothin' to do with Charlie. He was living with Dennis at the time. Dennis was just divorced; I suppose the life style appealed to him. Perhaps I have more sexual inhibitions, moral strictures. I wasn't into drugs at that point, which was Charlie's way of conditioning his little friends, turning them into egoless entities. I wasn't going for his pitch.

"Dennis ran up the largest gonorrhea bill in history the time the whole family got the clap. He took them all to a Beverly Hills doctor-it took something like a thousand dollars in penicillin.

"We've got several eight track tapes of Charlie and the girls that Dennis cut, maybe even some 16 track. Just chanting, fucking, sucking, balling… Maybe we'll put it out in the fall. Call it 'Death Row.'

"It was a million laughs, believe me."

Dennis said he didn't want all this mentioned.

"Just say Dennis was the farthest out in life-style of any of us, having known Charles Manson before he made the headlines. And that he requested you not to bring it up."

Carl remembers that Dennis did get in more trouble than the others. "Dennis is for sure the most physical of the group," he said. "He has the most nervous energy. I've never witnessed energy like that. His music, the music he likes to write best, is really serious. It's sort of like practical, you know? He's more sort of a physical earth person; he likes simple things, he likes gardening a lot. He's into nature quite a bit.

"There was a big drain ditch near where we used to live. It was really dark down there, and you could take it from right by our house all the way to the beach. We'd ride our bikes down it, and the trip was to see how far you could go without getting scared out of your mind. It was a daredevil thing. I believe Dennis probably did go in the furthest.

"Dennis was the best surfer and he was the one who really had the idea for the group."

According to Murry, this is how it all started. "They had written a song called 'Surfin'', which I never did like and still don't like, it was so rude and crude, you know? Dennis made them write it. He told them, 'Write a song about surfing.' He bugged them. He was an avid surfer. He'd disappear every Saturday and Sunday he could, without cutting the lawn – you might put that in, too – without cutting the lawn. He loved the sport.

"And so they kept saying to Mr. Morgan, Hite Morgan, my publisher, 'We've written a song about the surfing sport and we'd like to sing it for you.' Finally he agreed to hear it, and Mrs. Morgan said, 'Drop everything, we're going to record your song. I think it's good.' And she's the one responsible. It came out on the Candix label, and it was played on three stations in L.A. every hour, 24 hours a day Sam Riddle introduced it on KDAY, and Russ Regan – well known producer and record figure, who was then handling Candix and who gave them the name

Beach Boys – got it on KFWB and KRLA. And it went to 76 on the Top 100 chart.

"Then after 'Surfin'' the boys were off the air and they couldn't get back on the air. No one wanted them, they thought they were a one shot record. Al Jardine hit the road and enrolled in dental school. Mr. Morgan and I went to Dot Records and cooled our heels in the foyer, nobody would talk to us. We went to Liberty, and the big shots were too busy to see us. And finally I asked Mr. Morgan, who produced 'Surfin',' 'What'll we do?' He says, 'I don't know, Murry, you're their Dad and manager, lots of luck to you.' And he says goodbye. And that cost him $2,700,000, that statement. It cost him $2,700,000."

Murry was asked what he thought when the news came out about Dennis and Charles Manson. "I told my sons a long time ago," he said, "be careful who you choose as your friends."

All the Beach Boys except Bruce Johnston practice, to one degree or another, Transcendental Meditation, as personally introduced to them by Maharishi. But perhaps Carl, the youngest, just shows it more. Always the most even tempered of the group, he now speaks in an almost temperless cherubic voice.

"Maharishi, he's really fantastic to be with. Every time I've been with him I've felt very good. He's a very spontaneous person. How happy he is, and things like his laugh are very contagious. And very powerful.

"We were in Paris, doing a UNICEF show, and we met Maharishi there. We talked to him for several hours, and we were all initiated. I meditate regularly. It's helped me to cope with things. Things affect me less. Bad things affect me less-pardon me, I would rather say difficult things. I find that it relaxes me very deeply and gives me energy. I recommend it highly."

Possibly it is Transcendental Meditation that allows Carl to cope so philosophically with the difficult moments in the Beach Boys saga, such as the time Brian suddenly canceled out of the first Monterey Pop Festival, a move some feel stunted their careers for years.

"Brian was on the board, and it changed several times, the concept of it. And he decided, 'Well, shit, let's not play it.' And I think there were some people getting hostile about the group at the time, you know, about the surfing thing, and he figured, 'Fuck you,' or something like that, I don't know.

"I'm really glad the way things have turned out. I'm really grateful, actually, the way everything has happened. The most important thing was that we had a chance to sort of cool out and develop, you know? That was necessary for the group to really carry on and do anything. 'Cause you could make hits all week long, but it just wouldn't mean shit. As far as making good music, you need time, I mean some of us do. Brian advanced way beyond the rest of the group, and we really had to start to catch up."

Since then the others have caught up considerably, although Carl is quick to emphasize, "We're far from becoming Brian Wilsons, believe me." All but Mike Love can play many instruments, including the Moog, and Mike can play theremin. Each Beach Boy is capable of producing an entire song by himself – playing and singing all parts – and, theoretically, an entire album. Carl, perhaps, has grown the most dramatically and now unofficially leads the group both on the road and in the studio. And the future lies ahead.

"Speaking for myself," as Carl usually does, "musically I'm most influenced by Brian. I mean that's obvious. And I've been writing a lot of songs lately. Dennis is writing a lot of beautiful music, and Brian's writing some beautiful songs. Everybody's writing. I don't know exactly what's gonna happen yet. I just know there's gonna be a lot of music.

"The main trip is music for sure. Brian was always more into music as a vibration, a sound feeling and vibration, right? More than lyrics or anything words could ever say. And it's really true. Music, a really heavy vibration, says a lot more than a million words could in eternity say. As far as really holy sounds go."

* * * * *

"The music business has been good to the entire Wilson family," adds Murry. "And, this album, which has been mixed as emotionally as possible, retaining color, shading and warmth, is humbly offered to the public."
— Notes to *The Many Moods of Murry Wilson*

* * * * *

"See, THE whole trade has given Brian credit for everything. Truthfully – I'm not beating myself on the back, but knowing them as a father, I knew their voices, right? And I'm musical, my wife is, we knew how to sing on key and when they were flat and sharp and how they should sound good in a song. And we put the echo on they wanted, and we got the balance; we used Telefunken mikes and we surged on their power here and there to make them sound better. When they'd run out of wind at the end of the sentence, we'd surge on the power to keep the level of their musical tone the same. Or if they were singing a phrase weak, when Mike was singing 'She's fine, that 409,' we'd surge on the part. Without their knowledge, at first.

"A lot of artists think they're doing it all because they get in front of a mike and open their damn mouths. But most artists have an engineer, a smart engineer surging on the power here and there to help them when they're weak and tired and run out of gas, to put an echo on them here and there and make them sound like gods. He's got a lot of beautiful people, unsung heroes, under him, helping him make his career. Not to mention the record company and all the promotional people in the field, and the jobbers that push the records and everybody else that helps, you know? A lot of people. Artists don't make themselves."

That was Murry Wilson describing how he helped produce "409", one of the Beach Boys' earliest songs.

Here's Carl describing how he produced "Feel Flows": I played piano first and then I played organ. I played piano twice, overdubbed it, and used a variable speed oscillator to make the track different speeds so that the piano would be a little bit out of tune, sort of a spread sound, do you understand what I mean? You play the tape at 30 inches per second, and then you may slow it down to about 29 and 3/4 inches per second. It shouldn't be that great actually, I got my cycles mixed up with inches per second. But say at 60 cycles and then 59. So that makes the piano sound like the effect of a twelve string guitar, you know? When the two strings are at the same octave but just a tiny bit out of tune? You know that real ringing sound?

"And then I put the organ on and put it through the Moog at the same time, on that one side of the stereo had the direct organ sound and the other side had the return through the Moog synthesizer. It's sort of like a vibrato, but the frequency changes, there's a tone change like a graphic tone. Do you know what a graphic equalizer is? Well, it just springs out, you can amplify any particular part of a sound spectrum, like from 50 cycles to 10,000 cycles. The Moog did that automatically; there's a component called a sequencer and you can time it to react and go through a series of circuits all connected to a different frequency, and it does that back and forth. And therefore it sounded sort of like a vibrato or a wah wah, sort of both at the same time.

"Then I put on the bass, played the bass guitar. Then I put on the Moog for that part where the piano comes in by itself after the instrumental part, you know? Then we put on the bells, and a guy named Woody Thews played percussion on it, and I sang it. I put the guitar on about the same time.

"Then I think it was the next day Charles Lloyd came by and we did the flute and saxophone. And I might add, he heard it one time and then started playing, he started recording right away. It was really a thrill for me to have him play on it 'cause he's a gifted musician. It was really great. And then the next session we did the vocals, the background part, and that was it."

Why did the Beach Boys record monaurally for so many years?

"Well, Brian had control of all the production," said Carl, "and he liked it better. Plus he can't comprehend stereo, really."

He still can't?

"No, not with one ear. Only one works, you know. He had an operation but it wasn't successful at the time. Whenever his ear is fatigued, his bad ear, his right ear, will start to work. But it will be very painful and sound very low fidelity, like one of those tin can walkie talkies, you know? That's how he explained it, anyway, and he gets out of balance and everything. It's been that way for many years. Ever since he was an infant.

"I believe that his hearing is going to return. I just have a feeling. And he will be very inspired when it does."

"When he was 11 years old," Murry remembered, "Mrs. Wilson discovered that he kept turning his head. And she found out that he couldn't hear very well out of that ear. Then it got worse and he became deaf in that ear. He was injured in some … either a football game or some injury of some kind. Or it just happened, who knows?"

There's a rumor going around that you might have hit him on the ear when he was young.

"Oh, I spanked his bottom, you know, like any father would do to a kid, just whap him a little bit. No, I never hit my kid on the ear. No. No. I was too strong. If anyone caused that rumor, all I hope is that they have itchy piles for ten years. Because I never hit my son Brian on the ear. Never. No." Murry also denied the story of Brian's dumping on his father's dinner plate.

"No, that's absolutely not true. No, no. I don't know who said that, they're putting you on. In fact, we wouldn't put up with any of that crap."

What did you think when you read Brian had experimented with LSD? "I told him … we were driving to a recording session, and I said, 'I heard that you experimented with LSD. Is that a put-on to the newspaper, or did you do it?' And he said, 'Yes, Dad, I did,' and I said, 'Well tell me, Brian, do you think you're strong enough in your brain that you can experiment with a chemical that might drive you crazy later?' He says, 'No, Dad, it's opened a lot of things for me.' And I said, 'Brian, who you trying to kid?' He said, 'Well, I had weird, weird hallucinations, it made me understand.' And I said, 'Who you trying to kid, Brian? What did you understand, except seeing a bunch of different like nightmares in your brain, colors and things like that? And he agreed that he'd never do it again. And I said, 'You know, Brian, one thing God gives you is a brain, if you play with it and destroy it, you're dead. And we haven't heard the rest of this, there are going to be a lot of people killed and people in sanitariums, insane asylums, because they played, you know, they played with God.

"If you want to print it, I would be happy to have you do it. These guys that have to be freaked out on marijuana and other things on stage to become artists, should never have the privilege of stepping onto a stage to play for young impressionable people."

Murry paused briefly to light his pipe and muse over the proud feats of his first son. It was true, Brian, with the help of his father's strict family training, had resisted the temptations of success – pressures of performing, the phoniness, the dope, the tight pants – to devote his life to music.

"*Pet Sounds* is a masterpiece of accomplishment for Brian," said Murry. "The public doesn't realize it, most of them. But Brian took the masters, a lot of the masters, approached the music in his own way and put a rock and roll beat to it. He even got Stephen Foster in there – phrases that we used to sing when he was a baby, you know? And it's twisted around with his beautiful approach to rock and roll, and his bass root; his bass root figurations of the bass guitar is fantastic!

"*Pet Sounds* has been copied, chewed up, renewed – Negro artists have used it in band arrangements, commercials have used it. Every day you hear a commercial that has a Beach Boys sound in back of it.

"Every ten years or so there comes an arranger or musical brain that does this. Like Mancini did it for eight years right? Now Bacharach is having his heyday. Very brilliant young man, Bacharach.

"Mancini is a God given talent. And so is Brian Wilson."

Tales Of Hawthorne featured additional material by David Felton

Original Reviews Part 4

Live in London album.
"The playing here is rather clumsy, definitely rooted in the pre-psychedelic manner of hit groups doing their hits for 45 minutes..."

"the only real surprise is a brief accapella treatment of a pretty (if slightly mawkish) ballad called 'Their Hearts Were Full of Spring'..."

"...it's a necessity only to the most ardent fans."

Surf's Up album.
"The overall effect is one of perfection ...you can smell Brian Wilson's hand in it..."

"...better than *Sunflower*, but below *Wild Honey* and *Smiley Smile*..."

"Brian Wilson came to his senses and realised that his work was not yet over..."

"...a whole new passage in the Beach Boys' career...they have re-captured all the subtleties and beauty of *Pet Sounds*..."

"[As for] 'A Day in The Life of A Tree' it would be hard to imagine a more shattering and emotional indictment of the way we're letting the world rot around us. Working with Jack Rieley, with fuge organ and a voice of pained suffering, it is a song that will make you justly weep for man's folly."

"...miraculous, quite brilliant..."

Carl and The Passions: So Tough album.
"Let's get one thing straight right from the start: there are things on *So Tough* which no one else but the Beach Boys can do. There's music which makes your head dizzy with sheer loveliness, of the kind which belongs to them alone...unfortunately, the rest of the album is somewhat spotty..."

"*Carl and The Passions*, which is a simple and rock based album, was mostly Carl's project and as an entity is probably the least successful of the Beach Boys' albums..."

"If you buy *So Tough* (and you should despite it all) you get a bit of a curate's egg."

Bruce Johnston also wrote a review of this album at the time that he had left the band: "I don't think it's as good as *Surf's up*, and I don't think it matches anything that *Sunflower* did ... I would like to see more involvement with the Beach Boys and Brian Wilson ... he really didn't have too much to do with this album and I'm hoping that if he does come to Holland to meet the guys and get involved in recording in the summer we'll hear some more Beach Boy hits like we used to hear, but not repeating the old success formula, and we'll hear some 1972 Beach Boys with 1972 Brian."

Holland

The Beach Boys career has been notable for a series of strange twists and deci-sions, none more so than the move to Holland of the entire band, families and equipment in 1972 in order to record the album of the same name. The musical and technical aspects of the operation were recorded in a 16 page booklet called The Beach Boys: Holland, The Making of The Album, *now a collectors item in its own right. The text of this booklet is reproduced here for the first time.*

Until now, in a career spanning more than a decade, the Beach Boys have record-ed exclusively in California. They were the patron saints of surf boards, Hondas and cruisin'. With record sales in excess of 70 million (group sales second only to the Beatles), they spread the goodtime gospel all over the planet. The Beach Boys/California identity became so powerful that one virtually stood for the other. That proved a mixed blessing. And suddenly last summer they reacted on no less than a monumental scale, to a pressure that had built up over several years. Concentrating on their other widely recognised obsession – technological advance – they took off for Holland where the surf's NEVER up and went through some half a million dollars settling in and arranging for nearly four tons of recording equipment to be brought from America. The evidence of the whole incredible adventure is their new album, simply called Holland. Good vibrations.

The Beach Boys did not pick Holland for their getaway entirely at random. As they've often sung, they've been all over this great big world. They know precisely what they're looking for. In February of this year, they came to Amsterdam to appear on the Gala du Disc, a Dutch TV spectacular. They had not been to Holland since December, 1970. when they battled crippling logistics with sensational results. After being fogged in at London Heathrow, they scrambled for a jet at neighbouring Gatwick Airport. They could not get a flight to Amsterdam, so they landed in Brussels where they were met by a caravan of a dozen Mercedes. They drove like madmen to Amsterdam where a play-by-play account of their progress was being broadcast to the waiting audience. As dawn approached the band sin-cerely doubted there would be an audience if and when they made their destina-tion. But when they strode on stage at quarter past five in the morning, it was to a full and clamouring house. Most rewarding, from the band's viewpoint, was this crowd's enthusiasm for their new music. They weren't all screaming "Fun, Fun, Fun"; it left the Beach Boys with lasting good vibrations.

When the group returned for the TV special, it was thought that they'd stay only a week. The week turned into months when they gradually succumbed to the spell of Holland's all encompassing calm. They decided Amsterdam would be the base camp from which they'd administer their European tour, that the tour would wind up there and that they'd stay on to do some recording. The latter decision brought with it problems in logistics that made the '70 stunt look pale.

Room Service, Send Me a Room

The first person to suffer the extent to which this was not going to be easy was one Bill de Simone, erstwhile Hollywood PR man. His job was to fix houses and transportation for the entourage. (The rollcall below will indicate the toughness of being in Bill's shoes, wooden or Florsheim.) With no prior knowledge of Holland's critical and chronic housing shortage, Bill manfully tried to retain the necessary 11 houses in Haarlem, a handsome residential area convenient to EMI studios. In two weeks, he did well to find four. Inevitably personnel were scattered within a 30 mile radius of central Amsterdam.

The scatter-ees were Brian Wilson, his wife, two children, sister-in-law and housekeeper; Dennis Wilson with wife and child; Carl Wilson with wife, two children, mother, brother-in-law, housekeeper and two dogs; Mike Love with wife, two kids and a maid; Al Jardine with the same as Mike, Rick Fataar with wife and in-laws; Blondie Chaplin and girlfriend. For starters.

Then there was chief engineer Steve Moffitt with secretary and son; additional engineers Gordon Rudd and wife, Jon Parker and girl; and Thom Gellert and admirers; Russ Mackie, the group's traveling attache: Jack Rieley, Brother Records' senior officer and the man at whom the buck stops, his secretary Carole Hayes and her husband, plus Jack's dog. And not least, Bill, who sought shelter for all. In the end they were sprinkled through the Netherlands thus: Jack, Russ and Carole in Amsterdam; Carl and Blondie in Hilversum; Brian in Laren; Ricky in Vreeland; Jon and Thom in Haarlem; Gordon in Heemsted; Steve in Assendelft; Mike and Al in Bloemendaal – all converging on a converted barn in Baambrugge. Before the houses were ready, all were put up in hotels. The musicians' houses were each outfitted with rented stereo and piano. They rented nine Mercedes, one Audi, bought three VWs and van. Aging visibly as he speaks, Jack says, "Some day accounting will face a column just called 'Holland.'" Before they obtained their present Amsterdam office, Jack's duplex apartment a furnished summer rental, became Brother Records' European headquarters. The office was set up in the children's room, already resplendent with bears, dolls and tables not exceeding one and a half feet in height. A Telex was installed with an obliging Dutch answering service. It handled on the average, three quarters of an hour's messages per day, the printed sheets unfurling like an endless paper towel. So many transatlantic calls were placed that the international operators in Pittsburgh, through whom all such calls are relayed, got wise to the number and noted it to save time.

A Moveable Feast

As if things weren't hair-raising enough, there was the ticklish business of Brian. Brian had not budged in seven years and he is intensely shy – perhaps the more so for having been dubbed "brilliant" or "genius" by various admirers, ever since he gave up touring with the band. His hearing is difficult and painful. Any description of him as a homebody or private person would still fall short of the truth. He once retired to his room, somewhere in the rambling Edgar Rice Burroughs house in Bel Air, for six solid months. To further avoid even local travel, he constructed a substantial studio in the living room of this same house (a 30's Gothic affair, right down to the secret panels). With their passion for technological improvement, the group gradually made this studio obsolete by their own standards, and besides, Brian's wife thought it was about time to do some living in the living room. The studio was duly dismantled. Getting Brian to Amsterdam was every bit as touch and go as getting Bobby Fischer to Reykjavik. A miasma of false starts and silences. His wife, kids and housekeeper went over first. Twice Brian got as far as the airport and turned back. The third time he appeared to get on the plane. A phone call went through to Amsterdam to confirm it. But three hours after the plan landed there was still no sign of him. A search of the aircraft yielded Brian's ticket and passport, abandoned on his seat. Oblivious to the panic was Brian who had shuffled off the plane and fallen asleep on a couch in the duty free lounge, where he eventually was found.

Operation Supersound

Of course when the initial decision to record in Holland was made it was assumed that the group would use Dutch facilities. They learned soon enough, however, that the few existing studios were already overtaxed, and no way could enough time for an LP be booked. Still, they had come too far to turn back. They were sick of rush hour, poison air and nerves. So they rashly commissioned a 21st Century board, one borrowing liberally from the future, and set it up in sleepy, rural Netherlands.

Steve Moffitt was minding his own business somewhere in Santa Monica when he got a call from Amsterdam requesting a studio to be designed and constructed, then disassembled, shipped and reassembled in Holland. Steve, who had worked as engineer on the *Carl and the Passions: So Tough* album, had been involved in discussions of possibly recording in Holland one day, but certainly building a portable studio had never been proposed. When Steve assisted with breaking down Brian's living room studio, a "dream" console – a 24 channel quadraphonic monster – was conceived, but shelved for the time being.

Steve's call came in mid-March. He was given a deadline of June 1. His first move was to contact all quality console makers in New York and Los Angeles, requesting prices and specifications for standard models, and emphasising the deadline. The deadline was a dead end: none of the manufacturers could promise a thing in less than 90 days.

Steve's only alternative was to create a studio from scratch. Having made that decision, he decided to go the whole hog and attempt the "dream" machine fantasised during the Bel Air breakdown. He would need help. Friend and physics wiz Gordon Rudd was understandably reluctant, but he was the only man with whom Steve felt the project had a chance. Looking back, Steve says. "It was a ridiculous task to start with, with only two men working on it – even for a stock model. But the manufacturers were proposing ones twice the size with half the functions. Most of the people who design consoles have never actually had to use them".

"I Was Virgin Console"

When Steve and Gordon completed their design, construction took place in a 2,000 square foot warehouse / laboratory in the back of an "adult" movie house in Santa Monica. The place also served as an inventory of all Brother Records gear, including the earthly remains of the Bel Air studio. Once construction started, assemblers worked 24 hours a day in shifts to get the job completed.

As soon as he'd finished his coordinating work with the console in America, Steve flew to Amsterdam to supervise its assembly there. When the components for the custom built studio began shipping, Beach Boy equipment occupied every single flight from L. A. to Amsterdam (of which there are four daily) and, to correct breakdowns, every Amsterdam to L.A flight (of which there are three daily), for four and a half weeks. The specially made crates alone cost over $5,000. The heaviest single item, the racks containing the limiters, Kepexes, Dolbys and prodigious patch bay, actually cracked the tarmac as it was rolled out to the plane for loading. The gross weight of all parts was 7,300 pounds.

It was dodgy. Although the individual parts had been tested, the system as a whole had not had time for a try out, and now the condition of any part may have been affected by the extreme cold in the plane's freight bay. Even if they'd stayed in California, it often takes a full month to get a system compatible. They were flying blind.

Steve recalls, "We finally got it all hooked up...and NOTHING worked right!" He adds with professional calm, "You learn in electronics to expect anything". He and Gordon, who followed on to nurse the monster, began working 18 hour days trouble shooting. The aggregate delay of four and a half weeks scotched the groups plans for extra touring in order to defray the summer's staggering expenses.

The group meanwhile wanted to mix down a live tape from their spring European tour. The 3M-16 track was unhitched from the control room and taken to a studio in town, where it proceeded to blow up and all but catch fire. Steve was prepared with over $3,000 worth of spare parts – everything, in fact, except the one that was needed to fix it. A 3M man was flown over from London to put it right. It then behaved impeccably until the end of the Holland mission, when it blew up again as Steve was trying to make copy tapes.

Throughout the recording period, Steve tended the touchy apparatus exhaustively, vetting it out for four hours before recording began each day, and for another two hours after finishing up. It was a Herculean labor, but Steve stayed cool, meditating at home in suburban Assendelft when TV of a Friday evening affords a diet of Flipper, Zorro and Rod McKuen. And it was entirely worth it when he stood back and admired his creation – the streamlined, multi-colored console supported on two pedestals with no wires visible, glowing futuristically in the dark. It was a wondrous anachronism, sitting there in a one time farm building in rural Baambrugge .

The building had, in fact, previously seen use as a studio, with a 4-track used primarily for commercials and the odd Christmas album. Out front it still bears the imposing name BBC 2 (curiously, no relation to BBC 2 of Britain). Inside it was a disaster when Steve found it. The acoustics were dreadful. He began by having the floor relaid six inches higher so that the cables could run under it. Sand was poured between the uprights to avoid resonating. (Even the speakers had sand, Malibu sand at that, to prevent resonance.) Angles were built into the ceiling. which was covered with spun glass. The fiendish florescent lighting (strangely popular in Holland) was quickly replaced with a multitude of Study-Buddy lamps, stuck on the wall, covered with different colored gels and controlled by dimmer switches. The building's delighted owner rushed around taking home movies and garnering autographs, in between looking after the cows whose faces loomed directly out the studio windows.

Expensive Innards

Anyone with enough spare cash to buy a private jet or pay parking fines in New York City can now learn what is required to duplicate the Beach Boys revolution-ary control room at home. Start with a Clover Systems (Gordon's firm) 30-input console with 20 channel monitor system. Add 30 quad pans, 30 stereo pans and a 1,000 hole patch bay with 1,000 jacks to stick in it. (This will be the biggest patch bay on your block.)

From England you will need 20 Dolby Noise Reduction Units, which alone will set you back more than $12,000 (and to think, until a few years ago all records were made without them). Still, if you don't want that natural hiss tape makes dirtying up your sound, it's gotta be Dolbys (The Beach Boys studio is actually wired for 34 Dolbys, which they'll get around to installing when they discover a way to use all those 24 tracks).

Speaking of clean sound, for another four and a half grand you can get 16 Kepexes. These are not extinct birds, as their name implies, but rather magical devices which allow sound through to the tape only when the voice or instrument is performing, thus eliminating the normal hum and buzz that plagues idle but turned on equipment. They were supplied to Steve and Gordon by the clever wags at Alison Research, which is named after the wife of the guy who does the researching. From these same loonies, Steve and Gordon got four limiters, more standard equipment, inexplicably called Gainbrains. What limiters limit is the dynamic range of sound, diminishing too loud noises while beefing up weak ones, and, in particular, encouraging guitar notes to sustain. All the Kepexes and Gainbrains are adorned with little cameos of Alison herself, at no extra cost.

Fleshing out the Beach Boys control room are one Cooper Time Cube Audio Acoustic Delay Unit, two little Dipper filters; two SAE Graphic Equalizers (these are tone control devices analogous to the treble and bass control on home hi-fis, only more sophisticated); an Orban Parasound stereo mixer; and, to deal effec-tively with foreign power, three Variable Speed Oscillators to run the tape at 60 cycles; a crystal oscillator to run all the VSOs on 60 cycles; a 3M 16 track tape machine with VSO built in; and a 3M 2 track machine for mastering from the 16. For cue system and studio monitors Steve used Crown D60 amplifiers; for the con-trol room monitor, a pair of custom built Crown DC300 amplifiers. Two speaker systems were especially made for Holland, incorporating a concept he'd been

working on for five years. When mixing down, the group uses inferior speakers –
the object being to get the sound first rate on any home system.

Reviewing the particular qualities which he feels set this system apart from
other good ones currently in use, Steve first cites its modular construction.
Although it is is only "half" portable (it takes a week to disassemble), it does allow
for individual parts repair and replacement within a minute. Second, at the push of
a button, all equalisation from the main part of the console is switched into the
monitor system. Third, the peak indicating meters indicate with light rather than
needles, so they needn't be watched as closely. It is as if your car speedometer
turned from white to red as soon as you went over the limit. Fourth and greatest
convenience is the 1,000 hole patch bay which acts as a fail safe system, especially useful for mix down. Anything can be patched into anything. If an equalizer
breaks, you patch it out and patch another one in, you can reassign the position of
already recorded tracks, grouping them as you like. You can put a limiter before
or after faders, or anywhere you like. Steve said they had occasion to use it all.

As he packs up his things in preparation for another American tour, Carl
Wilson reflects on why Holland was such a good idea. "We've all been wanting
to leave LA. for a couple of years now. Holland is friendly in every sense. The
environment eliminates distractions. The only kind of tension is the good kind of
working tension – not the kind you get crossing L.A in rush hour. There is a subliminal feeling of safety here. We worked long hours to make up for the delay,
usually waking in the afternoon and then working 'til 5 in the morning. It was so
perfectly still at night. Sometimes we'd walk out and see Venus like a headlamp
– amazingly bright!"

Dutch Beef

There was one incident that temporarily threatened tranquility. A musicians' union
called ANOUK (a subdivision of one of the labor federations) was mighty suspicious of the Beach Boys' presence. They thought the band might be taking work
away from Dutch musicians, wanted them investigated and, if need be deported.
Brother Records prepared a dossier to explain they weren't doing any Dutch out
of jobs, that they were in fact using Dutch sidemen on occasion (for example, the
strings on "Only With You"), that they hoped their activities would give a boost
to to Holland's music scene. ANOUK was agreeable. Their only regret – and a fair
beef – was that Dutch musicians couldn't hope to do the same thing in America,
due to the notorious strictness of U.S. Immigration. Overall, relations with the
Dutch throughout the project were extremely good. The group recalls with amusement that fans approaching for autographs were given away by the sound of their
wooden shoes on the cement outside the studio.

Leader of the Packing

Approaching Baambrugge from Amsterdam it is at once plain why Carl described
it as "a really good change, a completely different experience". The drive takes

about 20 minutes along a four lane divided highway flanked on both sides by flat fields, cows and canals. Sea birds fly by overhead. The windmills are really there, just like in the pictures, turning with spatulate grace. The highway patrol drive Porsches and it is said that the gypsies drive Mercedes.

BBC 2 sits among a collection of unprepossessing farm buildings, adjacent to a defunct greenhouse. Just inside the door are stacked 15 empty cases of Coke – conclusive evidence of American occupation. In the studio proper JR is methodically packing the final bits. JR was the one who packed the equipment originally in L.A. for shipping to the Netherlands; now he has flown over specifically to re-pack the lot. After proudly displaying a handsome trunk he picked up in the Amsterdam flea market to cope with extras, he rhapsodises about Great Packing. He cites Dolbys and Thorens turntables as the apex of the art, swathed in in unending foam rubber and expanded polystyrene.

Everywhere the studio shows signs of recording's universal depredations – the carpet tiles littered with ash, empty cigarette packs, glutinous coffee cups, foul ash trays. JR carefully arranges the hardware in fishing tackle boxes. Assorted percussion gives a tell tale rattle inside its horseshoe shaped box. Inside each of the custom built crates is a neatly typed list of contents – as if if everything were going off to some unimaginable summer camp.

Of course over the months loads of stuff has accumulated that was not part of the original design – art supplies and empty reels, a crate of fat 16 track tapes and skinny 2 tracks, mike cord, headphones, giant rolls of jute cloth. The floor is deep in the tools of the packer's art – pliers, hammer, scissors, screwdriver, string, Magic Markers and the ubiquitous foam rubber. JR leaves his work for a moment and carefully undoes the cover to display the console, like Carter revealing the golden mask of the boy pharaoh – and there it lies, looking positively like God's jukebox. When it arrives safely home it will be reassembled and tested in the warehouse / lab, then dismantled once again for reconstruction at some as yet undetermined site – possibly Topanga or Malibu.

In their six month emigration to Holland to realize an album project, the Beach Boys have demonstrated both a broadened insight into being and a good grip on the purpose for contradiction. The decision to leave California, where the group had recorded all of its previous studio efforts, bore with it the challenge to rediscover "why" a land of 24 hour a day supermarkets could still hold value for humans anguished over their home's ecological condition long before linguists named it.

The contradiction of the Beach Boys is born in many forms. Most notable of late was the bringing of two South African blacks, Ricky Fataar and Blondie Chaplin, into "all that is American and white". However, in Holland the Beach Boys have imparted reason for that contradiction and served their audience with new ones as well: they left a land of water, California for a change, but landed upon the land stolen from water, Holland, where they recorded the cries of drowning men and floating images more imaginatively than any before them have attempted; they looked at the land they had spurned and praised it, returning to that land nostalgically but without hope of tomorrows.

Side One

"Sail on Sailor" is a Brian Wilson-Jack Rieley song with writer credits suggesting informal assistance from a wide range of characters, among them Van Dyke Parks. It takes the composers sense of rueful sorcery to a politically radical plateau, accompanied lyrically by one of the more blunt statements of the quality of being ever uttered by the Beach Boys. Blondie Chaplin sings lead, and Carl Wilson produced.

"Steamboat" is the adventure of sound as life's recreation – of recorded production as blood's pulse. Dennis Wilson-Jack Rieley written, the song is descriptive and chugging, like the vehicle for which it is named. Carl sings lead on this one and co-produced with Dennis. Tony Martin plays steel guitar.

California Saga

"Big Sur" marks the first time Mike Love has composed the music as well as written the words for a song, and is the first part of the trilogy *California Saga* which examines the ghettoized cloisters of what remains in dear California. Mike sings lead and Alan Jardine and Carl co-produced.

"The Beaks of Eagles" came originally from a poem by Robinson Jeffers which Alan Jardine found one day. In it a certain sense of natural nobility is portrayed, then praised in brief verse sung like a clear bell by Jardine, who singly wrote.

"California" which the author also also refers to as "on my way to sunny Cal-i-forn-eye-ay" – the line sung from the seldom heard vocal chords of Brian Wilson. In the song a certain flashback montage permeates a generally high descriptive lyric. Al Jardine composed the words and music and co-produced with Carl.

Side Two

"The Trader" is a two part Carl Wilson painting – his first effort since "Feel Flows" and "Long Promised Road" appeared on the *Surf's up* album. In it recorded production reaches new heights in glory and measure; like a many layered puzzle whose pieces are nothing singly but which, when put together, registers incredibly upon the sensory scoreboard. The Jack Rieley lyric condemns the imperialism of Holland's yesterdays and America's todays, both from the viewpoint of the perpetrator and from that of the victim. Carl sings lead and Carl produced.

"Leaving This Town" stalks ground of deep inner experience and is built of a beautifully simple structure created by Ricky Fataar. Unlike the composer's two earlier Beach Boys efforts (on the *so Tough* album), this song takes full advantage of the musical coexistence of diversity which Brian Wilson has for so long expounded. The integral quality of the recording is even more apparent when the credits are shown revealing back up writing from Carl Wilson, Blondie Chaplin and Mike Love. Blondie Chaplin sings lead, Ricky produced and also did the Moog solo.

"Only With You" is Dennis Wilson's beauty and wonder expressed in group form. Mike Love wrote the words and brother Carl sings the lead. Dennis' emotionalism is soft and gentle here, as it was on *Sunflower*'s "Forever" and *Friends'* "Little Bird". It contrasts both in form and effect from his contributions to *so Tough*.

"Funky Pretty," the last cut on the album, is one of the more descriptive titles ever laid upon a song. Brian Wilson composed this one, of course. It is equally the first and last word of its title. It incorporates every member of the group equally, and features no fewer than four melodies running concurrently through the verse. The Mike Love-Jack Rieley lyrics are at once humorous, mystical and perverse. Even the lead vocal is shared – by four of the group members. The song's tag incorporates perhaps a dozen moving parts. Brothers Brian and Carl produced.

And the Bonus Record

Those buying *Holland* are recipient of a so-called gift from Brian Wilson, in the form of a 45 that the Beach Boys like to refer to as his fairy tale. Titled "Mount Vernon and Fairway", it is in reality a post-Sartre essay on the nothingness of being, carrying with it a joy and exhaltation which evaporates time as nothing Brian Wilson has ever attempted before. It is not a rock opera, so it will disappoint some and insult perhaps a few listeners. It's the classic form of the fairy tale and nothing else. Nothing else, that is, except perhaps an autobiographical look at Brian Wilson's early planet. He wrote the words, music and text, and also provided the Pied Piper voice.

Dutch Treat

Was it worth it? Or was this all a very complicated dream, anyhow? Well, the Beach Boys stand behind the experiment, more than pleased with the results. Brother Records has become so enamoured of Holland that they have set up a permanent office in Amsterdam, an exquisite 17th Century house overlooking a mossy green canal. Upstairs, resounding among the antique furnishings, is the shiny black round thing that all the fuss was about. Carl is still too close to the business to be objective – that will take months. But the other listeners are smiling that knocked out smile, and it looks like the right idea was *Holland*.

Shelley Benoit, November, 1972

Original Reviews Part 5

Holland album

"This will very likely be hailed as the Beach Boys best ever…"

"The new album is very good, sometimes great, sometimes lame and occasionally diabolical. It is by no means as good as *Pet Sounds*…"

"I'd love to declare this as a supreme triumph in music, etc., but it isn't, which may be a blessing in disguise. After initial disappointment, I settled down to accept it on its own terms and discovered a very fine album indeed…"

"I've never been much impressed by the solo writing talents of Messrs Love and Jardine, but they provide the undoubted highlight of *Holland*: a long piece in three parts called 'California Saga'… The suite finishes with Jardine's 'California', a celebration so ecstatic that I was sure that Brian Wilson had written it…"

"the quality is excellent (and at £2.59 it should be!), but the quality has been just fine on all their albums. The money spent could surely have been put to a much better use?" [This last comment was from a fan letter at the time, rather than a review snippet – Ed.]

Hold On Dear Brother:
The Beach Boys Without Brian Wilson
by Peter Doggett

When a band has at its centre one of the greatest record producers and composers of the twentieth century, what do they do when he withdraws his involvement? Brian Wilson is still perceived by record companies, critics, and fans alike, as being the musical force of the band, even though he has been mainly absent from the Beach Boys since the mid-sixties. This specially commissioned article by Peter Doggett looks at how the band fared during Brian's long absences.

If Brian Wilson is the Beach Boys, as his brother Dennis once contended, then who are the Beach Boys without Brian Wilson? It's a question which has been in the air since late 1964, after Brian announced that he would no longer tour with the band. Three years later, when the grandeur of *Smile* dissipated into the anticlimax of *Smiley Smile*, the eldest Wilson brother withdrew into his California mansion – there but not quite there for the next decade and beyond.

"We've been talking about Brian for 25 years," says Bruce Johnston, who joined the band in 1965 to replace Brian on the road. "It's like he had this five year career, and we've been talking about it ever since." As the band's "in house adviser", Johnston was one of those presented with the task of hiding, and compensating for, Brian's absence: "It was like a great conductor, walking off the stage for 20 years. The orchestra can still play the parts."

Losing the most ambitious composer in pop history, who just happened to be a peerless singer, musician and producer, could have torpedoed the Beach Boys. Instead, they inhaled some of the era's self confidence, and taught themselves to become geniuses overnight.

The process began with the 1968 album, *Friends*. Though Brian was no longer in sole charge of the sessions, he was rarely far away when *Friends* was being recorded – simply because it was cut in his home studio, below his master bedroom. Dozens of Beach Boys sessions took place literally a few feet from brother Brian, who had no choice but to listen to what his brothers, cousin and friends were doing.

For the next five years, a complex game of double bluff was played out. As far as the Beach Boys publicity machine was concerned, Brian Wilson was a constant creative presence – his picture on every album, his name heavily represented in the writing credits, his absence from the studio hidden by the group's shared production credit. Little hint of the reality, that Brian spent more daylight time in bed than with his fellow Beach Boys, was allowed to creep out before the public.

At the same time, the rest of the group were locked in a battle of wills with their reclusive mentor. They used a mixture of emotional blackmail, animal cunning and naked pleading to persuade him to contribute to their records – a song, a vocal, an arrangement idea, anything that they could trumpet to the world as proof that Brian was still around. In return, Brian did his best to frustrate their plans, or at least to appear only when he felt like appearing – usually when he was least expected.

With no guarantee that there would be any Brian Wilson songs available, the rest of the Beach Boys had to become professional composers overnight. Dennis Wilson blossomed on *Friends* and its successors; Mike Love could lean on his experience as Brian's lyricist, plus the spiritual inspiration of his Transcendental Meditation; and Bruce Johnston had his apprenticeship as, in his words, "CBS's rock'n'roll department" to fall back on. Carl Wilson and Al Jardine swallowed hard and improvised.

With Brian contributing some key moments, *Friends* was a miniature triumph. Likewise *20/20*, once Carl Wilson had taken over the reins of production, and persuaded his big brother to allow the *Smile* fragment, "Cabinessence", to be revived.

The album which proved that the Beach Boys was a viable concept with or without Brian Wilson was *Sunflower*. "I think of *Pet Sounds* as Brian's solo album," says Bruce Johnston. "The Beach Boys' equivalent of *Pet Sounds* was definitely *Sunflower*. That was the best album we ever made."

All six Beach Boys peaked simultaneously during the sessions for this record – though its impact in the States was crushed by the complex political negotiations that were taking place between the band and Capitol Records. Several different track line ups were prepared, one of which included Al Jardine's wonderfully madcap exercise in harmony pop, "Loop De Loop". There was nothing quite that crazy on the finished album, simply a succession of superbly performed and produced pop songs that featured the richest and most satisfying Beach Boys vocals on any record. Even without Brian's *Smile* leftover, "Cool, Cool Water", and his sublime "This Whole World", *Sunflower* would have been a credible, not to mention exhilarating, feast of music.

Those two songs aside, Brian's contribution wasn't always quite what it seemed. For instance, he shared a writing credit with Bruce Johnston on "Deirdre". "I gave him 50% of the song," Bruce complains, "but it should have been 5%. He came up with two lines, that was it. He was suggesting things like, 'My friend Bob/He has a job', and I was saying, 'No, Brian'. I was kinda disappointed."

The momentum of *Sunflower* was maintained into the sessions for 1971's *Surf's up*. Dennis pulled his songs off the album, but Carl picked up the slack, debuting as a major composer and arranger with two remarkable songs, "Long Promised Road" and "Feel Flows". Mike Love and Al Jardine ventured into ecological concerns, and Bruce Johnston weaved a rich tapestry of nostalgia on "Disney Girls (1957)". But even in his virtual absence from the sessions, Brian Wilson still dominated the record. The *Smile* song "Surf's up" was disinterred against its composer's wishes; he's still complaining about it in the 90s. Out of nowhere, though, Brian produced "Till I Die", a stunningly beautiful, hauntingly poignant snapshot of where his heart and soul were at in 1971.

Another creative presence had entered the Beach Boys' orbit during the *Surf's up* sessions. Manager Jack Rieley persuaded the band that they should be appealing to a more adult audience, and trying to shed the candy striped shirts and squeaky clean image of their first decade. To that end, he penned some impressionistic, oblique lyrics for Carl Wilson's songs; to some insiders, Bruce Johnston included, he appeared to be wielding an unhealthy power over the Beach Boys' delicate personal relations.

Bruce quit early in 1972, and Rieley had replacements already lined up. Ricky Fataar and Blondie Chaplin were South Africans who'd escaped that country's repressive regime to seek fame as pop singers in England. As Flame, they and Ricky's two brothers had become the first – indeed, only – outside signing to the Beach Boys' Brother Records label.

"We'd been recording at Brian's house," Ricky Fataar recalls. "He'd wander in every now and then in his bathrobe and have a listen, then wander off again. Or you'd see him strolling around in the garden. He wasn't doing too much else." By late 1971, Flame were deep into a second album project for Brother but, as Fataar admits, "the band were splintering".

Fataar and Chaplin were offered the chance to join the band, not as sidemen but as fully fledged Beach Boys. "We were always going to be on the outside," Fataar says, "because the heart of the band was a single family. But we were made to feel very welcome, and we were always treated fairly on a business level."

To the bemusement of many longtime fans, Chaplin and Fataar made an immediate contribution to 1972's *Carl And The Passions – So Tough*. Though the album was named after an early incarnation of the Beach Boys, its title was also an admission that Carl had now replaced Brian as their guiding force. But the album was blighted from the start, when it was announced that it would form half of a double LP set – the other record to be devoted to the legendary unissued *Smile* album. That threat brought Brian Wilson down from his bedroom, and *Pet Sounds* was reissued instead. Longtime fans baulked at buying another copy of an album they already owned; critics compared the new with the old and found the Brian less Beach Boys lacking.

In truth, there were now three separate entities at work under the group's banner. Dennis Wilson was creating orchestral epics away from the rest of the band; Chaplin and Fataar were cutting R&B flavoured tracks that bore no relation to the group's heritage; and Carl Wilson, Love and Jardine were forcing fragments out of Brian. There were some sublime moments on *Carl And The Passions* – notably "Marcella", a Brian song about his intimate masseuse which was rewritten for public consumption, and Dennis's "Cuddle Up'. But unlike *Sunflower* and *Surf's up* it sounded nothing like the work of a coherent band.

To reintroduce a corporate spirit, Jack Rieley somehow enticed this most Californian of outfits to relocate to a barn near Amsterdam, to record *Holland*. "That was probably the first time that anyone took an entire studio somewhere else and recorded in a different environment," Ricky Fataar suggests. "While we were recording, we could only use certain parts of the mixing desk because it was still being built. We'd be in the middle of a take, and there would be a pair of legs sticking out under the console, doing some last minute wiring. That whole album was an interesting experience, in fact. We'd set up the equipment in a barn, and sometimes cows would come right up against the wall and start mooing loudly."

Dragged from the security of his Bel Air bedroom to the other side of the Atlantic, Brian Wilson was – not for the first time – a spectral presence during the *Holland* sessions. "We were constantly trying to coax him to come down to the studio," Fataar recalls. "Eventually he agreed, and gave us one lovely song, 'Funky Pretty'. He even played drums on that track."

The sessions over, Jack Rieley delivered the finished tapes to Warner Reprise – who demanded a hit single, preferably with Brian Wilson's name on it. A team of co-writers finally squeezed "Sail on Sailor" out of him, but once again, his degree of involvement in the finished record was ambivalent. "The basic track was cut back in Los Angeles by me, Blondie and Carl," Ricky Fataar remembers. "Then everyone else arrived to do the vocals, but Brian didn't turn up. Instead, he insisted on singing the parts down the phone to Carl, who translated them for the rest of us. We'd try it out, then Brian would call back and ask to hear how it was going. It was a strange way of making a record."

Equally bizarre was "Mount Vernon And Fairway", a children's tale included as a bonus disc with *Holland*. This was genuine Brian Wilson music, circa 1972, which is why it was ideal listening for children. Brian certainly never bought into Jack Rieley's concept of an adult Beach Boys. But the rest of the group achieved just that. Mike Love and Al Jardine concocted a three part "California Saga", incorporating poetry, mythology and a singalong hit single; Carl Wilson and Rieley bemoaned the effects of imperialism, no less, on the superb "Trader"; and Fataar and Chaplin offered up an evocative ballad, "Leaving This Town", for which Ricky produced a sinuous synthesiser solo.

After the false start of *Carl And The Passions*, *Holland* proved that the Beach Boys could function as a creative rock band beyond the self-imposed limits of their 60s hits. With Dennis Wilson already starting work on ecology songs like "Pacific Ocean Blues"and "River Song", the Beach Boys could have carved a niche as guardians of the planet's natural heritage – a transition from the teenage preoccupations of their early years into maturity.

It was a direction they were incapable of following on their own. The only man who might have forced their hand was Jack Rieley, but he'd elected to remain in Amsterdam after the completion of *Holland*, and manage the group from long distance. In January 1973, Carl Wilson flew to Europe to inform Rieley that he was being fired.

"In the middle of all the in fighting that afflicted the group, Jack was the person trying to hold everything together," Ricky Fataar comments. "It was a liquid situation: the conflict was really within the Wilson/Love family. You never knew where you stood, from one hour to the next. People shifted from one side to the other, and back again. There was always someone not talking to someone else in the band, and refusing to come to the studio because their enemy was there. Eventually, we realised that Rieley was very much into manipulating the arguments, starting stories and telling tales – a divide and conquer mentality. When that came to light, we had to let him go." Rieley remained in Holland, where he cut an album called *Western Justice*. Melodically slight, it was still closer to the spirit of *Holland* than anything the Beach Boys recorded thereafter.

Not that recording was their priority in the mid 70s. "The strategy was to play as many gigs as possible, and rebuild the group's audience," Fataar says. "When Blondie and I joined the band, they were on a downward slump. We had trouble filling 1,500 seaters. So we toured constantly, and one of our last gigs was at Madison Square Garden. The strategy paid off, but recording went out of the window. Dennis was always working on something, and Carl and I would go down to play with him. Otherwise there was nothing."

Aside from a live album, there was no new Beach Boys music between *Holland* at the end of 1972, and *15 Big Ones in 1976* – the subject of the ridiculous "Brian is back honest" PR campaign. By then, Blondie Chaplin and Ricky Fataar had both left the band, which returned to the original five man line up of 1961, and its pre-occupations.

"Blondie was fired after that Madison Square Garden show," Fataar explains. "He'd somehow got involved in a fight with Stephen Love, Mike's brother, who was now managing the band." Typically, ten years later, the group initiated a series of lawsuits against Love. Shortly after his friend's departure, Ricky Fataar quit: "Everything was dislocated and floundering. I was tired of touring, tired of not recording. There was nothing to stay for."

The Beach Boys' "solo" trip was over. In an ironic juxtaposition of events, Chaplin and Fataar left just as a collection of the group's 60s oldies, *Endless Summer*, began its climb to the top of the American charts. It contained nothing to remind the world that, for most of the last decade, Brian Wilson had been the silent Beach Boy. The last remaining songs from *Surf's up* and *Holland* were quietly dropped from their concert repertoire. Ahead lay two decades of diminished ambitions, the long descent from a vital, organic force into a travelling revival show. Ironically, Brian Wilson would once again absent himself from much of the group's future activities. But this time, no one had the nerve to pick up the torch.

The Son Also Rises: Rejuvenation, Disjunction, Regret and Reunion During the Making of The Beach Boys' *15 Big Ones* by Timothy White

Over the years Timothy White has written extensively and informatively about Brian and the band, and his books, which include the highly acclaimed The Nearest Faraway Place: Brian Wilson, The Beach Boys and the Southern California Experience*, and his articles have always placed Brian as the lynch pin of the whole operation. White's introductory essay is new to this book, and the three following* Crawdaddy *articles have never been re-published anywhere since 1976. All of these pieces have been chosen by the author himself as his contribution to this collection.*

"When you're young, growing up around the house, it's hard to express yourself, so it was a great release when I became a Beach Boy", mused Dennis Wilson, sitting at the stern of his sailboat in Marina del Rey during a chilly, overcast late January afternoon in 1976. His group had just embarked on a probative new project, a series of sessions at their own Brother Studio in Santa Monica, at which they were cutting cover versions of R&B and pop hits of the '50s and early '60s in an attempt to induce Dennis' troubled brother Brian to resume an active role in the group he founded 15 years ago.

The unusual tack represented a compromise at a stage when the Boys felt stymied as a unit and reluctant to commit their own recent or stockpiled individual compositions to a communal album that didn't mainly feature Brian's work.

"We have a lot of stuff in the can we could have put together and released", said Dennis of the tentative exploration of the oldies option, "but it just wasn't that. It's always left up to the writer of each song as to what will happen to it, and we couldn't agree on enough of the old material". He sighed in frustration. "It takes a lot of fun out of the creativity to have to release, release."

The band's current undertaking was mandated by a mutually ungratifying contract with Warner Bros., whose Beach Boys yield of six new albums to date since their 1970 signing (including *Sunflower*, *Surf's Up*, *Carl and the Passions – So Tough* and *Holland*, and a *Best Of* LP) had stalled after their peak 1973 success with the gold *The Beach Boys in Concert*.

Meantime, Capitol Records had enjoyed a No. 1 *Billboard* album chart triumph with *Endless Summer*, a two record anthology of the group's seminal '60s hits. Thus, Warner Bros. wanted to restore corporate as well as consumer faith in its investment, while Brian's brother Dennis wanted to restore the group's reticent, overweight leader to functional participation in the world around him.

"Brian, he's a timid, reclusive person now," said Dennis, scratching his dense, dark blonde beard as he flexed against the rigging of the fifty foot Harmony, his recently purchased two masted ketch, "but I can remember back when people were seeking spiritual advice from Brian, like in 1967-68. He was even a father to a lot of kids in L.A. who were home alone when their fuckin' parents couldn't take the responsibility of taking care of their kids. I don't even think Brian was aware of a lot of it at the time.

"But Brian had emotional needs like everyone else; he had HIS needs," added Dennis. "A guy in that position, always being faced with others harping that they needed help, after a while, hell, it can really blow you out." Dennis shrugged sadly. "Lot of responsibility being a genius, I guess."

Granted, but the maintenance required of late to keep the emotionally beleaguered Brian afloat, much less shipshape, had brought both the Beach Boys and members of Brian's immediate family to the brink of desperation. ("Marilyn, Brian's wife had given him an ultimatum," Dennis later confided. "If he didn't get active again, she was gonna leave him.")

At the end of each day's stressful round of band meetings over the winter of '76, Dennis tended to retreat to his boat to recharge himself.

In a way, the Harmony represented the apex and ideal embodiment of the dream of liberating success that Dennis, Brian, their brother Carl, first cousin Mike Love, and friends Al Jardine, Dave Marks and Bruce Johnston had each fostered during the ebb and flow of their various spans with the Beach Boys. The boat's blueprints had been drafted in 1950 in New England, its sails hand sewn in England, the custom brass fittings cast in Scotland, and its hull constructed in Japan, with the finished craft boasting mahogany from the Philippines, camphorwood from Taiwan, and teak from Burma – far-flung locales where, incredibly, the Beach Boys music had found an audience via touring, official releases, bootlegs, or venturesome fans who toted tapes while on safari. (By the '70s, most serious surfers knew bitchin' shore breaks existed throughout Southeast Asia.)

Decades earlier, the famously fleet Harmony schooner had been known for runs of over 150 miles in a single day of long distance sailing. As for the Beach Boys, their lengthiest chart run – 155 weeks with *Endless Summer* – was likewise owed to navigation skills of the remote past.

Between January and late March '76, at the kind invitation of Dennis Wilson, this writer – then the Managing Editor of *Crawdaddy* – would pass numerous days with Brian and/or the Boys at Brother Studios or at Brian's home in Bel Air. (Dennis had phoned *Crawdaddy*'s Greenwich Village office out of the blue shortly after New Year's Day, saying he read the magazine regularly and wondered if I'd want to cover the rejuvenation of Brian and the Beach Boys.)

I also passed an equal amount of time with Dennis, eating between-session lunches and suppers with him at the Mexican restaurant across from the studio (his favorite dish was a massive salad served in a tortilla bowl called the Guadalajara); cruising with him in his van to assorted haunts in Venice, Ca., or riding out to Marina del Rey to loll on the deck of the Harmony, his close friend/collaborator Gregg Jakobson or his comely fiancee Karen Lamb sometimes joining us to watch the sunset. Occasionally Dennis was exultant, often he was tense and pensive, and sometimes he choked back tears.

Dennis felt the tide was turning for the Beach Boys, not to mention the rest of the pop record business – which had openly calculated that a stream of charismatic and radiogenic rock acts could be counted upon to arise at reasonable intervals, most of the talent quite open to a modern imaging and marketing push.

Since the Beach Boys still consisted of blood relatives and boyhood friends whose many flaws and artistic preoccupations endured largely intact, Dennis fretted over whether the Boys' Brian-filtered sensibilities could fit into an era that now prized sheer productivity or a steady catalogue of albums aptly named with roman numerals.

"Take Elton," said Dennis one evening at dusk in the marina, his eye catching the nearby mooring of Madman, the huge white yacht belonging to Elton John and manager John Reid. "If Elton took his time and just made one great album, it would be phenomenal. He would sell as many of the one as he would putting out three mediocre ones. I'm not digging at him or Chicago or any of the people right now who are hot and putting out album after album, 'cause you know three or four cuts on their albums are gonna be good but the others just won't make it. Brian Wilson albums tend to hold you all the way through; he's a producer and a writer and the Beach Boys are his tools."

Yet the master craftsman had since retreated into the shadows, neglecting his kindred human implements, and now they beckoned to and even implored him to be taken up again. The aural impact of *15 Big Ones*, an album that was never actually intended to be issued in what became its final form, would prove the sound of iron sharpening iron, a frictive test of wills of the sort that only blood ties and adolescence-spawned trust could forge.

Much has rightly been made of epochal Beach Boys albums like *Pet Sounds* and the abortive *Smile*, but for the sheer humanity of the internal and external struggles suffusing it, *15 Big Ones* may one day be accorded a similar dramatic status in the Beach Boys canon. Hastened by heartbreak, shaped by disappointment, jump-started by commercial imperatives that ran parallel with survival impulses, it was and is an honest if disturbing document, emblematic of the group's need to find fresh purpose in the remnants of a worthy past.

What follows are three articles of mine that originally appeared in *Crawdaddy*. Published in the magazine's April 1976 issue, the opening piece was the first notice anywhere in the world of the endeavour that would transpire as *15 Big Ones*. It is followed by the review in *Crawdaddy* of the completed 15-track *15 Big Ones* album (recorded between January 30 and May 15, 1976 and released on July 5, 1976) that ran in *Crawdaddy*'s September 1976 issue. Incidentally, this review included interviews and was presented almost as a news analysis because of the great surprise and shock *15 Big Ones*' rough hewn nature elicited at the time, i.e., it was not the sort of record that anyone, including some if its participants, had believed would result from the oldies premise privately discussed by the Beach Boys at its outset. This circumstance is plain from the third piece, first printed in the November 1976 *Crawdaddy*, which unveiled in detail Dennis and Carl Wilson's own deeply felt post-mortems of *15 Big Ones*.

If some members of the band were disgruntled with *15 Big Ones*, others were determined to press onward, seeing the album as a dose of disagreeable medicine that had to be digested to get Brian & company back into working order. The latter outlook was of a piece with the Warner Bros. corporate perspective, as evidenced by its mammoth resultant "Brian is back!" promotional campaign.

In the end, it seems everyone was right, since the record was a sometimes unintentionally poignant/exasperating glimpse at a great band in transitional pain, yet it did contain the smash single, "Rock and Roll Music", a Top Five rendition of the Chuck Berry classic that became the Boys' biggest hit since "Good Vibrations" ten years prior. And *15 Big Ones* had another high charting single with "It's O.K", which climbed to No. 29 in *Billboard*'s Hot 100. Still, it also precipitated the abrupt solo career decisions by Dennis and Carl Wilson.

Readers interested in the full saga of the making of *15 Big Ones* and much of what occurred before and afterward may wish to seek out the newly expanded 1997 edition of my recent book, *The Nearest Faraway Place: Brian Wilson, The Beach Boys and the Southern California Experience* (Henry Holt, US; Pan Macmillan, UK). But these archival articles republished for the first time in over twenty years disclose the basic developments as discovered by Beach Boys fans and the general public during the slow dawning and bittersweet afterglow of that unforgettable summer of '76.

"Hello Brian..."
Checking In With The Bashful Beachcomber
by Timothy White

BEL AIR, Ca. – It's been over three years since the Beach Boys have released an album of all new material, but founder Brian Wilson, the reticent Hawthorne, Ca., teenager who immortalized America's itinerant sunburnt surf bum and sent a pallid nation scurrying to the drugstore for Quik Tan and Clairoxide, promises a new release this spring.

Reached at his California home Brian confirmed rumours of the forthcoming LP and appeared to have resumed his once active role in the studio, Judging from his heavy use of "we're" in his discussion of the record. He confessed, however, that the Beach Boys had been working on the project "only a month. We're not really working very hard," he offered timorously in his somewhat high, raspy voice.

Asked about content, Wilson said "oldies but goodies. We're not doing anything new yet. We're doing oldies songs: 'Blueberry Hill' and 'Palisades Park'. We're doing them in the traditional way; it will be like the old Beach Boys' harmonies."

Will the album contain new material?

"Yes," Wilson assured. "A song called 'Susie Cincinnati', which is an original and which is up-tempo harmonies and, aaah, that's all that I can think of right now. It was written by Al Jardine," said Wilson, and then offered a two line sample of the lyrics:

"Susie Cincinnati got a groovy
little motor car,
She lives for the night and her
husband's a security guard"

'It's about a female cab driver,' Brian explained.

(In January of this year, Carl Wilson offered Warner Bros. a "reworked" version of "Susie Cincinnati" for consideration as a new single, but later changed his mind. As for the current status of the song, which was released in 1970 as the 'B' side to "Add Some Music to Your Day", and later the 'B' side to the Beach Boys'

1974 Christmas single, "Child of Winter", we quote Brian Wilson: "There's a few cuts in the can we're gonna use on one of our new albums, like 'Susie Cincinnati', which was never on an album. I am working on a new version of it because it's a good song." Incidentally, Dennis Wilson has no recollection of the song having been released at all: "Did we release that? I doubt it.")

The 33-year old millionaire songwriter also said he intends to include Van Dyke Parks' "Come To The Sunshine" in the roster of cuts. "Yes, that's true," he said. "We're trying to get the tapes right now." (Parks told *Crawdaddy* that he and Brian were having difficulty obtaining from an undisclosed source a completed version of what he described as "a 24-track tape of the song.")

The new LP (the last all-new album was *Holland* in 1973) comes in the wake of an astonishingly successful glut of Beach Boys reissues and anthologies, particularly *Endless Summer*, a Capitol compendium of the group's biggest hits / favorites, which reached No. 1 nationwide in 1974.

The notoriously shy Wilson made no attempt to conceal his satisfaction with that unexpected development.

"I was very happy, as a matter of fact," he enthused. "The new kids, the new young kids are hearing a lot of these songs for the first time." Brian added that he also was pleased with the quality of the anthologies and the selection of songs. 'I thought they were very well handpicked," he said. "We're discussing another one now. They might try to come up with some more sides – I don't know if we have enough on Capitol, though."

A virtual hermit for the last few years both socially and professionally, the brains behind one of the most popular bands of all time seems to be emerging from the shadows. Asked about the possibility of any other involvements, he replied: "I'm working with Terry Melcher. He has a group called California Music, and we're working on some projects for that and we hope to get them going soon."

Wilson's new promises aside, a succession of proposed Beach Boys albums have repeatedly failed to materialise. Lack of songs reportedly isn't the problem, however; some say a large amount of unreleased tapes exists, but then there are the famous stories concerning Brian's casual destruction over the years of hours of recorded work. When is this latest effort supposed to hit the stores?

"We don't have a release date yet on it," said Wilson, but he vowed it would occur some time "this spring."

A spokesman for Warner Brothers Records, the band's label since 1970 seemed less certain. "That album has been on again, off again for a long time," he said. "Everyone is just waiting to see it happen."

Lost Surfari
by Timothy White

15 Big Ones, The Beach Boys, Reprise/Brother (MS 2251)

Boy, I sure do love a day at the beach, but – Ouch! – what a terrible burn I've gotten:

> I know it took us a long while,
> To go and find us a rock style,
> I know that we could take it
> One more mile!
> Because we're singing that same song,
> We're still singing that same song . .

© 1976 Irving Music, Inc.

Heck. With these ill chosen words, Brian Wilson and Mike Love make an embarrassingly self-conscious attempt to convince a waiting world that the Beach Boys' mythical Pendletons have dropped not a single stripe since the glory days. But jeeze, it's like painting over rust; the feeble whitewash that is "That Same Song" and the other 14 bleeding tracks on *15 Big Ones* betrays an artistic wipeout, as Brian, Mike, Carl, Dennis and Al rage against their destiny as the Beach Men.

Ever since Brian's creative withdrawal from the Boys in the years following the 1966-67 *Dumb Angel / Smile* snafu and the empty compromise of *Smiley Smile*, the rest of the group has devoted what must have been a considerable amount of time, money and mettle coaxing their reluctant mentor back into his leadership role. One senses that their courtship was as much a tug of war as a reasoned wooing; either way, Brian & co. seem shaken by the wear and tear.

Coming some three and a half years after *Holland*, the Beach Boys' last all new LP, *Big Ones* is a startlingly directionless item, its flip inanities exceeded only by its unspoken but pervasive theme: fear of failure.

In a grim effort to find the thread that might lead them back into their heavily anthologized heyday, the Boys have begged, chosen or allowed Brian to pilot the group again. Sadly, their anxiousness under big brother's benevolent dictatorship is thinly disguised, and the only time the fellas aren't holding their collective breaths is when they have no alternative but to harmonise.

Be assured, you get plenty of *ooh-wah* along with the ever present tambourine and chimes. Likewise, the thunking drums and the sweet, sweet organ that sounds likes a calliope and an accordion and a summer breeze – but you don't get any inspiration, not a single romantic mirage.

In fairness, it must be said that, given Brian Wilson's fragile nature, his return to an active role in the Beach Boys' recording schedule could merely have fallen prey to unsteady hands. But even a casual listen to *Big Ones* would seem to indicate that the problems here are not quite so ephemeral, and potentially are very serious.

Numbered among the mish mash of cuts are five apparent originals and ten "oldies but goodies" of various vintages, including a slightly reworked version of "Susie Cincinnati" (1970) and "Had To Phone Ya", one of four tracks that appeared on an early '70s demo by Spring, an ill-fated duo consisting of Brian's wife, Marilyn, and her sister, Diane Rovell.

The quality of the oldies is uneven, most treatments suffering from a hackneyed obviousness that robs them of much of their colour, musicality and lyrical/emotional intent. The new material with the exception of the puerile "The T M Song", is never less than pleasant, but none of it convinces on any level, save that of "See?! We're trying!"

Following the development of this album from it's confused beginnings last January up to its completion in early May, the most glaring shortcoming from the onset was the absence of any unity of purpose, beyond a hunger for product. This is not to say that the record was simply cranked out, devoid of any sincerity, but over the past few months the Beach Boys' prime motivation in the studio seemed to me to be the burning desire to gain a specific beachhead: an all Brian Wilson production in the 1970s.

Big Ones was originally intended to be an all oldies album: at least that's what Brian said he wanted last winter in order to "limber up" in the studio. The rest of the Beach Boys went along – albeit tentatively – with his wishes. A host of oldies (reportedly as many as 15), were cut in the space of a few weeks, but at least one member of the group was immediately dissatisfied with the outcome of the project.

"I hope they don't release the oldies album," Dennis Wilson confessed over the phone last March, speaking from his Zuma Beach home several days after the tracks were completed. "We recorded a mess of old stuff like 'Sea Cruise', 'On Broadway', 'Come Go With Me', 'Johnny B. Goode', 'Rock And Roll Music', 'In The Still of the Night', and all," he explained at the time. "But I don't think they're very good, and I hope they don't release it [the oldies album] before they release a new album. Really, I hope they don't put it out at all; we gotta give 'em something new."

Dennis had similar sentiments for "Susie Cincinnati". Sitting in his camper van at Marina Del Rey one afternoon last February, he played a cassette of the new mix of the song on his tape deck and then dismissed it, with a laugh, as a "silly piece of shit".

I pass along these anecdotes to illustrate the cross currents that shape and propel the Beach Boys, for in the end, what we have here is another *Smiley Smile* type compromise. Once again, Brian would seem not to have gotten his way. But then, the damage was already done.

The raw, wooden production on much of *15 Big Ones* is a throwback to the days of *Surfin' Safari*. There is nothing to indicate that Brian and the group ever cut a ballad as heartrending as "Don't Worry Baby", or a rock collage as awe inspiring as "Good Vibrations". It's as if *Pet Sounds* never existed; more to the point, the Boys are pretending they never recovered from their late 60s enervation with the altogether stunning *Sunflower*.

Mysteriously, we must endure cynical remakes of "Chapel Of Love", "In The Still of the Night", and the Six Teens' "A Casual Look", each accorded an unamusing exercise in nasal mugging and horseplay. Speaking as one who has often appreciated the Beach Boys admittedly sophomoric sense of fun ("Cassius Love vs. Sonny Wilson", "Bull Session with the 'Big Daddy'"), I find the aping of their "Help Me Rhonda" style Bau-bau-bau back up vocals misplaced and insulting, while Mike Love's falsetto histrionics are downright stupid. God help us if the Beach Boys lust after the Sha Na Na crowd.

Big Ones does boast several bright moments – but no brilliant ones. "Palisades Park" is a classic – Carl Wilson's abashed vocal notwithstanding – but it sounds as if it was recorded in 1964, and I'm distressed the Boys have to dig that deeply for an energy source. The raucous "Blueberry Hill" is marred by an insipid sax intro, but recovers thanks to the boisterous singing of Love et al, and an enticing bass line. Carl's studied cover of Little Willie John's 1958 hit, "Talk To Me, Talk To Me", is quite believable – until the mood is shattered by the intrusion of a disastrous snippet of "Tallahassee Lassie".

One of the strongest songs is "It's O.K.", which will probably be the second single off the LP. An unpretentious ode to good cheer, it succeeds in spite of its fatalistic homily:

Good or bad, glad or sad,
It's all gonna pass away.
So hey, let's all play,
And enjoy while it lasts . . .

Another favourite is Mike Love's "Everyone's In Love With You", a cryptic but airy ballad that features some sprightly flute and the most expressive vocals in evidence; but I would have enjoyed it a lot more if Love hadn't confided that it's about the Maharishi.

The album's biggest flops are Brian's croaking rendition of "Back Home", and a cover of the old King, Goffin & Spector collaboration, "Just Once in My Life". Throughout the record, Brian's singing is conspicuously sluggish, undisciplined and bereft of its early nuance and power. His failings are most obvious, however, on "Back Home", where the chain-smoking Wilson cheats on even the midrange passages as he rambles on about spending one's summer on a farm, feeding the chickens and hurrying to the dinner table to gobble up everything that's set before him. None for me, thanks.

The biggest disappointment is "Just Once in My Life". With a *Sunflower*-minded attack and at least passable vocals, it might have been the dazzler in this simpering stack o' tracks, but the Boys pathetically hoarse, wizened approach resembles the Righteous Brothers with strep throats.

Where is all the *primo* material I heard in the studio? What of Dennis' intriguing "10,000 Years", and Brian's eloquent "California Feeling"? Well, maybe next time. After meeting and observing the Beach Boys as they work, I am more convinced than ever that (1) Brian, for better or worse, remains the guru to the group and (2) the greatest obstacle the Beach Boys face is that of five divergent personalities, fraught with jealousies, fears, foibles, conflicting interests and basic stylistic disagreements. If one bears in mind that this is a family, composed of three brothers, a first cousin and a childhood chum, its easier to see how complicated their task can become.

15 Big Ones is the anti-climactic cap of a decade-and-a-half of joyful noise and occasional genius. And yet, any group capable of slapping together a product as nonchalantly adequate as this is, might have broken new ground had they taken a few more months and applied some elbow grease. It's a shame. After three and a half years of uncertainty, I, for one, would have been willing to wait at bit longer.

Little Deuce Coup: Two Beach Boys Sail Solo
by Timothy White

SANTA MONICA, Ca.-The Beach Boys' surfboards lay idle and ding-ridden until bashful Brian Wilson came out of retirement and patched things up with *15 Big Ones*. But as the sun slowly sets on a historic summer of fun, we find our heroes catching separate waves.

"Listen to this bass note," Dennis Wilson pleads coyly, his bronze fingers forming a chord on an electric clavinet in the Boys' Brother Studio. "You like that one? See, whenever I'm making music, I like to get everybody involved."

Wilson's latest involvement is still more history in the making: a Beach Boy solo album. Dennis had previously recorded some singles with Gary Usher (in 1963) as the Four Speeds and fronted a group called Rumbo in 1969 for an obscure British 45 called "Sound Of Free", but this marks the first time any member of the Beach Boys has paddled out alone for an entire album. The pioneering LP, co-produced by friend, Gregg Jakobson, will be released on Columbia's Caribou label, and there are certain restrictions as to who may ride on Wilson's mixing board.

"All of the songs on the album will be sung by me," says Dennis. "And I'm not allowed to use any Brian Wilson compositions *or* the other Beach Boys.

"I called up Mo [Ostin, President of Warner Bros., the Boys' label] and he was very understanding and gave me a release. The basic contract terms leave the amount of records up to me: I will only do one album a year, but I'd like to at least deliver three or four years' worth. Also, I'm not allowed to perform any of the material live unless it's with the Beach Boys on-stage."

Dennis' album arrives in the wake of months of rumours that all the Beach Boys were planning to record independently. However, the boyish Wilson brushes aside speculation that his move was influenced by the cool critical reception to *15 Big Ones*, the group's first all new LP and all Brian Wilson production in years.

"I've been planning this solo thing for four or five years," he demurs. "I was writing and completing songs, taking my time and never really feeling that I would do an album because no one was behind it.

"It was James Guercio [manager/producer of Chicago and head of Caribou Records] who convinced me," he says. "I called him up one day and said, 'Look, I wanna make an album with you,' because I really loved some of his ideas. But after he heard the tracks I had so far he said 'You do it and I'll get behind you and support you all the way.'

"I said, 'Uhhaahaayaayaa, shit! That's scary!'"Dennis mugs expansively. "But I finally said okay, and asked a lot of my friends to play on it, like Ricky Fataar, Jimmie Haskell, Jimmy Bond, Hal Blaine, Ron Altbach, who is the keyboard arranger for Beach Boys' concerts, and the Double Rock Baptist Choir.

"I've been in the studio from 10 a.m. until late evening every free day I've had," Dennis reveals, "and on some of the tracks, I play everything myself. There's one tune, called 'Time', that's all me, except for some trumpet by Bill Lamb. As for this title of the record, right now I like *Freckles*, 'cause they're nice – especially freckles and red hair.

"I'm working fast. Yesterday, I did a final version of 'Pacific Ocean Song' which I had cut several times, and tomorrow I'm working on a track called 'Honey, You and I'.

Among the tracks slated for *Freckles* are two currently called "Rainbow" and "10,000 Years", both of which Dennis had earlier considered for *15 Big Ones* or a future Beach Boys album.

"'10,000 Years' is about how man has changed and not changed in 10,000 years; the only real change is that we have roofs over our heads and we have toilets," he chuckles mischievously. "We're still murdering and lustful and all that crap, still paying to see *Deep Throat* over and over again."

The album's emphasis, however, will be on romance rather than sociology, consisting mostly of the tender ballads that Dennis has specialised in since he penned "Little Bird" (with Steve Kalinich) in 1968 for the Beach Boys' *Friends* LP. Other proposed cuts include "School Girl", "The River", a remake of "Only With You" from *Holland*, another untitled collaboration with Kalinich about the life of Helen Keller, and a love song presently called "Flowers Come in The Spring":

> Flowers come in the spring,
> All the love I can bring,
> Bring it for my lady,
> Falling in love, in love,
> In love with my lady.

15 Big Ones was only the Beach Boys' second gold LP since signing with Warner Bros., and it pleased their starved fans more than it did Dennis. While he says his burgeoning outside interests should not be construed as an intention to abandon ship, he is candid in voicing his disappointment with what he thinks should have been a monster record.

"I was unhappy with the oldies – absolutely," he admits. "The album should have been 100% original. We had enough Brian Wilson material to do it; I was disappointed [the group] wouldn't follow through with that. Steve Love [the Beach Boys' business advisor], Mike Love and Alan Jardine were pushing to get it out – it was just a big push. They'd rather just get it out there than take time with it and develop it. Carl and I were really upset.

"It was a total vote; everyone stood in the studio and raised hands over the tunes. I was blown out of the water, but I don't want to sound negative – just critical. I'm very excited for Brian, but I don't want him to lay back, the way he's been doing with oldies.

"I think his new stuff is better than his songs on *Big Ones*. He and Carl have a new tune called 'Good Timing' and it's fabulous. It's another 'Surfer Girl'!"

Later in the day, Carl Wilson stretches out on a chaise lounge on the sun deck of his beach house and seconds brother Dennis' emotional disenchantment with their latest product.

"The truth is, Dennis and I were hoping that Brian would go back to the main plan," Carl, begins. "Dennis and I had a picture of doing an album of oldies just as a warm-up and then doing another album. But as it happens, we started to do the new stuff and then Brian said, 'Well, I've recorded enough. I don't want to record any longer and the album's finished.'

"I believe that Brian was consciously under-producing the album, and that was his choice – we deferred to him. But when we voted to do it that way with those particular songs, I left the studio right there on the spot because I was very disenchanted. Thing is, then I came back and worked my ass off because I support my brother Brian professionally and personally."

Carl Wilson wished to further clarify published reports (*Crawdaddy*, July '76) that Brian is unusually dependent on his family for money and mobility. Expanding on his earlier statement that his 34-year-old brother's checking account was suspended because "he kept on giving people money to score," Carl alleges that "while people were saying they're trying to look out for Brian, [and] he didn't have any money, [and] he didn't have control – well, the fucking truth was that Sly Stone and Terry Melcher and all those people were hitting on him for like $1,500 a week so they could score coke, okay? That is the fucking reason why his name was taken off the checks. It's because he could not say no to people who have really heavy habits … the fucking vipers."*

Carl's latest project has been the singing career of Dean Martin's son, Ricci. The youngest Beach Boy worked on Martin's recent Capitol single, "Stop Look Around", and shared production credits (with Billy Hinsche) on his new Epic LP. Now Carl confirms that he too is considering a solo effort.

"I have a release from Warners to do other projects on my own, although I would not do a solo album, because I like to play with my buddies," he discloses. "So it would not be a solo – aah, maybe it would I don't know. I like company."

Although the Boys are still concentrating on making the most of *15 Big Ones,* they remain confident there won't be another three and a half year wait for the follow up. Dennis believes the next Beach Boys album could be out "as early as Christmas", and says he hopes "it will be all originals." During the *Freckles* sessions, Brian showed up to cut yet another oldie – "Ruby Baby" – but both his brothers insist there's plenty of fresh material on the way.

"Brian's got a lot of new songs," Carl says happily. "One is called 'Hey Little Tomboy (I'm Gonna Make You A Girl)', but they're all in the formative stages.

"We still owe Warners two albums and we're well aware of it. We think they're working really hard for us and we appreciate that" he submits, asking to be excused so he can play with his kids. "But the hype is kinda weird," he concludes thoughtfully. "There's such a lotta Beach Boys hype going on and it's getting strange – but we choose to be in this group. If we didn't want this group we'd all split right now, because we don't need it. I think people get off on enduring relationships, don't you?"

*Footnote
In a letter to *Crawdaddy* that was published in the January 1977 issue, Carl Wilson apologised for the angry statements, albeit quoted verbatim, that he made at this point in the interview, saying he

wanted to "clean up the matter of myself communicating so poorly ...The point in time was approximately three years ago and Brian was using coke...And regretfully in a blur of anger I blurted out Sly Stone this and Terry Melcher and on and on...and when I read this piece I felt very sad, because Sly apparently is clean... so it really hurt to think of bringing him harm in any way...Regarding Terry, I was so pissed when we were talking that I didn't even say what my problem with him was. Anyway it was not related to the drug syndrome...After years of reading things taken out of context at times and even bullshit, over and over, one gets fed up. The day we talked I dumped it on you, and Timothy I apologise."

Timothy White was Editor In Chief of Billboard *and also the author of the best-selling* Catch A Fire: The Life of Bob Marley, *and* Music to My Ears: The Billboard Essays, *winner of the ASCAP Deems Taylor Award for excellence in music journalism. At White's request, the fee for the above essay and archival material has been donated to the Surfrider Foundation in Santa Monica, California in memory of Dennis Wilson.*

Timothy White was quite simply a lovely man to talk to and deal with. He was a strong supporter of the idea for this book, was helpful with contacts as it progressed and was most complimentary of the finished product. So many people in the music business, including Brian, have written so fondly of him since his untimely passing in Summer 2002, and I simply add my voice to theirs. RIP Timothy. KA 2002.

The Healing of Brother Bri' – A Multitrack *Rolling Stone* Interview with Beach Boys Brian, Dennis and Carl Wilson, Mike Love and Al Jardine ... plus Brian's wife, His Shrink, His Mom and his Dad, the late Murry Wilson
by David Felton

This piece, originally from Rolling Stone *magazine (November 4th, 1976), was one of the first articles that really attempted to explain Brian Wilson's health problems. The cover of the magazine featured Brian on a beach dressed in a bathrobe, holding a surfboard and looking quite ill at ease. This was the time of the "Brian is Back" campaign – launched and promoted by the rest of the band.*

The Abominable Beach Boy

Everybody assumes that Big-foot, the legendary man beast who stalks America's Northwest, is one mean son of a – son of a *something* – just because he's huge and hairy and elusive and reclusive. Just because he makes few public appearances, and even on those occasions he's all naked and gross looking, they assume he's *anti-social*.

But maybe he's really just a shy guy. Maybe he's really gentle and sensitive and spends most of his time at home in bed because the public's so rough and grabby. Christ, he can't even wander out into the nearest clearing, to pick fowers or look at the blue sky, without some asshole snapping his picture and splashing his name across the front pages.

Reason I bring all this up, a few months ago I think I may have met Bigfoot in person – not in the Northwest but in southern California – and actually talked to him. Or it may have been Brian Wilson. It looked like either one – this huge, hairy "person" standing at the entrance of a rambling Spanish mansion in fashionable Bel Air.

Probably it *was* Brian Wilson. Recently several sightings of this abominable Beach Boy had been reported in the Los Angeles area, and some of these reports seemed quite authentic. Also, Sandy Friedman, the Beach Boys' PR man who was accompanying me, claimed the Spanish mansion belonged to Brian and certainly the figure at the door exhibited some of his famous traits. For one thing he kept yawning; and even before we crossed the threshold he explained that he could only spare 20 minutes, that he had to take a nap. It was 11 a.m.

As he spoke, his face betrayed little emotion – no smiles, no pain – but what he had to say was amiable, to the point and often quite personal. I conducted the preliminary interview under the assumption that I was, in fact, speaking to Brian Wilson; if it was Bigfoot, I hope the critter appreciates an honest mistake.

Right now there's the new album, the tour and the TV special. Why all this burst of energy?

BRIAN: I can only consider how my energy has bursted. I have refrained from sexual experience, I'm trying out this yoga – I read a book. It showed how if you repress sexual desire, not your kundalini but a similar type of energy is released when you don't have sex. It's been a couple months now I haven't had any sex. That's just a personal answer.

Very personal, I'd say.

BRIAN: Yes. Also because it was spring. To tell you the very truth it was spring-time. It's just like they always say, in spring you start hopping and we started hop-ing a little before the first of Spring – we got our album and stuff.

This is the first spring in a long time, though.

BRIAN: Yeah, right. Well, we started hopping a few springs ago, but we really hadn't been serious about it like we were this time.

Maybe it was the combination of spring and sexual repression.

BRIAN: Yes, I think that that was probably it.

Do you find it difficult to get into writing?

BRIAN: Yeah. Lately I have found it difficult as heck to finish a song. It's a funny thing. Probably not much of a song left in me, you know, if any, because I've writ-ten so many, some 250 songs or 300 or whatever it is. And it just doesn't seem as vast [yawn], the creativity doesn't seem as vast. That's why we did a lot of oldies but goodies this time on our album. That got us going as a matter of fact.

I haven't yet heard the album. Are you going into some new areas?

BRIAN: Not that I can think of. The only areas would be into Transcendental Meditation, using that as a base. We believe in it, [yawn] we feel it's our respon-sibility, partially, to carry the Maharishi message into the world. Which I think is a great message. I think the meditation is a great thing.

You've just recently become more involved in that yourself, haven't you?

BRIAN: Yeah. I meditate and I also think about meditation which is funny. I think about Maharishi, about just the idea of meditating. It gives me something.

Do you think that may help you write more?

BRIAN: Oh, yeah I think that's gonna he the answer. As it progresses, I think that I'm going to gather more peace of mind, I'll be able to gather my thoughts a little easier. I won't be as jangled in the nerves. I think it's going to aid in my creativity.

This difficulty in writing songs – would you describe it as a writing block?

BRIAN: Well, I have a writing block right now. Even today I started to sit down to write a song, and there was a block there. God knows what that is. Unless it's supposed to be there. I mean, it's not something you just kick away and say, "Come on, let's go, let's get a song writ." If the block is there, it's there.

Another thing, too, is that I used to write on pills, I used to take uppers and write, and I used to like that effect. In fact, I'd like to take uppers now and write because they give me, you know, a certain lift and a certain outlook. And it's not an unnatural thing. I mean the pill might be unnatural and the energy, but the song itself doesn't turn out unnatural on the uppers. The creativity flows through.

Well, why don't you do that?

BRIAN: I'm thinking of asking the doctor if I can go back to those, yeah.

But you believe writers really do run out of material.

BRIAN: I believe that writers run out of material, I really do. I believe very strongly in the fact that when the natural time is up, writers actually do run out of material. [Yawn] To me it's black and white. When there's a song there's a song, when there's not there's not. Of course you run out, maybe not indefinitely, but everybody runs out of some material that writes for a while. And it's a frightening experience. It's an awesome thing to think, "Oh my God, the only thing that's ever supplied me with any success or made us money, I'm running out of." So right there there's an insecurity that sets in. This is why I'm going through these different experiments sexually and all, to see what can happen, to see if there's anything waiting in there that I haven't found.

Is there much else you could do if you didn't write songs?

BRIAN: No not really. I'm not cut out to do very much at all.

[At that point Brian says he really has to take his nap but that we will talk again. After he leaves the room, Sandy Friedman starts making frantic erasure motions and whispers, "Don't believe that stuff about uppers; he's not taking uppers." But he didn't say he was taking uppers, I explain, he said he wanted to take uppers. Friedman smiles and does the erasure thing again. "He's not gonna be taking uppers."]

    This may have been, as the trades predicted, the bitchinest summer ever for the Beach Boys, what with their new album, their tour, and Brian Wilson finally getting out of bed. But as far as I'm concerned these last four months have been one endless bummer. I couldn't seem to come up with a new handle to their venerable rock legend. Let's face it, the Beach Boys are probably the most thoroughly written about, mythicised, analyzed, agonized over and deeply probed pop group in America. And this summer especially we've had Beach Boys up the ass: dozens of heavy feature articles in major magazines and newspapers; a dazzling, hour long TV documentary; a three month concert tour of stadiums and fairgrounds throughout the United States and Canada; release of *15 Big Ones*, the first album of new Beach Boys material in 42 months, in honor of the 15 years they've miraculously played, strayed, prayed and stayed together; and a scholarly sounding paperback entitled *The Beach Boys' Southern California Pastoral*, in which Cal State professor Bruce Golden puts the guys right up there with Dante, Cervantes, Shakespeare and Milton as masters of the pastoral form.

    Well, why not, it's a great legend, and just like nearly everything the Beach Boys ever recorded, I can never stop listening to it. Mainly it's about Brian Wilson, the partially deaf boy wonder turned mad genius who tuned his one good ear into the drone of middle class America and heard the lost chord of God. Until it drove him nuts and finally silent.

    So in June, when the word started spreading that Brian was ready to talk for the first time in half a decade I flew down to Los Angeles to conduct an official *Rolling Stone* interview. But it didn't work out exactly. Brian was ready to talk, all right, just as he was ready to walk or ready to start dressing himself; but there could be no definitive Brian Wilson interview because Brian Wilson was not yet definitively himself. Therefore I also talked to the other Beach Boys and to Brian's mother, his wife and his shrink. Plus in late 1971 I'd interviewed Brian's father Murry, while he was still alive, and I threw a little of that in somewhere.

The raw material, I think, is pretty good – some really touching stories, some laughs, hopefully some answers. But focusing it, as I mentioned, was a bitch. First I tried a musical analysis thing, portraying the Beach Boys as "primitivists" like contemporary composer Carl Orff. Both Orff and the Beach Boys ignored the virtuosic contrivances of established music and returned to the common, simple rhythms and harmonies of the people. They both orchestrated this folk element with layers of brilliant tonal color and ambiance to produce a music of incredible spiritual purity. I mentioned this to the Beach Boys and none of them had ever heard of Carl Orff. Which in a way, I thought, reinforced my theory but also sort of soured me on it.

Finally, in late September, I returned to Los Angeles at the suggestion of Brian's shrink, Dr. Eugene Landy. He wanted me to see Brian's progress since June. That day disturbed me a great deal, but it did provide an update and ultimately a focus for the story. For this in one sense is a story of gurus, of old and new methods of personal growth in the promised land called California. Brian's father was a guru of sorts, a frustrated songwriter and ruthlessly aggressive man who heard in his three sons the music he could never articulate himself, who as their manager drove them to such heights of success they eventually fired him. Then Brian took over as guru.

AUDREE: The way it really started, Brian, he started singing when he was just a little bitty guy, three years old he'd sing right on key. He loved to hear me play the piano, he loved the chords. And he'd say, "Play that chord again".

Brian just always had this incredibly marvelous talent. The other boys were a little slower, they were kinda like slow bloomers. Brian started writing arrangements when he was around 14. He loved the Four Freshmen – I know you've read that over and over – and he would make these incredible arrangements sorta like them, but he'll add what he wanted. And we'd sing the first two parts on the tape recorder, then play it back and sing the other two parts with it. That was great fun.

Did he ever take formal piano lessons or anything like that?

AUDREE: Brian took accordion lessons, on one of those little baby accordions, for six weeks. And the teacher said, "I don't think he's reading. He just hears it once and plays the whole thing through perfectly." Anyway at the end of six weeks he was supposed to buy a large accordion, but we couldn't afford it. And that's all the training he ever had.

Brian is deaf in one ear. Was he born that way?

AUDREE: We don't really know. Brian thinks it happened when he was around ten. Some kid down the street really whacked him in the ear. However, it's a damaged ninth nerve, so he could have been born that way; it's called the ninth nerve and there's nothing they can do about that. I think it makes him more incredible.

The way he arranges, produces and records – the ambiance and total sound – is something that two ears can really appreciate. He's never heard that and I guess he never will.

AUDREE: Ah, he hears. [Audree laughs in amazement.] He doesn't maybe hear like we do, but he does.

So when did your sons start to record?

AUDREE: My husband was in the machinery business, big lathes from England, and the people from whom he imported them were here to visit us. And we took them to Mexico City. When we left, the refrigerator was completely stocked and we gave the boys enough money to buy whatever else they needed. We came back and here they had gone out and rented a bass, a big standup, as tall as Al for sure, and drums and a microphone. They had used every bit of their food money. And they said, "We want to play something for you." They were very excited about it, and I thought the song was darling – never dreaming anything would happen.

And that song was "Surfin'".

AUDREE: Right.

Well, then they signed with Capitol and they started making a lot of hits. How did that change your life at home?

AUDREE: Well, it was really very hectic. Telephones never ever stopped ringing. And I was doing all of the book work. I was making all the forms for the musicians' union and I was going to the bank and being so careful that all five of them got exactly the same amount to the penny. And I remember cooking dinner and we'd have to leave. I remember dinners not even being eaten because we had to fly out to wherever they had to appear.

How did they handle their success?

AUDREE: Well, being a mother, I thought they handled it so beautifully for being that young. But their father had a strong hand as far as … well, they didn't always listen to him. Later he'd say, "Why didn't you listen to me?" And they'd say, "Well, I guess we were punks".

There was a night during or after the Austalian tour when they decided they didn't want their father to manage them.

AUDREE: It *destroyed* him.

Do you understand why?

AUDREE: Oh, I understood perfectly. That was a horrible time for me. He was just destroyed by that and yet he wasn't really up to it. He'd already had an ulcer and it was really too much for him; but he loved them so much, he was so overly protective, really. He couldn't let them go. He couldn't stand seeing anyone else handling his kids.

Those were terrible days, frankly, and he was angry with me. You always take it out on the closest one. He was angry at the whole world.

What did he say at the time?

AUDREE: Not too much. He stayed in bed a lot.

YOU NEED A MESS OF HELP TO STAND ALONE

Meanwhile back at the Bel Air mansion, Brian had just gone upstairs for his noontime nap when Dennis Wilson bounds into the living room. Dennis is easily the most infectious Beach Boy, the prettiest, wittiest, most outgoing and independent, the most, say his family, like his father. Not surprisingly, it's gotten him into a lot of trouble over the years, with his dad, his schoolteachers and later with his notorious roommate Charles Manson, to whom he now, bearded and prancing impulsively, bore a striking resemblance. (According to *New Musical Express*, Dennis told a reporter for England's *Rave* magazine in 1968, "Fear is nothing but awareness, man.... Sometimes the 'Wizard' frightens me. The 'Wizard' is Charlie Manson, who is another friend of mine, who says he is God and the Devil. He sings, plays and writes poetry and may be another artist for Brother Records.")

As Dennis sat down, Sandy Friedman handed him a local tattle paper with the Beach Boys on the cover. He glanced at it for a moment, then shrugged and said, "Come on, you can't read everything you believe." Then he stood up and walked to the center of the room for an important announcement.

DENNIS: I've just made a monumental decision. [Dennis pauses dramatically] I'm not guilty about masturbation anymore! [Then seriously, folks] I just started my own record company. It's like, I've been in one group my whole life. I always thought if I wasn't a Beach Boy I would fail. [Here Dennis sticks his arms straight out in mock agony.] So I called up my attorney and said, "Hey get me a record company," but my biggest piece of shit is, I'm gonna do a movie where I'm gonna be a flaming gay boy who wants to be a policeman.

So many positive things are happening to the Beach Boys' career right now. Let me tell you something about the Beach Boys ... we had a very normal childhood. Our father beat the shit out of us; his punishments were outrageous. I never saw eye to eye with him, ever. In fact I used to lie to him when I was young. I learned at an early age to be very protective of myself, I played a great mind game.

But one thing about my father – beautiful music would always melt my father's heart. You always wanted to sing for him. Dad was a frustrated songwriter, and I think Brian wrote his music through him.

[Dennis suggests we go to his VW camper in the driveway, where we listen to a cassette of two cuts from his planned solo album. They have a kind of a Beach Boys sound to them but rougher, more rock 'n' roll like, Dennis' voice and temperament. Actually, they sound great. Finally I get up enough nerve to ask him a question that has intimidated me for some time.]

I know this is an unpleasant subject but it's been a number of years now and I was wondering it we could discuss your experience with Charles Manson...

[But even before I finish Dennis is shaking his head.]

DENNIS: No. Never. As long as I live, I'll never talk about that. He gazes out the windshield of his camper. I don't know anything, you know? If I did, I would've been up on that witness stand.

[Just then actress Karen Lamm Wilson, Dennis' new wife drives up in a small sports car. "Gotta go guys" yells Dennis bolting from the camper and taking off.]

Inside, Carl, the youngest and most stable Wilson brother, had arrived, sporting, like all the Beach Boys these days, a full, rough beard, and like himself, a workmanlike jumpsuit. He owns a whole closetful of jumpsuits, in a spectrum of colors from grey to brown, and one suspects they are designed to ameliorate the last vestiges of a sweet baby chubbiness. Although he's occasionally made headlines in the past, resisting the draft for years before a federal court granted him C.O. status, his personality is basically shy and quiet. It was Carl who invariably kept his head while all about him were losing theirs, who took charge of stage performances after Brian left the road and who later took over record production when Brian could no longer handle that one.

Why was your father fired as manager?

CARL: My recollection could be kind of foggy on that. I just know it started in Australia – this was around '63 or '64. Brian, and Michael especially, wanted to not have my father involved because he screwed them up with chicks, you know? We'd want to find a girl to be with, the thing on the road, and he was really kind of prudish about it. Also, Brian really disagreed with the way he wanted things to sound. And I remember having a conversation with my dad in his bedroom at home. I said, "They really, you know, don't want you to manage the group anymore." When I think about it now, Jesus, that must have really crushed him. After all, he gave up his home and business for us, he was kind of crackers over us you know?

Would your dad be more likely to confide in you?

Yeah, we had a great relationship. He was crazy about Brian, but he and Brian drove each other nuts. You know, here Brian is really growing massively musically, right? And his old man's telling him how the records should sound. My dad would say do it faster, so Brian would say no, it's gotta be more laid back, have more feel to it. But he was a great man, very sensitive. I really loved my dad a lot. It about killed Brian when my dad died. He went to New York; my dad passed away, Brian split. He could not handle it.

He didn't go to the funeral?

CARL: No. That's how come he left, so he wouldn't have to be here and go. I think Brian hung onto that one for quite some time. I think he's okay with it now, maybe.

The area of questioning I find most difficult, it's so personal, is what we might call "Brian's problem".

CARL: Brian's behaviour?

Yeah, well, you once said he went through hell.

CARL: Well … a lot of anguish, a lot of anxiety, frustration, disillusionment. Brian worked really hard for the first seven years and he needed a break. I think he was pretty confused at the time by his environment. He just took a look and saw how fucked up the world was – he's not a dummy – and he said, "The world is so fucked up, I can't stand it; it's unspeakable how fucked up everything is." And I think it really broke his heart. He's painfully conscious. When it hurts, it hurts; he can't bury it and grow. I mean, he's one of the nerviest people I've ever met. He does exactly what he wants to do. I remember [*sits and laughs*] – this is so funny – when we did "Little Honda," Brian wanted me to get this real distorted guitar sound, real fuzzy. "This guitar sounds like shit." I said. "Brian, I hate this." And he goes, "Would you fucking do it? Just do it." When I heard it, I felt like an ass-hole. It sounded really hot. That was before fuzz became a big deal.

He's a true great, and his greatness has been a plague to him.

That afternoon Lorne Michaels, producer of the TV special, held a scheduling meeting at Brian's house. Most of Michaels' crew was there, including director Gary Weis and writers Danny Aykroyd, John Belushi and Alan Zweibel. All the

Beach Boys came too, except Brian left the room after a few minutes because he was "tired."

Actually he didn't miss that much – it was just a nice, friendly business meeting. The crew brought beer and pizza, and the Beach Boys played their new album. Michaels explained the shooting schedule for the next two weeks. Another meeting was announced for the following Monday.

Then an intense, tough-faced man who'd been sitting sort of off to the side suddenly assumed a peculiar authority. "Now, when you come back next Monday – no beer, no food, no anything," he announced sternly. "Today somebody was very naughty and brought beer. Brian's on a diet."

The scolding produced an awkward silence. Belushi shrugged and tried to explain the crew's transgression. "It was just a friendly gesture…"

"Yes, but Brian blew his diet. He had five beers," the man continued. "So next time you'll just have to drink coffee or nothing at all."

It seemed a bit embarassing, this explicit discussion of Brian's personal indulgence. "Who is that guy?" I asked Carl as the meeting broke up. "Oh, that's Gene Landy," he said, "Brian's psychologist."

A few nights later I phoned Dr. Landy at his Hollywood home and asked him if I could interview him. He was about to have dinner but since he's one of those brusque, hustling, snap-snap-snap busy people who like to do at least two things at once, he told me to come right over.

We sat down in his newly converted garage library, I with my tape recorder, he with a large green salad, a glass of wine, a phone and an intercom. He wore green pants with white stripes, boots and a flappy collared flower print shirt and looked really more like a record promoter than a shrink. In fact, years ago he did work as a promo man, for RCA, Coral, Decca, Mercury, and there still seemed to be a hard-sell, wisecracking, PR-bio feedback about him.

For instance, when I asked him, rather perfunctorily, who he was and what he did, Dr. Landy answered for 20 minutes, starting with the sixth grade. In short, he dropped out of sixth grade, unable to read, hit the streets, worked for the circus, fucked around a lot, worked for the record business, produced a radio show, went to night school and earned a bachelor's degree at the age of 30, went to med school but quit because of a liver disease, went to the University of Oklahoma and earned a doctorate in psychology, worked for the Peace Corps, Job Corps and VISTA, and finally, in the late Sixties, moved to Southern California and immersed himself in group dynamics. Also he wrote a book of hippie slang, *The Underground Dictionary*, a copy of which he now pulled from a shelf, autographed and handed to me without charge.

"My background," Dr. Landy summarised, is basically that of a hyperkinetic, perceptually disoriented, brain-damaged person. I'm also very bright, very intuitive, very sensitive, and I'm quite capable of reading what most people are thinking or doing.

I asked him how much he, a doctor, could talk about his patient Brian Wilson, and the question seemed to strike him for the first time. He immediately phoned a member of the California State Psychological Association's ethics committee, who advised him to phone Brian. He did, and Brian told him to do whatever he wanted.

Dr. Landy hung up the phone and laughed. "Brian would probably give me permission for anything."

How'd you get involved with Brian?

LANDY: They came to me, Marilyn, Mrs. Wilson, an appointment, she came in and talked to me.

Then you must have had some kind of reputation.

LANDY: Right, I've treated a lot of people. [*He laughs*].

Other celebrities ?

LANDY: Yeah, yeah ... the only one I can actually mention is the only one that went on television and said "This is my shrink" – Richard Harris – But I've treated a tremendous number of people in show business; for some reason I seem to be able to relate to them. I think I have a nice reputation that says I'm unorthodox by orthodox standards but basically unique by unorthodox standards.

Well, you sound like a pretty heavy-duty Hollywood shrink.

LANDY: Yeah, I guess. [*Gleefully*] I'm outrageously expensive.

How much do you charge?

LANDY: How much do you think I charge?

I don't know, $40 is what I've been paying, so...

LANDY: I'm $90.

Ninety? An hour?

LANDY: Fifty minutes.

How can you charge so much and get away with it? You must be very good.

LANDY: I am. I do unusual ... look at Brian he's a two year-patient, two and a half at the most. Nobody else would have taken him on for under five. I do a thing that says you don't have to spend a lot of time.

What's that?

LANDY: Well, I'm using a team approach, a team of people who work for me in the general, overall supervision and treatment. Let's see ... I'm a clinical psychologist ... there's a psychiatrist, Sol Samuels ... there's Dr. David Gans, the physician ... there's Joey, who's a shrink Arnold Horowitz, another shrink who's working on another part of the situation ... there's Scott Steinberg, that's six ...

Who's Scott Steinberg?

LANDY: Another one of the boys ... and the nutritionist is seven – I have a girl, Nancy, uh, whatever her name is, who does nutritional things. Anyway, Marilyn called me in late September of last year because she couldn't deal with the whole situation any longer. She has two kids that need to have their needs met. She has her own needs for her life. And, uh, Brian was basically withdrawn for a number of years.

What was he suffering from?

LANDY: Well, Brian was suffering from being scared.

Scared of what?

Just generally frightened. He was not able to deal with frightened or even have a response to frightened and therefore lived in the area of fantasy for a while. He's in the process of returning from fantasy every day more and more.

What happened to him in fantasy?

LANDY: [Shrugs] Nothing. [He laughs impishly]

So why hire you? There must have been something that was bothering him.

LANDY: Well, it wasn't bothering him, it was bothering her. And the kids. I mean, when someone lives in fantasy, they don't mind – they're enjoying themselves.

He wasn't unhappy?

LANDY: No. Why should he be? It was the people around him.

Because he wasn't being a real person, or ...

LANDY: Because he wasn't relating on the level in the society where we have expectancies of what we expect people to do. When you pick the phone up, you expect it to say hello. If you do something different, depending on how different, you frighten people around you. And if you're frightened yourself, you simply withdraw.

But the point is, what you had to work with was a serious problem.

LANDY: It depends by whose definition – not by an eight year old's, by a 34 year old's. We look at potential. When you stay at home and you can have the whole world if you want it, you're not living up to your potential. But who says you have to?

But he is a pretty weird guy.

LANDY: No, he's not a weird guy. Brian is absolutely one of the most charming people I've met. He only gets weird when he gets frightened. I see him as a really warm, loving, capable human being who when not frightened is a right on dude.

I guess what I'm asking is who are you working for? Are you working for Brian or for the people who would like to see Brian better?

LANDY: I was hired by Marilyn on the condition that I can do any thing, whatever it is. And she took that at face value. And that face value process has paid off. I'm working for Brian Wilson to have something he has not had, and that's an alternative ... that if he chooses to withdraw and be scared, that's as good as choosing not to, but to have the choice. And if Brian feels that he's better and likes better sitting in bed, then goddamnit, "Here's to you, Brian."

One thing that surprised me – when we were at that meeting with Lorne Michaels and the whole crew, you told them about not bringing beer next time. I expected a more traditional thing – you would have called Lorne aside, privately, and said, "Hey, look, don't have your guys bring it." But you said it right out in the open.

LANDY Well, if I only tell Lorne, he's gotta tell the others, and I don't know if the message gets across.

But my first impulse was, gee, you're treating Brian like a child. The fact that a private matter was being brought out – wouldn't that have a humiliating effect?

LANDY: I don't feel humiliated when I make it very clear that I can't be in the same room with people that smoke.

But Brian wasn't making it clear. You were making it clear for Brian.

LANDY: That's right. But that's what I'm paid to do.

I understand that, but is that therapeutic?

LANDY: Well, the whole point is that Brian had enjoyed five beers, and that's not therapeutic. Now, I sometimes assist him in things that he's not happy I assist him in. "No more beer." [Laughs] Sometimes I overassist 'cause I compensate for his overindulgence.

He sort of has a rebellious nature to him.

LANDY: Naw, it's indulgent, not rebellious.

I was thinking of the way he sometimes puts people on.

LANDY: Brian doesn't put anybody on. Brian doesn't have that much of a sense of humor.

But Brian is extremely bright, astute, competent, capable and just eats up information. You don't have to fight to get it in him. He eats it all up, he's just hungry. That's why we're moving so quickly. He just hungers.

* * * * *

It was high noon at Brother Studio in Santa Monica, and something of a showdown was about to disrupt the churchlike harmony of the place. The Beach Boys were there to record "I'm Bugged at My Old Man" for the TV special, but at the moment Brian Wilson was growing more and more bugged with Scott Steinberg. Scott, a short, thick young man with huge arms, stood guarding the entrance to a narrow corridor. He looked grim and unyielding. Brian faced him from about a foot away and looked absolutely ferocious.

"Where's my lunch?" Brian asked angrily.

"It's back there," said Scott, gesturing toward the corridor, "but you're not gettin' any."

Brian moved closer. Scott widened his stance and put his hands on his hips. "I want my lunch !" shouted Brian.

"No, Brian!"

"Why not?"

"You know goddamn well why not. You forfeited your lunch when you snuck upstairs and ate that hamburger."

"But I'm hungry!" bellowed Brian.

Scott cocked back his head. "You should have thought of that before you ate that hamburger."

After staring silently at this tough punk for another 30 seconds, Brian rotated his massive body and slowly lumbered back into the main recording studio. Then Scott relaxed, turned to an associate and snickered. "If he sings good, I'll give him the patty."

Scott is 19. Brian is 34.

WILD HONEY

When Brian first met Marilyn Rovell, she was singing with an all female group, the Honeys; later, with her sister Dianne, she formed a duo called Spring and recorded an album under Brian's direction. But the album bombed, as did several singles, and she's since devoted her time and energy to family affairs.

Mike Love has described her as "one of the most patient people in the world." And you can see why. As Brian's wife, Marilyn had to live with a man whose quirks, put-ons and indulgences were as celebrated as his pioneer writing and arranging talents. And that was when he was *healthy*. In recent years this small, resilient woman has had to manage a household of two young daughters and one sleeping giant pretty much alone.

MARILYN: Brian was always eccentric. From the day I met him I couldn't stop laughing. Just everything he did was funny. The way he lifted a fork was funny. [*Marilyn breaks up just thinking about it.*] He'd ride a motorcycle into Gold Star recording studios, I couldn't believe him!

Well, you know, he wanted a sandbox, so he got a sandbox. I mean, who am I to tell a creator what he can do? He said, "I want to play in the sand, I want to feel like a little kid. When I'm writing these songs, I want to feel what I'm writing, all the happiness." Brian wanted to experience it all. So he had this really good carpenter come up to the house – this was when we were living on Laurel Way – and in the dining room the guy built a gorgeous wood sandbox, around two and a half feet tall. And then they came with a dump truck and dumped eight tons of sand in it.

"I have the funniest story, about the piano tuner – have you heard it? Okay, the piano tuner, who we still use, walks into the house ... and the sandbox had been there awhile and I was very used to it. He says, "Okay, where's the piano?" I was busy in the house. I said, "Oh, it's over there in the sandbox," thinking nothing of it, right? There's this grand piano in the sandbox. He looks at me and goes, "Oh." All of a sudden he walks over to the sandbox and sits down, and he starts taking off his shoes and socks! That made me roar. He just took them off like, "Oh, sand, I got to take off my shoes and socks to go in the sand." And the sand, being that there is no sun, is freezing cold. By the way, the dogs had also used it – you know dogs and sand – and he puts up the hood thing, looks in the piano, and it was like he was going to have a nervous breakdown. "My God, this piano is filled with sand!" We had to vacuum it out.

I'll tell you another story about the piano tuner. One time after we first moved to this house, he came in and Brian sat down and hummed each note of the piano to the guy. Each note! It was Brian's tuning; he didn't want regular pitch, he wanted it tuned to his ears. He wanted the notes to ring a certain way – I could never explain it. But it was the greatest tuning job you ever heard.

How long have you two been married?

MARILYN: It'll be 12 years in December. I got married when I was 16 and he was 22.

And how did all that come about?

MARILYN: Well, we were like girlfriend and boyfriend for a year and a half – I already was totally in love with him you know – and yet he would never admit that there were feelings for me. And the time that he did do it ... the guys were going to Australia, and I remember sitting in the airport with Brian and Mike, and Mike – Mike was, you know, Mr. Joker; still is – goes, "Wow, Brian, boy we're sure going to have a good time in Australia." And Brian's kind of looking at me from the corner of his eye and he's going, "Yeah ... yeah, yeah, we are, aren't we." And I can't imagine why I said this, but I just went, "God that's great, because I'm going to have a great time too." You know, the typical childish things. And Brian looked at me like the first time I ever saw such an expression on his face like, "What? What'd you say?" Anyway, they went on the airplane for 13 hours, and that night when they arrived in Australia I got the call from him. Two telegrams had come in the meantime. I got the call, and for the first time he called me "honey." It was, like, "Marilyn", do you want to hear this?

Sure

MARILYN: I mean our love life?

I want to hear this story anyway. I'm not sure about your love life.

MARILYN: "Marilyn, oh I couldn't wait to talk to you," he said. "I don't know what happened but on the plane it just hit me, it was like an arrow struck me in the heart that I was going to lose you." He says, "I realize that, you know, that I need you and I have to have you as my wife, I've got to be with you, I can't stand the thought of ever losing you." And I mean, it was like four o'clock in the morning, and here I was just jumping like a rabbit. He phoned me three times a day each day – $3,000 worth of phone calls.

Actually, there is one thing I'd like to ask you about your love life. Brian mentioned he was experimenting with celibacy and I figured you would know if that's true.

MARILYN: Celibacy, what's that?

No sex.

MARILYN: No sex? Um … no, that's not true at all. I mean, I wouldn't say he was into it you know, like a master [She giggles.] But that definitely is not true.

He said he'd been refraining from sex for two months so that he would get more energy to do other things.

MARILYN. Let's put it this way, he refrains from coming.

Didn't Brian go through one of his most productive periods when you first got married?

MARILYN: Yeah … I remember him sitting in the sand box when he was writing *Pet Sounds. Pet Sounds* was so heavy. He just told me one night, he says, "Marilyn, I'm gonna make the greatest album, the greatest rock album ever made." And he meant it. Boy, he worked his butt off when he was making *Pet Sounds*. And I'll never forget the night that he finally got the final disc, when they finished it, dubbing it down and all that, and he brought the disc home. And he prepared a moment. We went in the bedroom, we had a stereo in the bedroom, and he goes, "OK, are you ready?" But he was really serious – this was his soul in there, you know? And we just lay there alone all night, you know, on the bed, and just listened and cried and did a whole thing. It was really, really heavy.

But *Pet Sounds* was not a big hit. That really hurt him badly, he couldn't understand it. It's like, why put your heart and soul into something? I think that had a lot to do with slowing him down.

But there you have a classic dilemma of popular art – the pressure to be creative verses the pressure to he commercial.

MARILYN: Brian has never … you can't pressure Brian.

Well, yes and no.

MARILYN: Well, you couldn't used to be able to pressure him. [*She laughs.*]

But isn't that sort of what's going on now with the new album and the tour – an answer to commercial demands?

MARILYN: It's that, but it's also something they need to do for themselves. You know, they're all just so happy to be back together. I mean, the thing that made me go to Landy was I couldn't stand to see Brian, whom I just love and adore, unhappy with himself and not really creating. Because music is his whole life, that's number one to him. So one of my girlfriends told me about Dr.Landy and I went and talked to him for an hour. I said, "I need someone who's gonna go to him, not where he has to go to you because he won't do it." And Dr. Landy said, "Yeah, I think I can do it." When I first met Dr. Landy, I knew I'd met someone who could play Brian's game.

The game plan, as I understand it, was that you told Brian it was actually you who Dr. Landy was coming to see.

MARILYN: Well, it was my problem to begin with. So Dr. Landy was coming to see me for a while, and Brian kept peekin' his head in "What are you doing with my wife?" you know? Then one day as I was talking to Dr. Landy, Brian just walked in the room and said, "Something's wrong with me, I need your help." And that started it all.

What was life like around then?

MARILYN: Well, it was a big drainer because of all the people coming around – too many weirdos coming over, drug people. And I've had it with drugs. Once we had our children I just said forget it, who needs it? You get all these drainers – that's my word for 'em "Hey Brian, I gotta song, listen to this," you know? "Can you help me?" I didn't know how to get rid of all these people. Everyone just – "Oh, Marilyn's a bitch, she won't let anybody come in." It got to the point where I was just yelling and screaming at anybody that walked in the door.

I could kill the guy that gave him acid. Really, that was the worst experience for Brian to go through. Jesus, do you realize how sick that is for people to give people acid? How can people play with drugs like that? Wait a minute, don't get me wrong, I once tried a tiny bit of it years and years ago, like a quarter of a thing. That was enough for me. I wound up with cramps all night.

But Brian's trip happened to be a very outrageous one. It was a beautiful experience for him and yet being so naive and pure, I just don't think he was ready for it. And who knows if he ever would be?

Before you went to Dr. Landy, was Brian spending most of the time in his room, that sort of thing?

MARILYN: Yeah, he spent a lot of time in his room. But I would say through the last seven years it's been in spurts. Like one week he'd be real active and want to go out, and then he'd spend two weeks at home and not go anywhere. And then maybe he would spend a full day in bed or two days in bed and just say, "I don't feel good I've got a sore throat," or something. It was difficult to find somebody who could help him 'cause I didn't know what needed to be helped. Sometimes I really thought to myself, is it me? Am I the one who's not seein' things right? And it was also difficult for the family to see it the same way, and the close friends, because everyone loved Brian and just said, "Oh, he'll get over it" – that kind of thing.

But I'm the one who had to live with him.

It must have been very rough.

MARILYN: It was the worst, the absolute worst. But it just got to the point where I said, okay, this is it. The kids are getting too old; it's not that good they see their daddy in bed. I know that Brian wants to be a good father. He adores them. They adore him. And he didn't have an easy childhood, he really didn't. He once told me, he said, "Marilyn, I want you to discipline the kids. I'll do it wrong." Because he had it really rough. He didn't want to do the same thing to his kids, therefore he backed out of it totally. That makes me the mother and father both. And that's too hard, it's too hard. And so Dr. Landy assures me that I will have my 34 year old husband soon, you know?

Gettin' Hungry

There's a directness about Brian Wilson that can be alarming. He doesn't mince words. Like he'll walk into this really posh Chinese restaurant, wave aside the niceties of cocktails or menus and simply ask,

"Ya got any shrimp?" He's not being rude or childish, just getting the job done and the food there faster. And that's how he conducts interviews – dutiful, businesslike, wasting no time with small talk or unnecessary emotion, often prefacing his answers with the last words of your question, like some kind of oral exam. Sometimes you think he's joking because he says outrageous things from the corner of his mouth like Buddy Hackett. But usually he's quite serious. I think.

We were at the restaurant because Dr. Landy had set up a luncheon interview between me and Brian, which was nice of him except that he invited all these extra people – Marilyn, Audree, Dr. Landy's friend Alexandra and another shrink, Dr. Arnold Horowitz. Things looked bad for the interview, but Brian, in a remarkable act of quick thinking, solved the problem. Dr. Landy suggested we all move to a quieter table in the back. Everyone peeled off one by one, then Brian suddenly announced, "I think we'll stay right here." At first Landy was pissed. "Fine – you can pay your own bill," he snapped. Later, however, he told me on the phone, "That was tremendous, Brian really asserted himself. I thought that was marvelous."

At any rate, it allowed us to do the interview in relative privacy, away from family and shrinks and bodyguards. As it turned out, Brian may have had his own reasons for wanting to be alone.

Why don't we talk a bit about "Good Vibrations."

BRIAN: That would be a good place to begin. "Good Vibrations" took six months to make. We recorded the very first part of it at Gold Star Recording Studio, then we took it to a place called Western, then we went to Sunset Sound, then we went to Columbia.

So it took quite a while. There's a story behind this record that I tell everybody. My mother used to tell me about vibrations. I didn't really understand too much of what that meant when I was just a boy. It scared me, the word "vibrations." To think that invisible feelings, invisible vibrations existed, scared me to death. But she told about dogs that would bark at people and then not bark at others, that a dog would pick up vibrations from these people that you can't see, but you can feel. And the same existed with people.

And so it came to pass that we talked about good vibrations. We went ahead and experimented with the song and the idea, and we decided that on the one hand you could say, "I love the colorful clothes she wears and the way the sunlight plays upon her hair. I hear the sound of a gentle word on the wind that lifts her perfume through the air." Those are sensual things. And then you go, "I'm pickin' up good vibrations," which is a contrast against all the sensual – there's what you call the extrasensory perception which we have. And this is what we're really talking about.

But you also set out to do something new musically. Why this particular song?

BRIAN: Because we wanted to explain that concept, plus we wanted to do something that was R&B but had a taste of modern, avant garde R&B to it. "Good Vibrations" was advanced rhythm and blues music.

You took a risk.

BRIAN: Oh yeah, we took a great risk. As a matter of fact, I didn't think it was going to make it because of its complexity, but apparently people accepted it very well. They felt that it had a naturalness to it, it flowed. It was a little pocket symphony.

How come you used four different studios ?

BRIAN: Because we wanted to experiment with combining studio sounds. Every studio has its own marked sound. Using the four different studios had a lot to do with the way the final record sounded.

Did everybody support what you were trying to do?

BRIAN: No, not everybody. There was a lot of "oh you can't do this, that's too modern" or "that's going to be too long a record." I said no, it's not going to be too long a record, it's going to be just right.

Who resisted you? Your manager? The record company?

BRIAN: No, people in the group, but I can't tell ya who. We just had resisting ideas. They didn't quite understand what this jumping from studio to studio was all about. And they couldn't conceive of the record as I did. I saw the record as a totality piece.

Do you remember the time you realized you really had it ?

BRIAN: I remember the time that we had it. It was at Columbia. I remember I had it right in the sack. I could just feel it when I dubbed it down, made the final mix from the 16 track down to mono. It was a feeling of power, it was a rush. A feeling of exaltation. Artistic beauty. It was everything.

Do you remember saying anything?

BRIAN: I remember saying, "Oh my God. Sit back and listen to this!"

At that time did you feel it was your most important song? Did you think in terms like that – reaching a new plateau in music?

BRIAN: Yes I felt that it was a plateau. First of all, it felt very arty and it sounded arty. Second of all, it was the first utilisation of a cello in rock & roll music to that extent – using it as an upfront instrument, as a rock instrument.

Not to mention the theremin.

BRIAN: It was also the first use or a theremin in rock&roll.

By the time you did "Good Vibrations" you had matured your artistic concept far beyond the sort of thing you were doing say in "Surfin'." Was there any particular time when you realised that you now were totally into creating music on your own terms?

BRIAN: Yes. *Pet Sounds* would be that period when I figured that I was into my own ... via the Phil Spector approach. Now, the Phil Spector approach is utilising many instruments to combine for a single form or a single sound. Like combining clarinets, trombones and saxophones to give you a certain sound, rather than hearing that arrangement as "oh, those are piccolos, oh, those are trombones."

How much was Spector an influence on you, artistically and competitively?

BRIAN: Well, I didn't feel I was competing as much as I was emulating, emulating the greatness of his style in my music. We have a high degree of art in our group. We've come to regard Phil Spector as the greatest, the most avant garde producer in the business.

Yet he's not really a composer of songs.

BRIAN: Well, I'm a firm believer that he wrote those songs and gave the others credit. In order to produce them the way he did, he had to write them.

Mike Love mentions the time you composed "The Warmth of the Sun" within hours of the John F. Kennedy assassination and how it illustrated that even during a very negative time you could come up with a very positive feeling.

BRIAN: Yeah, it's a strange thing, but I think we were always spiritually minded and we wrote music to give strength to people. I always feel holy when it comes to recording. Even during "Surfer Girl," even then I felt a bit spiritual.

What's the nature of your spiritual outlook today? Does it present you with a kind of attitude toward the world?

BRIAN: No, not really. I'm not as aware of this world as I should be.

Is that necessarily a bad thing?

BRIAN: Yeah, because I think if I became more aware, I could structure my lyrics to be a little more in tune with people.

Are you working on that process right now?

BRIAN: Yes, I'm working on that right now, I'm working with people who I know know where it's at. Like Van Dyke Parks – he's a guy who's a link to where it's at for me. He keeps me very current on what's happening.

At one time you and he were working on a revolutionary album called Smile which you never released.

BRIAN: Yeah, we didn't finish it because we had a lot of problems, inner group problems. We had time commitments we couldn't keep. So we stopped. Plus, for instance, we did a thing called the "fire track." We cut a song called "Fire" and we used fire helmets on the musicians and we put a bucket with fire burning in it in the studio so we could smell smoke while we cut. And about a day later a building down the street burned down. We thought maybe it was witchcraft or something, we didn't know what we were into. So we decided not to finish it.

Plus I got into drugs and I began doing things that were over my head. It was too fancy for the public. I got too fancy and arty and was doing things that were just not Beach Boys at all. They were made for me.

Ever consider doing an album just on your own ?

BRIAN: No, I haven't considered that because I didn't think it would be commercial if I did.

Well so what ?

BRIAN: Well, maybe I could do that then. I think I might.

What's this program with Dr. Landy and his team designed to do ?

BRIAN: Well, it's basically designed to correct me from taking drugs.

You've had a problem with that ?

BRIAN: Yeah, I had a problem taking drugs. Up until four months ago I was taking a lot of cocaine. And these doctors came in and showed me a way to stop doing it, which is having bodyguards with you all the time so you can't get to it.

What do you think of that approach?

BRIAN: That approach works because there's someone right there all the time – it keeps you on the spot. They catch you when you're ready to do something you shouldn't do. It works until you have finally reached the stage where you don't need it anymore.

Why did you consent to this program?

BRIAN: Because my wife called the doctors and legally she had the right to call them.

In addition to guarding you all the time what else do Dr Landy's people do for you?

BRIAN: They teach me socialisation, how to socialise. They're just teaching me different social graces, like manners.

Didn't you at one time know those?

BRIAN: I did, but I lost them. Drugs took 'em away.

How could that be?

BRIAN: It just was. Drugs took 'em all away. I got real paranoid I couldn't do anything.

Were you unhappy then?

BRIAN: I was unhappy as all heck. I knew I was screwing myself up and I couldn't do anything about it. I was a useless little vegetable. I made everybody very angry at me because I wasn't able to work to get off my butt. Coke every day. Goin' over to parties. Just havin' bags of snow around, just snortin' it down like crazy.

But aren't drugs just a symptom? There must be something else. Carl said that at some point you looked at the world and it was so messed up that you just couldn't take it.

BRIAN: I couldn't.

But the world is messed up. How do you deal with it?

BRIAN: The way I deal with it is I go jogging in the morning. I goddamn get out of bed and I jog and I make sure I stay in shape. That's how I do it. And so far the only way I've been keeping from drugs is with those bodyguards and the only way I've been going jogging is those bodyguards have been taking me jogging.

So in one sense you're not yet fully committed to the idea.

BRIAN: It's just that once you've had a taste of drugs you like 'em and you want 'em. Do you take drugs yourself?

Yeah, I experiment.

BRIAN: Do ya? Do ya snort?

Sure.

BRIAN: That's what I thought. Do you have any with ya?

No.

BRIAN: That's the problem. Do you have any uppers?

I have nothing on me.

BRIAN: Nothing? Not a thing, no uppers?

I wouldn't lie to you. I wish I had 'em, but I don't.

BRIAN: Do you have any at home? Do you know where you can get some?

See now I guess you gotta get to the point in the program where you're not going to ask me more questions like that.

BRIAN: That's right. You just saw my weakness coming out. Which I don't understand. I just do it anyway. I used to drink my head off too, that's another thing. They've been keeping me from drinkin', taking pills and taking coke. And I'm jogging every morning.

Had your wife not gone to see Dr. Landy and got him to work on you ...

BRIAN: I'd have been a goner. I'd have been in the hospital by now.

THE OLD MAN

When did you first notice something was wrong with Brian?

AUDREE: It was just that he'd stay in his room all the time. I would go over there, and there could be a houseful of people and he just wouldn't come down.

When you talked to him in his bedroom, would he make sense?

AUDREE: Oh, of course, perfectly. He just wanted to be alone. Sometimes he would say, "I'm really so tired," or, "I'll be down in a little while." And I'd think to myself, "You might or you might not, and if not, that's okay with me." I knew he was in trouble. I knew he had a problem.

Did he seem depressed?

AUDREE: Oh yes, I think so. He didn't show his depression to me that much because if I'd go upstairs to say hi or give him a kiss, he would always be sweet to me and say, "Hi, mom. How are you?" or, "I'm tired," or, "I have a cold," or, "My stomach is upset," or just anything. At that time I didn't believe it, I just thought, he wants to be alone. I would never – oh God – no way would I bug him. I figured if he wanted to talk to me he would tell me.

Do you think Brian's creativity began to be a burden to him?

AUDREE: I do. I think that he just went through a lot of pain. I think it was very painful for him to live up to this tremendous image that had happened just like that [snaps her fingers]. All of a sudden he felt he couldn't do it anymore, he felt like he had reached the pinnacle – and what was left?

And then for a number of years did he just sort of deteriorate?

AUDREE: Well, he went through stages. In fact, Marilyn would say, "Oh, Brian's so much better, we this or we that". I'd be happy to hear it. So it was kind of an up and down thing.

Carl says that he was the closest to his father but that Brian and Dennis had a difficult time communicating with him.

AUDREE: Yes, they did. But in the later years, Dennis and his father had a great relationship. Well, they held some thing in common. They both loved to fish, they both loved boxing.

Dennis said when he was young his father used to beat the hell out of him sometimes.

AUDREE: Yeah, he really got the short end of the stick.

How did you feel when you heard about Dennis' involvement with Charles Manson?

AUDREE: Oh my God, absolutely horrified. Terrified.

First of all, when Manson and his family, the girls, moved in with Dennis, Dennis had this beautiful, beautiful place at Will Rogers State Park, right off Sunset. And he befriended them. They were just hippies and he thought Manson was the nicest person, a very gentle, nice guy. Murry had a fit. He knew there were a bunch of girls living there.

I went there one day. Dennis was at the recording studio in Brian's house, and he said, "Will you take me home?" And I was very hesitant because I thought, "Oh God, Murry's not going to like this." But I took him home, and he said, "Will you just come in and meet them." Come on, they're nice." And I said, "Dennis, promise me you won't tell Dad."

So I went in, and Charlie Manson was walking through this big yard with a long robe on, and Dennis introduced me. And we went into the house, and I think three girls were in the house, just darling young girls, I thought. I zipped through the house, got back in my car and left. And wouldn't you know that Dennis told his dad"

Did you get heck for that?

AUDREE: Yeah, he didn't like it. He was pissed.

How did Charlie strike you when you saw him?

AUDREE: I just thought he looked older than he supposedly is, like an older man, and I thought he had a kind face. That was the only impression I had. And I did think they were a bunch of leeches; Dennis had been through that before. He could never stand to see anyone who needed anything or anybody who had any kind of a problem ... he was right there.

At that time nobody knew who Manson was.

AUDREE: No idea. In fact, when that horrible story came out about Manson's arrest for the Sharon Tate murder, Annie, Carl's wife, called me. And she said, "Ma, do you realize ...?" I did not connect at all that that was the same person and the same family who had been with Dennis. When she told me, I just totally froze.

Well, it must have been a shock for Dennis as well.

AUDREE: Horrifying. I think the next day was his birthday, and he was at Carl and Annie's. I went there and we had dinner. And we were all very quiet. And somebody said something, and Carl said "I don't think we should talk about it." So we just watched television and had a very quiet evening. We were totally terrified. I remember Carl saying, "Mom, let's all go back and stay at your house." And I said, "Carl, everybody knows where I live. What good would that do?" So I stayed at their house a couple of nights. And see, when they left Dennis' house Manson or somebody stole Dennis' Ferrari, and they stole everything in the house that could be moved. Everything. Stripped. Dennis had kicked them out because they were into heavy drugs and he just wanted them out. And Manson, of course, had music he wanted published, and he wanted money, quite a sum, 10 or 15 thousand dollars. And Dennis turned him down. So Manson threatened Dennis, he said, "If you don't give it to me" – I'm paraphrasing – "something's going to happen to Scotty." Scotty was Dennis' first wife's son, and Dennis just adored him. He was really like his daddy. But that was a terrible period.

You said that Dennis and his father later became much closer.

AUDREE: They were buddies. You know, it's the most amazing thing ... the year that he died, Dennis called his father on Mother's Day and Murry told him, "I'm just going to live about a month." Which Dennis didn't tell me, thank God. I didn't need to know it. But he could tell Dennis that.

He'd had one heart attack.

AUDREE: He'd had a heart attack and he was just getting along famously. And six weeks later, it was in June, he just ... well, it's weird the way that happened. I was waiting for him to wake up, thinking, "I wish he'd wake up. I wonder if he's really okay." I was standing in the kitchen, watching the clock, thinking I'll be so glad when he wakes up. And all of a sudden he woke up, and we had a great talk. He was in a good mood. He seemed to feel fine. And we talked for quite a while, about so many things. He said to me, "I'm so glad I've never had to take nitroglycerin." And I was glad, too, because I knew that would be frightening. That's for the pain. He said he wanted to take a walk – he'd been able to walk around the house but not outside yet. And I said, "Great, if you feel like it." So I was going to drive him down to Whittier Boulevard to walk. I went into the kitchen to make cereal for him, and all of a sudden I heard him yelling for me. I started dashing down this long hallway. He was in the bathroom sitting on the toilet. And he said, "Nitroglycerin," so I grabbed it and said, "Put it under your tongue." But he just sat there, very pale. And he said, "Cold water." So I got a cloth with real cold water on it and kept going like this on his forehead, and then held it on the back of his neck. And he still just sat there. I said, "Are you okay?" And he said, "I don't know."

I got up next to him to hold him – he was much bigger than I am – and he just toppled over. So I turned him over – I don't know how I did it, but I did it. And I realized he was really in bad trouble. In fact, I thought he was gone. By that time his face looked very gushed and his eyes ... I knew he didn't see me because I went like this [pats her cheek] and said, "Baby, baby." All I said to him was, "Baby, baby, I love you." I ran into the bedroom and called the fire department. I never went back in that bathroom.

I locked the house, got in my car and went to the hospital ... and sat there for quite a while. A doctor came out once and said, "We're doing everything we can." And I said, "I'm sure you are." And I knew that that was it.

Brian did not go to the funeral.

AUDREE: Nope. I understand that perfectly. You know, Carl was very angry that Brian didn't go to the funeral. And I said, "Carl, I understand perfectly." It didn't bother me. Brian couldn't face it. No way.

Do you think he'll go to yours?

AUDREE: I'd be surprised. You know, I don't know if he's ever been to one. To me, so what? I don't believe in funerals, frankly – the most barbaric, outmoded bunch of ... [censors herself and laughs]. Anyway...

In general you seem to have been much looser than your husband.

AUDREE: Oh yeah, a great deal more. He took life so seriously, really. It was hard for him to have fun. Once he said to me, "Sometimes you can be so mad or in some kind of mood, and somebody comes over and you can laugh and have a good time. Maybe I'm jealous of you." I used to think it would be so nice if he could just loosen up. But he was what he was, you know?

About ten years ago everyone started getting into drugs and marijuana and I'm sure your boys did too. How did that affect you ?

AUDREE: Well, I had a horrible problem with my husband about that. He was so, sooo against it, so mortified – I can't even think of a strong enough word. They all went and told him that they were smoking pot and, oh, he just thought that was the end of the world, the most horrible thing they could do. And of course he was angry with me. In fact he was so angry he wouldn't allow them to come to our house for quite a while. And he told me I couldn't go see them.

But now, of course dope is much better understood. Have you ever tried it?

AUDREE: Frankly, I did try it. In fact, I just zonked out. I was at Carl and Annie's house and I walked into the living room and I couldn't get up. I didn't like it at all. Then one other time, though, I tried it and I've never had more fun in my life. Laughed and laughed and laughed, just had a ball. This is since Murry's gone.

How old are you ?

AUDREE: Thirty seven. You know I'm lying. Should I tell the truth ?

Let's see ... you said you got married when you were 20 ... and you had Brian after four years and he just turned 34 ... so you're about 58.

AUDREE: Exactly. Rats.

So what are you doing with your time?

AUDREE: Not as much as I should.

You mean not as much as you'd like?

AUDREE: Well, as I'd like and should for my own good, because I'm lonely a lot and that's ridiculous.

Do you still play music?

AUDREE: I don't like to play by myself. And I should because I just adore it. In fact, the other night some of my relatives were here and they were watching Gone With The Wind and all of a sudden I just got bored and I went into the living room and I played the piano for a while. And I played the organ. And I was comfortable because I knew there was somebody here. But by myself I'm not comfortable. I just don't have anything in particular going for me.

Talk about Good Vibrations, Mike Love's seven-acre spread near Santa Barbara is positively infested with them. There on a bluff overlooking the blue Pacific and a tiny surfers' cove, Mike spends his few non-working day of the year surrounded by Jasmine, bougainvillea, wild strawberries, exotic chickens and a small community of serious transcendental meditators. These radiant, gracious people, most of whom help run the place when Mike's away, were heavy into abstinence abuse – no booze, no drugs, no tobacco, no meat.

Naturally I could only take it for about 24 hours, but I understood why Mike would dig it. When you spend most of your time performing or recording in front of giant speakers turned up full blast, you need some refuge where the ringing stops. Also, Mike, of course, is a stone Transcendental Meditation zealot, teaches it, preaches it, writes songs about it and has practiced it twice a day for the last quarter of his life. All the Beach Boys have practised it off and on; Brian, in fact, was the first. But only Mike, in late 1967, flew to Rishikesh, India, where the Ganges leaves the Himalayas, to sit for a month at the feet of Maharishi (and at the side of the Beatles, Donovan and Mia Farrow). That experience convinced him that TM could not only change his life, it could change the life of the world.

"I didn't want to just come home 30 years later," he recalled, "sit down in front of the TV, pop the top off the beer can and sit there feeding my beer gut like so many millions of people were into."

Now, on a shimmering, starlit summer night, Mike sat down in his redwood hot tub in front of an infinite ocean, slurped the top off an organic fruit juice fizz, and remembered a really neat vision he once had in Rishikesh.

MIKE: I was in my room and the mantra assumed a little melody. I was sort of singing it to myself, or singing it in my mind, and all of a sudden, from some other part of my mind, I was thinking, "Well, I'm in India, so there's a little sitarish impulse to the melody." And then I was thinking of the black kind of impulse – African, rhythmic drum impulses. Then the expression of the Latin kind of rhythm and sound, and the Chinese sort of singsong approach, and the Irish sort of hillbilly Appalachian music – all elements all around the world, Eastern, Oriental, Indian, African and Russian, that whole heavy, dramatic influence they have there, the Slovakian kind of thing. I mean, it was amazing; simultaneously this one little original melody was being played in different instruments and voice expressions and rhythms, until that one sound built to total cacophony, but it made sense.

The whole world, in other words, in its expressions of the same sound, was in harmony, although there was a difference in each one. And then once the whole world had attained that harmony, it became in harmony with the universe and the cosmos. And what I took it to be was a really far out lesson that once everyone – starting with the individual – once all the nations and races became harmonious, even with their differences, only then will the world be in harmony with nature.

But anyway, it was neat to hear that melody building like that, like a symphony of nations. Like on the new album, "That Same Song" – the whole substance of that song is this:

"The rock of ages built that rockin' sound, till more and more people started to come around. They worshipped in church and built that great big choir, it grew and grew until it spread like fire."

I'd like to personally thank the Beach Boys for breaking from their hectic schedule to put up with another crazy idea of mine – a group interview conducted in Brian's music room. We'd all had misgivings about the project. John Belushi, in town to film the TV special, had warned me, "Forget it. Group interviews never work." I suppose he was right. We'd hoped the group thing might put Brian more at ease, but it seemed to do just the opposite. We'd hoped to discuss the music, to get a feel of the music down on paper, but it became painfully apparent that that sort of thing is beyond words.

Yet there is a feeling here, of the warm brotherhood bond that has kept this gang together longer than any other white American band. That, and a sense of the good fart humor inspired years ago in the locker rooms of Hawthorne High.

First of all let's test the mikes and see if all this stuff is working. We'll just go around the room, and you tell me your name and something about yourself.

CARL: Okay. This is Carl. I'm a really groovy guy.

DENNIS: This is Dennis, and I want to know if it's going on the radio ... uh ... I'm Dennis and –

BRIAN: This is Brian.

DENNIS: I'm not done, Brian. This is Dennis and I'm the cute one.

[Everyone waits for Brian to speak again but he simply stares ahead, his face expressionless]

MIKE: This is cousin Mike, checking in over here on 99.9.

Al is a little late, but he should be at his microphone shortly. What I'd like you to do this afternoon is sort of informally discuss your music, what songs or segments or devices you are really proud of.

DENNIS: There's a lot of things – how a record will fade out. I love the way Brian has faded out some of his records.

Yeah there's a couple of songs "Wind Chimes" I think and "Little Bird" – where the part that delighted me the most was the fadeout.

CARL: "At My Window" is like that too, from *Sunflower*. I love the tag. We call fadeouts "tags"; we're big tag fans.

Do you remember when you started doing that sort of tag?

CARL: Oh golly – "Surfer Girl," "Surfin' U.S.A." – I think that's when Brian got the knack. Brian, would you like to comment?

[Brian says nothing.]

DENNIS: I think "Let Him Run Wild" was one of Brian's first tracks that he did a real stretch on. It was a real breakthrough .

CARL: That was on *Summer Days and Summer Nights*. The door starts to fly open on that album, musically speaking – the recording process and, you know, that whole total sound.

Brian with these innovations were they like planned ahead or did you just try them in the studio?

BRIAN: We'd just try it, like spontaneous; whatever worked out spontaneously we'd usually go along with.

DENNIS: [*Whispers into Carl's mike*] Hi, this is Carl … and I wanna say that … I like pussy.

MIKE: Bomp bomps, I guess, were the kind of little parts, the spontaneous inventions, Brian was talking about. We might have a song, a good pattern, a good chord structure, maybe a concept, maybe no lyrics, and the thing would come together in the studio. .

CARL: I think one of the most unusual background parts Brian came up with is on "This Whole World."

MIKE: Oom bop didit.

DENNIS: Like the new one Brian's working on – mow mama …

MIKE: Mow mama yama …

DENNIS: Mow mama yama holy

CARL: …hallelujah.

MIKE: [*Sings*] Mow mama yama holy hallelujah.

What's that song Brian ?

BRIAN: That's from a song called "Clang." We haven't really got it together yet, so we can't talk about it. It's a spiritual sort of rock 'n' roll song.

Some of your innovations in "Good Vibrations" must have struck people as a little unusual. Like taking six months to record it and using four studios.

DENNIS: Actually, that's when Brian started losing his mind and he couldn't tell which studio was which [much laughter]. You know, so he'd go to Columbia, and he'd go, "Oh, jeez, wait a minute… I lost the tapes."

CARL: I remember Dad was worried about the bridge section. You know, the time change, "They can't dance to it."

DENNIS: [*Humbly proud*] It's still one of the all time great standard rock & roll tunes. It was an honor to be able to take part in it. It was so superb. When there was all I could do to struggle to learn one line, one melodic line, Brian had eight or nine going. Brian had me in awe for a long time … 'till I figured out his secret.

Which was….

DENNIS: Shooting up acid.

[Dennis' masterfully timed punch line delivered with a sly pokerface cracks up everyone.]

MIKE: [*Embarrassed giggle*] Oh, God!

DENNIS: Naw, I was kidding.

[Everyone that is except, Brian, who continues to stare straight ahead as if he'd heard nothing. After a moment the doorbell rings and Al walks into the entrance hall. From the beginning of their career this smallest of Beach Boys, related neither by blood nor temperament, has stood apart from the others. Even today he readily admits that the Beach Boys are "not my whole life". For one thing he and his family live hundreds of miles up the coast in the remote Big Sur area of northern California. He is a "professional" rancher dabbling in honeybees and Arabian horses on a 75 acre plot he owns near Monterey. And he's something of a politician, shaking hands with Governor Brown and supporting community action to preserve the Pacific coastline.

[Yet his influence on the Beach Boys has been considerable. His early folk song background inspired the others to record, almost journalistically, their times and surroundings, in effect to write a new folk music for the Sixties, or at least the Sixties of Hawthorne. And to think he almost blew this profitable gig a year after it started when he abruptly quit the group to enroll in dental school.

[It took two semesters for Al to come to his senses, and when Brian phoned him in the summer of '63 and asked him to return, Al eagerly accepted. Brian explained that he didn't want to tour anymore, that he needed Al to replace him. And now as Al enters the music room there is a curious sense of deja vu. Brian suddenly stands up and leaves the room allowing Al to again replace him in the group.]

CARL: *[To Brian]* You're not participating much in this.

BRIAN: I did a long interview the other day ... let them go for a while. I'm just going to lay down. I got a little headache.

[Brian heads upstairs as Al sits down in front of the sixth mike.]

AL: This is Alan Jardine.

Did Brian tell you, Al, why he wanted to stop touring?

AL: I don't remember a reason. He just didn't enjoy going out there, and I think his weight had something to do with it even at that time. He was starting to get heavy he didn't feel comfortable. At times he seemed to enjoy it though. He always liked to hog the microphone, I remember that. If you were singing on the microphone with three people or even two people, he'd just move you right over *[laughter]*. He just wanted to make sure he got his part in, I guess. He's very aggressive in that way, and that's how he exhibited himself in the studio as a producer, with that very all encompassing and very dominant personality.

[Scott Steinberg enters the music room.]

SCOTT: Do you need Brian?

Well, he said he had a headache.

SCOTT: *[Scornfully]* Bullshit. *[Twists and shouts]* Come on down!

BRIAN: *[From his room]* I'm tired, I'm lying down.

SCOTT: *[Bounds up the stairs]* No, you said you had a headache.

BRIAN: I ... I said I had a headache to Felton.

SCOTT: No. We'll go downstairs now.

BRIAN: Well ... I do have a little headache.

[The group giggles affectionately at Brian's hasty excuses. Al continues.]

AL: But eventually Brian became worn down and tired from all the work, the producing, from what I've heen able to gather. And it was on our way to Houston, Texas I was sitting next to him on the plane, and he just broke down and cried, he just crashed right there. This was at the end of '64, right after "When I Grow up (To Be a Man)."

[*Scott leads Brian into the music room and directs him to resume his place behind the mike. Brian seems irritable and starts cracking his thick neck, twisting his head back and forth in his hands.*]

There's a couple of songs that I think illustrate the Beach Boys' sense of humour. Like Al, you wrote "Take a Load off Your Feet".

BRIAN: [*Gruffly*] I think we should move faster. I don't think you're asking the questions fast enough.

AL: I was wearing Birkenstock sandals, and I read the instructions that came with them; it was inspiring to read about how important your feet are to the rest of your body. And so Brian and I got carried away. He'd come down at night and sit and play the bottles, these Sparklett's bottles we had lying around. He walked around on the roof – there was this skipping sound on the end of the song, you know, and that was Brian on the asphalt roof of the garage. Skipping around in a circle.

Another funny song is Mike's "She's Goin' Bald."

DENNIS: I took that song in a very strange way. I thought it was more or less about oral sex. [*Mike bursts out laughing.*] You know, [sings] "Get a job, sha na na na, sha na na na na. What a blow...." And I thought, Jesus, that's funny as shit – [*moronic voice*] "Hey, it's about getting a blow job, huh huh huh."

AL: Well, that's what it was, right?

MIKE: We were stoned out of our heads. We were laughing our asses of when we recorded that stuff.

CARL: Yeah, a little hash.

DENNIS: [*Gently ribbing*] Brian used to have a great sense of humor. [*He looks at Brian for some sort of reaction but gets none.*] Michael, just tell me ... what is the esoteric meaning behind a bald chick to you? [*To the others*] Michael once told me that if I ever had a dream about a toilet, I'd be bisexual. [*Mike starts shrieking with falsetto laughter.*] He said, "Dennis, you ever dream about a toilet?" I told him I had a dream that my grandmother, Grandma Betty, went down the toilet. He said, "Dennis, that means you're gay." [*The whole group cracks up.*] And I believed him. I went, "You're kidding My God !" I went, [*moronic*] "Hey, Mom, am I gay?"

MIKE: [*Tries to regain his composure*] What ... what about the time I told ... [*but fails, explodes, spits, snorts, wheezes hysterically*] ... I told my mom you had syphillis?

DENNIS: She wouldn't talk to me for three years. I'd go, "Hi," and she'd go [*gasps, shrinks back, wipes deadly scum off his clothes*]. One time I got Carl on television. And the guy was asking, "The group had a lull, didn't it? What was the cause of that lull?" And I said, "Carl was in the hospital for four years for junk!" [Again the group breaks up.] Carl goes, "What?".

[Carl jerks backward in a fit, tears streaming from his eyes.]

CARL: Oh God, we're so straight, it's beautiful. Really, we are so straight.

I Do ... I Should ... I Will

On Saturday, September, 18th, Brian Wilson was nominated to the "Hall of Fame" on Don Kirshner's televised *Rock Music Awards* show. He didn't make it, but only because all the nominations in that category were ridiculously overdue and included other pioneers like Elvis, the Beatles, John Lennon and Bob Dylan. (The Beatles won. But Brian did receive his own tribute on the show, a standing ovation when he made a guest appearance to announce the winners of the Best Single and Best Female Vocalist categories. And he looked stunning, with a new tuxedo, a new haircut and a new figure, down from 250 to 215 pounds. He handled his few routine lines with style and confidence, and as he left the stage, a friend of mine watching the show shouted, "He made it!"

Step by step, Brian is making it every day. He still seems a bit timid and programmed in, say, an interview situation, but when he's in front of a TV camera or a piano, his recovery seems nearly complete.

It's not, of course, and a few days later Annie Leibovitz and I returned to Los Angeles at the urging of Dr. Landy. "You gotta come down," he'd said, "it's been three months, and what you saw is not what you get. We got a new model ... I think you'll be pleasantly impressed."

Well, it wasn't that pleasant, but in the end I was impressed. Bodyguard Scott Steinberg picked us up at the airport, and on the way to Dr. Landy's office he enthusiastically described Brian's progress in the four months he's been living with him. "When I first met Brian, God, he was very spacey," he said. "He was this big giant, he seemed like a gorilla to me." Scott, formerly a veterinary major at Los Angeles City College, knew about gorillas, but at first knew absolutely nothing about Brian Wilson, had never heard his music or his name. Which didn't really matter, his main job was to get him out of bed, take care of him and keep him clean.

"Basically he's a person now," said Scott. "Like even getting dressed for the *Rock Awards* show – he did it himself, he took his own shower."

At the office I asked Landy if there was any one time when Brian started to withdraw. "Yes, one time, one time in specific," he said. "It's all related to his use of acid. Acid attacks the limbic region of the brain, the part that affects one's whole emotional response. With someone like Brian, who had a predisposition toward psychosis, all it takes is one hit."

Landy's plan was for all of us to go to the same Chinese restaurant as before, affording a more scientific comparison, then to the Century West Club to watch Brian work out in the gym, then to his home to hear some new songs he'd written. At the restaurant I had a chance to ask Brian a few more questions, but this time he seemed slightly more tense, or, understandably, impatient.

One thing that puzzles me is why you consented to this interview at all. There've been so many stories about your personal life – doesn't that bother you?

BRIAN: No, that doesn't bother me.

Why not?

BRIAN: Any article's good. Long as it's publicity, I think that's all that matters. I think it's advancement for my career.

You went through two years of really intense withdrawal, but you started getting a reputation for being reclusive or eccentric long before that. You must have read all those reports of your being kind of nuts.

BRIAN: It bothered me, yeah, because I figured, "Why are they calling me nuts?" I didn't feel I was nuts.

Just weren't too active.

BRIAN: Right.

Last time we talked about the Smile *album, and you said you'd gotten too fancy for the public. I was wondering if perhaps today the public might not be ready for it, and if so, don't you have an obligation to find out by releasing it?*

BRIAN: I do … I should … I will.

Do you know when?

BRIAN: I don't know, probably in a couple years.

There's been the conjecture that when you heard yourself being called a genius, it frightened you.

BRIAN: Yeah, it gave me a weird feeling, an eerie feeling

But didn't you sort of agree with it, too ?

BRIAN: Yeah, I did

I think you must be fully aware of your contribution to music.

BRIAN: I am.

During lunch Brian committed an infraction, nothing big really, but it resulted in Landy yelling at Brian and Brian cringing back, his eyes smarting. Landy subsequently asked me not to write about the incident, that it was not typical of Brian's present behavior, that his reading about it might be harmful. When Landy left the room for a phone call, I asked Brian if such public admonishments didn't embarrass him. "That is embarrassing to me," he admitted. "Don't you object to that?" I asked, and he said, "I just feel brought down".

I felt brought down myself, and it occurred to me that Landy might be as concerned with his own image as he is with Brian's. (At one point Landy said, "Did you read the thing in New West? I don't want to appear like I did in that.") Later at the gym we were going up an escalator, Brian and Scott and Annie and me, and Scott asked, "So, what did you think of Brian today? Did he seem any different?" I couldn't answer him, I couldn't continue this game of dissecting Brian, mulling over Brian, in his presence, as if he wasn't there. Why do they have to do that? Why keep slamming him in public now that he's so much better? I mean, there's plenty of evidence Landy's method is working. I just hope that when Brian's fully healed, when he's finally in touch and he's learned all those good manners, I just hope he's strong enough to teach Dr. Landy a few.

Fortunately Brian had cheered up by the time we reached his home. He sat down at an old upright in his living room and whipped off three songs he'd written since June. He seemed amazingly confident, singing various parts, playing the piano, even smiling occasionally. One song was called "Hey, Little Tomboy" ("time you turned into a girl"). Another, "I Want to Pick You Up" ("'cause you're still a baby to me"). The third, the one I liked best, was a tribute to his wife and was entitled simply "Marilyn Rovell". The words are pretty homey, the music –

pshew! – days later I was still humming it, it was so delicious. And that was just Brian and the piano; who knows how great it'll sound with the Beach Boys' voices and those funky instruments and the sound effects and echo and some kind of fantastic fadeout?

That is the miracle of his music. It just grabs you and follows you around like a little angel. It makes you feel good and gives you hope. It certainly gave me hope for Brian. In June he feared he was washed up as a writer, now here were three gems in three months – talk about progress! By the time I left his house I was convinced that, despite his sickness, despite his cure, Brian Wilson shall rise and shine again.

The Tag

Brian stands barefoot in the sand near Trances Beach wearing a flowing bathrobe and carrying a surfboard that somehow looks like a tablet. It is June 20th, Father's Day, Brian's 34th birthday. He is there to film a spot for the TV special, a comic bit called "Brian's Nightmare" in which he's arrested and forced to surf. (Brian's fear of surfing and water is well known.)

Soberly he plods forward, accompanied by Danny Aykroyd and John Belushi in highway patrol uniforms. About 50 yards from the ocean they stop, and Aykroyd steps out to direct the breakers. Then he nods to Brian and says, "Okay, Mr. Wilson, here's your wave."

A small crowd of friends and crew people watches nervously, silently, as Brian carries out his sentence. His feet touch the surf but he plunges ahead up to his waist then dives in, his whalelike body atop the board and totally immersed in the cool, clear water. The crowd cheers like crazy.

Suddenly on the mind's horizon six giant figures appear, floating over the blue Pacific. They form a pyramid. At the base stand Carl, Brian and Dennis. On their shoulders stand Mike and Al. At the top stands Murry Wilson. He pulls a pipe from his jowly face, and as he begins to speak, the boys begin to chant in harmony with the universe.

BRIAN, DENNIS, CARL, MIKE, AL: Mow mama yama holy hallelujah, mow mama yama holy hallelujah, mow mama yama holy hallelujah, mow mama yama holy hallelujah....

MURRY: I'm sure these guys didn't give you the facts right. The first record, called "Surfin'" – which I never did like and still don't like, it was so rude and crude, you know? – was the first song lyrically about surfing. It was just like a gold mine waiting to be opened. And my boys were so hungry and thirsty to prove how good they were.

My kids would whine, and I'd bawl them out. They were so exhausted I had to make them mad at me to get the best out of them. There's more than one way to give love to kids, you know? I drove them harder because they asked for it. They said, "Help us, make us famous, help us record. We need you, Dad."

I think the Beach Boys have been instrumental in changing the style of music to a great degree, not only with songwriters but also with band arrangements, with

Negro artists, as well as the listening public. They're using Brian's *Pet Sounds* format, and his approach to bass root arrangements and his style of changing keys without any rhyme or reason. Without knowing it, he's created a monster – actually, he changed the concept of music.

BRIAN, DENNIS, CARL, MIKE, AL: Papa oom mow mow, Papa oom mow mow, Papa oom mow mow, Papa oom mow mow...

MURRY: We were driving in a car, going to a recording session, and I said to Brian, "I read in the Times that you experimented with LSD. Is that a put-on to the newspapers, or did you do it?" And he said, "Yes, Dad, I did." And I said, "Well, tell me Brian, do you think you're strong enough in your brain that you can experiment with a chemical that might drive you crazy later or maybe you might kill somebody or jump out of a window if it ricochets on you?" He said, "No, Dad, it made me understand a lot of things." I said, "Who're you trying to kid, Brian? What did you understand, except seeing like a nightmare in your brain, colors and things like that maybe?" And I said, "You know, Brian, one thing that God gave you was a brain. If you play with it and destroy it, you're dead, you're a vegetable. And we haven't heard the end of this. There are going to be people killed and people in sanitariums and insane asylums because they played with God."

BRIAN, DENNIS, CARL, MIKE, AL: Mow mama yama holy hallelujah, Mow mama yama holy hallelujah ...

MURRY: I lost my left eye in an industrial accident at Goodyear, and I wear a plastic eye. But I'd like to add that it made me a better man. When I was 25 I thought the world owed me a living; when I lost my eye I tried harder, drove harder and did the work of two men in the company and got more raises. I put $2,300 on my Hawthorne house, went into my own business and succeeded against millionaire dealers. Now you figure it out. Guts.

And that's what the Beach Boys have – guts. And talent. And I'm proud of them. I've been down on them a few times when they would make mistakes or not do what I figured was the best. And I never quit reminding them that they got a big break and "now get out there and earn your money. Don't whine to me, get up on that stage. So you're tired – you asked for it. Dennis, don't you miss a beat on the drum again. Quit looking at the girls and get on the ball." I drove 'em and I'm proud of it.

I don't know if you admire any of them or their accomplishments, but I think it's one of those success stories that can happen in America. And it isn't all talent – it's guts and promotion and just keeping at it even when you make mistakes. You can't be right all the time. But the ability to fight back, come back and create again is America. In other words, they're just Americans, they're like any one of you. Got it? Got the message?

BRIAN, DENNIS, CARL, MIKE, AL: [Fading out as the sun begins to set] Oom bop didit, oom bop didit, Mow mama yama holy hallelujah, papa oom mow mow, papa oom mow mow, mow mama yama holy hallelujah, papa oom mow mow, mow mama yama holy hallelujah, hallelujah, hallelujah, hallelujah, hallelujah ...

Original Reviews Part 6

In Concert double album

"Who would have thought that a group who came to the top on an early sixties craze would still be going strong today?..."

"... their somewhat weak live sound has been a handicap in the past...but now the six man caucus, augmented by others, have the 'oomph' they've always needed..."

"... oddly enough, it's the complicated numbers like 'Good Vibrations' which come off best, whereas the relatively simple 'Sloop John B.' seems lacking in zip...a minor quibble though on a totally fantastic album...."

"hmmm, very nice... 'Marcella' is a shade tatty...a rambunctious, rip roaring, riveting rollick of an album."

15 Big Ones album

"What the little deuce coupe is going on round here?...a gaggle of cover versions of songs which might be called 'classics' if you were feeling generous and / or drunk..."

"Welcome back Brian...a simple summer album for a nice, hot summer...can a distillation of the best of 15 years make for big bucks today? Who knows?...as an entity the Beach Boys still kick ass, Brian still kicks ass ..."

"... just what kind of menopause, re-evaluation, or plain laziness has gone on in those years since *Holland* noone has been airing to the public...the first reaction to *15 Big Ones* is gross disappointment..."

"Reprise decided that the magic ingredient needed was Brian Wilson back in a lead creative role...[but Brian's] professional collapse cannot be ignored..."

"The Beach Boys only succeed in jumping several steps sideways and ten years backwards...grimly disappointing, spotlighting a group desperately trying to retain the spirit of their early gorgeously naive youngblood sunflecked Californian 'essence'."

The Beach Boys Love You album

"Brian Wilson is alive and well and constructing unique, catchy and absolutely joyful pop songs again..."

"... one first reaction to this news of Wilson's renewed creative hyper activity is one of extreme elation mixed with a certain trepidation...This is easily the best Beach Boys album since *Sunflower*, but it's no *Pet Sounds* ... a goodly half and half situation really..."

" 'Solar System' is a splendidly dumb ride across the universe...[and] 'Mona' is a hit single ... an overwhelming proportion of the tracks are simply spiffing..."

Mike Love: 14 mins with a Beach Boy
by John Tobler

This short interview first appeared in the October 1976 issue of Zigzag, *and is interesting as an early take on Mike Love's perception of the direction in which the band was heading at the time. It also shows his genuine appreciation (at least at that time) of Brian's musical talent and leadership.*

Mike Love was recently in London for an all too brief period (as will be seen) the reason being that the group have made an hour long video programme which is due to be shown on American TV soon, and presumably in an effort to sell it to interested British parties it was previewed in London. Before we get to the meat, let me recommend the video in the highest possible terms – it has a prodigious quantity of great music, humour (Van Dyke Parks is amazing in it) and lots of other stuff that I'll leave as a surprise. See it if you possibly can…
    The interview which follows wasn't quite what was intended. You'll see.

ML: Keith (Richard) is in the hotel if you want to interview a real funky rock star.

ZZ: I'm more interested in you.

ML: You're just trying to flatter me!

Why would I bother? I'm as old as you are.

(After age comparisons). I'm your senior so treat me respectfully if you will please. OK what is your first question? My first question is where are all those beautiful Oriental girls who walk around the streets here?

What is this thing that Americans have about Chinese people?

I don't know about other Americans but I love Oriental girls.

You're not the only one. Ray Manzarek is married to one I believe.

Is he really? Dirty dog! That's it – if I marry one it'll probably break the fixation.

I would imagine so…tell me please about David L. Marks. A gentleman who is much neglected in Beach Boys history.

He is sorely neglected and unjustly so, for he's a fine gentleman – a nice person and he's also studied classical music at a music school in Boston. Went from playing rhythm guitar with the Beach Boys, to Dave Marks and the Marksmen, a small band in Southern California. He returned east to study in the conservatory of music but now he's back on the West Coast, doing what I don't know because I haven't talked to him for the last couple of years. When I last saw him about three years ago in Boston he was doing very well, feeling good, he'd grown up very handsomely and nicely; and he wasn't the same snotty punk kid he was when he was in the group!

He was with you while Al [Jardine] was away for a while wasn't he?

Al went away for about a year. He had pretentions, ideas of going to dental school but he soon figured – I could have told him this and saved him a lot of trouble –

that he could look down a whole lot more mouths at one time on stage with the Beach Boys than one at a time in a dentist's chair.

How many albums was David Marks on?

Surfin USA, *Surfer Girl* and *Shut Down*.

What influence did Murry Wilson have on the Beach Boys?

What influence does any father have on his sons?

You're not his son so you're in no position to answer.

I'm his nephew. Or he's my aunt. Was. He's deceased. He had very little influence on us day to day... his influence was mainly genetic in relationship to the Wilson boys; and the fact that he was...you'll see in the Special that he's spoken of rather irreverently by Dennis. He was a harsh man, an aspiring songwriter, and he would have been a stage mother except he was more of a father. He aspired to write music, and he at least created a musical climate, an atmosphere behind the group. He was our first manager – at first he didn't think we knew what we were doing, we were just kids, we didn't know anything. And then finally, somehow, we got a hit record, and another one, and he took these few songs that we recorded to Capitol Records, and got a contract with Capitol Records, which was actually what you call a slave contract. They used to have indentured servitude, you remember that? In the 1700s, you'd leave England, and go to work in the cotton fields for a while. But then in 1961, they called indentured servitude a Capitol Records contract, and we were living under that miserable spectre (and I don't mean Phil) for about eight or nine years until we finally got out of it, and into a decent contract with a respectable company, and one that is not a flagrant prostitution of our beautiful art!

I can only follow that by asking you whether you approve of Endless Summers, *after that little diatribe. I gathered that the Beach Boys are co-operating fully with Capitol in their reissue programme.*

We have nothing to say about it, I met with Capitol Records on *Endless Summer* which is a reason that it's so terribly successful, of course, but the fact of the matter is I hoped they would do an anthological kind of approach, rather than *Oldies* or *20 Golden Greats* or something, and so we got 80% there, The artwork was, I thought, meagre, to say the most about it – to be nice about it, it could have been done a lot better, but it accomplished, it took the edge off what they had planned. *Endless Summer*, the very title itself, that was the title I gave it, is better that *20 Golden Mouldies*, because to me it implies two of the most important qualities of the Beach Boys – timelessness, the eternal quality of the music and summer,- *Endless Summer*.

You're saying that you didn't have anything to do with Spirit of America?

Nothing. We were just doing our duty.

So did you approve of it in any way, the track choice, for example?

I approved of the fact that it sold about a million.

So you're not keen on Capitol, but you're taking the money?

No, I'm saying that we had a lousy royalty rate. They promoted us very well for the first four or five years then they failed miserably in promoting that change, which would have been very commercially sensible on their part, but they didn't ever do it. In '68 or '69, they were still promoting us as the number one surfing group in the USA. How relevant was that after "Good Vibrations", *Pet Sounds*, *Smiley Smile* or Vietnam and everything else? It was not, I tell you; right in the middle of psychedelia, they were talking about the number one surfing group in the USA. It's obnoxious corporate intellect! Just because a certain style sells in one year, it's going to sell in the next – not necessarily so, and we weren't fixed to that. We'd moved on, evolved and changed as much or more than anybody, sometimes pressing the legal limits and sensible limits of credibility with our peers. Look at "Good Vibrations", when it first came out, the number one disc jockey in New York, Bruce Morrow, Cousin Brucie, said to me that it scared him, He said he hated it – he hated "Good Vibrations" because it was so different. He wanted to hear "I Get Around" or "Surfin' USA" one more time, or "California Girls Part Two". When "Good Vibrations" came out, it was rather logical and sequential after *Pet Sounds* which was rather sequential and logical after "I Get Around", witness the first verse: "I'm getting bugged driving up and down that same old strip, I got to find a new place where the kids are hip", meaning awareness, you see, so we could see the seeds of rebellion as early as "I Get Around".

1964, August, when my first daughter was born.

Was that 1964 August? That was when Mick Jagger came back here on "Ready, Steady Flipout" or whatever was happening at the time, and he said "Oh great mumble mumble mumble record, "I Get Around". He came back and he actually mentioned it. He still couldn't get no satisfaction!

[At this point in proceedings, a brief but hilarious exchange occurred, which has been removed, as lawyers already seem to make quite enough money without our assistance.]

I gather that at one stage there was a move to change the name of the Beach Boys to simply Beach...

Where did you hear that?

I read it in Rock Marketplace.

In that case it couldn't be wrong. That and *Roget's Thesaurus.*

A great similarity...

Although I must say I've never read *Rock Marketplace*. I swear I haven't, but that doesn't mean anything. I don't read a lot of rock press. I read very little.

Tell me about it then...

The rock 'n' roll press? I don't know anything that is going on. I'm very naive about what's happenings.

Very good at evading questions as well! Was there an idea that you were going to change Beach Boys to Beach?

Alright, I'll tell, I'll tell! No, that was a statement that I rather facetiously uttered in jest with some dry and caustic humour, when once upon a time I was asked if we had ever thought of changing our name, and I said "Well, we've thought about dropping the 'Boys' – to call ourselves The Beach would be very hip and psychedelic in 68 or 7 or something, with flower power, lover of the Beach" ... and then Elton John comes along years later, and "The Beach is Back" and we're OK, you know. "It's OK", as a matter of fact.

(An obscure reference to the latest, and very fine single by the Beach Boys, I expect you'll all have realised).

Tell me about Brother Records and who else is on it.

Nobody. We had the Flame there for a while, but that was a glorified label deal. That was a logo, if you know what I mean. Logo.

I know exactly what you mean, why haven't you got anybody else? What's the point of having a label which is only you?

Did you ever hear that song on the *Holland* album, "Only With You"?

You're evading the question again.

Because we spent enough time doing the Beach Boys, on tour, in the studios and stuff. Why the hell were we going to spend the rest of our lives promoting and producing other people? Besides that, we didn't have the mechanics or the proper management and promotion people around us at the time. We had a couple of leeches and frauds and never do wells, and so the ideas that we had to develop Brother Records and stuff, which were very good, were never translated into sound business practice. We never got immersed that deeply like the Beatles, who did Apple Records, to where we lost millions of dollars... we stopped short of it. We said "Well, the only way you're going to be a record company is if you have your own distribution, sales and promotion. Just making a royalty deal with a major record company to to distribute a product is nothing more than a distribution deal for your production company, so you really have no mastery over your own destiny. We saw that immediately after we'd signed it, so we said "Oh shit, we've had it!"

So there was the intention originally to put Flame on it, and what about the Redwoods?

The Redwoods! Those people were Three Dog Night. The thing is, that was one of the stupidest fuck ups in the world of recording. Three Dog Night sold more records, singles that is, than anybody in the world, and Brian Wilson produced them originally but you know, it was funny. They'd go in, and they wouldn't sing good enough for him; he didn't want to hear any sharps or flats; he was at that period of his life when he was horrible to live with. But he's great musically, that is why our music has lasted, because he was a great stickler for perfection, and he would hear them sharp or flat, or they didn't have the quality. It's not just a note being sung, but the particular pitch and timbre, and subtle overt and covert implications that Brian is looking for. Who knows...cosmic or whatever, but the fact of the matter is that he had them in the studio for several days, and he was really funny. They didn't meet up to his expectations, but they went off and made billions.

Was the theory that they were going to be on Brother?

Yeah, that was the idea.

And was it true that "Darlin'" and "Good Vibrations" were written for Danny Hutton originally?

Yeah.... "Good Vibrations"? Not Danny, take it easy, I mean really not. That sounds like a Bruce Johnston quote. "Darlin'" was originally going to be Three Dog Night. Which they'd sound great doing too.

    At which point we were joined by a gentleman named Warren Duffy who was accompanying Mike on the trip.

WD: Gentlemen I'm afraid that I have to interrupt.

ML: What time is it?

WD: It's 5.30.

ML: We've only been here five minutes.

Is there any possibility of carrying on after the film? I have a million other trivial questions to ask.

ML: How many millions?

About forty but they're not all trivias – there's the Van Dyke Parks question for instance. We've had about a quarter of an hour of tape and only covered about six points.

WD: And you want to ask forty? Impossible. Please understand we have literally been besieged and Mike, and I must speak on his behalf, has been very patient. We can only work so long and we started quite early and it's going to go on quite late. Tomorrow we have to fly from here and he has to be back on stage to do a show tomorrow night back in America. I would appreciate your understanding. We have two more interviews to do tomorrow while we're packing and getting ready to go to the plane so we have squeezed in as much as we can. Everyone would like to have an awful lot of time, and it's impossible.

ML: I'll tell you what we can do. If you want to write down those questions and give them to Warren sometime...

WD: You're going to be at the film tonight. We can record them on cassettes and mail them back to you.

If you'd do that I'd be most grateful.

WD: I'd be more than happy to do that for you. He only has half an hour now. (To ML) I'll have to speed you along to meditate, to shower and to dress because the car's coming promptly at six. As a matter of fact we're supposed to be there at six and it's 5.30 now.

And that is what happened. I'm looking forward with great interest to getting the tape back when I hope to be able to deny or confirm a few more of the many rumours that exist surrounding the Beach Boys. I repeat they are my all time favourite at weathering all kinds of musical fashions that crop up consistently able to sound fresh despite the passing of time and a joy forever. Additionally I strongly recommend that you ignore the rantings of critics of *15 Big Ones* and invest immediately at the same time getting yourself a copy of *20 Golden Greats* on Capitol which has to contain some of the finest music you'll ever hear, music which only plant life might be unable to appreciate.

M.I.U. Album Review
by Richard Williams

In the 60s Richard Williams was one of the few British writers who really understood how the Beach Boys worked, or didn't as the case may be. In his review of the M.I.U. Album, *he eloquently sums up the personnel problems within the band, and his words have as much resonance in 1997 as they did at the time..*

The initials of the title stand for Maharishi Institute University, where the album was partly recorded, but their significance is greater by far than that. In recent years the Beach Boys have been split into two factions: The Transcendental Meditators (Mike Love and Al Jardine) and what might be called the Sceptics (Dennis and Carl Wilson). The Meditators, having been greatly impressed with Capitol's success with the *Endless Summer* and *Spirit of America* repackages several years ago, believe that the future of the group is in its past: in a perpetuation of the cars and surfing image, which involves performing either genuine oldies or new songs that sound like oldies. The Sceptics believe that a continued trust in extraordinary (by pop music standards) creativity which gave birth to "Good Vibrations", "Heroes and Villains" and "Surf's up" holds out the promise of greater fulfilment.

These warring factions have been involved in a bloody struggle called The Battle For Brian Wilson's Mind, for both sides share the belief that therein lies the key to the group's success (not to say the key to the bank vaults of major record companies).

The title of this album tells you unmistakeably who's winning. For the moment, at least, Brian is firmly corralled by the Love / Jardine camp; the younger Wilsons are mere bystanders, going with the flow, one assumes, of the greater good....

How tragic that Brian is saddled with other people's imagination, that he should be reduced to the role of hack, setting his impassioned melodies and arrangements to laughably juvenile lyrics....those songs of which Brian has sole charge exemplify his dilemma: he is obviously encouraged to deliver the adolescent pap of "Hey Little Tomboy", so that the dark emotions and warm textures of "Diane" are thrown into even higher relief. Should you choose to ignore the rest of the album, at least hear "Diane" and be reassured that the spark still glows... Love and Jardine tried to offer the *M.I.U. Album* to Epic, as the first delivery under their new deal. That they were turned down, on grounds of quality, is a tribute to Epic's discretion. Here's hoping that the company holds out for as long as it takes to get an album by the real Beach Boys: the brothers Wilson.

Original Reviews Part 7

Pacific Ocean Blue – Dennis Wilson album

"Dennis, with his true blue Beach Boy pedigree, … flexes his manhood all over the gatefold sleeve…- an incorrigible romantic, sensibly deriving maximum kicks from the sea, sex and rock 'n' roll."

"I wish I could wholeheartedly recommend this one, but no way. [*POB*] is further proof that Brian is / was the real creative force [in the band]."

"[With] heavy handed orchestration [*POB* is] a sort of miscalculated Spector wall of sound with ethereal choir swamps."

Going Public – Bruce Johnston album

"No way is the progressive market going to absorb this pap, most of which is rougher than the bottom of a parrot's cage … even numbers of undoubted merit, 'Dierdre' or 'Disney Girls', make you realise how much he needed the Beach Boys for ideas to attain fruition…"

"The record suffers from disastrous compromise, total non-contributions from the likes of Curt Becher, Caleb Quaye and Gary Mallaber siphened over an unremitting sweetness that would make carrion crawl in gagged horror … asinine lapses of taste…" "Johnston won a Grammy for 'I Write The Songs' which is enough to shatter anyone's confidence."

"These days Bruce is happy to be very MOR…"

"The fall of the house of Gary Usher…"

Brian Wilson: High and Bri'
by Nick Kent

Nick Kent wrote the extended three part article "The Last Beach Movie" for the NME *in 1975. It was to become the best known piece written about Brian and the band in England, and was rumoured to have had quite an effect on Brian. It can be found in full in Kent's own retrospective book* The Dark Stuff – *the entirety of which is essential reading. This piece is a slightly rewritten version of a later* NME *story. Written in the early eighties, it paints an eloquent picture of Brian's 'problem years'.*

"When you work in my business, it's all scary." Brian Wilson.

One day in the summer of 1980 I awoke from a deep disorienting dream to hear my letter box rattling. Through it had been placed a telegram on which the following message was written. Epic records' publicity department had received word from the Beach Boys' new manager, Jerry Schilling, that Brian Wilson was very much on a personality upsurge, had rid himself of the various quirks and kinks previously bedevilling his troubled temperament and was ready to talk at length about himself, his music and his problems. The interview would take place at Wilson's home where intimacy was assured. Was I interested in firing the questions? Yes, of course … I suppose.

It had been almost five years to the day since I'd last set foot in Los Angeles, back in 1975, determined to turn the city upside down in order to find out what really happened to Brian Wilson. What I discovered wasn't pretty. Banished from his sprawling mansion to live in a small changing hut by the pool because his degenerate behaviour was having too negative an effect on his two daughters, Wendy and Carnie, Wilson would spend his nights snorting cocaine, sometimes mixing it with heroin, as well as boozing to horrific excess. Wilson's family had finally to freeze his bank account in order to curtail his drug spending. Consequently he took to wandering the streets of LA, spending much of his time getting thrown out of massage parlours, when he wasn't closeting himself away with drug buddies.

When allowed in his own house he would stay in his room for days on end, lying in a huge bed surrounded by pornography and junk food. He'd reached the point where music no longer held any interest for him. Though he would fitfully work up scraps of melodies on the piano, he'd almost always fail to complete them. Then in '76 the protective wall around Brian Wilson was suddenly demolished. The previous year the Beach Boys' career had suddenly encountered a dramatic lift off owing to the success of a compilation album of oldies released by Capitol (the label they'd left five years ago so they could instigate what subsequently became a stormy liaison with Warner Bros.). *Endless Summer* sprinted to the top of the U S charts and scored platinum sales on the strength of four sides of classic sixties Brian Wilson songs finding favour with a new generation of American teenagers. An EMI compilation *20 Golden Greats*, released in Britain at the same time was similarly successful. The Beach Boys' commercial renaissance was finally coming to pass. Yet all those new found converts wanted to know just one thing: where was Brian Wilson?

In other words, the Beach Boys needed Wilson to truly cement this rediscovered fervour. To this end a psychiatrist was employed to draw him out of his shell and get him back to the piano, where it was presumed he would again bash out new compositions as if all those years lost in some psychic twilight zone had never really existed. This psychiatrist, Eugene Landy by name, thought he'd achieve all this by instigating a programme of bullying tactics. He bullied Wilson into acting the role of "responsible member of society"; bullied him into writing songs, bullied him into going on stage with the group (even though Wilson's natural shyness of live shows had originally triggered the first of a number of nervous breakdowns); and bullied him even into performing humiliating solo performances on network US television. To get full mileage out of this specious ploy, Brian was also made to do interviews. Most of them were farcical.

One of the most revealing appeared in *Oui*, where Wilson – who is nothing if not candid stated, "Today I want to go places – but I can't because of the doctor [Landy]. I feel like a prisoner and I don't know where it's going to end ... he would put the police on me if I took off and he'd put me in the funny farm ... I'm just waiting it out, playing along. That's what I'm doing. [Pause.] Do you have any uppers?" (In most of these interviews Wilson would deliver maybe twenty minutes of badly remembered facts before asking his interrogator for cocaine or speed and then suddenly claim to be feeling ill before skulking back to his room.) His presence on stage with the Beach Boys was equally painful to behold. Terrified, he couldn't sing properly and his piano playing and occasional bass work were rarely in sync with the song. The band simply and corruptly used their extremely confused former leader in order to make themselves more money.

The public was briefly fooled into going along with this whole sick charade, but soon enough it back fired on the group. *15 Big Ones*, the album around which the whole "Brian's Back" campaign was constructed, went gold but was such a wretched piece of product it turned innumerable Beach Boys fans – old and new – against this shoddy, over promoted soap opera of a group. Utterly uninspired and weary sounding, the album was clearly intended only as therapy for Wilson's long dormant production talents. Through pressure and greed it was released, resulting in both Carl and Dennis publicly airing their grievances and criticisms.

The superior 1977 follow up, *The Beach Boys Love You*, was what the record should have been in that it actually contained twelve new Brian Wilson songs. Unfortunately, bad feeling within the group meant that Brian Wilson and Carl were the only two Beach Boys featured on the record at all; and to compound misfortune, the group's plan to leave Warners and go with Epic / CBS was discovered just before the release of *Love You* and so the record consequently got negligible exposure, condemning it to meagre sales.

The group's inner relationship quickly deteriorated into two rival factions: Mike Love and Al Jardine's grotesque transcendental meditation versus the increasingly spaced out Carl and Dennis with the hapless Brian as prized pawn in the middle. This backstabbing antipathy reached its climax in '78 when Love and Jardine tried to sack Dennis and so make Carl's clout within the group ineffectual. Somehow a compromise was reached, but the dreadful *M.I.U. Album* – the band's final Warners release – was instigated by Love and Jardine. Both critics and the record buying public alike ignored the product's pitiful contents.

In 1979 there was an uneasy truce with the release of the *LA Album* beginning the band's contract for Caribou (CBS). With this record Bruce Johnston returned, having been ousted eight years earlier, and took on the producer's mantle to juggle together a collection of songs spotlighting all five members in equal portions. In other words, it was more mediocre pop, even including an extended disco re jig of "Here Comes the Night" that the group felt obliged to apologize for whenever they performed it live.

After the group had experienced the terrible wrath of CBS president Walter Yetnikoff ("Gentlemen, I think I've just been fucked" was his opening remark to them at the meeting), they went in to record *Keepin' Summer Alive*, another album mostly given over to new Brian Wilson songs, but the critics had become so irritated by the group and their constant, tacky bickering that most reviews slammed it more out of instinct than anything else.

At least Schilling and the record company seemed finally to be facing up to all these prejudices. Consequently a vigorous promotional push had begun, with everything from Carl Wilson's earnest claims in *Rolling Stone* ("Remember that slogan, 'Brian's back'? Well, Brian wasn't back then. But now he's really back!") to a TV special entitled *Going Platinum*, a grotesque and fawning documentary of the *Keepin' The Summer Alive* sessions about to be broadcast all across America. Needing to attract an audience for several huge concerts set for Britain that autumn, Schilling was craving some serious column inches in the UK media. That's where I came into the picture.

Not that I was feeling too comfortable with any aspect of the upcoming journey. Back in 1975 I'd written a 30,000 word profile of Brian Wilson for the *NME*, using much of the information and many of the quotes gathered in these preceding pages. [The author is here referring to the revised version of the *NME* pieces appearing as parts 1 and 2 of "The Last Beach Movie Revisited: The Life of Brian Wilson" in *The Dark Stuff*.] The Beach Boys had hated it and had instigated a long drawn out communication breakdown with the paper lasting a number of years. Bruce Johnston even went so far as to state in a rival music paper that Brian Wilson had read the articles in question and had become suicidally depressed as a direct result. So did the group know I was coming over to do this interview, or was it some sort of set up?

I finally boarded the plane to Los Angeles a day late (but that's another story). Fifteen arduous hours later I was just checking into the hotel when the English press officer approached me with bad news to report. Two other writers had already done interviews, not at Brian's house, but at the Beach Boys' offices. There, a wild eyed and anxious looking Wilson had been surrounded by brother Carl, manager Schilling and about five other record company people silently scrutinizing his every nervous twitch. One guy from a British Sunday paper got twenty minutes of halting, stammered quotes punctuated by an array of embarrassing silences. Another from a music journal got maybe five minutes, most of them catatonic, before Wilson jumped up and ran out of the room, never to return. Both journalists still claimed to be fans of his music, but both were quite adamant they never wanted to find themselves in the same room as Brian Wilson again for as long as they lived.

Now the press officer was apologetically explaining that it was looking unlikely that Wilson would in fact do that promised "definitive" interview with me. As I'd suspected, Bruce Johnston had not been alerted to my arrival until the very last minute and was now apparently in hysterics, berating manager Schilling with terrible warnings about the possible consequences of my encountering Wilson. So what was I supposed to do? Well, first thing tomorrow there was to be a screening of a new Beach Boys promotional film. And then, later in the day, I too was to be "screened".

"Hey, honey, do you remember the time that guy at the airport said to Brian, 'Don't you get tired of being referred to as a genius?' Brian just stared at him, shrugged his shoulders and said 'No.'" Carl Wilson looks at his girlfriend for confirmation. "Oh yeah," she laughs back. "Uh, didn't he say, 'Nah, it doesn't bother me'? Something like that anyway."

At four in the afternoon Carl Wilson has been talking for, well, goodness gracious, it's been almost two hours about the Beach Boys. Just one hour later singer Mike Love will storm into the office and scream in a very loud voice to Schilling and the girl at the switchboard (who's actually Priscilla Presley's younger sister and who can't tell one Beach Boy from another, "It's the beards," she tells me) that, goddammit, let the press get a good look at all the group's dirty linen. Hell, let them see for themselves that Brian's a vegetable, that Dennis is a drugged out no talent parasite (who we've sacked) and that the only guys on the ball here are cleanliving talent free Al Jardine. And Mike of course. But this kind of outburst ... Well, it's just not Carl's style at all. Dubbed "the Henry Kissinger of the group" by Schilling, he understands the power of diplomacy. In fact, he's a master at the art of the inscrutable understatement. Most of the time he fields questions some innocuous, some rather more weighty, using his natural technique of "Gee, yeah. I can see your point but you've got to understand I'm just an easy going kinda guy and hey, that's just the way it is" self effacement. Very occasionally he lets the mask slip a little and an utterly cynical chuckle slices through the veneer. Carl and I are playing a game called "tactics", or more specifically "How do I prove myself inoffensive enough to get a shot at interviewing Brian Wilson?" The judge is Jerry Schilling, who sits quietly at his desk just a few feet away, well within earshot. Both he and Carl exercise that precious right of access to the eldest Wilson brother who, although officially "suffering from a bug he's pretty sick", will be wheeled out if the conditions prove conducive enough. I play my role close to the chest with three fairly innocuous questions to one actual "relevant" query. The latter category involves thorny issues like the uneasy truce 'twixt the two Love/Jardine and Wilson factions, the reasons for Dennis Wilson's current absence (too much cocaine, but Carl doesn't tell me that) and, of course, the subject of Brian Wilson.

The dialogue always returns to Brian. The recent *Rolling Stone* quote regarding his eldest brother's full creative resurgence with the music on *Keepin' The Summer Alive* is mentioned, along with a reference to the dreaded Dr Landy. Carl dodges the latter topic altogether, remarking with a certain strained nonchalance that, "Back then [1976] maybe it should have read 'Brian's almost back'." He smiles to himself, then quickly adds, "No, but Brian's real well now. I mean, he's totally into playing live. Don't you recall" he turns to his girlfriend again "Brian saying, 'Being on the road is my real home. It's my whole life now.'" She nods.

"Yeah, right! Brian's so into touring. He's always there in the office asking Jerry when we're playing."

Had this new attitude towards touring come about because of Brian's recent separation from his wife Marilyn? After fifteen years the marriage had just recently collapsed, with his former spouse filing for divorce and taking their two daughters with her.

Carl simply evades the issue yet again. "It's hard to say just how that's affected Brian, y'know. But Marilyn brought Wendy and Carnie to a gig in San Diego not long ago."

Talking about what's emphatically known as "Brian's problem", Carl continues, "He's coping much, much better. I don't know. Maybe it was a bad acid trip he took that caused all this inner turmoil. That's what I figure, y'know. But, like I said, he's so much better now. He's back into his music and he's ... he's on this big health kick. He's got these hot tubs in his new house, a jacuzzi, sauna . . . you name it."

Finally, our two hours have passed. "Wow, that went really fast. Enjoyed talking to you," Carl remarks, ever Mr Sincerity. Schilling hovers and I request a short interview. And so he talks in a somewhat disconcerting whisper mainly about himself. Previously he worked for Elvis Presley, first as a stuntman and stand-in when Elvis couldn't make it on to the set and later working for Presley's manager, Colonel Tom Parker. He remarks that Parker and he are still close – that the latter's offices are a mere two doors away.

"I figured when Elvis died that the Beach Boys were the next biggest legend in American music," he opines. And he talks about re-establishing the Beach Boys "as a real contemporary American music phenomenon ... I think the Colonel's mistake was to keep Elvis too cloistered away from his audience."

Also, there's the idea of movies. Schilling is really into film production and is currently working with Parker on an Elvis tribute. The final touch comes when Schilling mentions that he also wants to do a film of the Beach Boys. Even now a script is being written by the same guy who wrote the Elvis film.

"Nothing's certain yet but we were thinking of maybe getting Jeff Bridges to play Brian."

Fade. Cut.

We leave the Beach Boys' office at five in the afternoon. I've played every wild card I can pull out of my sleeve. Schilling just nods silently. He'll see what he can do, he promises. Two hours later I'm informed that we'll be driving over to Brian Wilson's house in half an hour. Schilling simply asked to keep the interview short as Brian needs to get to bed early to be fresh for a business meeting the next day.

In the final years of the hellzapoppin' sixties, when he was the hermit recluse living in Bel Air with his sand box and purple meditation tent, Brian Wilson wrote and recorded an absurd little song entitled "Busy Doin' Nothing" in which he gave the listener exact directions to his house: just drive down Santa Monica, take a left on Sunset, a few more detours and there he'd be, waiting for you standing by the gates of his mansion. Times and locations change. It takes us an hour to find Wilson's new house. An emergency stop at a country club up in the hills finally gives us the right direction and we duly arrive at a small, unimpressive two bedroom Spanish style building located well off the beaten track out past Santa Monica.

From the car you could already make out Brian Wilson's bulky silhouette through the bay windows. A black woman with fiery eyes opens the door to us (us being the press officer, a photographer and myself) and we walk into a totally unfurnished living room. Right away, something is very wrong here. Wilson, who must weigh at least 280 pounds, is eating a vegetarian salad, a fork in one hand and a cigarette in the other. He awkwardly begins trying to play the genial host. He apologizes for the starkness of the house and clumsily goes around shaking hands. Obviously ill at ease, his discomfort is instantly contagious.

"Uh ... yeah, now who's doin' the interview? Oh, you! Oh! [Laughs self consciously.] OK, man ... uh [he stops to look at me.] Say, how old are you? Twenty eight ... Wow, I'm thirty seven. Maybe I should interview you. you look more like a rock star than me." He lets forth a disconcerting bellow, then checks himself.

For my part, at this precise juncture I'm willing to strike up any sort of rapport with Wilson, whose sense of discomfort is becoming ever more imposing. I remark that Carl just mentioned that this new house is fitted out with hot tubs, a health spa and a ... (I start stammering out the word) jacuzzi.

"Jacuzzi?" The word seems to totally unnerve him for an instant.

"Jacuzzi??" He looks first mystified, then quite horrified.

"Jacuzzi???" Then suddenly he leaps up off the couch on which he's been slumped. He is a very, very big man.

"Hey! I'll show ya something really great about this place. Wanna see it?" He immediately motions towards the large bay windows. "This is really neat," he says, sounding like an excitable little kid about to show his parents a brand new party trick. Then he simply opens the windows and gestures out at the night.

"See? Air! Fresh air! Ummm! Healthy!! Let's keep 'em open, yeah?" He breathes in and out, vigorously. "Ummmmm ... Neat! Outasight! . . . Healthy!"

Brian slumps back on to the couch, and it's only then that I suddenly notice the presence of a third party in the room.

"Oh ... this is Diane," he mutters by way of an introduction to his blonde companion, who looks about sixteen. Actually, her real name is Debbie, but I won't find that out tonight because she won't bother to correct Brian, so absorbed is she in maintaining this vacant, bedazzled grin on her face, even during those excruciating moments when her beloved Brian's own face is contorted with pain. She looks exactly like a Robert Altman version of an acid casualty waitress working in a health food restaurant, except Altman would probably end up naming her Starchild or Munchkin. This vision of inane serenity – all teeth and cut off jeans – beams forth throughout the interview. I find myself wondering just what she and Wilson must talk about when they're alone, and then shudder at the thought.

"OK, fire away." Another awkward chuckle.

So I start by asking him about some of the songs he wrote just prior to *Pet Sounds*, but, before I get the first sentence out, Wilson is looking pained. Then he speaks.

"Hey, emotional! Wow, all those are so emotional! Maybe too ... No, I forget ... Yeah, when you make music that emotional it can really get to you, y'know."

Before I can ask another question, he starts going off on weird tangents. First, he wants to know all about Paul McCartney's recent drug bust in Japan, suddenly seguing into comments like, "Say, what's the weather like over in England? Boy, I'm lookin' forward to comin' over. I haven't been to London since ... oh, wow

... 1964! Yeah, wow! Long time." (I don't bother to remind him that he and the Beach Boys played London in 1977 at a CBS convention.)

With a small transistor radio placed next to the couch – the only sign of music in this desolate room – blaring out some anonymous AM hit as we speak, I ask Wilson if he listens to the radio a lot. Does he check out new sounds?

"No, I've only been listening to the radio for a week," he replies, sounding suddenly very melancholy. "Ever since the new album's been out. Haven't heard it played much. Don't know why! Seems like we're going through a real bad spell."

Wilson keeps referring to "we" constantly, presumably meaning the Beach Boys. Considering that he spent much of the seventies in exile from the group and at one point tried to break all ties with them, I enquire whether he still views his musical career in any terms beyond those of the Beach Boys. Once again he looks pained, then pensive.

"No, not at all. It's all I've got, y'know. The group."

So what gives him the most pleasure in life?

"Well, I'll tell ya one thing," he blurts out aggressively. "I'm not into women anymore." Then he pauses. "Music probably. Yeah, definitely. I like to sit down at the piano, y'know. Playing those chords. I love the way they look.

"Plus playing live ... that's the biggest thrill. It's real spiritual."

When I ask him to define the term "spiritual" a little better, he looks at me as if I'm completely crazy. By now the pauses are getting longer and the photographer's camera clicking is causing Wilson to flinch automatically as if torturous electric shocks were being triggered through his central nervous system. He keeps struggling to articulate himself but at the same time it's so obvious he is in terrible psychic pain. Certain references to his past suddenly make him visibly shudder. I name a song from the new album that I particularly like and he literally screams.

"I hate that song! I hate that song!"

So why did you put it on the record?

"I didn't," he stammers. "Bruce ..."

This is becoming steadily more and more horrific. So we talk about ego – something Wilson once had in excess and now claims to be utterly devoid of.

"Yeah, I used to be real competitive," he shudders. "Not anymore, though. Ego can be dangerous. All that drive can destroy you. It almost killed me. It almost drove me insane."

Wilson is now chain smoking, flicking the ash into his halfeaten salad. Occasionally he digs a fork into the mess of chopped vegetables and cigarette ash and puts it in his mouth. When he is coherent, he talks like a man drowning in all the sorrow that this world can visit on one lost and sorry soul. This is what he has to say:

"I don't see my mother much. She doesn't like the Beach Boys. Not since father died ... My father and I, we never got on. He used to come down really hard on me. We used to fight all the time ... No, I don't see anything for me beyond the Beach Boys. It's like they're all I got, y'know ... No, I don't want to make a solo record. I just don't see myself making music as strong as most of the old stuff ever again.

Why, I keep asking back.

"Why? I don't know why. You dry up, I guess. It's like ..."

Suddenly he shudders again, this time buckling over as if about to vomit violently. But nothing comes out. So instead he leaps up from the couch as though on fire and starts to stammer out an apology.

"I-I-I ... I'm sorry. I-I ... I feel real tired. It's late and I've got to see my psychiatrist real early tomorrow. M-maybe we can talk some more then."

So, finally, I've got my Brian Wilson interview. All thirty minutes of it. Feeling numb, somewhat nauseous myself and desperate for fresh air, I walk straight out of the house to the waiting car. As I look back, I see the press officer standing staring at the house. He is quite speechless and will remain that way for the rest of the night. Meanwhile, the equally stunned photographer can't stop himself taking useless shots of the empty living-room from the outside of the house. Seated in the back seat for the long return journey, I start feeling like an utter parasite for having intruded upon Brian Wilson's private hell. Then I snap out of it, go back to the hotel and start to write this story.

Holy Man and Slow Booze: Dennis Wilson
by Peter Doggett

It is wrong to think of the Beach Boys as entirely a vehicle for Brian Wilson. All the various members have added worthwhile and lasting music to the band's catalogue over the years, but it is the work of Dennis which has made the most lasting impression. In all things, Dennis went his own way, and this new piece by Record Collector *editor Peter Doggett explores his highly individual artistic growth.*

"I'll never make the headlines or the evening news", Dennis Wilson sang in 1977. Six years later, he drowned at the age of 39. He was, so the papers said, the original Beach Boy, a golden child of the sea and sun trapped by the natural world he loved. In the second wave of stories, the mood darkened – he was an addict, a bum, a drunkard, a serial womaniser, a one man dissipation of those good vibrations.

Neither strand quite caught the real man. What they missed was his soul, obvious to anyone who ever saw him wield a drumstick, throwing his body into every beat. But ultimately no one knew Dennis Wilson who didn't know his music. The Beach Boys were Brian Wilson's band, and Dennis, after all, was only the drummer. But the same spark of flawed genius that powered Brian also touched Dennis. In fact, for a decade between 1969 and 1979, it was Dennis, not Brian, who was the prime creative force in the Beach Boys. But nobody cared to recognise the fact – least of all his colleagues in the band.

The Wilson boys were a study in fraternal isolation. If his elder brother Brian had the aura of an eternal child, while youngest sibling Carl was born with the brain of a middle aged diplomat, Dennis swaggered like an adolescent kingpin. He was, as Beach Boys myth recounts, the only surfer in the band, a party animal who seemed to belong on the beach, with a trail of flaxen-haired beauties in his wake.

Dennis shrugged off the endless arguments that constituted his relationship with his father, Murry, emerging battered but not outwardly scarred. Brian switched between challenging and trying to pacify his dad; Dennis rode the punches with the assurance of a man who knew that his true kingdom awaited outdoors.

While Brian and Carl watched enviously, Dennis straddled a surfboard with ease, attracted a flock of eager jock disciples, and captured the heart of every teenage girl in Southern California. His passion for the sun, the sea and the surf inadvertently transformed the lives of all three brothers. When Brian Wilson began to compose songs in the early 60s, Dennis suggested that Brian should write about him and his friends. The eldest sibling thought himself into the mindset of his athletic junior, and the Beach Boys' career was born. Not that Dennis was envisaged as any kind of musician. His husky baritone voice lacked the fluidity, grace and range of his brothers', so when Brian and Carl Wilson, their cousin Mike Love and Brian's school pal Al Jardine first discussed forming a band, Dennis was never in the frame. "I begged them to let him join," mother Audrey Wilson revealed years later. "Brian and Mike didn't want him, but they agreed, purely for my sake."

"If there wasn't the Beach Boys," Dennis admitted years later, "and there wasn't music, I would not even talk to my brothers. But through the music I fell in love with them." And America fell in love with Dennis Wilson, who was sidelined as the (virtually non-singing) drummer, but still garnered more teen admiration and lust than the rest of the band combined. Pulled down front to sing "The Wanderer" or "Do You Wanna Dance", Dennis was bathed in pre-orgasmic screams. He quickly accepted them as his birthright.

In the studio, his influence in the early years was minimal. Sessionmen usually handled the drums, and his voice was buried deep in the harmony stack. But his untutored style gave "Do You Wanna Dance" an insistent power, and on the same album, *The Beach Boys Today*, he showed for the first time an awareness that his voice could be a blunt emotional instrument. On "In The Back Of My Mind", his erratic croon cut straight to the heart, with an urgency that his more precise brothers could never have matched.

During the creation of *Pet Sounds*, "Good Vibrations" and *Smile*, Dennis was effectively absent as a creative presence. But no musical contribution could have been as vital as his unstinting support of his brother Brian. While Mike Love, Murry Wilson and Capitol Records competed to undermine Brian's confidence in his expanded musical imagination, Dennis forcefully backed him every inch of the way. A decade later, his faith hadn't wavered: "Brian Wilson is the Beach Boys. He is the band. We're his fucking messengers. He is all of it. Period. We're nothing. He's everything ."

Ironically, the intervening years had suggested quite the opposite. After 1967, Brian Wilson gradually eased himself out of the band's creative loop, shadowing their sessions from an upstairs room and occasionally gracing his brothers with a song fragment or a harmony line. Every single member of the Beach Boys responded to the challenge, but none with such flair and – whisper it – genius, as Dennis.

A 1963 drum showcase aside, Dennis's first real songwriting surfaced on 1968's *Friends*. Amidst the album's lazy serenades to domestic bliss, he and co-writer Steve Kalinich prepared two gentle vignettes – "Little Bird", and the mantra like "Be Still". Half ancient wisdom, half romantic sweet talk, "Be Still" was a duet for the barest of organ parts and Dennis' inexpressibly tender and fragile voice. "Your life is meant for joy", he sang. "It's all so deep within." It was a philosophy he carried to his dying day.

Over the next two years, he became the Beach Boys' most expressive voice. Though rowdy rockers like "All I Want To Do" (*20/20*) and "Got To Know The Woman" (*Sunflower*) expressed nothing more than his lust for life (and wife), his other work on those albums opened multiple windows on his soul.

"Be With Me" on 1969's *20/20* was his first orchestral epic. While Brian painted with delicate brush strokes, Dennis's approach was a splash of technicolour, emotionally overpowering. Its dramatic flourish added a psychic dimension to a lyric that was little more than mundane.

What had unshackled Dennis's artistic spirit? Drugs, certainly, plus close proximity to brother Brian, but also his involvement with the man he called "The Wizard" – cult leader, ex-criminal and budding Beach Boys songwriter Charles

Manson. Dennis was entranced by Manson's psychological power, especially when it involved carnal knowledge of a coven of eager young women.

It was the era for quasi religious gurus, and to Wilson, the slight but commanding Manson offered a more attractive fantasy than the Maharishi, who'd entranced the rest of the Beach Boys. Neither was Manson the talentless psychopath beloved of journalists. Though his songs were lyrically one dimensional, he could weave an enticing melody line.

For a cash sum, which kept the guru's commune in drugs and food, Dennis bought the rights to Manson's "Cease To Exist". With the mildest of rewrites, it emerged on *20/20* as "Never Learn Not To Love" without a mention of its original composer.

Even in augmented form, "Never Learn Not To Love" bore an unrelenting message – its audience commanded to "give up your world" and reminded that "submission is a gift". And whereas the Beach Boys' music customarily evoked the emotions of the heart, Wilson's ominous, overpowering production conveyed a menace previously unheard in their work. Six months after the song was released, members of Manson's "family" committed a series of brutal murders in Hollywood. Thereafter, Dennis Wilson refused ever to discuss his friend again.

Its chilling aftermath aside, the "Never Learn Not To Love" saga taught Dennis another lesson: the visceral power of music. He unleashed another torrent of sound at the end of the disarmingly cheerful "Celebrate The News", a 1969 B side. But it was 1970's *Sunflower* that confirmed him as a talent to rival, if not match, Brian's.

His "Slip on Through" introduced this most luscious of Beach Boys albums, with a surge into falsetto that was both erratic and soulful. "Forever" was the killer, though. Co-written with his friend Gregg Jakobson, it set up a mood of utter melancholy, juxtaposed with lyrics of romantic idealism – all the more poignant because you knew that they'd be in vain. In 1983, the song provided a fitting epitaph for its creator: "If every song I sing could fill your heart with joy, I'd sing forever".

The summer of *Sunflower* also brought the first genuine Beach Boys solo record – Brian's "Caroline No" in 1966 having been merely a marketing ploy to pull two singles off *Pet Sounds* simultaneously. "Sound of Free" was credited to Dennis Wilson and Rumbo, the latter an alias for keyboardist Daryl Dragon, who later scored a run of hits himself with The Captain And Tennille.

But the most remarkable aspect of this compelling but unassuming track was its composer credit: Dennis Wilson/Mike Love. Brotherly love might have cemented the Beach Boys for more than three decades, but there was little family feeling between these two cousins. "Dennis is not a kind of person who you can give another chance to," Mike Love reflected in the late 70s, "he's not the kind of person who's trustworthy". "I hope the bad karma will fuck up Mike's meditation forever," Dennis replied. But three times in the 70s, the pair did manage to collaborate on songs of passion and beauty.

In a more generous mood, Love once noted that Dennis "did come up with some good melodies and great moments. Feelings were his strong suit, I think." All of Dennis's work in the early 70s took feelings as its touchstone. In the chaos that surrounded the compilation of *Sunflower*, one song remained a constant: "Fallin' In Love", which (retitled "Lady") eventually emerged as the flipside of "Sound of Free". It might have backed Mike Love's judgement that "he was not verbally facile", but the pained splendour of the music, and Dennis's eternally soulful voice, belied any lyrical flaws.

"Sound of Free" and "Lady" were feelers for a project that could have altered the course of Beach Boys history: a Dennis Wilson solo album. "Dennis is into strings and things," Mike Love noted at the time. "He wants to do classical things." Or romantic things, to be closer to the truth, as the bulk of the material that Dennis composed around 1970/71 comprised heartbroken ballads, supported by overpowering string arrangements.

Like his brother Carl, Dennis had also fallen under the spell of the Moog synthesiser. "What I want to do," he explained, "is instead of renting a bell for $10, to try to get a bell sound with the Moog – or the sound of a snail crawling, or the noise a liver would make inside an alcoholic. But it takes time. I've only been at it a year."

The Beach Boys had long been augmenting their personnel on record and stage with session musicians, and when Dennis stuck his hand through a plate glass window in 1971, severing vital nerves, his career as the group's drummer was halted. 'I can't play any more," he revealed. "The last song I'll ever play drums on is 'Riot'" – alias "Student Demonstration Time" on *Surf's up*. Working separately from the rest of the group, Dennis had several tracks finished in time for that summer 1971 album. But after an argument about the sequencing of the record with Carl, he held them back for his solo project. Lost in action were "4th of July", an overblown paean to Independence Day, and "Carry Me Home", an agonising evocation of the death of an American soldier in the Vietnam War.

It might have been the moment to quit the band for good, but as ever in the Beach Boys' saga, blood triumphed over artistic ambition. For the moment, the solo album was quietly abandoned. Unable to drum, Dennis wandered desultorily round the stage of their early 70s shows, playing some rudimentary keyboard and chipping in an occasional harmony. But as his contributions to 1972's *Carl And The Passions: So Tough* showed, his vision was way out of kilter with the rest of the band.

"Make It Good" and "Cuddle Up" were extravaganzas of doomed romanticism, with Dennis's cracked voice just another instrument of emotional turmoil in a huge orchestral arrangement. They were magnificent epics, explorations of the heart in sound, but they had little connection with the R&B based material that dominated the album.

During 1972, Beach Boys manager Jack Rieley enticed the band to tape their next record in Holland – which duly became its title. While Brian Wilson remained defiantly on the fringes of the project, Dennis set one of Rieley's Americana lyrics to music ("Steamboat"), and revived his unlikely partnership with Mike Love on the plaintive, compelling ballad, "Only With You".

It proved to be the last time in which Dennis took an active creative role in a Beach Boys album project. As the group stepped back from the present into the comforting warmth of the past, and reinvented themselves as a touring oldies band, he recognised that his musical ambitions could only be satisfied outside of the family concern. That didn't preclude him from singing with the Beach Boys (indeed, his rapidly coarsening growl was all over the 1977 album, *Love You*), but his songs were saved for himself.

From 1973 to the end of the decade, Dennis divided his time unequally between hedonistic delights (notably a growing cocaine habit which stripped away any remaining smoothness in his voice) and exploratory studio sessions in Los Angeles. Gregg Jakobson was a constant companion for the latter, with Carl Wilson also lending regular support. Dennis's longest lasting wife, Karen Lamm, helped him write lyrics, while he also enlisted collaborative help from a young songwriter called Jim Dutch, for whom Dennis was supposedly producing an album.

In the summer of 1977, when the Beach Boys were racked by internal conflict and Brian Wilson's all too obvious traumas, Dennis finally released the solo album he'd been threatening since 1970: *Pacific Ocean Blue*. It was a stunning record – an effect felt by none more deeply than his fellow Beach Boys. In particular, Mike Love and Al Jardine were said to be jealous that it was the least committed of the group's original members who should be winning critical plaudits, at a time when the Beach Boys' own stock was falling fast.

Like the group's effort that year, *The Beach Boys Love You*, *Pacific Ocean Blue* was a unified suite of songs. Unlike *Love You*, it sounded like the work of a mature, albeit deeply emotional, adult. The album was awash with musical subtleties worthy of Brian at his peak – delicate beds of vocal harmonies, rich swathes of bass harmonica, cello, or bassoon – but the weight was carried by that most fragile of instruments, Dennis Wilson's voice. Anything beyond a single quavering octave was now out of his range, but the emotional impact of his ragged crooning more than compensated.

"River Song", awash with rich layers of harmony, and "Pacific Ocean Blues" were laments for the spoilation of nature, but the bulk of the album was devoted to the subject that perennially teased at Dennis's mind – the impossibility of love. It pervaded the record with an air of bittersweet melancholy, all the more poignant after 1983. Everywhere, there were hints of elegy – in "Farewell My Friend" and "End of The Show", most obviously, but elsewhere in the images of death, loss and parting that seemed to bind the record together.

Pacific Ocean Blue charted briefly in the States, but its biggest impact was on the Beach Boys community – the band themselves, their entourage, and their most loyal fans. With Brian slipping back into self-destruction, and all of Carl's energies turned towards the group's very survival, Dennis seemed to be the last bastion of the Wilson brothers' idealism.

His artistic dominance would have been even more evident if the Beach Boys had been allowed to release their disastrous *Merry Christmas* album in 1977 – for which Dennis had composed the gorgeous "Holy Evening", which combined the textures of *Smile* with the spirituality of Brian's "Till I Die".

The following spring, work began on a second solo album, provisionally entitled *Bamboo*. Besides the songs left over from the *Pacific Ocean Blue* sessions – "Tug of Love", "Taking Off", "School Girl", "Time For Bed", "10,000 Years" and "Holy Man And Slow Booze", to name but a few – Dennis had composed a batch of material with his friend Carly Munoz.

If *Pacific Ocean Blue* was a cry from the soul, then *Bamboo* would have been a celebration of Dennis's other preoccupation, the body. "Companion" sizzled to a rich Latin disco score; "Wild Situation" was a baffled and finally obscene story of desire; the revived "School Girl" paraded Dennis's lust to the world.

But the spectre of loss was never far away. "Baby Blue Eyes" and "It's Not Too Late" both borrowed the angelic voice of Carl Wilson as counterpoint to their composer's gruff tones: desperately sad, they lifted the spirit and then drowned it in the same expansive motion. Only on "Love Surrounds Me" did romance, rather than sex, seem to offer any consolation.

The manic powerplay that afflicted the Beach Boys in 1978 briefly saw Dennis sacked from the band; then the Wilsons regained dominance, and as a gesture of fraternal love, Dennis gave "Baby Blue Eyes" and "Love Surrounds Me" to the group, for the ill fated but often inspired L.A. (*Light Album*).

With that gift, *Bamboo* died. So, too, did Dennis's active involvement as a Beach Boy. His final years were an ongoing crisis – doomed romantic flings, culminating in his marriage to none other than Mike Love's daughter; binges on drink and drugs, followed by desperate vows of abstinence; and a refusal to accept responsibility for his own life, let alone those of his brothers.

Thrown out of the group one last time, he grasped at the lifeline of self restraint, and reappeared for some final shows in the summer of 1983. His athletic frame was now bloated, his eyes puffy and distant, his voice a hollow rasp; but he could still stagger to the microphone to deliver a valedictory chorus of "You Are So Beautiful" to his loyal fans.

That December, he was drinking, laughing with friends and diving for booty from a boat in Marina Del Ray, California. Several times he resurfaced with keepsakes from his own boat, which had sunk in the harbour. Then he dived again, and never came back. For years he'd surfed in, and sung about, that ocean; now it reclaimed him as its own. The original Beach Boy was dead: so were the Beach Boys.

Requiem for the Beach Boy
by David Leaf

If Brian Wilson represented the musical heart of The Beach Boys, then Dennis Wilson was the band's spirit. His full frontal attack on life showed a way that perhaps many of us would like to, but dare not, follow. David Leaf's affectionate and moving piece, which originally was adapted from an article in BAM (Bay Area Music)*, was included in the 2nd edition of his book* The Beach Boys and the California Myth *published in 1985.*

In November 1983, after the Beach Boys' opening night concert at the Universal Amphitheatre, I spoke with Brian Wilson backstage. During a long conversation, Brian asked me whether I liked the way the group had performed "Surfer Girl." As their harmonies had been mediocre, and as I've never deliberately hurt Brian's ultrasensitive feelings, my answer was evasive. But it was also the truth.

"Brian, I don't know why, but it was on that song that I missed Dennis the most. You know, the way he stands at the microphone, with his hand in his ear, his eyes closed, singing and swaying with the music. It's just not the same when he's not there."

Dennis would never perform with the Beach Boys again. He died just a month later, weeks after his thirty-ninth birthday. And if you had seen Dennis in the last year, his death really wasn't a surprise.

I last saw him in April 1983 at the Meadowlands Arena in New Jersey. It was obvious that something serious was wrong. He could barely speak, let alone sing, and his once muscular surfer's body seemed doughy. Describing it to friends, I called it "beer bloat."

Whatever the L.A. County Coroner ultimately concludes, my feeling is that Dennis's death wasn't from alcohol or drug abuse so much as a cumulative overdose of life. Nobody I've ever known lived a more intense existence. When Dennis Wilson worked, it was nonstop, for days at a time until he would collapse from exhaustion on a studio control room couch. And when he played – well, let's just say that in recent years, he was more a "player" than a worker.

The night he died, a South Bay newspaper reporter asked me to characterise Dennis. I told him that Dennis's most fascinating personality facet was his intense curiosity. Dennis wanted to know everything through experience, and he attacked life with a combination of blind faith and childlike innocence. He lived his life with a freshness and vitality, all that really mattered was this one, wonderful moment of now. Dennis was a perpetual bad child, but he could always win your forgiveness with his smile.

Incredibly, it was not an act. Dennis had never been taught how to deceive people, and he was genuine. In his dealings with the media, Dennis was easily the most candid and revealing member of his family and the group. A rare combination – intensity and honesty; and Dennis didn't lie – except maybe to himself. As with Keith Moon and other dead rock stars, chronology is relatively meaningless. Dennis Wilson lived more life in a month than most people do in a lifetime; we need not feel badly just because he died so young. We mourn not only for his youth but the waste. He had much to give, and he only tapped a fraction of that. On albums like *Sunflower*, Dennis bloomed, and his emotional artistry would later see its first (and last) major expression on his impressive debut album, *Pacific Ocean Blue*. His music was adult and maturing, and there was the promise of more to come. Sadly, he never really knew how much his music was appreciated.

Dennis seemed uncomfortable with his talent (who wouldn't be, in the shadow of Brian?), and while insisting that his brother "Brian, is the Beach Boys," Dennis overlooked the fact that he, Dennis, was *the* Beach Boy. He, with his sandy hair and winning grin, was the one the girls screamed for.

In his personal life, Dennis acted as if he feared nothing, including death. Some people said he was self-destructive, but from what I saw, Dennis approached almost everything he did as a challenge. Maybe he pushed himself beyond the limit so that he could prove that for himself, there were no limits. And for Dennis, there was so much to try that it was inevitable that he would cross the boundaries of "acceptable behavior."

Not that this is an apologia for Dennis. He could be rude and irresponsible. But when he was sober, Dennis often exhibited to his fans a modest charm and unexpected thoughtfulness. He made everybody he was with think they were the most important person in the world at that single second. He was sincere, but like a child, would move on to a new toy. Maybe worst of all, Dennis didn't know how to say no.

There were qualities he kept hidden, too. Perhaps most moving was the remark one of Dennis's children made after Dennis died. "Mommy," he cried, "things will never be the same again. No one can make me laugh like Daddy can."

When I heard that Dennis had died, I was determined not to dwell on the sadness; and when *BAM Magazine* asked me to write a reflective memoir on what Dennis Wilson meant to California music, I began to flash back to the times when I had seem him or been alone with him. Like the day I had watched him vigorously perform his promotional duties for his pride, *Pacific Ocean Blue*; that night, he took me and a bunch of other writers into Brother Studio to sing on "He's A Bum," teaching us that making records was hard work.

Later that night, Dennis was at the piano in his beachside house. He pounded out "Heroes and Villains" at the piano, and then smoothly and with a musical wink, moved into "River Deep, Mountain High." By three in the morning, he had me writing lyrics to a new song of his. And as the night wore on and I fought sleep, he told me a little about his time with Charles Manson, and the fear he still lived with. As dawn broke, he was on the phone, rousting friends.

There were also the concerts in the early '70s when Dennis would sit at the piano and humbly play his beautiful, haunting love songs like "Barbara" and "I've Got a Friend," as if to say, "I know they're not as good as Brian's, but ..." or at the end of the show, when caught up in the crowd's excitement, he peeled bandages off his hand and jumped onto his rightful perch – the drums.

Possibly my favorite memory is the time he called me at three in the morning. He was reading the book I wrote about the band, [*The Beach Boys and the Californian Myth*], and he had been hurt by something I'd written. He demanded to know the source of a fact. "Dennis," I softly replied, "normally, I wouldn't reveal a source, but in this case, I'll make an exception. Your mother told me that."

Dennis countered with "Why did you listen to her?" We both erupted in laughter. I think that was the last time I spoke with him.

I certainly don't claim to have been a close friend of Dennis Wilson's, but the time I've spent with him and his music has always been precious. I hope that I've absorbed just a little of his spirit. He was *alive*!

In death, I pray he finds his peace.

David Leaf has requested that his fee for this article and his other articles in this book be donated to "Heal The Bay", a local charity that he feels is particularly appropriate for this book. "Heal The Bay" was first formed in the mid-1980s to fight for a swimmable, fishable Santa Monica bay. Now in its second decade, the organization primarily focusses its efforts on enhancing and restoring L.A. County beaches and coastal waters for people and marine life. Those L.A. County beaches, of course, include the legendary "South Bay", where Dennis surfed and the other Beach Boys either did or didn't "catch a wave". To make a donation in Dennis Wilson's memory to the organization, send an IMO to "Heal The Bay", 2701 Ocean Park Boulevard #150, Santa Monica, California 90405, USA.

A Dennis Wilson Discography of Officially Released Material
Album track or single (Dennis' contribution)

"Little Girl (You're My Miss America)"(1)
"Hawaii" (From the Album *Surfer Girl*) (2)
"Surfers Rule" (1)
"This Car of Mine" (1)
"Denny's Drums" (3, drums)
"Auld Lang Syne" (From the *Christmas Album*) (spoken message)
"The Wanderer" (1)
"Do You Wanna Dance" (1)
"In The Back of My Mine" (2)
"You've Got To Hide Your Love Away" (1)
"Little Bird" (1,3,4)
"Be Still" (1,3,4)
"All I Want To Do" (1,3,4)
"Never Learn Not To Love" (1,3,4)
"Celebrate The News" (1,3,4)
"Slip on Through"(1,3,4)
"Got To Know The Woman" (1,3,4)
"It's About Time" (3,4)
"Forever" (1,3,4)
"Sound of Free" (1,3,4)
"Lady" (1,3,4)
"Make It Good" (1,3,4)
"Cuddle Up" (1,3,4)
"Steamboat" (3,4)
"Only With You" (3,4)
"Had To Phone Ya" (2)
"In The Still of The Night" (1)
"Mona" (1)
"I'll Bet He's Nice" (2)
"I Wanna Pick You Up" (2)
"My Diane" (1)
"Angel Come Home" (1)
"Love Surrounds Me" (1,3,4)
"Baby Blue" (1,3,4)
"San Miguel" (3,4)
"Sea Cruise" (1)

Albums:
Pacific Ocean Blue (1,3,4)

Key: 1 Lead vocal by Dennis, 2 Lead vocal partly by Dennis, 3 Written or co-written by Dennis, 4 Produced or co-produced by Dennis

PART THREE

Hang On To Your Ego

Writing With The Wilsons
An Interview With Steve Kalinich
by Kingsley Abbott

Most people with more than a passing interest in the Beach Boys are aware that many of their best known songs were written with the help of outside lyricists. Tony Asher's work on Pet Sounds *and Van Dyke Parks' work on* Smile *have been well documented elsewhere, but the collaborative contribution by Californian poet and lyricist Steve Kalinich, is much less well-known.*

This exclusive interview with Kalinich was conducted in the summer of 1997, and highlights the fact that he was the only songwriter outside the immediate group, to have written with all three Wilson brothers.

KA: How did you first meet and get involved with The Beach Boys?

SK: I was living in the YMCA, and I had a partner named Mark Buckingham and we started writing songs. We wrote a song called "Leaves of Grass" that was inspired by Walt Whitman. Then Arnie Geller from Brother Records heard us and loved the song and the poetry; I wrote a lot of poems back then. Arnie took me to meet Brian Wilson, who loved my stuff so much that Brother decided to sign me. Carl produced that "Leaves of Grass" record at Studio B at Capital. Everyone loved it, but no one wanted to play it because everyone thought it was about marijuana even though I didn't go near the stuff. In the end the song never got released, but it was a lot of fun recording it.

My first encounter was with Dennis, I was the first one ever to write with him. I was like a catalyst, as he'd never finished songs before. We did a lot of songs together. Some of them got recorded, some of them didn't.

When you co-wrote "Little Bird" and "Be Still" with Dennis Wilson, was he specifically trying to move in a different direction to the rest of the band?

No, not at all. Things just came to him. "Be Still" came from a Christmas card I got from a Unity minister that said, "Be still and know that I am God". Dennis and I sat down at the house on Sunset, and I wrote the lyrics. For the music I think he followed the direction of the lyrics and how spiritual and how beautiful it felt, almost like a hymn. Later on, I wrote a poem "Be Still" which I recorded with Brian on a poetry album.

With "Little Bird", I was looking out the window of Dennis's house on Sunset and I saw a little bird in the tree and I got that idea of a little bird up in a tree who looked down and sang the song to me of how it began. I just wrote the lyric and left it on his piano, and six or seven weeks later it was out all over the country! Again I think the musical direction came from Dennis following the lyrics. But one thing about "Little Bird" that is not well known is that Brian added the musical hook to the part that goes, "Where's my pretty bird, he must of flown away; if I keep singing, he'll come back some day." That part, Brian added the musical hook there, but never gave himself credit. He also changed the lyrics around, and never gave himself credit, but I know it's him. He's never said it; it's never been stated publicly, but it just wasn't Dennis' style of doing a hook. So, I'm indebted to Brian, and so was Dennis.

Dennis and I used to sit up in his tree hut and talk about how we would like to change and help influence the world towards world peace, towards helping all of the sick kids in the hospitals and things like that. Despite all the things you read about Dennis, there was that side of him that wanted to give. We did another project later which was called "Life Symphony" which never got released either, but some day I might do something with it.

What was the "modus operandi" of working with Dennis? Who did what?

I did almost all the lyrics; he did almost all the music. The way I worked with Dennis was sometimes he'd pick me up (I was living a motor hotel then) at midnight. I'd throw my blankets in the car and we'd go to the house on Sunset and we'd write all night. We would cruise the streets and go around in a chauffeur-driven brown Rolls, and we'd have a ball. But we also did some great songs, and I used to just recite poems to him. We talked, we walked, and some times Brian, he and I would walk the streets and the piers of Venice, and we just had a great time. We were like brothers. There was never talk about money or success or death. There was only talk about the work, the creativity. They used to love to listen to me recite poetry, which I love doing. I thought it was fantastic.

How did you come to work with Brian and how did it differ from working with Dennis?

Well, Brian heard me do a poem: "The Magic Hand", he loved it so much, we ended up doing a poetry album together called "A World of Peace". He would love to hear me recite poems, and he got the idea to do some background voices and vocals and things like that.

Unfortunately, the album never got released, a lot of people heard it though and Mo Ostin considered putting it out. The way working with Brian differed from Dennis was that Brian let me do all the lyrics without restraint, and he would just sometimes put music to my lyrics rather than have me fill in lyrics to the music. But they both had a great capacity, and neither of them said "It's going to be a hit!" They just went for the real feeling. Dennis, as much as Brian, got in to the classical, the feeling of the beauty of music, and he wanted to influence and change people with music. There were other differences working with them. Dennis was quieter working, not as confident, but he treated it with a reverence, like it was almost God, or spiritual, the way he entered the realm of music. Brian did that, but Brian also had the commercial feel of it. But, I'm not negating what Brian did, because I think he had the other capacity too.

"California Feeling" is one of the best unreleased songs. Can you tell us specifically about the writing of this song?

Well, I wrote the lyrics walking down the beach on a surfing trip to San Onofre. I wrote that lyric and I took it to Brian and we went into the studio and recorded it. We were so excited! There's other verses that I have, and I've added some new ones, and some day I'd love to get Brian to record it, or somebody great to record it. I think it's a great song; you can feel the warmth of the California feeling. I came up with the whole concept, the whole lyrics; the Beach Boys had nothing to do with it, although Brian did like it and identified with it. I have that feeling of

California being open, as being a place where a person can still come and find their identity, express themselves and do something different. This was my intent in writing this song.

Two other songs co-written with Brian were copyrighted on the same day as "California Feeling" on 30th December 1975. They were "You're Riding High on The Music" and "Lucy Jones". What can you tell us about these? Were they recorded?

They were sort of recorded with Brian, but not in a formal kind of way. "You're Riding High On The Music" was a combination of Brian and me. I did all the lyrics, except the part; "Don't tell your Ma, don't tell your Pa." Brian added that. We wanted to record it, but it never saw the full light of day. I always loved that song, and people did want to record it. "Lucy Jones" was (sings) "Woppin' and a boppin' with Lucy Jones. This is the story of Lucy Jones, five foot tall, she's skin and bones. She rides a motorcycle and she rides a Jeep, she's up all night, when everyone else is asleep." Anyway it was just a funky song, and Brian and I were having fun.

How did "Child of Winter" come about?

Brian and I decided we wanted to do a children's song and we somehow combined "Here Comes Santa Claus" with Gene Autry; I came up with this lyric about a child of winter and Brian put music to it, and then we went in to Brother Studio and recorded it. Wendy and Carnie sang background, and I played the kazoo. It was funky, with that crazy voice of Brian's at the end. It was funny at the end, (sings again) "Ding dong ding go the bells," and all that stuff. We just wanted to do a Christmas album. I remember I wanted to release this, but the Beach Boys didn't think there were enough harmonies, and they kind of sabotaged a major release. People never got behind the song, and so the song never really happened big. It got a lot of airplay so Warners told me, but it never got the full promotion, and the Beach Boys never really got behind it. Maybe there should have been more voices, maybe not, but it was a good record. I think it still has a lot of potential, but it never got a chance. It's another one that hasn't seen it's full day, but hopefully one day it can.

What can you tell us about a song written for Pacific Ocean Blue *about Helen Keller? Did Dennis record it?*

I did write a song about Helen Keller, Dennis put music to it, but it never was specifically for *Pacific Ocean Blue*. It was maybe for that album, and it was "She touched me in stillness, no sounds could she hear, no stars could she see, yet she smiled as she walked, as if something within gave her eyes, gave her ears, gave her hope. And I who could see the morning sun rise, and see the ripples in the gentle stream, did not see in life as much as she, could not hear the many silent voices." There were other parts: it was a tribute to her. Dennis loved it and put a beautiful melody to it, which is hidden somewhere in some drawer. Dennis may have had a rough tape of it, but I don't think anyone ever saw it.

The song "Rainbows" (on POB*) was written with Dennis and Carl Wilson, thus making you, I think, the only family outsider to have written with all three Wilson brothers. How did this unusual partnership work?*

Dennis and I wrote "Rainbows"; I guess Carl must have added something after. I did work with Carl too, and yes I think I was the only outsider to write with all three Wilsons. Carl and I had collaborations; he produced "Leaves Of Grass", and he helped me on other things. Carl was always friendly with me, always helpful, always encouraging. I would go to Carl's house, and we would talk about things. We did not write much together, but we did have this one exchange, although our parts were done separately rather than together on this particular song.

Are there any other songs written that we do not know about?

There are many songs written that you do not know about, probably. There are literally hundreds of other songs, and at some other point, when I can jog my memory, we can come up with them.

Are there any other retrospective thoughts that you have about The Beach Boys?

I wish that the direction I was trying to go with "Little Bird" and "Be Still" could have had more support from the group, and I wish I had had more encouragement with the "California Feeling" idea and some of the other ideas. I brought some strong ideas, and strong poetic concepts which were really never given a full chance, but I think with Brian's abilities and with Dennis's abilities, that we could have gone in the direction of Sgt. Pepper's "Within You Without You". We could have made many more major symphonic kinds of pieces.

Overall, working with them was a wonderful, exhilarating experience; they really seemed to love my poetry and they picked up on my concepts of wanting to see the good within people. I think their hearts were good, but I think their bottom-line orientated management worked against them. Basic survival and human interests like money, and all the secretive things that go around that, can protect the person in the wrong way, even protecting what could be good for them. Only when I got a little older did I even think about money or anything like that, and by then I realised that, either through lack of advice or management, I had given away most of my publishing.

Inspite of that, it was a great time. I'm still all for the Beach Boys' idea of California, of open roads, of Walt Whitman, of all the extension of the west, of lovely beaches and lovely possibilities which are still here. I think underneath all the beauty though, there was the crumbling of values, and the Beach Boys were one of the last signs of a kind of music from a more hopeful, a more optimistic time which I'd like to get back to, but with a new awareness of all the problems too. I loved it, and I wouldn't trade any of my other experiences with it.

Editor's note: The poetry album with additional vocal backgrounds by Brian that is mentioned in this interview was completed, and does indeed still exist, but remains unreleased to this day.

Editor's note, 2002: Since 1997, the poetry album is still unreleased, but some moves have been made towards its possible release. Of even more interest is that during summer and autumn of 2002, Stephen Kalinich, always a close personal friend, has begun to collaborate once more with Brian. He is excited and stimulated about the prospects, but at time of writing no fruits of their labour have emerged.

Original Reviews Part 8

L.A. (Light album) album

"The Beach Boys are not dead, as this fine album proves ... the sound of the album is beautiful... beautiful changes... the harmonies are as well sung as ever... The production, by Jim Guercio and Bruce Johnston, strives unashamedly to please the ear..."

" 'Here Comes The Night' is a disco record, a Beach Boys record and a great record, in no particular order."

"...short, melancholy, exquisite ballads ... songs with positive messages that make you feel sad ... that they communicate irony without bitterness, without hopelessness, is the mark of their art..."

The Beach Boys 1985 album

"The warm Californian sun is still beating down on the rolling surf, but nowadays The Beach Boys look like they'd prefer a round of golf ... their music has aged gracefully but it does sound very old; echoes from another era ..."

"Whilst the harmonies are intact, the actual lyrical input treads the well worn path of 'lurve' and introspection, the inevitable L.A. themes. 'Maybe I Don't Know' is certainly the worst offender..."

"... a digitally recorded, drum programmed, synthesised and computer-aided Beach Boys album ... [with] all manner of technological hardware [that] ... somehow manages to sound old and cosy."

Two Soulmates Touching In The Dark:
Brian Wilson, Gary Usher and The Wilson Project.
by Kingsley Abbott

The book, The Wilson Project *by Stephen McParland, chronicled in great detail the period from May 1986 to June 1987 when Gary Usher worked with Brian Wilson on what was supposed to become Brian's first solo album. Although Gary got Brian working again, the eventual release bore no resemblance to the music recorded in these sessions, and there was no mention of Usher on the album. This previously unpublished piece revisits that short period, which as well as reuniting Wilson with one of his earliest collaborators, appears with hindsight as a micro-cosm of the whole Landy era.*

It was a sad time for all those involved.

The whole idea should have worked. It probably would have worked had it not been set in America, where financial motivations and people's litigious natures are further advanced than on British shores. Perhaps it would have worked had it not been for the characters of the three main players involved; for the combination of those three vastly different personalities at that time of their lives was almost bound to fail.

The idea, probably not thought out fully by anyone at the outset, was to aid Brian Wilson's return to health, fitness and musical potential by letting him work with a very old friend in a non-threatening environment and to see what might develop musically. The very old friend was Gary Usher whose connections with Brian went right back to 1961 when they each had their first tentative recordings released within weeks of each other. After late teen social links were made, Brian and Gary began collaborating musically on several songs that formed the back-bone of the Beach Boys' first album, and thereafter on some of the best known songs in the early canon: "Lonely Sea", "409" and "In My Room". Jealousies from within the band and suspicions from Brian's father, Murry, meant that Gary's working relationship with Brian was quite quickly curtailed. However Gary, who was by then confident enough to feel that he had a place in the music business, went on to write, sing and produce prolifically in the pop harmony vein over the ensuing years. His output can be found on a huge number of singles and albums, put out under a variety of names on a variety of labels. In fact, he probably rode the surfin', draggin', bikin' era longer and more successfully than anyone, including Brian. By the mid 60s Gary was working as a staff producer at American Decca where he helped develop the folk rock genre before he moved over to Columbia and The Byrds to produce *Younger Than Yesterday, Sweetheart of The Rodeo* and *The Notorious Byrd Brothers* followed by work on his own projects such as Sagittarius and Celestium.

The catalyst for the initial meetings in 1986 was the writer David Leaf, who had suggested to Usher that his involvement would be great for Brian. Usher said that he would love to do it. His guiding motivation throughout what was to become The Wilson Project was to "get back not so much the good old days, but just get

Brian Wilson music out; perhaps update it … I felt I was one of the few guys to do it, and I would love to do it."

With a producer with a proven track record, who was also an old friend, things looked set for a productive and pleasurable spell in the studio for Brian. What actually happened from this point is recorded in meticulous detail in the book *The Wilson Project* by Stephen J. McParland. This Australian writer/historian had been in contact with Usher for some time, and was collaborating with him on a major book on Usher's extensive work and the whole genre of California Music. Usher had been very impressed with Stephen's depth of knowledge, and had begun to keep a journal of his activities to aid the eventual book. When the contacts with Brian and Dr. Landy began, Stephen urged Usher towards even more detailed recording of events. This Usher did throughout the whole project, to the extent that full daily records were kept together with tapes of all the musical "work-in-progress". The net result led to as good and truthful a description of the main players' motivations in that era as anyone could possibly want. McParland's recording of Usher's journals, and his visits to him in California, became important enough to involve Stephen in subsequent court cases involving Brian and Landy, and later, Brian and Mike Love.

The initial contact that Gary Usher had with Brian was of course through Dr. Landy and was very tentative. Landy was feeling Usher out and wanted to check things out first before letting Brian anywhere near. Usher was a trifle sceptical even at the first meeting on Saturday 24th May 1986.

"Landy really got lost coming over to the studio. He used his car phone and I actually had to talk him down the street. I found that very interesting because I gave the same directions to Brian (when he finally came over later) and Brian drove straight here without any problem; yet his psychologist got lost!"

Eventually meetings at Usher's home and studio began to take place with Brian always being accompanied by minders whose job it was to report in full detail back to Dr. Landy. Brian's condition musically and socially varied a good deal during these initial visits, but it gradually became clear that he was happy and excited to be working with his old friend again. Usher was quickly aware that, although his voice had suffered over the years, Brian's musical talents were still evident but often locked in behind personal problems and the restrictive regime that he was under. To help his old friend he was prepared to take things slowly and see how things developed.

However, from the beginning, Dr. Landy was extremely hostile to the project and expressed suspicions that Usher was using his contact with Brian to manoeuvre himself into a producer role with The Beach Boys. Usher adamantly denies this:

"I had no desire to work with Mike Love or any of The Beach Boys… I really wanted to make a great album with Brian."

To Usher's way of thinking this meant waiting until Brian was taking a lead that he could follow and embellish. He was not very impressed with the song ideas and demos that Brian had at the outset of the Project, but he was happy to work on them to help get the thing rolling. This relationship, with the producer slightly holding back, is one which Dominic Priore touches on in his piece towards the end of this book. He identifies producers who have worked with Brian and tried, intentionally or otherwise, to assume too much of a leading role in the relationship. Priore sees success with Brian coming with someone who is prepared to let his spontaneity have full reign. This seems to be what Usher was trying to do, and also, what Andy Paley has done when he has worked with Brian in the nineties. However, what made things difficult for Usher was that there was no formal agreement or contract as to how things would proceed.

In fact, nothing was broached financially until some two months into the project, during which Usher had given freely of his studio, equipment, house and food. It was not until the end of July that anything was made public, or put on something like an official status. When this did happen, Usher saw it as a vote of confidence, but still did not see any money for his time. It was also evident that Landy was casting himself in the role of Executive Producer and was drawing up agreements to ensure that he got 25% "off the top" of any new material that Brian and Gary might write.

In the meantime, however, the musical relationship was developing. Brian was excited and stimulated by his old friend's talents and songs, and was evidently feeling relaxed and contented most of the time at the studio in a happy home atmosphere. Sometimes he would arrive with instructions from Landy that they had to work on this or that song, often one that Landy had some lyrical involvement with. Usher was very unimpressed with these efforts, and these sessions were rarely productive. However, at other times with other songs, Brian was stretching himself much more. From Usher's journals, McParland observed:

"The problem Usher could see was that Brian was taking these nonsensical lyrics and writing nonsensical music to them. A definite pattern was emerging. Brian was reacting to what he was given. If he was presented with dumb, simple and childish lyrics, he wrote dumb, simple and childish music. However, when exposed to something more substantial, like 'So Long' or 'Heavenly Bodies', his creative juices flowed."

Over the ensuing weeks it was evident that Landy felt uneasy about not having direct and full control over what was going on. He had tried, and was still trying, to push his own musical involvement through his lyrics, but things really came to a head when Landy's main "assistant" Kevin Leslie told Usher that the master tapes for each day's work were to return with him to Landy. Usher, who had been happy to send copy cassettes of the "work-in-progress", really dug his heels in over this request. He had still seen no money, and now he was to supposed to surrender his own master tapes. Leslie remained adamant; he had his orders. While Brian looking on, Usher refused, railing:

"What do you guys want from me? You haven't paid me a cent. I've cut literally half an album; I've absorbed ALL the costs and ALL the expenses. You cancel half your sessions with little if any notice and now you want to walk out of here with the master tapes. Give me a break!"

He went on to define the key issue as he saw it:

"You call Eugene and you tell him that he can get a Paul McCartney, he can get his Phil Spector; he can get the hottest producers in the world, but…you'll never get a producer who knows Brian like I do; who understands him like I do and who cares for him like I do and who will take care of him and protect him like I will. Other producers…will set him back ten to fifteen years… relay that exactly to Eugene Landy!"

It is doubtful that the passion and feeling in this outburst was ever exactly conveyed to Landy, and even if it had been it is perhaps unlikely that Usher's personal feelings would have been understood in the way in which they were intended.

The net result was that very little changed in that Usher continued to be used as a part of what could, in retrospect, be seen as the evolution of a Landy masterplan. As 1986 wore on, difficulties persisted regarding work schedules, and whilst some money for Usher was eventually forthcoming, it was never enough to cover his real outgoings.

In November things took an interesting turn. Suddenly, after months of uncertainty and cancelled or missed sessions, Landy introduced a planned and regular work timetable for Brian and Usher to work to. One of the reasons for this apparent change of heart soon became clear when it was announced that various Beach Boys, though initially just Mike Love, would be turning up to add to the sessions. This put Usher in somewhat of a quandary. As a successful producer with a wonderful portfolio of proven work, it was obvious that should he ever have been asked he would have been interested in working with the whole band. In many ways it would have been a natural choice for them, but Usher's deep seated suspicions of certain band members remained an obstacle.

It soon became clear that both Landy and Mike Love were working to their own agendas: Landy wanted Mike's vote at Beach Boy meetings for matters involving Brian, and Mike was anxious to check out just how good Brian's new material really was. Mike Love's motivations at this stage might have been quite convoluted. Had he considered the new material strong enough, he might have sought to get more involved in the Wilson Project in a writing and planning capacity, or to have taken the best songs for future Beach Boys product. After all it would have had Brian's name all over it in the roles of writer, performer and co-producer; all ideal for advances on record deals. In fact, the work-in-progress that seemed to fulfil both parties' agendas was "The Spirit of Rock And Roll", just the sort of commercial title that would strike a chord with Love. The song was eventually used at the end of a Beach Boys television special, but although no credit was given to Usher, Love and Landy both failed to get the co-writer credits they had sought for themselves. Landy had also threatened to withdraw Brian from the show if the song wasn't used for at least one minute before the credits rolled. In the end the band and their management agreed to keep Brian as part of the show, but there was no mention anywhere of Usher, nor was there for the production work that he hurriedly completed soon after to merge various Beach Boys voices onto an existing Fat Boys track of "Wipe Out", which was subsequently a huge hit single on both sides of the Atlantic.

As Usher became increasingly marginalised, the extent to which he was being used as a pawn in the surrounding power and money struggles, became more and more apparent. Unfortunately, there was very little he could do about it. Usher's only leverage was that people knew Brian responded well to him, both musically and personally, but this did not alleviate the financial difficulties he was starting to experience. Usher was turning down other paid studio work in order to continue working with Brian, but without any money coming from the Wilson camp, he was severely out of pocket. It is frustrating to read the account of his poor treatment documented in Usher's journals: as his treatment gets worse and worse the obvious question is why didn't he just walk away. The obvious answer is that Usher was naive. But if certain sections of McParland's journals are more closely scrutinised, it appears that Usher was simply unable to separate the business side of the Project from his friendship with Brian. His initial motivation of helping Brian never wavered, and even if he emerged from this episode with nothing else, Usher maintained a high sense of morality throughout.

Eventually the inevitable happened, and the project ground to a halt. It appeared that Landy had pulled the plug on it after almost a year of hard work, although at the final meeting Landy had with Usher he tried to shift the blame for the split onto Sire Records and the deal that they had on offer. Thus in the end it had become a clash between an artistically motivated approach and a financial and power based one, and as such reflected much of what has always characterised Beach Boys activities and decision making in the past. If anything good did come out of the Project, it was that Usher's meticulous journals formed a part of the court case that eventually freed Brian from the grip of Dr. Landy.

And the music? Of the seventeen songs that were worked on during The Wilson Project, mostly co-written by Brian and Usher, only "Let's Go To Heaven in My Car" released as a single (together with is B-Side), and the track "Walking The Line" which appeared on Brian's 1988 solo album, ever saw the official light of day. The tracks were technically proficient and the songs were interesting, but in retrospect they were very guitar and synth driven productions which never came near the subtleties and delightful variations of some of Brian's best work. Usher's part is perhaps best appreciated as a paving of the way for the much better work Brian has produced since. We can only speculate about what might have emerged from these sessions if Brian had been under a more benign regime, and if those around him had had a genuine interest in redeveloping his production, writing and arranging skills, rather than simply using him to their own ends.

On May 25th 1990, Gary Usher died of lung cancer at the age of fifty one. A month before his death, Brian ventured over to see him. It was a Thursday and it was Dr. Landy's Brian. He sat and talked. The following day he returned. This time it was the Brian Gary remembered from their youth. He had brought with him a CD copy of The Ronettes' "Be My Baby", Brian's all time favourite song. He played it five times. He held his friend's hand and he cried...

Editor's note: The final paragraph of this piece is taken directly from McParland's book with his permission. It could not be improved upon.

Appendix

The following extract represents legal evidence prepared in Oct. 1987 from Gary Usher's journals, as reported in the *Wilson Project* book, for possible use in the court case against Landy. By agreeing that such stark revelations could be used, Usher effectively put an end to the possibility of ever working with Brian again.

Summary of Most Pertinent Evidence in Diary
[Background Gary Usher apparently wrote songs with Brian Wilson in the early 60's, when both were in their early 20's. Apparently they were best friends for a period of time then, prior to Brian's dropping out and heavy drug use. It is this past rapport and friendship which apparently made it possible for Usher to obtain Brian's confidence during this recent songwriting experience 1986-87].

A. Brian's Feeling That He is a Prisoner Under Landy

During a time when Brian expressed to Usher his frustration about the Landy program, he said this even in the presence of the omnipresent guard (Kevin), who Brian knew would have to report what he said back to Landy:

"Since I started in Dr. Landy's program I have never been alone once. I can't even take a ride with my friends. I can't even call. I can't do anything. I'm a prisoner and I have to be that way for the rest of my life." (5:27)

[Brian then expressed his feeling about this as follows: "Sometimes I wake up in the morning and I put the pillow over my head and I scream." [Usher's comment: "And he made a screaming sound. Brian said 'I scream so loud... the pain ... it hurts me so much because I'm so screwed up that I can't live and conduct a normal life." (5:28).

Usher continued: "Then [Brian] went back into another tirade about Dr. Landy ... how he does-n't like to be told everything to do and he doesn't like to be totally as a prisoner ... [quoting Brian again: 'I'm a prisoner. I have no hope of escaping.'" (5:28; emphasis added).

"Brian said ' ... Now I live in a strange hell. I'm under 24 hour psychiatric treatment and I'll prob-ably be that way for the rest of my life because I'm not responsible enough to handle the every-day things of life.'" (5:27)

[Torrance comment: That Brian is aware of all of this says a great deal about his mental state; i.e. he is not so out of it that he is unable to resent the treatment by Landy].

B. Brian's Awareness of What Landy is Charging

Brian is apparently aware of how much Landy is costing him. [Usher] asked [Brian] how much he paid [Landy]. [Brian] was complaining about how much he paid [Landy]. [Brian] said 'It's over $200,000 a year.'" (6:11; emphasis added)

C. Best Evidence Yet of Dual Relationship; Landy Admits He Receives 25% of Copyrights

One of the key charges that we intend to make is that Landy is involved in a dual relationship with his client, which is gross negligence. The dual relationship is that he is serving as business man-ager as well as therapist. Landy made the following admission to Usher in the presence of Usher's manager, who is also willing to testify as a witness:

"[Landy] explained ... that years ago ... Brian, ... being out of money ... couldn't afford Landy full time but needed Landy and his services full time for obvious reasons. ... Landy wouldn't and couldn't work for free ... I don't know if you know what it costs for a full time psychiatrist twen-ty-four hours a day year round ... but you're talking very big bucks; more money than Brian has available. Landy made a deal with Brian's people. The deal being: that Landy would work for, not so much free, but essentially free; paying the cost of an assistant to always monitor Brian and for Landy being on call 24 hours a day; in return for 25% of Brian's copyrights." (2:31; emphasis added).

D. Evidence of Brian's Condition

(1) Brian mentioned that he tried to commit suicide while swimming in the summer of 1985. (3:31).

(2) Brian said that every fourth day has been a down day for the past 5 years (Torrance comment: the Landy program has been the last 5 years).

(3) Brian told Usher that he had taken cocaine every day for a five year period, $300-$400 a shot. (5:26).

(4) on one occasion, Brian suggested to Usher that what they needed was a shot of morphine ( ) and on another occasion he said the same thing about a shot of heroin. (2:5).

E. Further Evidence of How Landy Controls Brian

1. On one occasion, Usher and his wife double dated with Brian and his date in a limousine driven by guard Scott Steinberg. Near the end of the date, the phone rang in the front seat and Usher could hear Scott talking on it. The girl who was Brian's date, a girl named Melinda, could also hear. It was Landy on the phone telling Scott to tell Brian to walk Melinda up to the door goodnight and to make sure and kiss her.(3:30)

2. While in Hawaii for the taping of the 25th anniversary Beach Boys concert in Dec. 1986 (shown on TV in Mar. 1987 and viewed by our experts and me on videotapes of it I have), Landy gave an ultimatum to the Beach Boys; either include the song which Brian did actually sing at the end of the 90 minute telecast (over the credits), or he would pull Brian out of Hawaii and he would not be available for taping on any of the rest of the concert. The Beach Boys acquiesced to the threat and the song went in. (6:35)

3. On one occasion, Brian told Usher he wanted to make a phone call, then turned to guard Kevin and said, "do you have to listen in?". (5:4).

4. Usher never saw Brian without one of the guards, either Kevin, Scott or Evan (Landy's son). The guard regularly took notes and wrote down everything that happened; also there were usually 40-50 phone calls between Landy and the guard during a 6 hour recording session. On one occasion, when Beach Boy manager Tom Hulett took Brian backstage at the Moody Blues concert to introduce him to some of the members of that band, the bodyguard (Scott) insisted on going into the dressing room with Brian, and Hulett became upset. Scott insisted that his instructions were to go everywhere with Brian. (3:23)

5. Usher observed Brian talking on the phone to Landy on one occasion, where Landy was telling him what to say at the forthcoming Beach Boy meeting later that evening. Usher observed "him shaking at times; holding on till his knuckles were white … it almost looked like [Brian] was going through withdrawals." (4:28).

6. On a couple of occasions, Brian begged Usher not to get Landy mad, or Landy would pull him [Brian] off the project, and Brian wanted to finish the songwriting project with Usher. (5:8) On another occasion, Brian suggested that if Usher was mad at Landy, Usher could tell Brian and then Brian would relay the negative feelings to Landy. (5:10)

7. "Brian told Usher that it really hurts him when [Landy] gets mad at him because if things don't go well, [he] is not happy and he can't create and he can't have things." (7:17)

Trouble in Mind – A Revealing Interview
with Brian Wilson
by Jerry McCulley

This interview and its introduction date from the August 1988 issue of BAM *(Bay Area Music magazine), about the time of the release of Brian's first solo album, when he was still under Dr. Landy's influence. The interview is perhaps the fullest and most revealing Brian gave in the eighties. Jerry McCulley has also written a short piece drawing parallels between Brian and the American composer Charles Ives, who is known as the father of "Modern American Music".*

"After years of inactivity, Beach Boy Brian Wilson has ended his monk like retreat. With the help of psychiatrists, 'bodyguards' and family, he is again producing the joyful, visionary music that advanced the art of recording and captured the soul of middle-class America."
Rolling Stone, "The Healing of Brother Brian" November 4, 1976

That's how the curtain went up a decade ago on Brian Wilson's troubled personal life. It was a splashy debut for a supposedly rejuvenated musical genius that had been carefully orchestrated by his then struggling band, a public relations powerhouse and his sternly innovative psychotherapist. Brian was Back.

Back from a decade of unfulfilled musical promise and psychic quicksand. Back in the studio with a band that had long since become a monument to the American, and more specifically, the California Dream. Back before the prying camera lenses and microphones of journalists whom he sometimes seemed to mistrust, occasionally misinformed and could always live more peacefully without.

Sure enough, the Beach Boys soon had their first Top Ten album of new material in a decade. But within months Wilson's ambitious therapist had run afoul of the band's management and was promptly sent packing. The cameras and microphones moved on to cover the Next Big Thing. And Brian was Back again, to that terrifying place within himself that no one else could quite fathom.

Whatever wreaked havoc with Brian Wilson's soul had twice turned him into a chemically ravaged hulk who seemed to insulate himself from a threatening world with layers of superfluous body tissue. By 1982 his once absurdly prolific musical output was but a long cherished memory.

The statistics behind Wilson's contributions with the Beach Boys (a dozen Top 10 singles and ten Top 10 albums from 1963 to 1966 alone) tell less than half the story of his music. And the words come even harder in trying to adequately convey the strangely emotional responses that "Good Vibrations" and *Pet Sounds* can still evoke in listeners two decades on. There was something about Wilson that enabled his music to plug directly into the soul. Most critics called it genius, a word that would come to haunt Brian Wilson for two decades.

And yes, after an intermission of twelve years, Brian Wilson is Back again. So, incidentally, are the public relations machinery and the shrewd psychotherapist,

Dr. Eugene Landy. The Beach Boys, it is assumed, are waiting in the wings with anxious curiosity. What's different? Brian Wilson is different; an overdue solo release that has thrust Wilson back into the pop limelight, seemingly overnight. A project that consumed a year and $1 million in production, Wilson's solo debut received production assistance from veterans Russ Titelman and Jeff Lynne as well as Sire A&R rep Andy Paley and Warner Records president Lenny Waronker.

It is an album whose first single, "Love And Mercy," seems to pick up where *Pet Sounds* left off. It then veers frequently into that timeless pop ethos that Wilson seems to have been issued a permanent passport to, before ending with the flourish of "Rio Grande." A lush eight minute suite, "Rio Grande" at last publicly validates the experimentations of the legendary *Smile*, the "lost" Beach Boys album that many feel would have beaten the Beatles at their own (*Sgt Pepper's*) game, and whose troubled production may have been the beginning of Wilson's long, dark road.

Dr. Eugene Landy, with whom Wilson shares a multi-layered business-mana-gerial-collaborator relationship, re-entered the musician's life in 1982 at the behest of the Beach Boys and Wilson family. Landy reinstituted his controversial 24 hour day therapy, a program in which the therapist and his team gain virtual-ly complete control over their patient's every move and decision. The physical results of Landy's program, which reportedly cost Wilson upwards of $500,000 annually, were impressive: in the five years since Landy resumed control, Wilson shed over 100 pounds and began to function in public again. But as Wilson's recovery progressed, so seemingly did Landy's involvement with the singer's musical and business affairs. Landy is credited as the executive producer of *Brian Wilson*, and shares writing credits on five of the album's eleven cuts. Indeed, the line between Landy's therapeutic services and business aspirations have blurred to such extent that the California Attorney General's office recently filed charges against him following a lengthy investigation. Landy vows that he will pursue the case to the Supreme Court if necessary. His argument: "The ethics don't meet the Situations".

And it is clear that there are precious few aspects of Brian Wilson's life that the good doctor has not exerted some influence upon. Arriving at Wilson's modest (very modest by Malibu Standards) beach house, one is greeted by Wilson's per-sonal assistant Kevin Leslie. The blond, pony-tailed 24-year-old makes regular reports to Landy, records all of Wilson's interviews at Landy's behest, and other-wise assists in household "chores." When asked how he got the job, Leslie is forth-right; he's a friend of Landy's son.

In a few minutes Wilson himself, trim and toned in white jeans, windbreaker and running shoes, bounds downstairs and extends a hand in greeting. It trembles slightly. "Congratulations" is all this writer can muster; it seems succinct yet appropriate. The interview takes on a relaxed, conversational tone and Wilson's habitual stiffness gradually subsides .

As we talk, our conversation is punctuated by the frequent electronic chirping of a phone in the back of the house. Leslie attends to these calls in the course of his duties. A second phone in the nearby dining area, this one with a loud bell more akin to a fire alarm, rings twice during the course of our conversation. This is apparently Brian's hotline to Dr. Landy. And, in this case, vice versa.

The conversational Brian Wilson can, if taken strictly at face value, present a puzzling enigma. In Michael Goldberg's recent *Rolling Stone* article, the musician talks disturbingly about the voices in his head. "I get calls in my head," he said, "from people in the vicinity or maybe ten, twenty miles out." A relapse of dormant psychosis? No, suggests a long time Wilson friend, merely Dr. Landy checking in via his car phone .

And if that's merely an example of Brian Wilson's playfully off-centre intelligence, brace yourself for more. Wilson approaches his subject matter from above, below or behind – whatever direction he deems necessary. Sometimes he'll appear initially to avoid a question or remark entirely, only to cut directly to its crux twenty minutes later in his preternaturally hip '60s patois. Press him too hard on a subject (as Landy did during one of his calls) and the responses become clipped and cliched. Give him room and the quotes take on an artistic expansiveness that can be a challenge to decipher. But then, that's why he's Brian Wilson and we're not.

Let's start with the basics. How did this record come about?

It all started with Dr Landy, Gene Landy actually. He puts his name on my records as Eugene Landy. Eugene Landy, my executive producer, told me that he would like to do a solo album with me, that he'd like to help produce it. A Brian Wilson solo album outside the Beach Boys, well, it just so happens that it hit home with me. I said, "That's a great idea, I think I'll take you up on that".

Because after all, making an album is an excursion into creativity. No real true loopholes or things standing in the way when you get into creativity. Creativity cuts a hole right in glass. It can cut through glass, it can cut through steel. Nothing stops creativity. The creative urge in mankind is somewhere way up on the totem pole of human experience. Some people might think that sex is the highest experience you can have. I tend to think that music is.

How did the other people who worked on the album – Lenny Waronker, Russ Titleman, Jeff Lynne and Andy Paley – get involved?

Lenny Waronker originally conceived of an idea. He called Andy Paley and myself both and asked us if we would go to the piano and the guitar and write a song about cowboys and Indians. And then Gene dropped the big one on us that he wanted us to make it a five or six segment suite and he wanted to call it "Life's Sweet." We ended up calling it "Rio Grande."

It's an interesting structure, kind of classical, that isn't used much in pop music anymore....

Well, the first time we tried it was quite a sensation amongst us. It went over beautifully. And then we tried it again and were ecstatic.

Tell me about Andy Paley. He's obviously made quite a contribution to the record.

He was referred to me by Seymour Stein and Lenny Waronker. And then Andy Paley and I started working and cutting. The directions we took were like boom, boom, boom. He's a real swift guy. Real fast. A very brainy guy. He puts a lot behind it, let's put it that way. He's a scary guy when you get right down to it.

Are you a competitor?

Only in that I want to live up to my name. Probably so, yeah. If you analyse me, which isn't fair because then you would expose me like tooth nerves to the air, as to what I'm all about. Say I wanted an image, well, I'm a competitor so you write that down or it goes on the tape and then in the article.

You've always had a reputation as someone who kept an eye on the charts and checked out the competition.

I don't check them too closely, but I always check numbers one through five. I have the drive. There's a lot of drive there. But there's also a lot of singing going on. You look around the industry, and you hear what's being sung, and it's amazing. Listen to Phil Collins in "One More Night"; "Give me just one more night...." Imagine where his voice is coming from on that song alone. Not to mention Lionel Richie or Diana Ross or different singers that are custom made throats. They were born to sing, that's all there is to it. Spector's acts, Ronnie and the Ronettes, they were born to sing. Not to do anything else but sing. Among other things, I guess they were born to get business together and do this and that. But I say when people bring music into the world, it's a gift. It's a spiritual gift, regardless of who sings it.

What's that group, Three Dog Night? I can never remember their name. I knew Danny Hutton. And his stuff. Who else? Like Frankie Valli, John Sebastian, Frank Sinatra, my ex-wife Marilyn. I spotted some heavy singers and I've got them in view now. I know who they are. Although my ego has flipped out a little bit. I flipped out. But I'll be alright.

What did you flip out about?

My perspective in relationship to the rest of the business. I flipped out. I kind of got carried away with ... See, all dogs have their day. I've had my day and I'm still trying. I'm getting a second wind with this record. Another day maybe. That's what I meant to say. It's fast, it really is. There's a lot of great stuff.

Since you started working the pace has changed dramatically.

How do you mean?

Bands don't have the longevity they once did. And musicians don't seem to have the creative lifespan. Now a band will put out two or three albums, the singer will go solo and everything will change.

Yeah, they certainly will. Dramatically.

Obviously you've experienced some of that.

Yes, I have in my life. I don't know. I think what the change is, is that you go in there, stamp a record out on the press, you say here it is, here's my record. Goes out, moderate hit. Go out and do a moderate concert. But never being totally satisfied with your career. Always thinking that this very next single will satisfy me. Or this next venture, this next cycle of waves that are developing, will bring me satisfaction. Mentally. And emotional and spiritual satisfaction.

But of all those that I just mentioned, spiritual satisfaction is the one that most interested me. I want people to feel satisfied with my music when they hear something. Their souls are satisfied. They hear the lyrics, they hear the lead, the way it all comes together in a song. I hope that people feel satisfied, like that Phil Collins song, "Give Me One More Night." That's one of the prime examples of spiritual music.

I have my ABCs down pat in my music. But as a liver of life ... The spiritual quality comes through in the background voices, the choir, the sweet oohs and aahs. I think that's where you hear it. I never want to go for that big lead sound. I like the lead to be more average and let the background sounds become more spiritual so that they sneak in. It's what glues things together.

Some people say love glues things together. I believe that. You wonder how things are glued together. Have you ever been through that? Wondering what keeps it all together? Some people say love, other people say sex. Other people say money. That's a big one there – money.

I worry about money, although I don't make much anymore, not like I used to. I make enough money to pay my bills and keep a few cents in the bank. I'm a millionaire on paper.

But you should have been a little better off had things been handled differently. Do you ever feel bitter about that?

At times. I just say, "Ah, why couldn't it have been this way? Why the hell not?" I don't know. It's like a dead end. It really is. It's a dead issue. Just accept it when it comes in and not worry about how many millions you're gonna have next week, next year or ten years from now.

How's your sense of humour these days? Yet another reputation to maintain.

It's there. It's alright. It's not as funny as it could be though. Damn, it could be funny.

Do you ever try to express it musically?

I've tried that. I can't get it in the music. I can get it in a personal thing. But the music is different. Unless I made a loud sound in the middle of a record. A firecracker going off would be fun. Other than saying that music is cool and spiritual, then your funniness can always take place a little later.

Humour is a very spiritual thing too.

Well, it all is then. But humour ... of course. (silly laugh)

Do you follow all the things that are said and written about you? You have a cult following, shall we say.

A cult?!

Well, maybe not a cult. They don't appear to come over and worship in your driveway.

A following. I do have a following.

Some [of those followers] are influential. Some have written books and have had a lot to say about you.

My followers are what helps shape and mold me. They help me to mold myself. Oh yeah, I get feedback from them all the time. Sometimes it's like looking in a mirror. It's not a real tangible thing. An off the cuff remark from somebody I might pick up in a different kind of way. But somebody comes up and says, "Hey, I've really liked your music for a long time, I've been a fan of yours for years," that to me is feedback. It helps me out. It gives me strength to carry on. When things are rough and the pressure's on it's hard to deal.

Do you think a lot of the stories of legend were blown out of proportion?

Oh yeah. Some were.

And then they become part of the legend too.

Yeah, that's true. It's a funny trip. It happened to me.

When did you feel like you had a grip on what the problem was?

About half a year ago. I have just recently gone to a higher plateau mentally within myself. Now when I speak with people I kind of speak in conventional patterns because I don't want to sound abstract. I want to give direct answers. Logical and sane answers. I don't want to branch off into an illogical bag, it works better for me when I'm logical and sane, rather than illogical and insane.

In that period when you were having the identity problems, did you ever lose your desire to make music?

Yeah, I did. There were times when I didn't even want to go to my piano. I didn't want to get down and make records or songs when my heart wasn't into it. Those were times when my conscious mind was fucked up. I couldn't consciously concentrate on songs.

I went through about a four year writing cycle. I was writing all the time for four years. I was in my music room at my piano a lot of the time, at least once a day.

What years are we talking about?

83- 4-5-6

That was the genesis of the album?

Yeah. We had 130 songs, then weeded it down to 20. We recorded 18 of those and chose 11 out of the 18 so that's how it was during that time. It was like the old grinder. A lot of it was that I was scared that something wouldn't go through. But then you really do – uhh! – get it together and nail a new bag, something you just thought of, the momentum does not stop for anything. There's total self-control involved.

Obviously that was a very productive period of songwriting. How would you compare that to, say, that early Beach Boys period when you also really had the momentum up?

It's comparable in an energy output standpoint. The quality of the music is different. It's different music, obviously, because I'm not using any of the Beach Boys vocals. So the quality sounds different than the Beach Boys.

What is your relationship with the band like now?

Business. The personal we've sacrificed a little bit in order to keep business going. We're doing it for the furtherment of the group's popularity and institutionalization. And we're sacrificing some, "hello there, how are you?" and all that stuff.

Do you still consider yourself a part of that band?

Oh yeah, of course. I formulated the band. I made them famous, and they know it and are appreciative of it. They pay me one fourth of all the income of the tours that they take.

Is there an artistic direction that you want to go with them? Or is it "separate but equal" as the saying used to go?

Yeah. Separate and equal.

Do you think your solo album will affect the way you work with them in the future?

Yeah, I think so. Gene told me yesterday that he thinks it's entirely appropriate that they sing some of my solo album songs on stage. If they want to. That's up to them. I can't tell them to do it.

Do you want them to?

Sure. I think it would be good for both of us.

What kind of relationship did you have working with the band in the '70s?

A very good relationship. I cut my hair all the way down, almost bald. I was in a strange space. But it worked out well because the guys always liked to be creative. They always welcomed new songs and new sessions. It's just the way they are. They always welcome anything I do artistically. They like my stuff and think it's good.

Didn't you have some friction?

There was a problem with Mike, but we got through it. He told me I was fucking around, that I wasn't serious. I cut a track with swing music. Remember swing music? I cut a swing track for one of our tracks and he got mad. He said "What are you doing messing around for?" I said I'm just trying to do what I like, what I think is right for now's times. That was about ten years ago.

Do you ever feel like you get second guessed a lot, or that your judgement isn't trusted?

Oh yeah all the time. Sure I do. I mean everybody in my position does. It's a racket. Being in the music business is a racket. You suddenly find yourself surrounded by people who are very picky, almost power mad.

And everybody's an expert...

Yeah, everybody's an expert. Dr. Landy is a total life expert. He's an expert on life. He's an expert on music and he's an expert on production. And he's an expert on executive production.

How did he get to be an expert on production?

How? He just did. He just came into his own all of a sudden. He came out of nowhere to take over my life. It was really quite dramatic. It was really something that I could never quite want to talk about because it meant opening up too much. Opening up some wounds and some sensitive areas that I didn't want to open up. Although I was vulnerable to those ideas it was kind of hard to open up to them.

Where do you draw inspiration from these days?

My inspiration comes from girls. It comes from people. It comes from the need to be spiritual for people. It comes from the need to give music to people who need it.

Music is really a truly spiritual idea. The idea of music; there being different things that make up a whole – bass, drums, guitars, pianos, violins, horns. And all those things working together make up what we call music.

The records on the radio all symbolise, represent different rates of sound vibrations. Each of those songs reach a person's subconscious mind, or his intuitive process. Although he's listening with his mind, his heart hears it too. And this is the tricky thing about music, music goes in a person and heals a person without them knowing it.

Your music seems to have a way of going in the ear, bypassing the brain entirely and going straight to the heart.

Yeah. That too is a great intuitive process that happens. This is what I would like to do with my album. I hope that I can create these kind of conditions where you have a listener who says, "Gee I like that song. I really like it!" Meanwhile, the song has played right to his intuitive process. Gently moving his insides back and forth and all around, wherever the harmonies go. It's a beautiful process. Music is beautiful. Nobody knows that.

Well, of course, a lot of people know that.

But they don't think about it. Not consciously. Maybe subconsciously. But it's a fun process. It's something that we all need and are going to need for some time.

But I've run out of melodies. I'm on a dry cycle right now. I've run out of melodies. I can't write any melodies! And goddamn it, that's my business and I've gone dry! I can't seem to write any melodies and it just pisses me off.

But you've gone through those spells in the past, haven't you?

Yeah, but this one is the worst. Ever. I go through these dry cycles, dry spells and I say, "Ah, it'll come back around, just give it time." I'll go to the piano, nothing (makes popping sound). Nothing. And I say give it time, just like I did before. I'm always referring to my past. I said I did it then and I can do it now. Isn't that really what it is when you're faced with a dilemma? You did it because you've done it before.

Do you still draw on any of the classical composers for inspiration?

I listen to Gershwin. I like "American in Paris." "Rhapsody in Blue" is probably one of my very favourites. You've got to look up to those guys, those classical composers because they created music that nobody else could create. They really did. Those classical composers created stuff that's like far beyond what anybody can conceive of: the form, the way it's put together, the sound of it, the tonal textures.

It can speak without lyrics.

They have something that no one can quite capture. That's why they live throughout the ages. They still stand because they created something that cannot be equalled. So therefore mankind worships it and builds it into a godly kind of thing.

How do you feel when someone compares you to one of those composers?

I say I hope you're not comparing the music. I can understand your comparing our names together, put them in the same sentence. But not our music. Some of that music is far superior to any music I could ever make. I make my own kind of music. I don't try to make classical music.

They made their own kind of music too. I don't think their intent was to be classical.

They couldn't probably make our kind of music either. Although our music is much simpler. I don't see how they could, how Gershwin could write "Be My Baby."

You might be surprised.

He might be able to write it but I think there's something else.

I can almost hear old George at the piano...

Cranking out those rock n roll, melodies, right?

A lot of the songs he wrote weren't that far off from...

From rock 'n' roll. I know that. I'm very aware of that. I've heard his backwards and forwards and I'm very familiar with it. I noticed in the "Rhapsody" there were parts that even now, even in today's market, the bass lines are as hip as any that have been written in modern rock 'n' roll days.

Do you want your music to outlive you? That seems to be a hallmark of classical music.

I suppose that if there's any spiritual weight to my music in the 2,000s, after I die, I would imagine that my music would make people happy for a long time. I just know it.

What's happening with Smile*? ...It seems like that project will hang over your head someway until it's dealt with. Maybe not in your mind, but certainly in the minds of the people that really follow your music.*

(Avoiding the question) The album had a lot to do with my programmer Michael Bernard. He was the most productive programmer I've ever worked with in my whole career. He gets these great new creative sounds for me. Guitars and pianos could never mix together to make a sound like that.

It was an experience recording. I had a lot of frustration and a lot of pressure while I was doing it. But I liked it because the pressure I had I wanted because this is what makes me do better, this very pressure I had. This drives me on. And I got those attitudes together and it really did work. I accumulated speed and strength during those pressure days of the production of the album.

Do you have problems with the technology involved now? .

I'm learning it. I still don't understand digital that well. I went to a sound convention last year down in Anaheim and I couldn't believe all the new instruments they had. So many new instruments and machines.

Do you prefer to work with that equipment or with acoustic instruments?

I work with the synthesizers. I gravitate toward that kind of sound for my records.

We started to talk about Smile*. Capitol issued a press release that indicated you were working on it again.*

We started to and then got side-tracked with some business. But we're going to go back and do it. We're going to fix up *Smile* so that it's in the right sequence. I have to figure out the sequence of what it's supposed to be. We're going to release it as sessions not as an album.

Does it excite you at all to work on that project again?

I'm wondering if it would sell. I don't know. It's not quite your conventional kind of album, so I don't know if it would sell. I have no idea. I think it stands a chance to sell, just like the solo album.

If that doesn't sell, something will. My second album might have some oldies but goodies on it. I'm shooting for the older songs next time. This one was the new, then comes the Mike Love kind of, he has a "come-go-with-me" kind of thing, his voice. (Sings) "I'm pickin' up Good Vibrations". You know.

He's got a little bit of a hang up for me though. He doesn't like ... Well, let me explain what happened first so that you'll understand what I'm talking about with Mike Love. He wrote part of "California Girls", half, and he never got credit or money for it. And it was all my fault. I knew that my dad made a mistake by putting my name on there only. My dad was the publisher. His name was Murry Wilson. My dad put me on there as the sole writer and he paid me the whole thing. So in other words we have our problems but it's OK, they're worked out. I worked it out with him.

Is the band going to be involved with Smile*'s resurrection? Technically, it's called a Beach Boys album, but is it or isn't it?*

No, it's not a Beach Boys album.
  (To a passing Kevin) Is *Smile* a Beach Boys album?
  KEVIN: It's whatever you want it to be. I have no idea.
  BRIAN: I don't know.
  KEVIN: Technically, you did it all.
  BRIAN: Technically I did it all so it could very possibly be a Brian Wilson album. But I don't know. I really don't know.
  (Again changing the subject away from *Smile*) I like McCartney. I like McCartney's stuff.

Have you ever considered working with him?

I thought we could do it. He's pretty high energy for me. I guess I could gear up a little and work with him. But it would be kind of hard because I'm in awe of the guy.

And he's seemed in awe of you.

He loved *Pet Sounds*. He thought it was the greatest album in the world.

He's claimed that album was the reason the Beatles cut Sgt. Pepper.

(Laughs)

How do you feel about that? That's almost the ultimate compliment.

He complimented me many times, not just once. And he said that *Sgt. Pepper's Lonely Heart Club Band* was inspired by *Pet Sounds*. I don't see how. Maybe on a basic level of competitiveness. I don't see how the album influenced it. The music of *Pet Sounds* didn't inspire *Sgt. Pepper's*.

It seems as much philosophy as music. A philosophical approach to pop music where you say, OK we don't need just drums, guitar and bass. It's OK to have strings.

Yeah, right.

That's where the influence is, in my feeble mind anyway. What were you trying to do on Smile*? Weren't you just trying to take that philosophy a little bit farther down the road?*

Yeah, I was. I wanted to take that philosophy a little farther down the road and arrive at a place, a meeting ground in my head, just to see what everybody else thought. Sound people out to see where I was at musically, I guess I got goin' on it pretty fast, I don't know. I know inside of my myself that I certainly did get going very fast on the project.

The *Smile* album was a bits and pieces kind of album that didn't have hardly any songs or lyrics over it, just background tracks. That's why I'm wondering if it would sell. We might add a couple more.

How do you foresee the next couple of years? Are you going to try and put out an album a year or does that depend on how the current one does?

Probably two albums a year, I would think. Not just one.

That's a throwback. Artists don't put out two albums a year anymore.

Really? Just one? Are you sure?

Ask Kevin. We'll out vote you I think.

(Laughs) Alright, one album a year it is then. I wonder how many Phil Spector records come out in a year. None, you know? He doesn't release records.

I could hear an album by Spector. I could stand to hear that. I could stand to hear an album by the Four Seasons. I thought their stuff was great. I idolised them. I just said *more! more!* to the Four Seasons 'cause I thought their stuff was great.

Tell me about that post Pet Sounds *era (*Smiley Smile, Wild Honey, Friends*). That seems like a generally overlooked period of Beach Boys music. What kind of relationship did you have with the band then?*

Drugs. The boys were into drugs then. But they all got off, they're all clean we all cleaned up. Three out of five of us were taking drugs. That's a majority, right? So you could say that the group was taking drugs at the time. But they got off drugs. Al and Bruce were clean. Dennis and Carl and I ...*Nah! Two* members actually, Dennis and I. So the whole group really wasn't taking drugs. But we influenced the group by taking drugs. The group couldn't believe where we were coming from. Really coming from an artistic place. But that's all I call tell you, 'cause it's just a phenomenon of creativity.

I'm not scared to step out and do a new thing. Why should I be scared? I'm a sensitive artist. But because of that, because of that sensitivity I've developed immense defenses against being hurt. I have a lot of defense mechanisms that I use in my life. Inside my head, of course. I'm always towing the line with people, being cool with people. But I do have those defense mechanisms that I use.

I try not to get too hurt in the process of making records but I always get hurt. I don't like it.

Nobody does. Obviously you bruise easier than the average person. But that's probably the price you pay for the kind of music you make.

Oh, for sure. That's why I say ... But the difference between me and a lot of other people is I don't care as much if my records make it. I care for "Love And Mercy." That's the one release I think is... I call it symbolic. I conjure up in my mind that what is at hand here is a symbolic release of a love message. And I said that's a stroke in my favour. That's something I'll remember in my life, as the time I released "Love And Mercy."

But, as for the time "Love And Mercy" was a smash record, I'm not looking forward to that. I don't care. Because I'm not going to put my hopes up. I refuse to put my hopes up about this record. I just refuse to do it. I refuse to identify with it to the point where I say, "This record is a smash!" I like that kind of attitude, but I don't have that attitude at all.

Did you used to have that attitude about your records?

No, not really. Wait a minute ... you mean the Beach Boys records? Oh *yeah*! On all of them I said this is a *smash*! This is a number one *smash*! And that's how I used to talk to people. I'd talk to Mike Love, I'd say we've got a Top Ten *smash* on our hands! On *Billboard*, on *Cashbox*. And that finally it'd go to number one and I'd call him and say, "We made it to number one!" And he'd go, "Whoa!" We'd get excited, right. We couldn't help it. It's an exciting thing to get a number one record. A number one record is like the first time you ever fucked a girl, it's a thrill. You know what I mean?

Was that perhaps the beginning of some of your more serious problems, when Pet Sounds *was accepted critically but not commercially? That must have increased the pressures.*

It was both combined. I incorporated my artistic attitude with the enthusiasm of the guys and the company, Capitol Records. I incorporated it beautifully and it worked great. There was a lot of ambition around, and pressure too. But there was so much creativity going on inside my brain that I had the overall feeling of walking into a studio and cutting a number one record inside of me. And I proved it to myself that I could do it. It's like the flu: it catches on. It's contagious. Where you pick up the spirit from somebody you have to do something with it 'cause it's so heavy. Like when Mike would say, "You gotta write a number one record!" I would get like (whistles) that feeling and I'd go do it, 'cause it was contagious.

Almost like the huddle of a football team .

Yeah! It's that, "C'mon guys, let's get a touchdown!" And it happened. Now we bombed a couple of times, too...

How did you react to that pressure?

It was a fight between ourselves and the record company, who was putting a lot of pressure on us. And we said, "look, leave us alone and we can get this record going.'' And the company said, "Look, we don't care what you say, we have a schedule to meet here. We have to have a Beach Boys record in ten days.''

You don't want to be scared all the time. There are other emotions besides fear. You've got anger. You've got jealousy. You've got joy. You've got fascination. You've got jealousy. You've got anger. You've got frustration. You've got hunger. You've got all those emotions.

But that's how it's strung together. We strung all these hits together. One hit, strung it together. Another hit, strung it together. Another hit, strung it together. And pretty soon we had a string of hits.

What happened in that Pet Sounds, Smile *era? Did something change?*

Pet Sounds didn't sell that well for us so we panicked and we went into the studio and did *Smile*. I did actually, there's only a couple of cuts where the guys sang. There's at least 15 or 16 things on there that are just background music where the Beach Boys did not sing on them. And so that's how it happened that it was an incomplete album.

I said I don't want it, I don't need it. I can't stand it. And it went away. The insecurity of a certain kind of thing went away. And it stayed more or less an even place for me and all that were concerned. All my friends and all the people that were happening with me. The guys, the company, my manager, our manager. That's how it all worked. *Smile* is a good album. It's good music. Have you heard it?

Just the pieces that friends have given me on tape.

How did it hit you? What did you think of it?

It's great music.

It's nice music isn't it?

I've played it for my girlfriend, who is not really a Beach Boys fans, she was raised in a different generation of music, and she loved it.

Whew...that's great. That's a good sign. Maybe it will be a hit then. I don't know. I have a situation where I'm so hot to trot – to get something rolling.

But then there's the back catalogue where everyone is saying, "Come on Brian, we've got to get this done, too."

So do it. why not do it now? I'm not saying that *Smile* is done. I can't tell you that I'm done yet. We might put a couple of other songs on there besides what's there. But what I have to do is improve on it a little bit and then I've got to get the guys to come in and do the vocals on it, and it's gonna be one epic of an album when we're done. But at this point, no it's not done. There's not enough on it.

How would they react to your wanting them to work on it, or do you even want to guess?

I don't think I could guess. I don't know how they'll react to it. Probably negatively. Probably say, "Well *Smile's* just bits and pieces." Well maybe we can make it better.

Anything is just bits and pieces without some bolts to hold it together. Some glue here and there...

It's got to have some glue. I think we'll get it too. That's an unfinished project, so I hope that I can get somebody excited with a couple of ideas I have although it's such a dilemma. I mean I can't work with those guys comfortably knowing that we don't even say "hi" on the phone hardly ever. That's the hardest part. For me the Beach Boys are among my very hardest people in the world to be with. I find it more difficult to be with the Beach Boys over say 95 percent of the people I know in this whole world.

Is it because you know them too well?

It's that plus ... It's a long story. It's just that they all had to read articles with Brian this and Brian that. You know the articles. You know the pattern the articles took. The interviews we did over the years: "Brian is the genius of the group". "Brian is the group." All this stuff. And the guys ... What a drag man.

How did you feel about that?

I felt guilty.

Really? Why?

'Cause I felt like I was pigging the show.

But you weren't trying to do that.

No. I felt like I was pigging the show. It wasn't my fault. What did I do? All I did was go in and give them number one records and then all of a sudden the inter-views revolved around my name all the time. And the guys resented it, obviously.

Do they somehow hold you personally responsible for that?

No they don't. They just resent the fact. And it's difficult to talk to the Beach Boys because of all that.

There's a lot of water under that bridge...

Yeah there is. It's a bitch of a persona conflict trip going. We sacrificed that in order to get those hit records and to get those hit tours. We go out there and we work together. When I'm working with the Beach Boys, I'm not comfortable just sitting there thinking, I'm talking to myself saying "What am I doing up here? I don't even feel comfortable playing with these guys." (A loud phone rings once and then stops.) And I say to myself I like it though. What am I doing playing with these guys? And then I turn round and say I love playing with the Beach Boys. It goes back and forth, you know what I mean?

If you could change something to make your relationship with that band better, what would it be?

...Oh God, what would I change? That's a lot to lay on me. Overall, that's too overall for me. I can't answer that question.

What would it take to work in a studio situation with them again?

I think maybe it would take some self-control and some logic and sanity. And some understanding. Maybe a little understanding.

Do you think they feel threatened by your solo record?

Oh no, I don't think so at all. I think they're proud of me. You know, I never thought of that. Maybe they do feel threatened by it. I don't know.

Here you are putting out a solo record and getting a lot of press again. It just seems like that situation could build again.

Some of that part of it will. The jealousy part will keep going just fine. Then it would be ... I think it might be a fight. A hassle, I mean, in my head. It's a fight inside my head to keep my sanity with the Beach Boys. I'm very much alienated to the group personally.

And yet you still want to be a part of them

I want to be a part of them, yes. I don't want to be forgotten on stage and in the records. The Beach Boys did a record without me called "Kokomo" [from the Cocktail soundtrack]. It's coming out this week.

What was the working relationship like for the last studio album?

I was close to the producer and I was close to Dr Landy. Eugene Landy was our executive producer on that. Steve Levene was the producer and we were the artists. We got along good. We spoke to each other...There were no hittings or yellings or anything like that. It was ok.

   It was fairly alright except that I was confronted with something that I didn't like: being with the Beach Boys. That's what I didn't like. But at the same time I love being with them.

But in some way it seems both statements are true. It's like a stormy relationship with a woman that goes back and forth.

It certainly does. That's what makes life go 'round – everybody has that. We all have a taste of feeling left out and then we feel like we're a part of it again. Like a girl might feel left out. That might be a problem with a woman. But I don't know I love the Beach Boys and I like being with them although sometimes I feel that I'm uncomfortable with them. Let's drop that subject, 'cause that's a rough one. That's the one subject that I wish I could master. If I could just master that and get it all together. Someday I will.

Now let me invent a subject: What is it like to produce a record? Would you like me to talk about that?

Sure. There are only a couple of tracks on the album that are solely credited to you as producer. So tell me...

What it's like to produce a record is this: you have what they call the bigger picture of the record in your mind. Your brain sends signals out to people, "Hey, I wanna cut a record," and they pick up on what you mean. You say I wanna cut a record but your brain sends out messages besides just, "I wanna cut a record." It sends out subliminal waves that people pick up. You can say, "Well, why don't we cut a record?" Who knows, maybe it'd be a hit. That kind of thing. They pick up on that too. I want to do something creative; they pick it up. It's like a subliminal thing you're sending to people. That's why some people are called winners. You say that's a winner person because that person knows how to send out those waves. And he knows how to talk to people. His attitude is contagious, too. So that's what I do when I talk to the Beach Boys. If I'm talking to Dr. Landy or somebody, anybody, whoever it might be, you know, doggone it that I'm gonna be telling that person what I truly feel. In other words I'm gonna say, "I wanna cut a record." I think I've got a number one fuckin' record besides 'Love and Mercy'. I wanna go in next week and cut again. And like that.

That's what you call transmission of ideas from one person to another. It's also the intuitive. It's not just what you say. It's the intuition that comes behind it. It's like when you watch a newscaster some nights you say, "Hmmm, yeah." And other nights you go, *"Yeah!"* You know? What is that? It's intuition he's sending out because he's in a better place that night. One night he's on a bummer and he doesn't like doing the newscast and you can tell he doesn't.

It's like when you're a producer, the task of the producer is to make the artist feel comfortable so that they can do their thing. You allow the artist to do his thing. That's what I've learned about production. I learned it from, God, a number of people.

Don't you think the producer's role has changed in the last 30 years?

Oh yeah, it has. Artists these days have more reign. Artists are just so high and mighty. The producer's a background kind of guy. Before, with the Phil Spector kind of producer, it was like *The Producer*. Featuring so and so on *production*. Producer Phil Spector on "Be My Baby". When records featured the producer, that was the heyday of the producer. Nowadays it's not that way. Nowadays the artist runs away with it.

But as far as your role on the records, you made the decisions?

I did, to an extent. (Sighs) Unfortunately the Beach Boys are a very record-conscious group and they all pitch in ideas. When we did "Good Vibrations", I had *ba ba ba bom ba ba ba*, you know, the chorus part where the cello plays. I had that. And Mike came up with (sings) "I'm pickin' up good vibrations." And Carl said why don't we use a cello. I instantly decoded it into a triplet thing. But that record came together beautifully. I wouldn't want to go back and do it again.

You recorded a lot of different segments to that song. Was it difficult to piece together?

No, that was instant. I was a very fast person. I was a quick decision-maker. I knew what I wanted. I was mad. I was a madman making a record, you know what I mean? My very reputation was on the line because a few records had gone down by the time we did "Good Vibrations", and I was challenged to do a great record.

I wanted to do a masterpiece record. I kept working on it and molding it and shaping it and finally we got down to the *ba ba ba ba ba bom ba ba*, the choir part at the end, and as soon as we got to that part I said, "This is a masterpiece record".

What about this story that at one point that song was going to be offered to Wilson Pickett?

Wilson Pickett?!

That's what some of the books have claimed.

I don't know anything about that. (Laughs)

You're going to have to spend some time proof-reading.

You know what I should do, if I really were smart, I'd probably go in and start another album, right away. Although there's an option now I understand with the group, they might come back with an offer to let me produce another album. They're getting hungry for an album. They, we, haven't had an album since 1985, that's three years. Label? No label. They just have a one-record deal for "Kokomo". But they don't have any contracts now with anybody. No advance money or anything like that. Who wants to put money out for a group that hasn't been around for awhile? Who in the business would invest in us? Three Dog Night can't even get a contract...

But don't you think you're going to be a sort of negotiating chip in that whole process?

A negotiating chip? What does that mean?

A label might be more willing to sign a deal with you producing the band than if they came in without you.

It would help. It would add to it, wouldn't it? They'd make a stronger position. I think what it might be is ... The old waiting game is the most fun of all. A lot of times I wait and I wait in fear sometimes. And sometimes I wait with a little anger in me. I start feeling, wait a minute, where are things? What's going on? Like that feverish feeling. And it works. If you allow yourself to be that way, you can. Like a mad scientist.

The down time seems to drive you crazy.

What I do then is just chew my teeth and then spit 'em out and grow new teeth. I do all kinds of weird trips.

(The phone rings; it's a loud bell once again. Brian quickly rises to answer it. It is apparently Landy, checking on the progress of the interview. Brian offers some assurances and returns to the couch.)

Why don't you ask me about some of the cuts on the album?

Well, we've talked about "Rio Grande", Walkin' The Line" and "Love And Mercy." Is Dr. Landy worried that we're not talking enough about the new album. That it?

Yeah. He wants us too.

We've covered quite a bit, actually.

I know. We really have. If we can just get into the album a little bit, it might be good for the publicity of it.

It just seems like a bigger story than so and so's new album.

Why don't we do this, why don't I just tell you about the songs.

OK. "Little Children"

"Little Children" is a song that has a playful sound to it, a background track of a youthful nature. And it's all about how little children are marching along. They're just doing their thing and making progress in the world. Little children are recognised as part of life just like everything else. Adults would say, "Huh, look at those cute little kids." Where nowadays they take a little more square, fair look at them.

"Couldn't Get His Poor Old Body To Move" is not on the album. It's the B side to "Love And Mercy". It's a message all about how you should exercise because you can stay alive longer and how you should move around instead of sitting in a chair feeling hypnotised. It's an exercise message song. It may not reach very many people, but at least, it's worth a try.

What's the intent behind the a cappella piece, "One For The Boys?"

The intent was to bring a kind of harmonic beauty to it … to change it right in the middle of the album. To bring about a change of vibration. A change of sound. A prettier sound. Something more beautiful.

Is the title a kind of wink?

The title's humorous almost.

"There's So Many" is about this guy who has a lot of different girls he could think of. And he goes into a thing, "the planets are spinning around". It's trying to say that the planets spinning around has a lot to do with a guy's love life. You wonder why you lose a girl and two months later you're with another girl and his girl got mad at you. And the guy gets all fucked up about it, and he winds up with an ego problem over it.

Sounds like a great movie.

It's pretty rugged making these records with the lyrics 'cause you've got to sell a lyric. Like my father used to say "Get in there and sell! Sell that song!" He was a real forceful kind of coach. He was a combination coach and … there's a private, what's the other one? A general?

A sergeant?

He was a combination coach and sergeant. He was pretty cute with the way he did that, 'cause I actually did what he said. It's almost like being hypnotised by your dad. That was weird when I lived with my father. He had a lot of things to say, "Uhhhrr! Uhhhrrr!" like that kind of stuff. He really hit pretty hard, he really did. The man just hit really hard with the psychology. I went sprawling half the time.

Did you have a lot of self-doubt going into this project?

Yeah, I did.

At what point did you overcome that?

I got over the self-doubt after a period of a month or two. It took me a while to get used to it, because I was making a solo, not a Beach Boys album. Gene knew I was nervous about it. And I knew he knew I was nervous about it. There was nothing to hide. I couldn't hide anything. My emotions were out there on the table. I said, "Hey, I'm in a positive mood, I want this to succeed and it's gonna do it one way or another." Or solo album number two will do it.

Author's note – Special thanks are due to David Leaf, whose book *The Beach Boys and the California Myth* is essential to a true understanding of Brian Wilson's music and the Beach Boys phenomemon.

Bittersweet Insanity:
The Fight for Brian Wilson's Soul
by Bill Holdship

This view of the tail end of the Landy years originally appeared in the December 12th 1991 issue of Bay Area Music *magazine. It should be noted that this writer has bucked the trend by largely championing the unreleased* Sweet Insanity *album, planned as Brian's second solo album, whilst most others who have heard the various versions have panned it.*

"One day we were driving through Santa Monica and I asked him 'Brian how does it feel to be a rock star?' He replied that he really doesn't think of himself as a rock star. 'I really think of myself as a hero', he said. 'Every day I do battle with these tremendous fears. And every day I conquer those fears I think that makes me a hero.'" – Todd Gold

Brian Wilson is having lunch at 72 Market Street, the exclusive Venice Beach restaurant owned by Dudley Moore. The beautiful grand piano at the front of the dining room is the one that Moore frequently uses when he visits the establishment but the hundred or so patrons on hand this afternoon are hoping that the guest of honor seated at the main table – the "mad" genius behind the Beach Boys – will grace them with a song or two. The occasion is a luncheon for *People* magazine advertisers; Todd Gold who helped Brian write his new Harper Collins autobiography is a *People* staff writer, and he has invited Brian to autograph copies of the book for the advertising dignitaries.

Brian seems especially stoked this afternoon absolutely radiating positive energy. Perhaps it's all the loving attention he felt earlier when signing the books but he seems excited about everything. There's even zeal in his voice when he chooses the chicken salad over the restaurant's meat loaf special. One would never know that this is a man about to enter a major court battle with Irving Almo Music, the publishing arm of A&M Records to regain songwriting copyrights to an amazing volume of work including such hits as "Surfer Girl" and the classic *Pet Sounds* LP (his late tyrannical father, Murry, sold the multi-million dollar catalogue in 1969 for $700,000). Meanwhile members of his family – including his mother Audree, daughters Carnie and Wendy (of Wilson Phillips) brother/Beach Boy Carl and cousin Stan Love (Beach Boy Mike Love's brother) – will have him in a different court room soon during which time they will ask a judge to declare him incompetent and to appoint a conservator to handle his affairs. The conservator case is contrary to his well expressed wishes – but Brian Wilson's best wishes have seldom been taken into account during the course of his life.

According to Dr. Eugene Landy, the controversial therapist who triggered the conservatorship case by becoming Wilson's business partner and song-writing collaborator several years ago, there are two factions within the Beach Boys camp, with Carl, Audree and the immediate family on one side and the Love brothers on the other, each vying for conservatorship of Brian – a position that became even more powerful in regards to business affairs when brother Dennis Wilson who almost always sided with Brian on artistic and financial matters drowned in 1983. There have been several press releases stating the family looks forward to the day when Brian can write with Mike Love again. According to Landy the Beach Boys do not have a recording contract and they cannot get one unless Brian Wilson agrees to write and produce 80 percent of the band's material. Even though the Brian-less Beach Boys scored a hit with "Kokomo" in 1988 at the same time that Brian's critically acclaimed debut solo LP failed to make a huge dent in the *Billboard* charts, the Beach Boys have managed to release one song in the year and a half since they named Mike Love "recording captain"- an embarrassing version of "Crocodile Rock" for the Elton John-Bernie Taupin tribute LP *Two Rooms*. Brian wasn't invited to the sessions.

It would appear to be stressful enough when artists have to deal with these sorts of things strictly in business terms. In Brian Wilson's case however, familial concerns enter into his problems – and Brian doesn't have a history of reacting well to stress. On top of all this Sire Records recently rejected *Sweet Insanity*, Wilson's second solo LP, on the grounds that the lyrics written primarily in collaboration with Landy weren't strong enough. The label then agreed to release Wilson from his contract. Plus some journalists are suggesting that Wilson – an artist who not only created *Pet Sounds* but works as gorgeous as "Love and Mercy" and many of the cuts on *Sweet Insanity* – is incapable of writing his own autobiography. Nevertheless, Brian Wilson seems very upbeat these days. He hums and sings "Mountain of Love" to himself during the lunch. He smiles a lot. He answers questions intelligently. Other than a few extra pounds he's put on in the paunch area, this man shows few signs of stress at all. He looks much more emotionally secure and much less pained than he did even five years ago.

January 1987. I'm at a Spago party when a tall slender goodlooking impeccably dressed man with blonde hair is pointed out to me. My God! Can it be? Not the same man who weighed over 300 pounds when I saw him onstage eight years ago? Rock's most famous "nutcase" and predicted next casualty. The man who is rumored to have once stuck his head between two pieces of bread in a restaurant. I tell him something about *Pet Sounds* being one of my favorite albums ever and how all of his music – right through *The Beach Boys Love You* has brought me so much joy. He stares at me for a moment. "What year is this?" he asks. He has a bit of a facial tic and he tends to talk from the side of his mouth; it looks like he may have recovered from a stroke although one later notices that he talked that way – albeit not as pronounced – even as a youth since being deaf in one ear he's talking to the other ear that can hear sounds outside of his head. "Well it's been over 20 years since I did *Pet Sounds*. And I'll tell you I could make an even better record than *Pet Sounds* if I could just go into the studio for a week. But I can't right now because I have to see my psychologist every day. I ask about an interview. He tells me to write a phone number down. "Write 'Brian Wilson' at the top of that" he says. I assure him I won't forget whose number it is. "No. No. Write 'Brian Wilson' Because you never know. You might forget…"

72 Market Street. Nearly five years later I'm sitting next to Brian at a table that also includes Todd Gold, his wife and Brian's personal assistant Kevin Leslie.

I've encountered Brian numerous times over those five years – running a gamut from formal interview sessions to listening to *Sweet Insanity* several times in the Brain & Genius studio, to numerous other Hollywood parties including one at Mick Fleetwood's short lived blues club at which I not only saw Brian's daughters walk right by their father without acknowledging him, but also watched Brian sweetly flirt with my brother's girlfriend ("Do you have a boyfriend?" he asked in the presence of Landy, whose worst critics have always claimed that he doesn't allow Brian to have girlfriends); still this luncheon seems to be the first time that Brian is actually starting to recognize me. I compliment him on his shirt "Thank you," he said. "I bought it yesterday at the Westside Pavilion where I went shopping with my girlfriend." Brian doesn't want to mention her name, except to say that she's "pretty" and an "inspiration" for his music. "Kevin and his girlfriend came with us, and, you know, I don't feel fear anymore when I go into those stores".

He asks if I've ever interviewed Paul McCartney, and when I tell him I haven't, he responds, "Well, when you finally interview Paul McCartney, he will probably tell you that Brian Wilson was an inspiration on the Beatles." I respond that nothing can mean more to me than the opportunities I've had to interview Brian Wilson. He smiles, and there is incredible joy in his eyes. It's almost as though he needed to hear that to believe it.

Late November, 1991. Photographer Robert Matheu and I are at the door of Brian's modest, three level, beach front, Malibu home. Brian greets us warmly, using both hands to shake ours, as has become his custom. "Come on in," he says. "It's really good to see you guys. There's no one home right now, except me. I just got off the phone with my friend, Danny [Hutton, of Three Dog Night], and, damn, I'm fired up! He and I can really relate to each other now, and there's no craziness. No more jealousy and it's great! Would you like something to eat? Something to drink? How about a nice, big banana?" Matheu accepts, and Brian, ever the gracious host, peels the banana before handing it to him.

"Go ahead and turn on your tape-recorder, and we'll talk some more," he tells me. "It's never a wrong time to do an interview". He pauses. "So I understand you guys want to wrap me up like a mummy." We explain that the idea is to drape him in recording tape but if that's what he'd like to do… "Well, listen. I'm not in favor of it. Because I'm scared. I don't really like having my arms and legs confined. But if you can do it, and you can guarantee me that you'll let me out, I'll do it. I mean, if I said, "Hey, let me out of this thing," and you guys split and left me on the beach, that would be a pretty wild trip! I mean, I'd be stuck in all this tape down on the beach…" we laugh, explaining that we'd never do that to him. But he isn't laughing.

"What we're doing here is working for world peace," says Brian, totally unsolicited, while Matheu is on the phone. "Every day. Like crazy. Because Gene [Landy] and I are crazy people. I want to try to create vibes that would at least embody some of that spirit. Usually you think, 'If I were to tell that person I'd like to help them along, that person would get suspicious,' right? It's human to act negatively. But I'm trying to create some good vibes. And trying to do some good. And just working every day." I tell him that his music has such beautiful melodies and harmonies. It's sorta like if there's such beautiful harmony in music, why can't there be harmony everywhere? He sighs, and his eyes drift away, dreamily. "Yeah. That's true." Then he laughs hard.

"So you see what I mean! There you go! Hey, I don't have the answer to life. I just know that when enough voices combine, you've got the sound of heaven. And it can be very liberating. It's the sound of an angels choir. You really can't fuck up in music. I told myself that back in the '80s. There's no fucking up in music, because music is perfect. And just like in heaven, there's no fucking up. But, you know, I really can't see another '60s revolution coming along. I think it's probably metal forever. Heavy metal forever... I like Joan Jett's heavy metal. She does a good job. But other than that, I really don't like metal." I ask if he's familiar with Guns 'N' Roses and Motley Crue. "Oh, yeah. I've watched MTV. Literally, all the time, and I've gotten very familiar with that kind of music. But it looks like it's totally saturated itself, do you know what I mean?"

Heavy metal plays a small role on "The Spirit of Rock 'n' Roll," a marvelous track on the unreleased *Sweet Insanity*. In the midst of a wailing saxophone, Beach Boys-like harmonies, and Brian's everything but the kitchen sink Phil Spector-isms, is a loud metal guitar, which may or may not be courtesy of Lou Reed / Alice Cooper / David Lee Roth axeman Steve Hunter, just one of the cut's huge cast. "The Spirit of Rock 'n' Roll," unabashedly celebrates the innocence and power of Brian Wilson's kind of music in a way that only he could get away with in this jaded day and age. ("I love rock 'n' roll," he says. "It's a very exuberant music. It's up, and it's full of life. And it has loads of energy in it. I mean, anybody who has ears should like rock 'n' roll. Even a little tiny baby could love rock 'n' roll.") And only a genius would recruit Bob Dylan ("a real cool breeze guy," according to Brian to duet on the track, singing the lines, "Once it's in your blood, you won't be the same no more" and "It's in the heart of every boy and girl," giving the track even more validity in the process. (The duet also obviously meant a lot to Brian: a photo of the artists together is his only star momento, sharing a wall with an auto-graphed Garry Trudeau lithograph of the Doonesbury series that dealt with AIDS patient Andy Lippincott having a chance to hear *Pet Sounds* on CD before his death.)

Sweet Insanity is, indeed, a wonderful album. In many ways it's an even better album than *Brian Wilson*. For one thing, Brian's vocals are many times stronger and more confident than they were four years ago. ("Oh, yeah," he agrees. "Well, I've gotten my chops back up a little bit since then.") And those *songs* – "Love Ya," an umpteenth rewrite of "Heart & Soul," which is exhilaratingly magic; "Water Builds Up," a pop lover's dream song; "Don't Let Her Know She's an Angel" and "Rainbow Eyes," both stunningly beautiful ballads; "Do You Have Any Regrets," which has Brian going head-to-head with the Beach Boys' mambo sounds on "Kokomo", and beating them a thousand times over; and even an inten-tionally hilarious rap song called "Smart Girls" that samples from – of all things – his Beach Boys hits. Co-produced and co-written by Landy, *Sweet Insanity* definitely has a few minor flaws. And even so, it's still the best album I've heard this year, and one that would be cherished by Brian Wilson fans the world over. The album also captured the imagination of super-producer Don Was:

"What I like best about *Sweet Insanity* is that it proves musically [Brian's] still intact. Whatever damage he may have done to himself over the years it didn't carry over to anything musical. And clearly when you listen to that record you can hear that he's still very creative,and he's got wonderful ideas. And he'd like to build even more on that. I think he needs to write even more songs. And that's my intention. Not so much as to use those 10 songs when we finally start working together but to use his creative momentum."

Still, Sire Records has declined to release it.

Malibu. Still playing the perfect host, Brian takes his visitors on a tour of his house, finally ending up in his piano room on the bottom floor. He talks philosophy, and tells stories. He mentions that he recently met with brother Carl in a motel near LA. "We didn't talk too much about the conservator case," he says, "but we did work out a couple of problems as brothers. He said one thing is he doesn't want to put me through the trauma of a trial."

And he plays the new song he recently wrote with Carole King on his piano. Clearly, as was pointed out, this is a man who still has some amazing musical chops. "Have you heard my version of 'Proud Mary'?" he asks. He plays it for us, and even though we've heard versions of the same song a million times in the two decades since John Fogerty wrote it, it still sounds incredible.

JOHN FOGERTY: "I'm a big admirer of Brian Wilson, and, in a sense we kind of had the same role in our bands. A long, long time ago, before Creedence was a success, and we were still known as the Golliwogs, we were trying to get a record released on the former version of Fantasy. You know, it used to be a jazz label, and they were not very successful at all. I was arguing with one of the owners – this kind of beatnik guy – over a point of recording and making records and things. And he just looked at me and said, 'Well, everybody just tries everything'. He said something like, 'If you throw enough mush up against the wall, some of it sticks, and sometimes it becomes a hit record.' And then he finished, 'Because nobody knows what a hit record is.' And I looked him right in the eye, and said, 'Brian Wilson does'. This was probably about 1966. And I still believe that. I mean I don't know if Brian does right now, at this moment. But at any given time, there are a few people who just know. It's not luck. I've always remembered that. That was the esteem I held Brian Wilson in, and still do, actually."

Brian has pulled the new Phil Spector boxset out, and he's playing selected cuts. "In reality, I never beat him," he says. "I never whipped him at record production, but I showed him that I had the ability to take what little he had showed me, and make it work on a grand scale." The opening strains of "Be My Baby" blare from the speaker, and he looks blissful. "Phil always made music that was mono," he says, "but I could only hear one channel anyway. My hearing is totally gone in my right ear. I feel a little ripped off about it sometimes. But not that much." He grins. "Laugh your way right through it, right? That's what it's all about. Humor. You let go of something, and you gain some thing else. You inherit something else. It's not like you've lost something forever, because you'll always get it back in another form. We as people get hung up saying, 'Oh, boy! I got ripped off! I don't have that anymore!' That isn't true at all! You always gain something from losing something."

Matheu tells Brian how much he loves the Beach Boys' version of Spector's "Just Once in My Life" from *15 Big Ones*. "Wasn't that a great song?" asks Brian. "Carl sang that, didn't he?" When told that, in actuality, it was Brian, Carl, and Dennis singing, he looks confused and sad. "No, not Dennis. Dennis drowned…"

His response is surprising given that Brian had discussed that very song in accurate detail with me several weeks earlier at Market Street. And he can rattle off trivia like a walking rock encyclopedia. However, this is not the first time I've seen this phenomenon. Once I told Brian that *The Beach Boys Love You* was one of my favorite albums of the "70s, and the artist said he didn't remember the record. But as soon as I mentioned "Mona," Brian began happily singing the song. Several months later, I again mentioned the *Love You* album, and Brian recalled everything in great detail. Of course, it's often hard for an average person to remember every detail of his life, let alone one who at one time literally experienced psychotic visions. "Oh, wait a minute!" he exclaims "You're talking about *15 Big Ones*? 1976. OK, OK. I'm thinking back to when we recorded that song..."

I re-enter Brian's living room from the outside patio, where the Ronettes' "Baby, I Love You" is blaring from the speakers. Matheu stands in utter fascination as Brian blissfully dances around the room the way a child might dance to a favorite record. "It's psychedelic! I see beautiful colors, and people, and *everything* in my head when I listen to this music!" He's purely ecstatic. It's a truly wonderful moment to see. And definitely one to cherish.

TODD GOLD: "I was really wary of doing this book because I didn't know how much Brian should remember or could remember. Whether he would be anecdotal or remember enough so I could fashion anecdotes. And during the initial interviews it seemed that my worst fears were coming true. He was monosyllabic or he spoke in very short cold sentences. Just saying stuff like, 'Yes I wrote that song in 1961', and then not embellishing anything. What it really was was a process of him coming to trust me and feeling comfortable with what he was doing. And me learning how to communicate with Brian. And learning that he responds best to direct sentences. That I had to learn not to always rely on him for every anecdote, but if I could do research and then bring a historical fact to him and ask him to embellish it he could do that. And once he got into it – several months into it – he trusted me and we got to know each other better, he became much more forthcoming.

"I read the other books and old articles about Brian just as anyone who writes an autobiography with someone would try to do. No one – even those with a healthy, sound mind – remembers everything about their life. And so sometimes stories were brought to Brian and he commented on them. When he absolutely didn't remember and it was important to have something about it in the book, things were paraphrased from other material. Or from other outside interviews. It should be noted that other people were interviewed – Van Dyke Parks, Tony Asher, Danny Hutton, Bruce Johnston, Al Jardine and Landy. In the end Brian was given chapters as they were finished – three or four at a time and asked to approve them or correct them.... Ultimately it was up to him to go through and change things if they were incorrect. And he did. There are copies that exist where he went through them with his pen. So if there are errors in the book it's ultimately not from any grand design on Landy's part. It comes from the fact that Brian didn't catch them.

"You know, Landy doesn't really know anything about Beach Boys history. He really is surprisingly ignorant of all that. And happily so. Landy was never ever around when I interviewed Brian and neither of them were ever around when I was at my computer working on the book.... Brian had already spent a year going over his life intensely with a team of lawyers involved in the A&M suit. So his story was very in tune to their case… But what you're getting is Brian's feelings and point of view.

"And of course I observed things. I accompanied Brian on the road for a 10-day tour with the Beach Boys during the summer of 1990. He was filling in for Mike Love who was at a TM conference, learning how to levitate. When Brian arrived that night he asked Carl to do an interview with me for the book and Carl's response was "Let me talk to my attorney." Earlier in May of 1990, shortly after the conservatorship suit was filed Brian flew up to San Francisco for a couple of gigs two nights in a row. He walked backstage to the dressing room and not having seen these guys for months, Mike's response wasn't 'hello', but rather to walk up to Brian and stand as close as possible, intimidating Brian, and playing up to Brian's fear of Mike. And then the first words out of his mouth were: 'Those shoes look hideous'. When Al Jardine walked up and said to Brian 'What are you doing here?' Brian said 'I work here. These are my songs.' Al was quiet for a moment and then said 'Well just don't sing them like you're a Vegas lounge act.' And Carl didn't say a word to Brian that whole night. He just kept his distance. So Brian was treated as the ultimate outsider. It was unbelievable to me. Equally unbelievable was that during the second show Al Jardine left in the middle of the concert. He just walked off the stage because he had a plane to catch. Throughout the first half of the show he just kept looking at his watch. And then he put his guitar down and walked off the stage."

During an earlier interview with Brian he was very pained when discussing the Beach Boys. He rolled his eyes back in his head as he sometimes does when unpleasant subjects are approached and he answered with little more than a "yes" or "no." Today however a much happier Wilson seems especially forthcoming on the subject. " I want to produce them again someday but not rightaway. Not until I think … Look, somebody deserves for me to produce them but maybe Mike and Carl don't deserve it! I don't know. I'm getting emotional now, but I don't think the Beach Boys deserve to be produced by me, at least not at this point. Because of some of the bullshit they've done to me. Their attitude has hurt me immensely. And I have a theory that they're doing this because they want Dr. Landy out of the picture. I guess those guys don't like him.

"I don't understand this whole image people have of him as a villain or something. He used to yell at people a lot four or five years ago. He still yells, but not as loud. But there's no brain control here at all. I think of it as education. I'm much happier now, more self-sufficient, and much more self-controlled. If I think bad thoughts now, I take care of them with my head. And I'm not a prisoner. I do think that life is like a prison to the spirit but Dr. Landy does not represent a prison to me. And Kevin Leslie is my personal assistant, and my very good friend.

"I have kept myself away from my relatives. I've purposely kept myself away from my daughters out of guilt, because I feared I wasn't a good enough dad to them. And my mom put her name on the original conservatorship papers that Stan Love sent to her. She endorsed it. She's aware of what a conservatorship could do to me, so I stopped calling her. But my family still says that Dr. Landy won't let me see them. What good would that do? Why wouldn't he want me to see my family? There's no logic in that."

I ask Brian if he could sever ties with Landy anytime he wants. "Sure!", he laughs hard. "But that wouldn't happen. I love Gene, and I think Gene has taught me more than any other person in the whole world. He's taught me so many things about life. He's taught me what it's like to survive, how to use logic, and how not to let your emotions rule you as much. They do sometimes, but I can keep my brain on top of it a little more than I did before. For a couple of years, he did have a fathering influence on me, but then when he saw I was OK, he said, You're on your own. I just wanted to teach you these things, and show you that there is good parenting. He taught me by parenting me that I could do what he said I could do. And then when he saw I knew that, he stopped parenting me. He saw I was OK. He pulled back, and that's when we became partners. Creative partners."

We're back at Market Street in Venice, and Brian is finally treating his captive audience to several songs on Dudley Moore's piano. He's perfectly charming as he runs through "California Girls" and "God Only Knows". Just him, plus voice, and his keyboards, he proves as someone once claimed, that he still has the best left hand in the business. But even though the Beach Boys classics are genuinely moving there also seems to be something remotely obligatory in Wilson's performance of them.

"This next song, I've had a few cries over, let's put it that way," he says, "It's a very beautiful song. Unfortunately, it didn't sell or the album it came from, *Brian Wilson*, didn't sell. But I must say that the song I'm about to play has a lot of intrinsic meaning in my personal life. Like a lot of people in the mid '60s, I took LSD, the acid, and had a lot of revelations about myself. And I developed a Jesus Christ complex, which was weird. I mean, a lot of people do, though, because to live is to be a Christ, to be alive. But after taking those kinds of drugs and knowing that I did have a lot of music inside of me, this song probably best exemplifies the Christ that's in me. The part that wants to give love to people". And he then performs a version of "Love & Mercy" that is truly transcendent.

After the performance, Brian once again speaks into the microphone. "I have a Dr. Landy syndrome," he tells the crowd, which has obviously seen some of the negative Landy / Wilson press. "Now, that's not hard to develop – a syndrome when you're around another person, and a person that you might build up to be your demi-god or a god in your life. Very most definitely, I have done that with Dr. Landy. And I didn't want to leave this meeting without you all knowing who he is and who he's been in my life. He's very definitely one of my absolutely, favorite, godly people in this whole world. Dr. Landy". He looks and sounds as though he's about to break into tears as he momentarily exits the room.

Outside in the parking lot, Brian is saying goodbye "Where are you going now, Bill?" he asks. I respond that I'm going to interview John Mellencamp, but it won't be as interesting as this has been "Oh, no. It'll be fun," he says. "So Phil Spector won't do any interviews?" he asks in reference to something said earlier in the day. "That's too bad." Kevin Leslie suggests that perhaps Brian should try to interview Spector himself. "Oh, I don't know that I could do that," he says. And then he grins widely. "But that would really be something, wouldn't it?"

[Editor's note: The Wilson-Landy relationship was terminated on all levels shortly after the interviews for this piece took place, following the "Conservator" case.]

Up Close and Personal With Mike Love
An Interview by Melodye Dorst

Dating from June 1994, this U.S. fanzine interview (Surf Patrol #10) catches a relaxed and verbose Mike Love as he tackles some of the often asked Beach Boys questions. Mike's answers reflect his concerns at a time when he was involved in the court case with his cousin Brian over songwriting credits and royalties. The answers also show just how much he is aware of the commercial aspects of his activity.

The following interview took place on June 25, 1994 in Charlotte, North Carolina at the Park Hotel.

S.P.: With over 30 years in the entertainment business, what would you consider to be the highlight of your career?

Mike: The highlight of our career, in personal appearances anyway, would have to have been July 4th in Washington, D.C. That was probably the highlight to see between a half million and a million people on a national holiday and getting a standing ovation as you walked onstage. That's gotta be quite an uplifting experience, you know, because here you are coming from a normal (whatever normal is), an average, middle class background in Southern California, and here you are in Washington, D.C. on July 4th with all these people applauding for you and you didn't even do anything. And that, I think, is probably one of the greatest, if not the greatest, high point of concert appearances.

Although, there are many different moments like that. I remember Czechoslovakia back in 1968 or '69. The Russians invaded Czechoslovakia; they came in and suppressed their demonstrations. They were trying to become a more democratic society. We performed there. I can remember the intensity with which the Beach Boys were received in the concert hall. Because we represented America and freedom to them. As a consequence, the reception was unbelievable. They have a habit of whistling there, hooting and whistling, and you know, it was deafening really. But that was another kind of special occasion.

The first time we ever went out onstage as the Beach Boys in 1961 was a thrill, too. It was a different kind of thrill. It was a nervous thrill because we were scared and nervous wondering how we'd go over. And I made up my mind that night to not get nervous anymore. I just said forget it, I'm just going to do as good as I can, and if that's not good enough, that's too bad. So I kind of willed myself not to get nervous and haven't felt nervous ever since.

There are all kinds of thrills. Then there's the access to places and people that are out of the ordinary. Like for instance, we went to Paris in December of 1967 to do a UN Children's Emergency Fund Unicef Benefit show, and Marlon Brando invited us to go out to breakfast with him at like 2:00 or 3:00 in the morning.

Another really high point was the time we were all instructed in TM by the Maharishi. It was a different kind of experience. It wasn't a public experience; it was very private. It was a real deep experience because when you learn to meditate... it's a different direction. Instead of being outwardly directed, you're taught to go inwardly. When you transcend, you go beyond thoughts and all these moods and things that are going on in your mind, and you attain this deeper level of self which a lot of mystics and spiritual people have talked about for thousands of years. But to actually experience it, you have to be taught by... at least the TM procedure... you have to be taught by an instructor. So that was a real high point. Then, a couple of months after that, I was in India at the same time as the Beatles, Donovan and Mia Farrow.

It was interesting to be at the breakfast room table when Paul McCartney came down to the table playing "Back In The U.S.S.R.," at least most of it. He played the verse, and I said, "Well, on the bridge there, you ought to talk about all the girls around Russia," which he did. We had some pretty nifty discussions. He was telling me...we ought to take more care with our art work on our album covers. Here is the guy behind *Sgt. Pepper* and it made so much sense. I mean, that was one of the greatest album covers ever, you know. It was clever and thought out and had so many intricate parts to it. So anyway, he gave me a little lecture on that, and I told him how to write a song! He's always been very gracious about the Beach Boys, too. Especially remarks about the *Pet Sounds* album (which is good because it was quite an astounding achievement). So, we've got things that happened in concert appearances, things that happened in personal levels, things that happened in the access to the bigger world that we wouldn't have had if we had just stayed in Southern California. We've been very blessed by the exposure to some of these... and benefitted by quite a bit, I think. There's still a lot of places on the planet that we haven't seen, and I hope to get to those in due time.

What would you consider to be the biggest disappointment of your career?

Disappointment... professionally that would be, honestly, my Uncle Murry not giving me credit for writing songs that I did write. Because I wrote all of the words to "California Girls," but my name does not appear on the label. I've never been paid anything for that. The same with "I Get Around." I wrote most of the words to "I Get Around." In fact, I came out with, "I'm picking up Good Vibrations. Brian has gotten, deservedly, a lot of credit, but I haven't been given the credit I deserve. Professionally speaking, that's the most personally impactful thing I can think of when your own cousin and your own uncle cheat you, it's a real drag. Brian has his excuses, I guess you say, or excuses could be made, or it could be rationalised because he's had a series of mental problems, nervous breakdowns, and he's diagnosed as a paranoid schizophrenic. He was awfully afraid of his father, and they sometimes didn't communicate very well, but he's had other opportunities to rectify that. But, most of his adult life he's been under the control of other people which is sad.

As far as the group itself is concerned and also the family, you'd have to say death is a major disappointment. By that I mean Dennis Wilson. His problem was his attraction to alcohol and drugs. Although the rest of us in the group tried as best we could to get him to stop abusing alcohol and drugs, he was the type of individual who would not take advice. He wanted to do what he wanted to do, when he wanted to do it. And unfortunately, some of those things are addictive. Maybe it was his father's influence on his mind because Murry was abusive, and maybe he was trying to medicate himself. Or maybe he was just trying to live life on the edge, which he did. Unfortunately, it didn't work out, so that was a drag to see people in your life get involved with drugs. So drugs and death, and impairment in the case of Brian, has been a real disappointment because I think the talent and energy of the Beach Boys together including Brian, of course, and Dennis with his energy on the drums and his spirit... if you were able to remove the influence of drugs and alcohol you would have, I'm sure, the most powerful musical entity in the world, and the most vibrant and alive. But unfortunately, those drugs did take huge, enormous tolls on those two lives to the point of ending one and severely impairing the function of the other.

What is your favorite Beach Boys album and why?

I guess *Pet Sounds* is my favorite because of the orchestrations and arrangements. Because it's not just about cars or girls or school, but it's about feelings; however, I think there was a screw up on that which was that they didn't include "Good Vibrations" on that album because it was being worked on about the same time. Had that been included, it really would be my favorite. As it is, I'd have to say it's a darn good album. It's sort of a landmark album. It's an album that was so evolved for its time.

Are there any other artists that you would like to see as guests on future Beach Boys albums?

Yeah, I want to do an unplugged album. I call it *Unplugged In Paradise.* I want to record it in the Caribbean or Hawaii or both or a couple of different beautiful places. Could be in a forest, part of it, but primarily the tropics. I would really like to do some '50s and '60s ballads, (do-wop kind of things), and have Aaron Neville guest with us. He has such an amazing lead voice. I'd like to do the "Duke of Earl" and "I Only Have Eyes For You," "In The Still of The Night" and those kind of songs that the Beach Boys grew up on. And then there's a little more up tempo kind of boppy thing you can do. I'd like to do something with Billy Joel. He's a great artist. And he's very versatile and has an ear for the same kind of music. He's a little more commercially minded and disciplined than the rest of us are, but he'd be great to work with. Uh, who else? I don't know... I think it would be great to do "Back in The U.S.S.R." with Paul McCartney. He'd sing a Beach Boys song, we'd sing a Beatles song or two that he's written. If we could get him, and get George to come along and do "Here Comes The Sun". You know, George Harrison and the Beach Boys. That'd be kinda neat stuff. Do it all in a lower voltage, unplugged context. Phil Collins is phenomenal. I'd like to do something with a major country singer. Like Clint Black or somebody like that.

Many fans would love to see a new live album. Do you see any chance of that?

I think what we ought to do is this *Unplugged in Paradise* and go from there. And see, between the box set and *Unplugged in Paradise* and the new stuff from "Summer in Paradise" and all the other stuff we've done, there'd be a great album, I'm sure, a great double live album.

Is this Unplugged in Paradise *a working title? I mean, is this something that is happening?*

Yeah. It's something we've been talking about, and we have to get together with Capitol Records and see if they want to do it.

Has Brian expressed any interest in recording with the Beach Boys now that his recording demands are over?

Oh yeah. He's controlled right now by a couple of attorneys. They won't let him anywhere near me because of the ongoing litigation stemming from the things I was telling you about, about the song rights. It results in something that happened in 1969, so I don't see it as relevant to today, but they do. Because they feel that if Brian is with us, he'll get too friendly and be too easy to influence, I guess. I'm assuming that's the case. Anyway, he's been scared off of being around us, although he's always welcome. He came to my wedding to Jackie in April. He's welcome to come anytime. It's just that he's... whether it's his own fears or the fear instilled in him by others... he's not felt free to do so.

With all of the enormous talent in the Love and Wilson families, I have always found it funny that only Carnie and Wendy Wilson seem to be interested in music. Are any of your children interested in following in your footsteps?

My son, Christian, has got a band. He calls it "Alex's Caine." They're out of Santa Barbara, California, and it consists of three players. Drums, guitar, and Christian plays the bass. And he makes up most of the songs, too. He's a songwriter! I call him a "Stingaholic!" He's very influenced by Sting. He even sounds a little like Sting. He plays the bass, the whole thing. He's a very goodlooking guy. He's a very highly individualistic person. He's a surfer, volleyball player. I mean he really lives the life that we sang about. The real deal there! One of my desires is to help him sort through songs and be of some help in not only recording the songs and videoing them, but getting him placed with the right people and stuff. So Christian is very much into music. So is Matt Jardine, by the way, who sings in the band. He's also recording an album little by little, song by song. He's recorded four or five things. He's working on it.

He has an incredible voice, doesn't he?

He does. He's a really good singer.

What is the biggest motivation for giving up your summer every year and going out on the road?

Money! Because then we don't have to go very far the rest of the year because we make enough money during the summer to relax and do some other things during the winter. That's basically it. The reason for that time period is that the State Fairs are going on then which aren't normally, and the amphitheaters are active then that aren't the rest of the time of the year. So, between the State Fairs, amphitheaters, and baseball (concerts after baseball games), there are three or four elements out there that aren't there for us in the winter, including the weather. We prefer to tour at a time, even though it's a little muggy and hot in a lot of places, in the East and Midwest during the summer. We still prefer that to freezing cold blizzards! Being from California, we're sissies when it comes to that stuff. Weather and finances are the driving forces in it. And availability. Not only availability, but demand for the group from all the State Fairs and amphitheaters; they all want to book us during that time.

I guess everyone in the band still enjoys going out and doing it.

Yeah, we do enjoy doing what we do for a living, and we try to make it reasonable. I mean we don't do 90 days in a row. We do three or four weeks and then take a couple weeks off, then do another three or four weeks.

By the time you are 60, do you still see yourself out on the road?

I don't look at it as a problem. My voice sounds quite similar to what it sounded like in the '60s. If it keeps sounding similar and we can still do the songs and the desire's there and we're able to evolve and encompass a few more things of meaning to us. Such as we began to do with "Summer In Paradise," the song. If we're able to mature and evolve those concerns that we naturally have for our life, the planet, our children, and what have you, then I say yeah, there would be a purpose to it. Whether we do it as the Beach Boys or some different offshoot, I'm not sure. It would be nice to improve or repair the damage or the schisms of the past; these would be Brian and ourselves and the group wigwam. At least for some studio work, at the very least, become I think that would be a really nice opportunity to close the chapter on separateness and negativity and open up a new chapter of harmony. Endless harmony, as Bruce would say!

When your page in the history books has been written, what would you most like to be remembered for?

You mean personally?

Personally and as a group, as well.

Personally, I'd like to use my creativity and energy, once I got in the position with the right people to do so, to evolve some new systems of entertainment. Films, music, and television that promotes positive things in life and actually fund things that are needed in life. There's a lot of ignorance out there. Not enough education. So there ought to be people smart enough to figure out ways to educate everybody, to feed everybody, to take care of everybody healthwise and stuff. But there is nobody yet that's surfaced that's smart enough. So I'd like to be a part of those groups that are smart enough and committed enough to create new ways of doing things and make enough money to get rid of the problems either through invention or new distribution methods or whatever. If I could do a film which is a half a billion dollar grossing film, and three quarters of it went to a fund for education, we could get a lot of people educated, if we did that with 50 or 100 films. So, it's a dream I have, and that's one of the things I'd like to do with my mind and time and energies… to build a better mousetrap. Create our way out of the situations that affect the earth. Including deforestation and so on. I'd like to have enough money to buy endangered forests so there wouldn't be any problem. So that's on a personal, spiritual, and/or philanthropic level. Those are my main goals.

With the group, I'd like to see if the group could, like I said, evolve and grow and start to communicate some values that are a little bit more evolutionary and maybe necessary at this point in time in life. If the Beach Boys can be evolutionary and mean something, that's great. I think nature will support that, and we'll feel good about it. If we don't, then I think the Beach Boys will be like a loving anachronism. Meaning, it has nothing to do with reality. We made some great music together, but it ended at a certain point and time. It's kinda like a geological time period like an epic or something. And if we can give life extension to that era by doing something from this era, this point and time with its concerns and values and needs, and if we can communicate something, then it becomes relevant.

Wouldn't It Be Nice?
Brian Wilson and Tony Asher reunite for *Pet Sounds'* anniversary
by Jerry McCulley

Once again Brian reunited with a previous collaborator to work on new music. This time it was with the Pet Sounds *lyricist Tony Asher, although at the time of writing, no new songs from this partnership had emerged. This short article appeared in the Spring 1996 issue of* Grammy *magazine.*

Does time indeed heal all wounds? In 30 years Brian Wilson and the Beach Boys' *Pet Sounds* album has gone from commercial disappointment (although it reached #10 on the charts in 1966 it was the first album of new material since the band's 1962 debut not to earn a gold record) to being celebrated as one of the greatest artist achievements in pop music history. The multi faceted musical talents of Wilson, *Pet Sounds'* writer / arranger / producer have long been enthusiastically endorsed by scores of other musicians songwriters engineers and producers. "If there is one person that I have to select as a living genius of pop music I would choose Brian Wilson"; an impressive compliment – especially coming from legendary Beatles producer George Martin in 1996.

"I'm not a genius" the NARAS member once said with typical modesty ''I'm just a hard working guy". Capitol Records' *The Pet Sounds Sessions* boxed set should help settle the argument; the four disc package is the most gratifying documentation / dissection of a single recording project yet attempted.

Taking a break from dubbing his distinctive high harmony on an upcoming Beach Boys country music project, Wilson collapses on a couch in the control room of Capitol's historic Studio A and briefly reminisces "I feel like I was born at Capitol Records" he mumbles, initially seeming trapped in a familiar TV commercial as he comically struggles to talk through a mouth-full of saltine crackers – got milk?

"We held prayer sessions, (my brother) Carl and me praying for the birth of an album that would bring spiritual love to people," Wilson says of *Pet Sounds'* evolution. Indeed Wilson with the unlikely lyrical collaboration of then struggling young advertising copywriter Tony Asher bravely eschewed the stereotypical sun 'n' fun formula of most previous Beach Boys records on *Pet Sounds* creating an emotionally introspective, musically haunting masterwork "We were in a space where we wanted to do some good. We wanted to do good for people. In that way we were holy, but in other ways we were square". Wilson puzzles "How do you size it up?"

But Wilson admits spiritual concerns were tempered by no small amount of competitive spirit. Socialising with friends in late 1965, Brian recalls sizing up the competition: "They sat down and said 'We want you to hear something by the Beatles [*Rubber Soul*] that's going to blow your mind.' I said 'I doubt it!' just being playful. But after I heard 'Girl' I said 'Oh my God, not that! Not the

Beatles!' So I said I'm going to go in and do something great like the Beatles. It really was a challenge."

"If you take it song for song *Pet Sounds* is an album with (a lot) of 'single' type songs on it. We released 'Wouldn't It Be Nice' and 'God Only Knows' from the album and they did fairly well. 'Caroline No' was released as a single under my name but it only went to No. 32 on the charts. The album didn't sell really all that well but it did have quite an impact on the recording industry. Because of that I was very proud of the feedback." And what feedback: "My influence [on *Sgt. Pepper*]" said Paul McCartney "was basically the *Pet Sounds* album. John was influenced by it.... It was the record of the time you know?"

Lyricist Tony Asher who's since pursued highly successful careers as a writer, jingle producer, advertising executive and marketing consultant, remembers that the creative genesis of *Pet Sounds* involved no small amount of business trepidation. "Both of us have some concerns that we would leave a big part of the Beach Boys' fans out. I can remember a conversation which Brian and I had after we had finished writing a song and he was just sitting at the piano playing it – the lyric was complete so he just sang it through one more time – when it was over he looked at me and said 'Boy, people are going to know that this is not a typical Beach Boys song.' It was not business as usual, I had that sense. But I didn't know if that was good or bad. Initially I think our only criteria was 'gee I hope this sells a lot of records.' And of course it wasn't as successful as any of the previous Beach Boys albums had been, so to that extent we were initially disappointed."

"But in a way maybe it was okay that that happened. If I had to choose between having what most albums of course do – they're tremendously successful initially, then as time goes by they just sort of evaporate – I guess I'd take [the fate] we got which is quite flattering."

Potentially more gratifying is the out-of-the-blue offer Wilson made Asher during the course of a joint interview for the *Pet Sounds* box set: the renewal of a songwriting partnership that had been dormant for 30 years. Is working with Wilson in 1996, as Yogi Berra might say, deja vu all over again? "It's very similar," Asher says. ''Remember when this partnership began he hardly knew me. Whatever kind of reputation I had with him was second hand. Frankly, I think there was a certain amount of desperation [then], he needed somebody to work with because he was getting pressure from the label. Now when we're getting back together he has a little different feeling about me, partly because of what we did before and also because of what he knows about what I've done since then. I feel like it's a more equal kind of experience and I'm really enjoying it for that reason. And there's a whole other layer of satisfaction which comes from the fact that Brian's excited, he's enthusiastic and he wants to get in the studio."

"Tony's grown a lot" Wilson says of the man who gave *Pet Sounds* its distinctive emotional language. "I guess we all evolve together in a sense. He's a very business-like person. He has fun but his work means so much to him that he sacrifices a little of the 'ha-ha-ha' kind of fun because that's just his nature."

Given the largely unfulfilled promises of past "Brian is Back" publicity campaigns and the mythic aura that surrounds their first collaboration, both men are understandably cautious in discussing their new music. Asher nonetheless braves comparisons with his own musical legend. "It's similar in this respect" he says of their songwriting reunion "this was true the first time and it's true now; we are not saying 'hey what's hot today and what can we do that's what people are looking for or expecting today?' We never thought about that [writing *Pet Sounds*], never played records and said 'gee that's the hottest record on the charts let's try to do something in that genre.' We didn't try anything based on what was happening at the time."

"There are no deadlines," Wilson says of his current efforts. "All we've got to do is do what we do and it'll be cool, all the scared trips that I go through will pass. I was scared as hell back [in 1966] because I felt like something was on my shoulders to keep moving with regards to what was going on in music then. But by and large, by 1995 I had realised that to blend into something is more important than to try to be something great yourself. The challenge for me now is to blend into the song rather than try to do a big deal with it. And that's hard." God only knows.

When Two Great Saints Meet... (it's a humbling experience.) The Creative Resurgence Of The Brian Wilson and Van Dyke Parks Team
by Domenic Priore

About 30 years ago at a backyard party thrown by the son of Doris Day, a time-less collaboration began. A Los Angeles session pianist was overheard by a famous record producer, and the rest is history in the making ... 30 years from the fateful moment. Though this collaboration resulted in only a few songs released prior to 1995, a wellspring of suppressed creativity has finally risen to the surface.

It's not as if notoriety has escaped the artists in question. Brian Wilson was responsible for no less than a major migration to the West Coast of America. His early songs foretold of a land where the warm weather precluded a bevy of scant-ily-clad youth cooling off in the surf to those outside our realm. The self-contained sunburn culture of these kids called for a flippant attitude toward conformity. In 1979 Joey Ramone reveled at "cruisin' around in my GTO," and nothing could be further handed down from Chuck Berry than Wilson's depiction of the surging thrill of surfing's boom era.

Van Dyke Parks' impact has been more subversive. Starting out with his broth-er Carson (author of Frank and Nancy Siniatra's "Something Stupid") in a pretty straight folk combo (The Greenwood County singers, on Kapp Records), Van Dyke left for the greener pastures of session work at about the same time Jimmy Page had done so in England. The work of both men reached beyond their own participation, coloring oodles of similar sounding records during the '60s. If it did-n't have a crunchy guitar, it may have featured the Elizabethan pop harpsichord, which Van Dyke Parks embodied on records like The Byrds' psychedelic deter-minant *5D* or The Beach Boys' masterfully Baroque *Pet Sounds*. *Sgt. Pepper* spread it from there.

None of this has anything to do with 1995, but then neither does *Orange Crate Art*, the first new collaboration released by Wilson and Parks since 1972. As a mat-ter of fact, this new release has nothing to do with 1966 either, other than its when these guys met and collaborated for the first time. All that comes to mind when lis-tening to the album is Stephen Foster and John Steinbeck. Maybe that's something we should have expected from a 50 year old Brian Wilson and Van Dyke Parks. Idle artistry itself has the feeling of continuation and coming full circle. But the roots of this work are imperiously bound to a high flying gestation rivaling the greatest works of recorded music itself, and which remains available mostly in bootleg form. That production, the most famous unreleased record known to mankind, is *Smile*.

Simply put, *Smile* was not released in its time (early 1967) due to legal com-plications between Capitol Records and the Beach Boys. Since then, *Smile* has become more legendary than most released LPs, a haunting 50 minute mosaic on the production level of its lead single "Good Vibrations." The group was attempt-ing to form its own label and as a ploy withheld the music from Capitol until it was too late. This meant that by the time the courts cleared things up The Beatles had released *Sgt. Pepper* and the Monterey Pop Festival had forever changed the course of radio airplay. Wilson and Parks' masterwork would have suffered unjust comparison to The Beatles in the wake of psychedelia. *Pet Sounds*, "Good Vibrations" and the work for *Smile* were influential to *Sgt. Pepper*. Wilson would not have *Smile* mistaken for an imitation.

"It was a very sad experience but I don't dismiss it" Parks admits. "The reasons for my re-approaching Brian were certainly not basically musical, they were personal, highly personal; I wanted to take care of something before I moved on. I felt it was time to do it." Parks has no illusions about the level of accomplishment on *Orange Crate Art*. "This music is not the product of a man in his 20s. It is not that brilliant, it is not that hyperactive and accomplished, it doesn't have such heights of invention and creation. It doesn't dazzle like *Pet Sounds* or *Smile* may have. It doesn't have that sense of novelty. This record is a thing of supreme unimportance. But it is very important to me and I hope it is to Brian, because it will have put a lot of things to rest. It does things to me that represent a solution and holds dear the continuity that an old friendship offers."

Certainly it is the best singing Brian Wilson has done since 1968 in his final heartfelt creation with The Beach Boys, the beautifully understated *Friends*. Once a man with perfect pitch and a beautifully resonant voice to match, Wilson's lead vocals had taken on the feeling of intentional sabotage for the projects he was forced to do in the '70s and '80s. The whole "Brian is Back" fiasco perpetrated by The Beach Boys in 1976 is where the hoarse nose-dive began and later a much improved voice appeared on *Brian Wilson*, his first solo album in 1988. But we were still hearing the sound of a forced Wilson vocal, most likely in a quiet rebellion against the svengali-like dictatorship of Eugene E. Landy, who had attempted to admonish his own "psychiatric" work with Wilson in a foiled Broadway play on the level of the Helen Keller Story. Thankfully, those days are over.

Brian Wilson humbly acknowledges Parks' role in his return to form in the vocal department.

"[Van Dyke] had his leadership in the studio … wonderful. A very great producer, and a very great leader, and he's also able to write music tailor-made for the artist that he's writing for, which is another thing people don't realize. Not only were those songs tailor-made for my voice, but the productions were a perfect frame for a nice picture. Really quite becoming, and very warm." I remind Wilson of his favorite Beach Boys album *Friends*. and the warmth inherent to that project "*Friends* … whooh! Talk about vocals! That's exactly it. Simple things are said in the songs [of both albums]. What Van Dyke had said lyrically, however, was also very good for California."

Indeed like *Smile*, it's hard to pick up on initial listening, the deep seeded messages of the songs. They're deceptively simple. "Orange crate art popularized California" reminds Parks. "It brought in Anglo Saxons who crossed the divide, [believing] in their Manifest Destiny to make it to this Gold Rush country and beyond. Beyond the Gold Rush came Yankee colonization. After the early land and robber barons laid out the high stakes of railroads and oil, it was decided that these valleys should become an agrarian Eden. Basically, the citrus industry became possible with the rail. I remember as a child growing up in Mississippi, every Christmas, getting an orange – it was an exotic treat. So orange crate art became interesting, to me because of its power in colonizing California. It became a logo".

But it wasn't only the blue collar pop art of the 1880s setting the framework for these songs. Plein air art was developing in California at about the same time, and it had very much to do with the clarity of the atmosphere. "The French Impressionists got word of what was going on over here" Parks notes, "and many of them took this impression of California at the same parallel, the 32nd degree, the one that LA sits on. This really created a relationship between the California Impressionists and the French Impressionists. There's a great kinship, a highly interpretive, very personal kind of spin on the light that surrounds us". To interpret the soul of a long gone cultural exchange between Paris and Los Angeles, it may just take the vocal artistry of this century's best adman for California, Brian Wilson. The compositional spirit of Parks expresses a central preoccupation with what we are losing, and defends what we have not yet destroyed in our beautiful, but increasingly uglified, Golden State. Parks relates solutions offered beneath gorgeous music inspired by paintings; "I must tell you, there is nothing sentimental about this album. It is driven with anger, and it is in pursuit of justice. Its politics are green. It's a tree-hugging son-of-a-bitch, and it absolutely believes in the future. It seeks its torque, its strength and its resolve in a retrospective fashion. The idealised California you see in these paintings is a place of refreshment, and it's still within reach here, in our time." These California art pieces can be viewed in the books *Oh! California* (Chronicle Books) and *Second Nature* (te Neues Publishing Co.), for your pleasure and research.

It is rather mind blowing that Parks was able to access such a talent as Brian Wilson to accommodate his subversive artistic grasp. It's certainly the most melodic album Parks has ever done. Counting his debut LP for Warner Brothers in 1968, *Song Cycle*, the man has only released 5 solo LP's in 28 years. The first was an extension of the patchwork quilt method of melodic juxtaposition that had colored his work with Wilson on *Smile*. Since then the records explored various Caribbean, Latin and Asian rhythms, all married to Parks' lyrical sophistication. In writing for Wilson, one hears a return to his own personal roots, the folk music of traditional American Gothic sounds. *Orange Crate Art* is colored with ragtime, Gershwin and the aforementioned Stephen Foster feel. But in all honesty, Parks' first single for MGM Records in 1966, "Come To The Sunshine" (later covered by a San Francisco group, Harpers Bizarre on their *Feelin' Groovy* LP), speaks fathoms more as to just why this guy is able to write songs for someone with the supreme melodious talents of a Brian Wilson.

"I've never been produced, in 35 years, never been produced" exclaims Wilson. "I like 'Summer in Monterey,' I like 'Palm Tree and Moon'... what he had done, was he put a mood together. He had this mood, and you think ... it's quite heavy. What he did is, he wrote it out on paper, so he wouldn't forget. He'd take his manuscript in the studio and teach me my parts that he'd written out on the staffs. Then he'd go [sings] 'Eldorado' and I'd go 'Eldorado', then he'd teach me the higher parts, and another higher part. I'd find it, and he'd say 'right there.' 'O.K. roll tape...O.K. overdub that and put your voice on twice.' It's unbelievable, the process it took to go through the whole album. The fascinating thing to me is how he can make such great things so quick. YOU would wonder what the secret is".

Indeed, it took three years for the album to be completed. But one must remember what else was going on in Wilson's life. One lawsuit concerned Brian attempting to regain his publishing, which his father sold after forging his son's signature. Another was from his cousin Mike Love, who claimed authorship on some of Wilson's songs and won. The most important lawsuit of all these was the one that forced Landy to go away, and fortunately, that's the most important decision to have gone in Wilson's favor. Landy had set himself up for 100% of Wilson's inheritance, in addition to causing physical damage to Wilson. Landy had also begun to take control over Wilson's new music, which in its worst incarnation. was, thankfully, unreleased. Amazingly Parks got great work out of Wilson during an extremely transitional period in Brian's life.

"It was very refreshing when Brian got engaged to his now-wife Melinda, because that simplified everything" Parks says. "At one time, some of the people involved with Brian may have been necessary in his life. I don't know that, but I know that I don't enjoy working around people who are not specifically involved in the production. I think that privacy is very important in a collaboration; mutual respect and trust, and confidence, and editorial approval. All those things are important in getting a real sense of collaboration. We were completing this project just as that was becoming a possibility. He is in a very strong field of mutual love and exploration and curiosity with his new marriage, and it's a wonderful thing to see. I think that it will change his whole life, because no one is being hired to guard Brian's interest. The mice are no longer guarding the cheese...O.K.?"

Indeed? Melinda Wilson thoroughly understands the rare position her husband holds. As one of the four most enduring dreamweavers of the '60s, he is somewhat alone, with Bob Dylan, as the sole source of the music, unlike the teams of Jagger/ Richard and Lennon/ McCartney. All financially purging claws reach to both Dylan and Wilson, alone in their precarious perches. Melinda takes great care in helping Wilson handle the onslaught, allowing him the creative space he needs. "Brian is warm, he's vulnerable and he takes things personally. Therefore he's elusive, extremely shy, and extremely sensitive, and these people know that, so when they come on strong, he's like a turtle. He goes into his shell, and that's where people have taken advantage of him in the past. We're just beginning to overcome that, and it's starting to got better. We're beginning to see the good side of life."

"Yeah, 'San Francisco' (whistles the tune), that stuff ... is one hell of a great vocal. That was definitely the one that topped them all, that's 'San Francisco.' Number 1... number 1 record in the world, record." Wilson is staring at me with a fixed look of determination, confidence, and a sense of achievement. This is the Brian Wilson I grew to love, from seeing his confident direction on the back of the first Beach Boys album *Surfin' Safari* as a small child in the early '60s. In 1963, his band opened for Dick Dale and his Deltones at the Barnes Park Community Centre in Monterey Park (across the street from my house), and the next night turned on the juice in a perfomance at Mark Keppel High School in Alhambra, again, opening for Dale. It was 10 years later that I would attend this same High School, and that's about the time of the first Wilson/ Parks collaboration "Sail on Sailor," which earned great popularity on progressive FM radio in the Los Angeles area and beyond.

That record was one of those that actually donged the *Billboard* charts with little or no airplay during radio's transitional period from Top 40 formats to narrowcasted FM superiority. Brian Wilson is somewhat unaware of the fact that "Stairway to Heaven" and "Freebird" enjoy the Guinness World Record for airplay time with similar chart-slow records. He's spent most of his time since the 60s avoiding the mainstream, as it were, so we're getting an uninfected artist. One hopes he can take resolve in the fact that Top 40 is insignificant today, and that great music reaches a wider, more lasting audience through merit. In Wilson's heart, he's always known this; his ultimate goal is to make people happy with his music. "I want to do something good, that someone will like" he reflects, "I want to make music that people need, not just throw crap out there. It took a very long time to get those background parts. It was pretty rough, but so much fun to sing. I was buzzin'... I couldn't believe it."

"He had a constant struggle with commercialism – what is gonna sell, and what is gonna be on the radio – and what he really wanted to do, and he still has that conflict goin' on. He still does" Melinda reminds. "He grew up with that as a kid, so he's come to expect it." With any luck, it won't deter his artistry. Already, Brian has recorded over 20 brilliant productions with his sidekick Andy Paley that are pure Brian Wilson, in their vocal splendor and their dense, imaginative production. One must never forget that Wilson was the first self-produced artist of the '60s and that the primary reason his music tastes so good is the density and feeling of his unique backing tracks.

Unfortunately, Brian was informed separately by Carl Wilson and Mike Love, that they feel he is incapable of producing a new Beach Boys record. Mike and Carl's knight in shining armor is Don Was, who has gone on record as saying he wants to produce The Beach Boys because he "wants to collect the major artists of the '60s on my production resume like baseball cards." He's even offered to list his credit as "Executive Producer," as he planned to re-record productions already finished marvelously by Brian Wilson. In other words, thank your for your name, Brian, now go away. The Beach Boys need Brian's name (and songs) to get decent bucks for a contract, but they don't want his actual involvement. That's no surprise, it's been this way for years. But the proof is in the pudding. Wilson's 1988 solo album won him universal critical acclaim, a *Billboard* showing in the top 40 for LP sales, and a "Comeback of the Year" award in *Rolling Stone*'s readers poll. The Beach Boys dismal 1992 CD (sans Brian) faded without a trace, another public embarrassment that lost the corporation a lot of money (they couldn't get anyone to sign them, so they put it out on their own.) The pressure for Brian Wilson to re-record his new material with the bland MOR musicianship Don Was gave us on the *I Just Wasn't Made For These Times* soundtrack, matched with the plague of the lightweight post "Kokomo" voices of The Beach Boys would have been the test of Wilson's ability to say no.

This is part of a vicious-circle-of-abuse relationship between Wilson and his old band that began around the time of his initial collaboration with Parks on *Smile*. Neither Parks nor Wilson are too comfortable with the subject, but it's clear that both men have a renewed sense of friendship, and may soon come to terms with the fact that, through bootlegs and tape swapping and some legitimate release, a great deal of people have been affected strongly by their unreleased work from the '60s. When confronted with the reality that diggers like XTC have produced amazing, contemporary music directly influenced by *Smile*, and alternative bands such as Velvet Crush can lovingly title their most recent LP *Teenage Symphonies to God* (a reference to Wilson's simple explanation of the *Smile* music in 1966), both Parks and Wilson seem able to somewhat overcome the pain of what they consider a missed opportunity. "Yeah. I just have this to say," pontificates Wilson about this fine musical hour, "I say that, like, if … if what Van Dyke Parks and I did in the 60s means a lot to people, then I'm proud that I did it. Proud that we did it, if it helped out, meaning spiritually, or anything. We did some heavy shit there."

Parks continues, "This Vietnamese thing was just beyond the pale, and I think with the influence of this new generation of musicians, Brian Wilson wanted to transform his message from fast cars and the illicit underbelly of eroticism, and extend his focus to something of a different nature, representing his greater understanding. I say the effort we all made in the '60s was necessary at the time. The foolishness was incidental. We got something done: we got out of Vietnam, we redefined what a song can do. There's blood, sweat and tears, there are hard lessons learned, and I feel totally at peace with the product of our participation. The only rub for me was that Brian and I did not put out a record together, to completion. We did not bring a record to press. With *Orange Crate Art*, I thought this was our last opportunity, 30 years later, to indicate that I was still interested in participating in a record with him, and I hope it leads somewhere, somewhere else, but I'm happy with it in and of itself."

Two questions remain about this rare but stunning team; will they work, and actually write songs together again. "Yeah, I'd think so… I'd like to do that" Wilson says. In a separate interview, Parks uses similar verbiage. "If somebody lets us do something, and Brian suggests it, I'd be happy to do that." With the door open for both artists, we can only hope it does happen.

Further intrigue about their incandescent work together from 1966 is unavoidable. Today we can pick up the *Smile* versions of "Wonderful", "Cabinessence", "Good Vibrations", "Surf's Up", "Wind Chimes", "Love To Say Dada", "Bicycle Rider", and part one of "Heroes and Villians" at most any record shop. But we're still missing the true *Smile* productions of "Do You Like Worms", "Vegetables", "Holidays", "Look", "The Old Master Painter", "Child Is Father To The Man", "Mrs O'Leary's Cow", "Barnyard", "Well, You're Welcome", and the second part of "Heroes and Villains". That second list is available only on bootlegs. It'd be nice to have it all in one place, at an affordable price in record stores everywhere. Currently, that's a question no-one seems able to answer. It's pretty clear that Parks is the only artist who's collaborated with Wilson, who has been able to give back to Wilson in collaboration the brilliance Wilson can put forth. The songs that have been released from the Smile sessions and the current LP are testaments to the fact that we still have a lot to learn from our own recent history.

What It's Really Like to Collaborate with Brian Wilson, Today! An interview with Andy Paley by Dominic Priore

Andy Paley attended the Beach Boys fans convention in London a few years ago, and stayed behind after the main events to chat to several of us about his the current work with Brian. Andy's love, interest and enthusiasm shone through and it was evident that, as a producer, he sought to provide the atmosphere for Brian to take the lead. This short interview comes from Domenic Priore's Smile *book.*

D.P. *I've been reading a lot of things lately in the press, and in fan publications about the making of Brian Wilson's solo album that just don't ring true...can you help clear some of this up?*

A.P. The main thing is, that what these people [*BBA*, Tobler, Hilburn – ed] are writing stuff, that is wrong about how Brian Wilson's album was made, and about the pressures concerning his collaboration with people like me, and Jeff Lynne...I just want to tell the truth about writing with Brian Wilson.

...O.K. Andy, you did a lot of it... what was your personal experience?

First of all, the credits on the album are wrong. The writing credits, the production credits and musician credits are all inaccurate.

Does that bother you?

Well, I wrote "One For The Boys" with Brian, and you'll only see one name under it. My name stayed on "Meet Me In My Dreams Tonight", "Night Time" and "Rio Grande". In "Night Time", Brian came up with the chorus, and I came up with the verse, chords, and melody for the verse... a 50:50 collaborative effort, but there are probably 5 names on the credits. In "One For The Boys" there are little movements in the middle that I wrote. "Meet Me In My Dreams Tonight" was a 50:50 collaborative effort too...Same with "Rio Grande".

I remember that some writer had implied that you had written "Meet Me In My Dreams Tonight" by yourself, and that Jeff Lynne wrote "Let It Shine", etc...and it seemed that they couldn't believe that Brian Wilson could come up with songs, as if he were dried up as a songwriter...

Look, there were a lot of people helping on that record. There were collaborators, co-producers, six musicians. These people aren't bad people. All were working toward the same end, and if any of them tried to force anything out of me or Brian, it would have been a failure, because this kind of tragic can't be turned on & off like a faucet...

What's the best feature about writing with Brian?

Believe it or not, the best things about writing, producing & collaborating with Brian Wilson in general are his energy, creativity, and his brilliant sense of humor. He is always underrated as a lyricist, but I saw him come up with great lines all the time. By the way, he knows he's good, no matter what anyone else thinks. One of the main reasons we hit it off so well as a writing team was mutual respect and the fact that we shared a lot of the same idols and role models in songwriting.

Like who, for instance?

Goffin, Barry Mann and Cynthia Weil, Neil Sedaka, Gene Pitney … the list would also include Holland-Dozier-Holland, Smokey Robinson, Marvin Gaye, Don Gibson, Randy Newman, George and Ira Gershwin… I don't know, I can't think of all of them right now, but believe me, Brian and I have a great reverence for these people.

So tell us something about the lyrics in "Rio Grande"…

Well, certain lyrics he wrote, certain lyrics I wrote, but we split it up 50:50 … The thing that bothers me though, is to see that people say that Brian is manipulated, or that Brian is a Frankenstein's monster…and that these corporate people forced him to make a record… that's wrong…Brian Wilson never stopped writing songs in his whole life, and there's no reason to think that he shut himself off creatively, and these evil people came along and said "you have to do this, and you have to do that"…that's not true. These people just tried to help. It's not true that Brian was forced to do a *Smile* sounding track.

…You mean, "Rio Grande"?

That all happened when Lenny Waronker suggested to us that we should try and step out of the pop marketplace a little bit and try something a little unusual. For people to say "that's retro" or "that's bribing", or "that's un-natural"… that's not true at all. You could walk up to anybody today, say a painter, and say "try something a little bit different. I like the way you do these realistic paintings, but why not try and do something a little abstract?" Well, the guy might reply "I don't know, I don't ever do that" But the thing with Brian is that he's done it, he's got the facilities to do it, so why not fool around? There's nothing wrong with that, and Brian absolutely enjoyed it, I can guarantee you that. He would not pursue things that he really doesn't like … there's no point. For people to write that we went in and said "This has to sound like *Smile*"… That's nonsense. Songs like "The Tiger's Eye", "Magic Lanterns", "Heavenly Lover" and "Hotter" are pretty much straight ahead pop songs with that angle.

…I know that "Heavenly Lover" was once part of "Rio Grande"… What about this song "The Tiger's Eye" … what's that?

I think we got the title off a Sushi menu. It's about a guy who's worried about his girlfriend in the jungle and he's trying to find her; its got a scary mood to it, but it's got a Motown feel, and a nice climbing bass line in the bridge that I remember. It's spooky, but he's saying "Don't Worry". It's like "Running Bear and Little White Dove". (Sings: "You shouldn't be alone in the jungle at night no, sighin' and a cryin'and feelin' uptight now, so burn your fire bright, don't make a sound").

Brian never stops writing songs. I just don't like some of the things I've read where it makes it look like we said "OK Brian, bamm, bamm, bamm, go in and write a bunch of songs, make an album". It's not that way. And the guy is always writing songs anyway, it's not like someone has to tell him to do it. He does it because it comes naturally to him. Nobody's going around ordering him to write songs except himself … and God.

The Brian Wilson Productions, Mid 90s Style
by Dominic Priore

Written in July 1997, this article usefully sums up where Brian's art appears to be at, as this book goes to press.

In the process of compiling information for this article (originally commissioned by the *LA Weekly*) I had the opportunity to screen some new Brian Wilson productions. These are tapes that Brian paid for with his own money. He did it with a production schedule that was as spontaneous as his inspiration. In other words, Brian would write songs, get hot to do 'em, and went in and *did it*.

His main collaborator for these tracks was Andy Paley, who worked so well with Brian on the 1988 solo album. ("Rio Grande" and "Meet Me In My Dreams Tonight", especially.) The reason that the collaboration was so successful is that unlike the other "star" producers who've come in to work with Brian Wilson – Steve Levine, Terry Melcher, Gary Usher, Jeff Lynne, Russ Titleman and Don Was – Paley does not assume a leadership role. Rather, he lets Brian lead the session, and is also helpful to Brian in that Paley works well as a multi-instrumentalist. If Brian wants something now, which is usually the case, Andy can provide the sounds on call. Having been raised on Beach Boys records, and having worked with Spector in the 1970's, Paley is also a scholar on how to get the exact sound that Brian is looking for. What even die-hard fans fail to realise is that guitar and amplifier settings, tones and the various "musician" details that go into making the Brian Wilson "sound" are not simple to figure out, let alone attain. This has been the major shortcoming of all the aforementioned "star" producers. Lenny Waronker is an exception, but then again his availability – and sometimes, seriousness – is not conducive to Brian's creative whims. It was Waronker, however, who instinctively brought Andy Paley in to the Brian Wilson sessions in 1987, and this was one of the keys to that album's energy.

That said, the new material featured here is unexpurgated Brian Wilson, cut without "outsiders'" input. Beyond that the tapes represent an excited Brian Wilson, fresh from the awful situation with Eugene Landy. It was Landy who bulldozed Wilson into the lyrical psychobabble of *Sweet Insanity* – not to mention its antiseptic *sound* – and the contemptuous legal briefing that was the "biography" *Wouldn't It Be Nice*. Those days are over (Brian is still suffering from lawsuits concerning the biography; whereas some observers feel it should be Landy on the receiving end). Brian has always preferred to avoid hassles, toss off nefarious "business" and continue to create. That's what he did in the period when he made these tracks.

"I'm Getting in Over My Head"
This is easily the best lead vocal performance by Brian Wilson since the *Pet Sounds* / *Friends* era. It actually can be considered on a par with the material from side two of *Beach Boys Today*, vocally; it is that good (though it is a more "mature" voice, it is just as strong and beautiful). Part of the track's impact is in

the convincing nature of the lyrics. They could only come from a man with years of experience of romance's ups and downs. The chords are chromatic, the production dense, and the words display Brian's underrated lyrical ability. Initially the thought of getting in over his head terrifies the protagonist "right out of [his] mind", but upon further consideration of the strength of his love, he realises "maybe that ain't so bad". This track should satisfy anyone yearning for something "serious" from Brian Wilson.

"You're Still a Mystery"
With a basic rhythm track akin to the instrumental "Pet Sounds", this is a ballad full of soaring intrigue. We hear the cool track from Brian Wilson's sessions, but the vocals were cut with the Beach Boys at the Don Was session (it's the only way they would record Brian's new material). It's fantastic to hear Carl and Al singing unison backgrounds to a perfect falsetto lead vocal by Brian. We haven't heard Brian hit it this sweet on a lead vocal in over thirty years.

"Chain Reaction of Love"
This has a rather jarring effect on the listener (as did "Wind Chimes", "Don't Back Down", "Our Prayer" and the harmonica version of "Help Me Rhonda"). It's a good rocker with an infectious chorus, verse and middle eight. The track has a romping feel similar to "Mona", "Honkin' Down the Highway" or "Let Us Go On This Way". The big difference is that the vocals are great now, and there is more thought put into the overall production, especially in the drums and percussion.

"Soul Searchin'"
This is a zero-cool Fats Domino-style ballad. It benefits from a full blown Brian Wilson production, complete with his New Orleans-meets-Phil Spector horn arrangement, and features vocal sessions dubbed back onto it from the inferior Don Was session. Carl Wilson sings a beautiful, heartfelt lead vocal, and the backing vocals are deep and strong. This sounds like it could even be a "hit", without compromising to anything "contemporary" or "radio friendly". "Soul Searchin'" shows best what we are missing due to Mike, Carl, Al and Bruce's apparent lack of respect for Brian's current production ability. It seems they would prefer a *current* "name", radio friendly producer as less of a "risk". And yet, this track *sounds* like a hit. Go figure.

"It's Not Easy Being Me"
After an intro reminiscent of "Those Were the Days", Brian embarks on his most personal song on the tape. As the title suggests, this is Brian Wilson's address – a continuation of "I Just Wasn't Made for These Times" with thirty further years of *dealing with it* behind him. "The same thing haunts me endlessly" Brian sings, and he reminds everyone that "the man you want, is just not there, you'll never find him anywhere". Formidable stuff. He then offers the impossible situation "walk a mile in my shoes, then you'll see it's not easy being me". Brian is baring his soul to you, the listener. This honest song speaks fathoms about Brian's strange reality, and it communicates with the beauty of his economical art. In addition to the lyrics, the solo vocal is passionate, and the sound exquisite.

"Desert Drive"
A rocker based on the middle saxophone riff from "Salt Lake City". A very tough
Spector-like horn section makes it a joy to hear … that is, if you like the sound of
old Beach Boys albums.

"Saturday Morning in the City"
This is Brian in a humorous mode, and also at his most melodic. Brian's vocal is
low and campy (except in the background chorus), as he laundry-lists suburban
pleasures such as garage sales and barbecues, and reels off invigorating jumpy
intonations such as "We're gonna have a fun day".

"The Song Wants to Sleep With You Tonight!"
This one has been released on a CD 45, and it is from the same sessions. It's actually a bit slicker than the rest of the stuff, with a phased organ for an orchestra and
an angelic choir of Brian, Andy Paley and Danny Hutton. The melody plods compared to the rest of the stuff too, but you can hear the good elements at work here
– an excellent fender bass line and great vocals by Brian – and overall this is an
arresting cut.

"Market Place"
This is a personal favourite that has all the calm of "Busy doin' Nothing", and features tossed-off lines of genius like "the world's a zoo, what can we do?" I hum
this all the time.

"I'm Broke"
This is a great bluesy workout for Brian's voice, and he sounds great – howling
and shouting. You can hear that he's having some real fun at last.
   This is also the track that led Brian to take a *rare* stab at Landy in *LA Style* magazine:
   "Dr Landy docsn't like ["I'm Broke"]. He thinks it's too simple. He doesn't
think there's any song to it". Brian also referred to Landy implying one of his new
songs "might be a little outdated". "I didn't know what to say. Let me just say that
the kind of music I hear is *way beyond* having someone tell me I am out of touch".
   It is good to point out at this point that during these sessions synthesisers are
used very sparingly. If you thought that Michael Bernard's synthesiser playing on
the 1988 *Brian Wilson* album was a Landy ploy, you were probably right.
Bernard's playing swamped important parts of that album, and thankfully there is
no such problem here.

"Must Be a Miracle"
Here's one that goes to your heart, with a great sloping melody and words about
having a baby. Brian sings with Andy Paley in a straight-ahead (non-falsetto)
voice. It's the work of a grown, sweet man, and it could make you cry.

"In My Moondreams"
This is a slow, moody surf instrumental in the unique Brian Wilson style of

"Summer Means New Love". It was released in the US on the Del-Fi CD *Pulp Surfin.*

"Mary Anne"
Here's another fun one: great catchy pop that is spontaneous and unpretentious, and will make you happy that Brian Wilson is clearly *still with us.*

"God Did It"
Like "He Came Down", "God Did It" is Brian working in the gospel vocal style and having fun in the process. More great catchy pop.

"Some Sweet Day"
Ideally, this would be a guest slot by the Honeys within the context of a Brian Wilson album. His work within the girl group genre is a very important part of the Brian Wilson legacy, as "He's a Doll" (The Honeys) and "Thinkin' Bout You Baby" (Sharon Marie) surely prove. Besides, *no one* is getting that sound today. So technically, it would not be out of context to have a "guest" track on a Brian Wilson album because, in the case of the girl group sound, the producer is the artist, and the singer or group, the "talent". That said, "Some Sweet Day" is an exuberant, joyous rocker, full of innocence and rumbling power.

"Slightly American Music"
This is the goofy one in the bunch. It is catchy, but the predictable "nostalgia" lyrics about "Bandstand", "Ol' Bing" and "Buddy Holly" make this one embarrassing listening for me.

"Elbow '63"
This is a much better effort at recollection. Brian goes through a rediscovery of the social elements that gave him his competitive drive in the early days of the Beach Boys, and musically it's as if he remembers the fun in that drive too. A rocker, indeed.

"This Could Be the Night"
Released on the Harry Nillson tribute LP, this is a good run through of Phil Spector's classic production for the Modern Folk Quartet. It's also one of Brian's favourite songs.

"Goin' Home"
This is a medium tempo rocker similar to "Hey Girl", the Goffin and King tune by Freddie Scott, and reminiscent in feeling to Wild Honey cuts such as "Country Air" and "Aren't You Glad".

"In the Wink of an Eye"
This is more in the classic 1920's mode of Irving Berlin or George Gershwin. The kind of music you always knew Brian was capable of. Cocktail time, gorgeous.

"Everything's Alright in the World"

A plaintive ballad with simple lyrics, its overall message is that the outside chaos of the world is calmed due to a love affair – a clue to Brian's current happiness?

"The Boogie's Back in Town"
A 90's big band boogie woogie work out with humorous lyrics.

Summing up, the 22 Brian Wilson productions listed here would add up to the best Brian Wilson record of any kind since the 1960s. Crucial is the actual *sound*, which is really more than half of what makes a great Brian Wilson record. The rest is the actual songs themselves. Still none of these factors would have the same impact if the vocals were not as fabulous as they are. The *overall picture* is great – something that never was the case with the other producers who tried to graft *their* own sound onto Brian's songs. With Brian Wilson's talent, the arrangement and production are more than half of what makes his records good, and the reason is this: an average song can be made brilliant by a great performance, but a great song can be ruined by a terrible performance.

What Brian Wilson has unconsciously come up with on the aforementioned tapes reminds me of Nick Lowe's work on the Elvis Costello pinnacle *Get Happy*. The production sneaks everything and the kitchen sink through your spectrum, with 20 songs and no overload. Cross that with the unbounded joy of Jeff Barry's work with The Archies and the fun style of rock 'n' roll romp that could only come from Brian Wilson's way with words and structure, and you get an idea of the overall feel. The styles encompass *Friends*-type songs, Honeys-type songs, *Beach Boys Today* and *Sunflower*-type songs, and *Pet Sounds*-type songs, and are all mastered wonderfully here by a rejuvenated Brian Wilson. Many of the songs also feature lead vocals by Brian which range with the best he's ever done.

So, after many years of mixed and often patchy results from big budget sessions, with big name producers, Brian Wilson finally produces some of his best music since the 60s at a series of self-produced and self-financed sessions, with no actual record release in sight. Where does all this leave Brian Wilson as we approach the end of the 90s? It appears that there is a major disparity between Brian's art, and how it is perceived by his "advisors". The adult oriented FM rock production that is often heaped upon Brian's music, is clearly out of touch with the heart of his youthfully innocent music. His essential *honesty* is at odds with the mainstream corporate rock world. These days, Brian Wilson's cult audience is with Generation X kids who've learned about him through their musician heroes, and who value this honesty. People of Brian's own age have very set ideas of how the music of the Beach Boys or Brian Wilson should sound, and winning this audience over – be they also fans of Michael Bolton, Don Henley, or Bruce Springsteen or New Age Fluff – will forever be a tough call. Brian has already made an album that will reach the fans who appreciate *why* his art is worthwhile. Brian's mentors these days are surely unaware of all of this; indeed Brian himself appears unconscious of what he has managed to do. Thus far, the tapes I write of have been relegated to "storage".

The problem remains in Brian's advisory staff, whose taste seems to lean toward AAA (Adult Album Alternative, a radio format that will never accept Brian Wilson at the level of cult status) and AC (Adult Contemporary, in other words, Michael Bolton, Kenny G *hell*) Brian's involvement with Joe Thomas, (the producer who worked with Brian and the Beach Boys and a number of country artists on the 1996 album, *Stars and Stripes*, and with whom Brian has apparently signed a two album deal) who has produced acts along the lines of Peter Cetera, and who owns a high tech, state of the art studio, that to my mind is soulless, is now I feel the main stumbling block. Everything that comes from Thomas's Chicago studio sounds to me supremely sterile, and yet this is where Brian now spends most of his time; it's gotten to the point where a house has been purchased nearby.

The rub is this: Brian was offered a goodly sum of money by Seymour Stein's Sire label to complete the aforementioned tapes for release. Clearly Stein is a much better judge of Brian's audience than those who currently surround him – remember Seymour Stein is the man who signed The Ramones, who became one of the most influential rock and roll bands of the past twenty years. A second meeting with Stein took place where Joe Thomas was brought in, and Thomas offered to deliver newly recorded Brian Wilson tapes from *his* studio (this offer was thankfully rejected). What the Wilson entourage fails to appreciate is the real McCoy, and that what is already on the tape is the cat's meow.

Marilyn At The Typewriter:
A Short Marilyn Wilson Interview
by Kingsley Abbott

Marilyn Wilson has been asked to talk about The Beach Boys a thousand times. After all, in addition to being Brian's wife, she was involved musically and personally with the band for such a long time. As a member of The Honeys and (American) Spring she was produced by Brian, but she also sung uncredited on most of the Beach Boys albums. She has been prepared to answer questions once more for this book, and her answers are succinct, germane and finally celebratory of the music.

KA: *Could you give us some of your early impressions of Brian and The Beach Boys as a musical entity?*

MW: I thought that they were innocent and friendly. We were all around the same age, and it was great having boys interested in singing music, besides us (the Honeys).

What was it like for The Honeys when Brian took on the role of producer? How much input did you have? Do you have a favourite recording?

Brian was wonderful to work with. He loved each of our individual voices, and made us all feel uniquely special. He was awfully cute, and funny. As a producer, we just gave him free rein, and let the Master do his work. If we had a suggestion, he would listen, and maybe do it, but he already had it all figured out anyway. We just did what he said, and it was always so great! My favorite Honeys record was "The One You Can't Have".

The Honeys appeared uncredited on a large number of Beach Boys songs. What are your memories of these times in the studios? How were you involved? Any favourites? How much did you record directly with the Beach Boys other than Brian?

I was practically on every Beach Boy album, doing a background somewhere, during my marriage. I always loved singing with the guys. They were all so good, and it was such a full sound. I was just the extra needed voice. My favorite was "Rock and Roll Music". The Honeys also sang once in a while, and of course you know that we were the cheerleaders on "Be True To Your School". I recorded a little with Carl. Our voices blended together so well. It was kind of cosmic. We should have made an album together. Our blend was amazing.

In retrospect, do you think Brian could have coped, or been helped to cope with the pressures that came with success?

I think Brian would have been able to cope, if it were not for drugs. Anyone who knew Brian, pre-drugs, saw an eccentric, talented, beautiful, sensitive person, who made them laugh, and feel good. He was a beautiful human being.

The mid 60s is seen by most commentators as Brian's creative peak. What directions do you think he would have followed later assuming good health?

I think he would be known today as a top motion picture scorer, and would have had his own record company. He could have produced all the acts he wanted and been so creative. It would have been so easy for him. It is the only thing he really feels comfortable doing.

You were involved in the decision to bring in Dr. Landy to help Brian in the 70s. What are your thoughts on this chapter and how it affected Brian as a musician?

Dr. Landy was the only doctor I found that was creative and inventive enough and willing to accept the challenge of Brian Wilson. Who could predict he thought himself as the star too? Why couldn't he have just been a good doctor, charge regular prices, and have self satisfaction from helping someone so special? I think Brian put him on musically, just to appease him. I do not believe he inspired Brian at all, musically.

What do you consider to be the happiest and most productive period (assuming that those two go together) in Beach Boys/Honeys/Spring/Brian history?

The happiest and most productive period for The Honeys, with Brian, was the late 1963 and 1964. Happiest Spring was 1972, when we made our album, and toured Europe, while we were in Holland, and the Beach Boys were making the *Holland* album, As for the Beach Boys, and this is just my observation and opinion, it was the "Fun, Fun Fun" period. It was the most natural time. I think that there is no doubt, that the most creative period for the Beach Boys, who was Brian Wilson, was the time of Pet Sounds. It was the real masterpiece!

How do you judge all the pieces of writing from over the years about The Beach Boys? Is there a piece that particularly stands out in your mind (for whatever reason), or that you feel came close to illuminating the heart of the band? Did any of the band react for or against any piece that you know of?

There were things written and people just took the word of other people. I never thought that was fair. It was insulting! No-one lived our lives, and only we know the truth about everything that went on. I think that most writers out there, want people to think that they know, and want to make a buck, not caring who they would hurt. I wouldn't even give credit to anyone, by mentioning their names.

Several Beach Boys children are now musically active. What do Carnie and Wendy feel about their recent work with their father? Do you think there will be future projects?

Carnie and Wendy loved singing and being creative with their father. Not too many people know the joy you feel when you're all singing at the microphone, and your voices are all blending together. It is heavenly. I don't know what will happen next.

From a musical stand point, what do you think will be looked back on as the really key pieces of Beach Boys/Brian Wilson music in 100 years time?

That Brian and the Beach Boys brought innocence, beach, sun and the freedom to be mixed together with music. Their music is timeless. It makes you feel good, no matter what age you are. Brian is a musical icon, and he was born with a very special gift from God.

Postscript
by Kingsley Abbott, September 1997

In 1965 The Beach Boys released *Summer Days (and Summer Nights!!)*, which was to be their last album of "Summer Fun" that decade. The lead track on that album, "Amusement Parks U.S.A.", featured the voice of a circus barker inviting us to "Step right up to The Beach Boys' Circus – The best little show in town!" The analogy was very appropriate, and took on more and more resonance as the years went by. To briefly adopt this circus metaphor, the history of the act might have read thus:

Their early youthful keenness had given us all the thrills of a family tumbling troupe, with their father as the initial anchor man. As they matured, they struck out on their own with new and astonishing feats of daring. It was as if the oldest son, the new acknowledged leader, was climbing to the highest trapeze with the others holding the rope steady as they watched him attempt untried tricks without a safety net. But ... maybe he overreached ... maybe the crowd expected too much ... maybe there was too much white hand powder ... maybe some of those on the rope whispered to him that he couldn't do it ... he fell and became temporarily paralysed, with his confidence shot to pieces. The act continued, going back to the early, easier show which had always satisfied the crowds. At one stage they tried to bring their star back into the act, only this time it was in the guise of a dancing bear. The bear act was never going to work, so it was dumped again for the tried and tested tricks. The star withdrew again into the shadows, and many years passed with little activity or artistic stimulation, until eventually, he slowly and tentatively, blinking slightly, stepped back into the spotlight. This time though, he left the family tent and set out with some old acrobatic friends to try to work out a new, more mature act. The original show continued without their star but, as circuses often do, began to look a little tawdry and tacky. Even so, some parts of the act still thrilled new generations and recalled the glory days, but new tricks were non-existent. Those who knew the star well helped him towards a new life where, whilst he did not attempt the tricks of his youth, he was able to use his wealth of experience and talent in safer ways.

Brian Wilson and The Beach Boys were, and are, wonderfully talented musicians. They have continued to give us sublime popular music throughout much of the second half of the twentieth century. Much of their work – both individual songs and albums – has, and will continue to survive the test of time, remaining part of the canon of classic popular music as long as this term has meaning. *Back to the Beach*, through its choice of articles and essays, is above all, a critical appreciation of this fact. It is to be hoped that as much as is possible of Brian and the Beach Boys' creativity will continue in solo or group projects, and that their influence will continue to resonate through other, perhaps yet unborn, musicians.

PART FOUR

Goin' On

Carl Wilson
by Geoffrey Himes

After initially being the 'baby boy' of the group, Carl Wilson very soon matured to become Brian's unspoken deputy and heir to the throne. When a variety of directions beckoned and differing approaches to the group appeared, it was Carl who took on the mantle of on-stage band leader and off-stage anchor and conscience. This piece from Geoffrey Himes was published in edited form in Musician *magazine on 16 December 1982, and appears here in fuller form. It offers a full interpersonal and musical perspective of the group through Carl's eyes.*

No one is closer to the Beach Boys story than Carl Wilson, Brian's youngest brother. "Brian, in fact, did stay home and create a whole world at the piano," Carl recalls. A bushy, brown beard wraps around his chubby, cherubic face as he stands by the window of his house at Colorado's Caribou Ranch. The snow-capped Continental Divide looms through the window. "Brian made this whole picture, and people were mad to get to California. There was an awe connected to California and the beach and the way we lived. Those were the people who were really cool. But it wasn't the real California so much as the California in Brian's songs."

"I've always been the one who worked real closely with Brian," Carl claims. "I was his sounding board; I was his underling. I always tagged along. In addition to being one of the players in the studio, I worked with him in the control room, because he wanted my ear. Like on 'Good Vibrations,' he said, 'I want to put an instrument here in this register.' And I said, 'Cello.' And that's what plays those triplets in there. I just absorbed so many little details over years of recording. The most important thing was his way of dealing with musicians. He knew how to communicate with people about getting a piece of music across and how he wanted it played. And he listened. That was always the key for us; using our ears."

Carl was only a freshman in high school when his big brother Brian called him into the family den to teach him a new song called "Surfer Girl." Even as Carl learned the mid-range harmony vocal devilishly close to Brian's lead, he realised this ballad offered far more than anything on the radio. As the melody rose and fell through minors and sevenths on the triplet bass figure, it seemed to offer a world of utopian ideal romance to the young girl on the beach. As the song modulated up a whole step for the final verse it held out the promise that this utopian world was a birthright.

"'Surfer Girl' has a real spiritual quality to it," Carl says, using the present tense, for the song has not faded a bit in 21 years. "I don't know who he wrote it for, but there's a real heart attached to that. The chords are just so filling. For its time, the record was so advanced. It was really beautiful to be alive when that record was playing. That's what blows me away about music. You put this needle on this little plastic thing, and the whole atmosphere can be transformed. The way our voices sounded on that, the melody Brian wrote, the way he put the arrangement together, that might be the perfect coming together of all elements. It's an

R&B tune in structure with that slow rock beat. 'The introduction has Brian going the opposite way, one to three-minor and down to the sixth, and there's all those minor sevenths. It's very enchanting; it's very Brian."

The family drama begins at 3701 W. 119th St. in a lower-middle-class housing development in Hawthorne, a Los Angeles suburb five miles inland. It was a modest place of neatly mowed lawns, sidewalks and $2000 two-bedroom homes. "I just remember music was always present," Carl says, "My dad was a part-time songwriter, and we always had a couple of pianos in the house and a jukebox. We had a garage that my dad fixed up into a den. We'd all get around the piano; my mom would play, and later Brian started to play. By 10, he could already play great boogie woogie piano.

"I remember one day we had our kitchen remodeled; we had an island; that was the big thing in the '50s. My cousin Shirley came over and said, 'I just love this new record by Elvis Presley, 'Heartbreak Hotel'. That was the first I was aware of rock'n'roll. Another time I was down the street at a friend's and we were in the backyard, and the radio came on with Little Richard's 'Tutti Frutti. I thought I was going to jump out my skin; the record was so alive and energetic, I couldn't believe my ears. Frankie Lymon was one of everyone's favourites. 'Why Do Fools Fall in Love' was a powerful record for those days. American Bandstand was a great place to hear new records and see the pretty girls dance. My dad used to say, 'Turn it off, he sounds like he's going insane.' We had the same arguments with our parents that everyone had. I had a real normal background. I used to stub my toe a lot."

"When I was 10, I'd have to sing a background part he'd made up as a rearrangement of a Four Freshmen tune. The thing about that kind of modern jazz is the parts are very strange; it's not like singing Christmas carols like we also did. I had to listen real hard; I had to remember exactly how the notes went and all the notes were flatted or sharped; these weren't your regular three-chord tunes. If I'd make a mistake, he'd say, 'No, it goes like this,' and I'd have to do it again until I got it right. Just so it would be more fun, I started to learn my parts quicker. It was great training. By the time, I was 15, I could hear a part one time and have it."

The five young boys went to the local studio of Hite & Dorinda Morgan, friends of Murry's. They cut four songs, including "Surfin'." "It was my guitar," Carl recalls. "Alan had the upright bass, and Brian played a single snare drum with a pencil and that was it. Brian took his shirt off and put it over the drum because it was too loud. We did it all at once, with Michael on one microphone and the rest of us on another." The single, released on X and Candix Records, became a regional hit and broke the top 100 nationally. "Dennis was so thrilled," Carl says, "because he was living it. He went to school and his friends said, 'We were on our way home from the beach, totally exhausted from riding the waves all day. We heard your record come on and it turned us on so much we went back to the beach.'"

Dennis had never been much of a participant in the family singalongs, because he was a real rough-and-tumble, outdoorsy kid. He was the only real surfer in the group, though. "He was the only one," Carl concedes. "I tried it, but I could never get good, so I gave it up. Dennis was really living it; that was his life. I remember everyone was bleaching their hair; Brian tried it and it turned out a very unnatural orange-very funny. But Brian drew on Dennis' experiences. I remember Brian would drill Dennis on what was going on, really pump him for the terminology and the newest thing. Dennis was the embodiment of the group; he lived what we were singing about. If it hadn't been for Dennis, the group wouldn't have happened in the same way. I mean, we could have gotten it from magazines like everyone else did, but Dennis was out there doing it. He made it true."

The real break through came in 1963. "When we heard 'Surfin' USA', we just knew it was going to be an undeniably big hit that could be played with anything. It was the first time we were aware we could make a powerful record. Instead of a little hokey California style of music, Brian adopted a more universal style, and he got into the mainstream of rock for the first time. Brian had this idea to change 'Sweet Little 16' into 'Surfin' USA' We were total Chuck Berry freaks, and the original Chuck Berry record is a fabulous record, but we made it our own. Brian just transformed it into a Beach Boys record. You don't go, "Oh, that's the tune," which is unusual.

A large part of the record's power came from Carl's unique guitar style that blended the Chuck Berry R&B style with the Dick Dale surf style. Carl took lessons before the group started from a guy on the next street named John Maus, who later went to England and became one of the Walker Brothers. "My first guitar was a Kay," Carl explains, and John taught me the surf picking technique. Everything was a down stroke except the one-and-beat, which was up the second eighth note. I would mute the strings a bit to get that clipped surf sound. I'd just lightly hit the strings with the palm of my picking hand to give it more of a percussive sound. It was a style that became popular in Southern California with a lot of surf bands. I remember going to see Dick Dale and the Belairs. Most of them were guitar bands though, and that's why we surfaced, because we had the vocals.

"I combined that surf style with a white approach to the Chuck Berry style. Our sound was very clean; we had big amps that made a clean sound, while he was just turning his amps up and cranking. I used a Stratocaster on the early records. We were young and foolish; we wanted the biggest, best, newest, most powerful thing: Fender amps, Showman amps, Dual Showman. This summer I used a Gibson 335 and an Epiphone 12-string. Last year when I was rocking out more on the Doobie Brothers tour, I used a Stratocaster, one of the first Strats ever made. It has a great neck and makes a wonderful sound. The 335 is the loudest guitar we have; it's very comfortable and versatile. Brian played Fender Precision bass on the early records; it was a great recording bass. Dennis was into Camco drums for a long time. The snare was good and bright and it had a full range, He used Zecos for a few years; he still had a set to record on."

The group's real contribution musically, though, was its vocals. Though Brian wrote the arrangement, the records wouldn't have sounded the same if he hadn't had five lead quality voices. In much the same way he had trained Carl earlier, Brian trained the other three to follow difficult parts at perfect pitch by drilling them to exacting standards. Even today, when the group concentrates, they can achieve that of precision-tuned intervals that only seems to come from family groups like the Jacksons or Roches.

"Everyone senses his part," Carl explains. "When Brian would present a song to us, we would almost know what our part would be. Michael always sang the bottom; I would sing the one above that, then would come Dennis or Alan, and then Brian on top. We had a feeling for it. Michael has a beautifully rich, very full-sounding bass voice. Yet his lead singing is real nasal, real punk. It's not widely known, but Michael had a hand in a lot of the arrangements. He would bring out the funkier approaches; he'd decide what rhythms and syllables to use in the background, whether to go shoo-boo-bop or bom-bom-did-di-did-did. It makes a big difference, because it can change the whole rhythm, the whole colour and tone of it. We're big oooh-ers; we love to oooh. It's a big, full sound, that's very pleasing to us; it opens up the heart.

"Alan's voice has a bright timbre to it; it really cuts. Brian's voice is very complete. He's not using it now; it's really sad. But when he does, he has a very thick voice, a full sounding voice. Even when he sings falsetto, it's full. It's not a thin sound like Frankie Valli; it's a big, high note. I think my voice has a kind of calm sound, like the sound we got on 'God Only Knows'. But I also love to sing R&B, to sing real loud, gruff rock stuff, like I am now.

"As early as some of the very first records we did, the background parts took the modern jazz chords of the Four Freshmen and voiced them very much like the R&B records of the '50s. We listened to all those records blasting through L.A. on KOFL. Our vocals were voiced like horn parts, the way those R&B records make background vocals sound like a sax section. With an R&B quartet or the Four Freshman, you get a lot out of those voices; they make a lot of music. It's a neat concept to use four parts to really make it sound big. They're all within the same octave; that's really the secret to it. We didn't just duplicate parts; we didn't just sing at octaves; that sounds really lame, very square. No, the close harmonies sounded fuller because all the voices were within the same octave. He used a lot of counterpoint, a lot of layered sound; it had a real depth to it. Obviously, Brian's influence is now massive."

Through Brian produced "Surfin' USA," Nick Venet got the credit. This forced a showdown. "Brian was really the one making the records," Carl insists. "Nick would call out the take number, but he wasn't part of making the music. When Brian said he wouldn't work with Nick anymore, Capitol sent over this other guy. Then it became real clear to Brian, and he said, 'Look, I'm not cutting with these guys, and what's more, I'm not going to use your studio. We'll just send you the next record,' Now this was a big thing is those day, because record companies were used to having absolute control over their artists. It was especially nervy, because Brian was a 21-year-old kid with just two albums. It was unheard of, but what could they say? Brian made good records. He wouldn't work at Capitol because it was a crappy-sounding studio. It has a fabulous string sound, and it was great for those records that Nat King Cole made, but not for rock'n'roll guitar. So we recorded at Western Recorders, which was really our home.

"'Fun, Fun, Fun' is an interesting tune," Carl comments. "That was one of the first tunes where we used other players. I played that Chuck Berry lick from 'Johnny B. Goode' in the introduction. The harmonies are really full for a song that comes on that simple in the verse. It's a three chord verse and then we go to the chorus which is one to three-minor, and the instrumental break is in the five chord, and then it flip-flops back to end the song. My dad said, 'That tag sounds too funny; it might only make the record go to number 13.' The way those background parts go, 'Fun, fun, fun, till her daddy took her T-Bird away,' spreads the chord there. It goes E to A-flat minor, and then it goes to a B suspended over an A. It didn't do what anyone would think it would do. It resolves but it doesn't. It's like the end of that verse is the end of the verse, but it's also the beginning of the next verse.

"'In My Room' is a tune we've learned to appreciate more as the years go by. It's pretty autobiographical. You can tell it's getting pretty close to home for Brian, and all those tender, vulnerable things are coming out. It was unusual in the early records not to do the macho thing about cars and surfing and to lay it out like that.

"'California Girls' is a very artistic record for its time. The guitar part by Ray Pohlman and myself in the introduction was very different, very bizarre. Then you didn't expect a rock'n'roll record to come on like that, classical and majestic. Then it came on like gangbusters out of nowhere.

"'Girls on the Beach' completely modulates in the third verse. It's not your typical three chord song; it's definitely not country music. It's very lively and free; it just meanders and goes where it wants to go. 'Warmth of the Sun' is another one; so is 'You Know Me Too Well.' He was being very free in his use of chords and patterns. Instead of a three chord song, it might be a six or nine or twelve chord song. It was all easy to him, because he wasn't locked into a particular approach to writing.

"Brian was evolving very fast. We learned as we went. He was writing stuff that really needed to be performed; that's why he needed session players." The players included female bassist Carol Kaye, who had played on Motown and Phil Spector records. Other Beach Boys musicians who also worked with Phil were acoustic bassist Jimmy Bond, pianist Leon Russell, saxophonist Steve Douglas, pianist Don Randi, saxophonist Jay Migliori, drummer Hal Blaine, percussionist Frank Kapp and guitarist Tommy Tedesco, Bill Pitman, Ray Pohlman and Glen Campbell. Jim Gordon played drums; Billy Strange played guitar. Chuck Britz engineered the early records.

"You have to remember," Carl emphasized, "that most of the records in the '50s had been done in New York. Phil moved out to L.A. just about the time we got started, and before that there were practically no records made in L.A. So it was a wonderful thing for players in L.A. to come together and make records. The Beach Boys met Phil through their mutual friend, Lou Adler.

"Brian just adored Phil; he couldn't get enough of Phil. Brian started going to Phil Spector sessions, and it just blew him away. Phil would play things back so loud it was scary. I think the psychological and emotional impact of going in and hearing songs before they came out made him totally fascinated with Phil, under a spell almost. That was Brian's favourite kind of rock; he liked it better than the early Beatles stuff. He loved the Beatles' later music when they evolved and started making intelligent, masterful music, but before that Phil was it.

If you listen to *Pet Sounds*, you can tell that the person who made that record loved Phil Spector, just as you can hear Beatles records and tell they loved Buddy Holly and the Everly Brothers. Brian just took Phil's production techniques and applied them to a more refined, more evolved music. For all their production, Phil's stuff was mostly real simple tunes; Brian's were far, more complex. Brian did a lot with dynamics; his music would be big and loud, and then get soft and change colour and tempo. Phil was mostly loud.

"When Brian would hear a record, he would get it all at once; the first time he heard it, he'd get the whole thing. The rest of us would have to listen 10 times or so to really get everything that's going on. So when Brian would teach us our parts, he'd already have the total picture in his head. He'd sit at the piano, and we'd stand around or pull up a chair, and he'd say, okay, you do this part and this is your part. Brian would play the piano and hum the part to the person. There's no doubt he heard it in his head, because it was invariably almost perfect, almost exactly the way the record turned out when he taught us. It was so complete when he put it together, that he didn't have to keep going back. He just knew every particle of music that was supposed to be put down.

"I remember a date at Gold Star one night, and there were a lot of players in the room. They were making a big, big sound, and Brian went, 'Whoa!' because one little thing didn't happen; someone didn't ring an orchestra bell at the right time. He used to drive Michael crazy. Michael would be doing his lead vocal, and Brian would go 'Okay, scratch.' We'd go, 'No, Brian, wait a minute, we love that part.' and he'd go 'No-o-ope, 36,' and it'd be gone, and we'd have to do it again. But he was always right. He'd just identify what was wrong – that's flat or lay back on these lines or say these words like this. He wasn't just looking for notes, he was looking for texture."

At the end of 1964, Brian had a nervous breakdown and left the tour. "This guy had turned Brian onto pot and LSD, and Brian just wasn't set up for it; he couldn't handle it. The pressure of writing, producing and performing all had an accumulative effect on him. Earlier that year, the group had decided they didn't want to work with my dad anymore. There were some parts of fatherhood he wasn't willing to let go of. It's hard to have someone bossing you around and working for you too. It was impossible to work with him; there was so much friction. All these pressures and the chemicals took Brian apart. He flew home, and it was decided he couldn't go on the road.

'We were all broken-hearted. Michael started crying. We didn't know what it meant. We didn't know what he was going through. And he was our leader on stage as well as offstage. He led rehearsals; he made sure tunes got counted off and we were just doing our parts. We had the choice of continuing or not continuing. We just felt, 'This is too much fun to stop.' It got the group to discipline itself and really do good work on the road. I just assumed leadership; it seemed natural. It got down to the point where I knew it would get done if I did it. It was kind of a private directive from Brian too. I'd always been Brian's apprentice. That's really when I became the older brother. I had always been the baby until then. But in terms of getting information and sharing it, taking care of stuff and holding things together, I've in many ways been the older brother ever since."

While the band was on the road, Brian would stay home, write and cut rhythm tracks. "*Summer Days and Summer Nights* was a turning point; that album sticks out to us. Brian was really into a very expansive stream of energy. We could see that he was opening up and making very serious music, and it was serious rock-'n'roll music which made it complete. We did the *Beach Boys Party* album just to get the record company out of our hair so we could do *Pet Sounds*. They wouldn't stop calling Brian, so he said, 'Okay, come on, guys.' We went down to the big room at Western with some friends and a bunch of beer and cut it in three days. A silly record."

Brian hired a friend of his wife's Tony Asher, an advertising writer, to write the lyrics for a cycle of songs that described the awkward doubt ("I Just Wasn't Made for These Times"), the eager expectancy ("Wouldn't It Be Nice") and sense of loss ("Caroline No") that go along with the transition from adolescence to adulthood. The themes were backed with the richest music Brian was ever to get to the public.

"The disappointment and the loss of innocence that everyone had to go through when they grow up and find everything's not Hollywood," Carl says, "are the recurrent themes on that album. *Pet Sounds* was really Brian's baby; he did an awful lot of the singing on it. Singles weren't enough for him anymore. He wasn't getting enough out of the experience. Most of the albums at that time had one hit and 11 other tunes. He was really the first to make albums as a whole. *Pet Sounds* was far more adult and human. The whole album was integrated with this really high quality music recorded beautifully with all the big production. It was done over a long period of time.

"When I heard it, I just thought it was the best work he had ever done. The music was very grown-up, very evolved, very artistic, which really thrilled me, because you can only do 'I Get Around' or 'Fun, Fun, Fun' so many times. How many times can you make the same record? *Pet Sounds* had rhythm and power in it, and yet the chords and constructions were starting to get classical.

"The idea for *Pet Sounds* was Brian's idea; it would be his favourite sounds, his pet sounds. He was fascinated by sounds and collected them. I remember how he used to say, 'I want a different sound for this.' He would experiment with tapes; we'd laugh in key and try different things just to see what we could do. It's that old thing of going out maybe a little too far to find out what you can do and then pulling back a little bit to fit what else you're actually doing. You have to be willing to take a chance and sound like a jerk. You can always edit. Brian did a lot with instruments, without a lot of sound effects.

Like 'Sloop John B' had a real marching band feel. Brian walked into Gold Star one day and saw this weird instrument, and said 'What's that?' The guy said, 'It's a theremin; it goes oooh-wooo!' And Brian said,.'He-eey!' He used it on the date that night for 'I Just Wasn't Made For These Times.' *(Editor's note: It was not actually a real theremin, but an easier-to-play device made by player Paul Tanner to copy the oscillating sounds)* He would have string players play in a way they wouldn't be used to – play without vibrato, for instance. Another combination he discovered was organ and clarinet. The woodwinds had their sound and the organ had its sound, but the way he put them together made its own sound. That sound is all over *Pet Sounds*.

"The echoing percussion on 'Caroline No' was a combination of tape reverb and chamber echo. He got very good at that. Chuck Britz would set up the machines and then delay a chamber to get a tumbling effect. Frankie Kapp and Hal Blaine had a lot of incredible instruments, for example, a set of plastic milk bottles of different sizes. Brian loved those different sounds. He got real tired of just hearing a tambourine on a record. He loved bells, jingle bells, woodblock, orchestra bells, marimba, xylophone. He also used the bass harmonica a lot. On 'Wouldn't It Be Nice,' that's what follows the bass line and goes, 'aroom! aroom!'

"Capitol didn't support *Pet Sounds*; I think they tried to talk Brian out of having it. Can you imagine that album not coming into being? It was a glorious album in our ears, but the record company gave it a real lukewarm reception. That really worried Brian; it really bothered him. He'd put his heart and soul on the line." But

Brian pushed on and crafted his three-and-a half minute "pocket symphony," the biggest selling Beach boys single of all times, "Good Vibrations."

"'Good Vibrations' has a lot of texture on it," Carl notes, "because we did so many overdubs. We'd double or triple or quadruple the exact same part, so it would sound like 20 voices. There's a phase in your voice, and even if you try to sing it exactly the same, it's not exactly the same and more overtones and harmonics come out. It has a choral sound, a choir effect. When I first heard it, it was a much rougher sound; it had more whomp to it. Instead of making it bigger, bulgier and more raucous as Phil might have, he refined it and got it more even sounding. Brian had the idea of 'I'm picking up good vibrations,' but Michael didn't write the lyrics until the very last minute.

"We recorded some bridge sections at Western, went back to Gold Star and tried some verses there and did some choruses at Sunset Sound. Each studio had a good sound for a different thing. In the end, he'd use the section that sounded best; it didn't matter where it was recorded. Recording in sections was an innovation. It was pretty daring back then to take a chance and record a section and see if it would fit with another. We started to work over at Columbia, because they were the only ones in town to have eight-track machines; everyone else had four. By the time he knew how he wanted all the sections to fit together, he put on the cello and theremin. Some sections got cut out of the record; the song was originally longer. The 'keep those loving good....' section was originally a rock part with fuzz bass that went on for a couple of minutes by itself and really built up steam."

"Good Vibrations" was supposed to be part of a new album called *Smile*. *Smile* was to be Brian's masterpiece, the record that moved beyond *Pet Sounds* and *Sgt Pepper*. If *Pet Sounds* absorbed adulthood into Brian's imagined world, *Smile* would bring the larger world into Brian's musical realm with L.A. poet-composer Van Dyke Parks writing the lyrics, Brian planned to expand his vision to encompass American geography and history in songs like "The Grand Coulee Dam," "The Iron Horse," "The Barnyard Suite," "Old Master Painter" and "Cabinessence." He wanted to evoke the elements themselves in songs like "Vegetables," "Wind Chimes," "Mrs O'Leary's Cow (Fire)" and "I Love to Say Da-Da (Water)". *Smile* was never completed, never released and today it remains the most legendary and controversial lost album in rock history.

"*Smile* was a step beyond *Pet Sounds*, just as *Pet Sounds* was a step beyond *Summer Days and Summer Nights*. It was more in the same directions; it was even more so than *Pet Sounds*. But Brian just couldn't thread it all together; he couldn't make that full cycle and tie it all together. How finished was it? Half, I suppose. At that time, it seemed inconceivable to spend two years on an album. Just think, two years before, they wanted three albums a year. Now of course, you can take more time. Maybe Brian found we were only halfway through the project and it was taking too much time. If people heard the *Smile* tapes today, they'd hear a lot of themes that keep cycling back on each other. A lot of tunes were interchangeable; you could take a section out of one and put it in another. There were so many titles thrown around.

"The 'Fire' tapes just sounded like fire; it sounded like a bunch of fire engines on the way to a fire and the fire going, but it was all musical instruments: bells and violas and cellos, very scary ascending and descending strings. 'Grand Coulee Dam' was great stuff. It had the bass harmonica, tack piano, harpsichords. It was mid-tempo and then would go double time in parts. It was really a classical approach of 200 years ago applied to modern rock sounds. Dennis did a killer version of 'You Are My Sunshine,' which was incorporated into 'The Old Master Painter.' 'The Barnyard Suite' had chickens and sound effects in the background, just funky, hokey music. 'Vegetables' sounded more Disneyesque on *Smile* than on the released version; it was more arranged, more moulded sound-wise. The whole album had a Disney quality; it was very picturesque, and yet it was not square or lame in the least. 'Can't Wait Too Long' was another great song; there's a lot of finished material on that one. It was a simple, funky tune with a lot of heart and soul. 'Cool, Cool Water' had a lot more stuff than finally got out.

"To get that album out, someone would have had to have the willingness and perseverance to corral all of us and keep Brian to the task of completing the work. But the group didn't really have any management at the time. The record company was giving us a hard time. It takes a lot of concentration to stay on top of a project like that, and everybody was so loaded on pot and hash all the time, that it's no wonder it didn't get done. He was getting fragmented; he was starting to have difficulty completing things. And it was also a thing of, what if it didn't turn out to be great, what if it had totally flopped. That would have completely destroyed him. We would have lost him forever in terms of having any communication with him. Still I'd be very surprised if *Smile* never came out; that's what you make music for – so people can hear it. Except we didn't complete it, so what do you do? Brian might be able to heal a lot of stuff within himself by doing that, by moving through it in spite of the pain. Or maybe it'll be the field for some other guy. Maybe some very gifted person will hear it and it'll push them to finish it. But I think it's going to surface somehow, someday.

"In the middle of all this, Brian just said, 'I can't do this. We're going to make a homespun version of it instead. We're just going to take it easy. I'll get in the pool and, sing. Or let's go in the gym and do our parts.' That was *Smiley Smile*. It was as real dip-out album. I've always said *Smiley Smile* was the bunt, and *Smile* was the home run. A lot of the same songs were on *Smiley Smile* but they didn't sound the same at all. The melodies were similar, but the versions were more laid back. Maybe we'd do the melody, but nothing would be there of the original production. Brian just wanted to lighten up a bit, so he did *Smiley Smile* instead. He was trying to get away from the pretence of making a heavy art album. He had given up on it and didn't want to know about it. So we just had fun.

"I felt a little funny about *Smiley Smile*, because I felt we were dicking off, smoking too much pot and just laughing our asses off. After all this hype for *Smile*, *Smiley Smile* was such a dirty trick. And yet it was so great to see Brian having fun after he had been through so much. It was kind of a devilish thing to do, you know, hee-hee, making this silly little record out of this grand and beautiful project."

Seen outside the expectations for *Smile*, *Smiley Smile* is indeed a wonderful album that holds up very well today. It radiates good humour; there's even some laughing synchronised into the rhythm and key. The next album, *Wild Honey*, was even funkier than *Smiley Smile*; it was an out-and-out R&B record. It had a hit single, "Darlin'," a Stevie Wonder tune ("I Was Made To Love Her") and Brian's version of an Aretha Franklin tune ("Let the Wind Blow"). This too was dismissed by many Beach Boys fans still waiting for *Smile*. But when *John Wesley Harding* came out the following year, and everyone was exclaiming how Dylan had "pulled the plug" on art-rock excess and gone back to the basics, it struck many people that Brian had once again been ahead of the game.

Wild Honey had some great tunes by Mike and Brian, but Brian withdrew from the production responsibilities, and asked Carl to take over. The production credit went, for the first time, to "the Beach Boys."

"*Wild Honey* was underrated," argues Carl. It didn't have the polish and pizazz, but it brought out all our R&B influences that had always been there but people had overlooked. The best analogy is the Beatles' "Got to Get You Into My Life." Where Paul did that Stax horn thing, and it worked. I thought "Darlin'" worked the same way.

Friends (1968) was another folksy, homespun album with hidden charms. It reflected the group's growing involvement in transcendental meditation. It was the first album to feature non-Brian tunes from the band: two by Dennis. By *20/20* (1969) nearly every song had a different producer and a different composer. As Brian withdrew, the unity of the Beach Boys records evaporated. Carl was now doing the bulk of the producing. *20/20* included the nostalgia-style hit single, "Do It Again," and two *Smile* tracks: "Our Prayer" and "Cabinessence."

"*Friends* was light and airy," Carl says. "Brian was really encouraging us to write more. His actions were telling us, 'Why don't you go ahead and write; come forward now.' Just before *20/20*. Brian told me, 'Please you got to take over and help me out; this is obviously not the thing I want to do now.' And yet *Friends* was a family reconciliation. Brian asked Murry to help. My dad sang the big deep note on 'Be Here in the Morning'.

In the wake of the *Smile* debacle and the commercial flop of the subsequent albums, the band found that its original idealism could no longer sustain it. Their optimistic vision of American life seemed naive to those who were fighting to stop an increasingly cynical war in Vietnam, even though the Beach Boys' idealism helped shape the hope protesters felt Vietnam had betrayed. A family unit that had relied on Brian for leadership and income suddenly found themselves distanced from the ever more reclusive composer. Their efforts to emulate him somehow always fell a bit short. They lost a golden opportunity to re-establish their hipness when they declined an invitation to the 1967 Monterey Pop Festival. They lost a big bundle of money when their 1968 tour was abruptly cancelled due to widespread urban rioting in the wake of Martin Luther King's assassination. Largely abandoned by their leader, their record company and their old fans, the Beach Boys faced a most uncertain future at the end of the '60s.

"We were used as a reference point as to what was lame about that time," Carl remembers painfully. It was nonsense, but people still associated us with cars and surfboards. We've always had the predicament of boxing ourselves in, right? We've always been damned if we do and damned if we don't. If we do something different, people complain it doesn't sound like us. If we make a record that sounds similar to the other ones, people complain it's the same old thing. When the hits stopped coming, we all felt a lot of pressure. It was back to the real world after the fairy tale." Carl leans back in his couch and sighs.

"That was a scary time for us. We were trying to get free from Capitol, because we didn't think they supported the group anymore. We were really stuck; they wanted us to do another hot rod song, and yet the feedback we were getting from the universe was loosen up, do something funkier, more natural. Mo Ostin had always dug the group, so we signed with Warners. It was called 'Mo's folly,' because people at the label thought we were ridiculous. But Mo was incredible; he really supported us when we needed it.

"We did *Sunflower* , which we thought was one of our really good records, but that didn't hit either. On the first single, 'Add Some Music to Your Day,' the company tried to hype the system by fudging on the first shipments, and they got caught with their pants down by the radio industry and that killed it. And the record has too much bass on it. But it's still a very loving album, Brian was involved in the production again as a favour to Mo. It was a real team effort with people's hands on knobs together trying to help each other with the mix. It was a great time for Dennis; he was at the very height of his creativity, and it got stifled later. He wrote 'Got to Know the Woman' and 'Slip on Through'; damn, I wish he would do that again. Dennis, Brian and I did all the vocals on 'Forever'; it was a real Wilson Brothers record. *Sunflower* was a very good-natured album. It had a maturity too; it sounds like surfers grown up."

Sunflower didn't crack the top 100, and Brian's parallel *Spring* project with wife Marilyn and her sister Diane didn't chart at all. Once again Brian felt rebuffed and retreated "back to the bushes", as Carl describes it. The responsibility for shepherding the next three albums through production again fell to Carl. On *Surf's Up* (1971), Carl wrote his first two songs: "Long Promised Road" and "Feel Flows."

"Before that," Carl claims, "I didn't need to push the idea of writing songs. I felt if the song wanted to come out, it would. Brian's absence kind of pushed that along. But it was more a personal experience. I had a piano at the house; I was playing it a lot, and I started to write. The first song I ever wrote was 'Long, Promised Road.' I heard things as Brian would, so it was natural I would write as Brian might. The structure, the attitude, the musical approach were all in the Brian school of writing. The verses were gentle with some nice chord movement and an unusual bass line, but the chorus was more simple and funky."

Surf's Up includes a lot of work by jazz reed player Charles Lloyd (who launched the careers of Keith Jarrett and Jack DeJohnette). Charles, who befriended Mike through the TM program, dueted with himself on sax and flute in "Feel Flows." The album ended with Brian's three songs, including a salvaged version of "Surf's Up" from the *Smile* sessions and "'Til I Die," a stunning confession of human limitations. The album also features lyrics by Jack Rieley, the bands' new manager.

"Jack Rieley came into our lives," Carl recounts, " and really woke us up to a lot of social issues. He was a guy who worked at the Pacifica station in L.A. He'd go into the Radiant Radish, the health food store Brian was running when he took time off from the group, and shoot the breeze. He invited us on his show. He just seemed a cool guy to have aboard. He was very healthy for the group. We were real sheltered. We had hit the big time in 1962 and gotten quite isolated from the real world. We had our own protective bubble, The main thing Jack did was point out to the group what its good points were when we were a little fuzzy and didn't see things too clearly. He'd say, 'Look at this song, it's a great song; it means something important to a lot of people.' I thought Jack was a good lyricist. He also alerted us to a lot of political things that we weren't conscious of."

Carl had already been in court for refusing induction into the draft. But Jack encouraged the band to play at a major anti-war demonstration in Washington in 1971 and at a benefit for the Berrigan Brothers. He also convinced them to take on Ricky Fataar and Blondie Chaplin as new members. Ricky and Blondie were half of a black South African quartet called Flame, who played an appealing hippie brand of R&B. Carl was so impressed when he heard them in London in 1969 that he immediately offered to produce them. Carl got his first solo production credit on *Flame* (1971), an obscure but delightful album that sounds like Stevie Wonder singing Abbey Road. A year later Ricky and Blondie were Beach Boys.

They contributed two songs to *Carl & the Passions – So Tough* (1972), which was released in the U.S. as a double set with *Pet Sounds*. "Even without the *Pet Sounds* reissue," Carl argued, "I thought *Carl & the Passions* should have been three separate albums. Blondie and Ricky were going in one direction that sounded a lot like the Band or Stevie Winwood. I thought 'Marcella,' and 'Mess of Help,' two of Brian's best tunes ever, were another direction. If we had done eight tunes like 'Marcella,' it could have been a great rock album, almost a folk-rock album. I think Dennis' 'Cuddle Up' was great; that direction could have been a real romantic side to an album. I wish Brian had been strong enough to produce the record, because it could have been an ass-kicking, great record."

Instead Brian, then Dennis and eventually Carl succumbed to drug problems. "Brian was starting to get into the drug shit then and some really bizarre behaviour. We didn't know what was going on. It didn't ever occur to us that he was strung out on coke. Later, when I found out, I went, 'Holy shit! No wonder he acted like that.' We were real sheltered, we were dumb."

Endless Summer (Capitol, 1974), a two-record compilation of the band's pre-1966 material, sold four million units at a time the band couldn't get a new album inside the top 20. 'We were just vaguely aware of *Endless Summer*,' remembers Carl. 'We heard it was coming out. Then we heard it was going up the charts pretty good. Then it was number one. Then it was multiple platinum. We were so detached from it; usually you're real involved with recording and promotion on an album project, but we'd recorded the stuff a decade before and it wasn't even our company. It had a big impact on our audiences and how they saw us. So we just surrendered to it. We'd gone through so many changes over the idea of oldies over the years, and now it was real obvious what the people wanted us to play. Real obvious.

"Brian came out to see us play at Anaheim Stadium. He was sitting in the backstage bleachers and saw those 12-year-old girls singing "Surfer Girl" right along with us. It just blew him away to realise that these people knew all our songs and they weren't even born when they were written. We just got out of own way. We couldn't see the point of recording an album and competing with our past."

So there was a three year gap between *Holland* (1973) and *15 Big Ones* (Brother/Reprise, 1976). Brian was in a strict therapy program with Gene Landy, and the advance publicity for the album was "Brian's back.". "That slogan was simply premature," Carl states flatly. "Brian was almost there, but not quite. The original idea for *15 Big Ones* was to have an album of oldies and an album of new songs. But once we had finished a certain batch of songs, Brian said, 'That's it; put it out.' Dennis and I went 'Whoa, wait a minute, you said we were going to do a lot more work.' But that was it. That's why the album sounds unfinished. Brian just wanted to do one cut and capture the moment rather than working on something."

Ironically, Gene Landy's work paid off a year later in some of the most fascinating music of Brian's career. *The Beach Boys Love You* (Brother/Reprise, 1977) features 14 Brian originals making it the first all-Brian album since 1967's *Smiley Smile*. If his early records captured adolescence and if *Pet Sounds* captured adulthood, *The Beach Boys Love You* captured parenthood. The record has a crude, crayola texture as Brian shares his daughters' fascination with airplanes, skates, rollercoasters, bedtime, cars and Johnny Carson. If the productions are revealingly sparse, the compositions are rich. Changes in key, tempo and mood occur at surprising junctures; vocals are offset by counterpoint harmonies; bridges miraculously take songs in completely new directions.

Brian's next project was tentatively titled *Adult Child*. Working with arranger Dick Reynolds, who had arranged the Four Freshmen's best records and the *Beach Boys' Christmas Album* (Capitol, 1964), Brian created a Sinatra-like pop sound. It had the earmarks of a solo album, though, and songs like "Still I Dream of It," "It's All Over," "It's Trying to Say" and "Everyone Wants to Live" reveal Brian grappling with the loss of his original optimism and trying to reclaim a more workable faith. Though tracks like "My Diane," "Hey Little Tomboy" and "Shortnin' Bread" were released on subsequent albums, *Adult Child*, like *Smile*, remains unreleased.

"Brian was just getting back on his feet," Carl maintains. "He had been with Gene for more than a year. He was becoming a lot more productive. It was part of his therapy to make music. But Gene and Steve Love (Mike's brother and the group's business manager) disagreed a lot about what Brian should do. Gene was doing it from a therapeutic angle, and Steve had business considerations. So Steve terminated Gene. It was really a shame, because Brian regressed pretty much after that. The group was really fractured at that time. We really went through an explosion. A lot of stuff that hadn't been acknowledged and hadn't been dealt with surfaced. People outside the five guys were vying for control. With the assistance of some attorneys in L.A., I began to see things that were, how shall I say it, uncustomary business practices. They all caught on later, and now we have actions going in court. For a while, though, it was unbelievable: fights, arguments, many, many meetings, votes."

Probably the most perilous moment came in 1977, when business mismanagement and cocaine led to public announcements of the band's break-up. "That was a very rough time for all of us," admits Carl. "Relations were very strained and icy. Everyone was frightened and it came out as anger. Everything was falling apart in front of us, and we didn't know how to get a hold of it. What we had to do was just let everything fall apart and then realise, 'Now, wait a minute. Do I want to fight with my family and friends?' We got a chance to see if we really wanted to be a group or not. We got to re-choose. It became clear we should put it back together."

It was in this state of near-collapse that Beach Boys gathered in Fairfield, Iowa, at the Maharishi International University to make the *M.I.U. Album* (Brother/Reprise, 1978). The album benefitted from some Brian compositions left over from his recent productive period, but not from his production. Al produced it with Ron Altbach, one of Mike's TM friends and the keyboardist from King Harvest.

Bruce produced *Keepin' the Summer Alive* (Brother/Reprise, 1980), and on it Carl foreshadowed his solo work with two strong R&B-flavoured songs co-written with Randy Bachman (of the Guess Who and the Bachman-Turner Overdrive). Brian contributed six new songs, including the very strong single, "Goin' On," which talked about breaking through problems and persevering.

"The group was really okay on *Keepin' the Summer Alive*," Carl claims. "It's like we got our foot in the door and were going in the right direction. Some people tell us that was our best record in some time. We worked a lot up at Alan's place and loved being there. Brian got hot for about three days in the studio. He was singing like a bird. All the protection that he usually runs just dropped; he came out of himself. He was right there in the room. Michael got so excited he was singing several notes above his normal range. "Sunshine" and "Goin' On" were part of those sessions. I did an interview with *Rolling Stone*, and told them, 'Brian's really back this time.' It was just wishful thinking on my part because he had a couple of good days in the studio. It taught me not to speak too soon. I think we missed a little on the sound of that album, though. Like my tune, 'Keepin' the Summer Alive,' sounded a lot punchier on our live tapes than it did on record."

After 20 years as a member of the Beach Boys, Carl Wilson released his first solo album in 1981 and left the Beach Boys tour to do his own tour. After many years of acting as the organiser and mediator who sacrificed to keep the band together, Carl has finally pursued his own ambitions, and has now released his second solo album, *Young Blood* (Caribou). After being closely associated with his brother Brian's highly polished, lushly harmonic music, Carl has returned to his first love: funky, blustery R&B rock.

His reasons for branching off on his own are spelled out in "The Right Lane," a frankly autobiographical track from the first solo album, *Carl Wilson*. Over a galloping, guitar-driven rock beat, Carl sings; "Always believed I could take care of my brother .... I've been livin' in the right lane, seein' others cruise on by. I've been tryin' to do the best thing; think I'll give the passin' lane a try."

"I was never inclined to do a solo album until three years ago," Carl acknowledges. "I'd been offered the opportunity, but I never considered it; I thought more of producing other people. Yet I got to the point where I wanted to sing and make new music, and the guys in the band decided not to record and were playing the same old songs every night. I got itchy. I remember the last two weeks of the summer tour of '79, I was so bored I couldn't believe it. I couldn't believe it. It was horrible to go on sometimes, because there was nothing in it. That was the first time that had ever happened to me with the group."

Jerry Schilling, a Memphis pal of Elvis Presley and a longtime member of the King's entourage, had become the Beach Boys' road manager just before Elvis died. Carl hired Jerry as his personal manager in 1978. Jerry pushed Carl to do the solo project. And it was Myrna Smith, Jerry's longtime girl friend, who collaborated with Carl on writing the bulk of the material. Myrna was one of the Sweet Inspirations, a gospel-soul quintet that sang with Elvis (where she met Jerry), Aretha Franklin and Dionne Warwick.

"I asked Jerry if Myrna might like to write some tunes with me," Carl says. "So I took a cassette player, guitar and tiny amp over to their house, and we just started making up tunes. It was very easy and natural. She has a very pure sense – very gentle and yet funky." Carl and Myrna co-wrote all eight songs on *Carl Wilson* and seven of the 11 on *Young Blood*. Myrna also sang on both albums plus the solo tours. The music they produced was different from the Beach Boys' music; it was dominated by R&B rhythms, Carl's rock lead guitar and his shouted lead vocals.

"I didn't want to compromise," Carl maintains, "and make my solo stuff sound like the Beach Boys, just as I wouldn't want to compromise the Beach Boys' stuff either. I know all the guys very well: how they approach a song; how they sing and how they play. I wouldn't compromise that, which is not to say they would have done it less well, but it would have been different. I wanted it to be pure, whatever it was going to be.

"The R&B approach just came naturally. If I picked up a guitar, that's what would come out. It's a side of me that's always wanted to come out. I have this massive collection of R&B records. When we were doing *Pet Sounds*, I'd go home and put on my Stax and Aretha stuff. It's always been a big part of my life. So I did something I wanted to do. I wanted to rock out, sing loud and have a bit of a rougher edge. Also the stuff we had been doing on the road with the group was real stagnant, and I wanted to shake it loose. Also I've always been a reserved, quiet person, and I wanted to break through some of that."

Jimmy Guercio, the producer of Chicago, Blood, Sweat and Tears and the Buckinghams, had been a friend of Carl's since he managed the Beach Boys in the early '70s. In fact, Jimmy owned the Caribou Ranch where Carl lived. Jimmy produced the first solo album at Caribou Studios. To underscore the funky approach, the songs were initially cut with guitar, bass, drums and voice to see if they could stand up on their own.

"'The Right Lane' was pretty autobiographical," Carl agrees. "I was always the facilitator in the group. I was always the one who made sure we got our work done. I stayed in the background in a supportive role, real quiet, making sure everybody was able to function. I didn't really assert myself or impose anything. This certainly gave me a shot to sing and make up tunes. 'Hurry Love' and 'Heaven' are obviously the most Beach Boys sounding cuts. If the band had done them, they probably would have been less folksy. They would have had more voices, different voices; they'd have been more produced. Also the band would have used more keyboards, which gives a song more flexibility, while my album was more guitar-oriented."

The album didn't sell too well, less that 50,000, but "Heaven" got some airplay and even went top 5 in Miami. Carl embarked on a solo tour of showcase clubs in the spring of '81. Interviewers kept pressing the point about his future with the Beach Boys. Finally Carl issued a press release that said "I haven't quit the Beach Boys, but I do not plan on touring with them until they decide that 1981 means as much to them as 1961" He listed three demands: he wanted the Beach Boys to make a record of new songs, to rehearse thoroughly before each tour and to stop playing multi-night engagements at Las Vegas, Lake Tahoe and other resorts.

"It was the wish of Jimmy Guercio that my record would encourage the guys to get off their butts and do something. I wanted to get the guys in a studio and go for a record. As for rehearsing, it's real simple; you just get together and rehearse. But we hadn't had a full rehearsal in more than a year."

Carl saw the resorts jobs and almost exclusive oldies repertoire as a real threat to seal the band in the past forever. "The resort rooms are not very big, so you have to do a couple of shows a day. So the shows have to be very short. It's very seductive. You just slide downstairs, get there a few minutes early and knock it off in an hour. It ends up being a show of meat and potatoes, just the hits, and the audiences love it. But there's a real danger of going to sleep on your talent. It almost gets down to going through the motions. I'd like to see a variety of the later, more artistic stuff in the show. The up side is that when the group rehearses and plays challenging material, they give really powerful performances."

The band didn't respond, so Carl made plans for a second album in November 1981. Jerry suggested Jeff "Skunk' Baxter – the former guitarist for Steely Dan and the Doobie Brothers – who had produced Nils Lofgren, Al Kooper and Billy & the Beaters. Carl went to see Jeff play with Billy & the Beaters at the Whiskey and met him backstage.

"It seemed to me that Jeff would be real good for me," Carl explains. "I have a tendency to be cool and not put myself out too much, and I thought he could get me to come out of myself. He has a lot of energy; he's a wiry, go-get-'em kind of guy. I'm sure he was hyperkinetic as a kid. I mean his idea of relaxing after a big album project is to book a week of session work: commercials, records, anything. It's a form of meditation for him; he calls it being a 'studio sausage'."

Young Blood is much more versatile and satisfying than *Carl Wilson*. Though the end of side two drags badly, three cuts in particular stand out as important contributions to the Beach Boys' tradition. "Givin' You Up," co-written with Myrna and Jerry, is Carl's best composition since "Long, Promised Road." It begins with a quiet, sad verse about breaking up with someone you like and builds to a rousing call-and-response climax with a Beach Boys-styled production. "What You Do To Me" by John & Johanna Hall was added after the album was supposedly finished and was the first single. Val Garay gave Carl the tune when Val was considering producing a Beach Boys album. The song's melody soars at a brisk tempo, and Carl's voice chases it with giddy romantic excitement.

The title cut, "Young Blood," is a witty, spirited remake of the Coasters' 1957 hit. The all-star doo-wop quartet on this song (and "Givin' You Up") is Carl singing lead, Jeff singing bass, Timothy Schmit (of the Eagles and Poco) singing high harmony and Burton Cummings (of the Guess Who) singing middle harmony. Carl also updates "Rockin' All Over the World" from John Fogerty's 1975 solo album after the singer-songwriter left Creedence Clearwater Revival. The song was added to the Beach Boys' live shows that Summer in a looser, fuller version. The album's best ballad is "One More Night Alone" by Billy Hinsche. Billy, Carl's longtime friend and former brother-in-law was once one-third of Dino, Desi & Billy before joining the Beach Boys' show band.

"1981 was a good time for me to be on my own and grow up," Carl reflects. "I had a chance to slow down. I missed the guys and felt funny about not being with them, but it was the correct thing for me. By the spring of 1982, I got some communication that said, 'Come back and do some shows. The guys are willing to rehearse now and they're willing to record.' So I agreed to a few dates in April to check it out. I could see the group really needed a lot of work; there was no music in the music. Everything was very rushed; it was very mechanical.

"We all agreed to rehearse and put a new show together, but then there was resistance to that out of habit. It was very close; I thought that maybe it wasn't going to work after all. Finally it all came together at the last minute. At the end of rehearsals, in fact, Alan said, 'I wish we had another week'. They had just forgotten; they just got out of the habit of really stretching to put another effort into it. In 1983, there will be a lot more rehearsals, new faces, new songs, different venues. I may open some shows with my own band. It'd be good for the group; it would be one us playing new songs."

"I think the band has some options, " Carl suggests. "One option obviously is to just continue as we are, playing live shows. Another option is solo projects. One option I intend to look into is finding out if there are some other people I could work with in a band and have a different chemistry. I have no interest in making 25 Carl Wilson records. The field of possibilities is endless.

"But I'd like to see the group take another shot at making a really good record. Just one more good record. That's the thing we keep trying to do and can never quite pull together all the elements. But I don't think we'll make another Beach Boys album until Brian's healthy enough to produce again. I know we could make a real strong commercial record with an outside producer.

There are some great producers out there who have access to great material, and we still have the voices. So that's possible, but if you're talking about making a great record, 'Good Vibrations' class, you're talking about Brian with us. Anything else is bullshit.

"And yet, I don't mind if he doesn't make any more music. That's fine with me. I don't give a fuck if he makes hits or not. My interest in Brian is I love him as a human being and a brother as I love all my family. I want him to have some joy and satisfaction in life, and he's not getting that. I'm not discouraging him by any means, but the main thing is that he have a nurturing, loving life. That's all that matters anyway."

*****

Though several years passed from the writing of this piece to Carl's sad passing, I believe that his view of the group and what was important about it did not alter substantially. What would have been fascinating however, would have been his view on his big brother's solo work of recent years. Had Carl lived, I believe that he would have been the bridge between Brian and the Beach Boys that no longer exists here in 2002. Carl alone could have successfully straddled both camps in a way that no one else could. How he would have loved to have seen Brian receiving the plaudits and adulation of today, and how wonderful it would have been to have the stately figure and velvet voice of Carl appear as part of Brian's solo shows. R.I.P. Carl. [KA]

Pet Memories
A New Century Interview with Tony Asher
by Kingsley Abbott

I had planned to try to fit an earlier Tony Asher interview into the first edition of this book, but space did not allow it. Tony was incredibly helpful during my writing of my subsequent volume Pet Sounds – The Greatest Album Of the Twentieth Century *(Helter Skelter 2001), and so for this inclusion I decided to go back to him afresh in the light of the recent further elevation of the status of the album with Brian's live touring.*

So, there you were working in advertising, when suddenly in late 1965 you were writing an album with one of the hottest young musicians of his day

Yes, it all happened very quickly. We met through our mutual friend Loren Schwartz, and I was delighted and excited to be invited to spend time with Brian. He knew I worked with advertising and jingles, and as you can imagine I was thrilled when he said that we would write an album together.

How did you take to Brian personally?

Brian is one of the sweetest people in the world. We were of a similar age, and shared similar interests of girls and many aspects of Californian culture. Our relationship was a little stilted at first, as I adjusted to his time frame and sometimes sluggish starts, but soon it was going swimmingly. We found we were able to talk easily about our thoughts and feelings. We would reflect upon what had happened to us thus far in our lives, and discuss our personal philosophies that were still in formulation at that stage – like college days conversations! Brian and I found we could talk honestly, and I realised even then that he wished he could turn back to simpler times with less record company pressure. The earlier Beach Boys times of pure fun had passed.

What were the main features of your working relationship with Brian as you co-operated on what would become Pet Sounds?

'What would become' is quite apt, as there was no master plan that I was aware of at the outset. Brian spoke of wanting to write a very different style of music for the album, and to move away from what had gone before, and much of our first few days together was him playing me music-in-progress and discussing many things: spiritualist elements, relationships, feelings, and our thoughts about girls. Oh, and eating as well!! After this came the more specific work on the writing. In most cases, Brian would play ideas on piano and explain a desire for a particular song theme. We would bounce ideas back and forth, musical and lyrical ideas, and sometimes I would work on the full lyric back home and take it back to him a day or two later. Whilst I did make a few music suggestions, the lead role was certainly Brian's, but similarly he did often defer to me lyrically. His role then became more of that of an editor. My musical background did enable me to join musical discussions perhaps suggesting a route back to a bridge at a certain point or the need for a different section and sometimes Brian would take my suggestions and sometimes not. He would not always take my lyrics, but would certainly allow me to fight my corner! I would have to say that a sense of fun and laughter sometimes pervaded our writing sessions. At other times, the emotion of the subject we were writing about would take over. When we worked we worked, but we had an awful lot of laughs and good discussions as well.

Did you gain musically from the writing sessions?

Absolutely. There was a basic difference between Brian and myself in that I had a somewhat more formal musical education and he had not been beyond what he may have encountered in schooling. Consequently I would tend to write within traditional song structures of A-A-B-A and eight bars to a phrase, whereas he did not feel that restriction. He would thus entertain tangents more readily. I began to feel a new freedom through that experience, which may have enabled me to expand my writing somewhat. I would talk about chord changes that I thought would intrigue Brian, as exemplified in the jazz-like stylings of The Hi-Lo's and the Four Freshman, a group we both particularly enjoyed. As you know, Brian's chord changes are often surprising. As we would work on a song at the piano, he would play the bass line with his left hand. It established the feel of the song. The attitude. It took more prominence with more serious writing, and the songs of *Pet Sounds* lent themselves to it.

Brian's musical sense enabled him to hear things in his head that were very different to what I was hearing, or thought I was hearing. I was often not fully aware of what he was getting excited about, but eventually I heard and realised in the finished product. An analogy perhaps would be trying to describe a coloured painting to someone who can't see it.

Did you or Brian, at any point in the writing, realise just how important the album would become?

We were giving birth to the unknown and we didn't always know if it was really good or not. There was an insecurity in the creation, but I believe that the recording was very exhilarating for Brian as it gave him another time for excitement and spontaneity after the hard work of writing.

I was well aware that Brian specifically wanted to break away from the strictures of the Beach Boys' accepted music. He wanted to move towards more emotionally driven songs that had more meaning and weight compared to what had gone before. For my part, whilst I was thrilled to be part of it, I was certainly unsure that his move was the right one. I had this feeling later when I was in the studio as the group took on board the lyrics, and politely (well, it wasn't actually all that polite) made it clear they were concerned too. It was all heightened when the initial US sales were disappointing, but then I suppose the album began a very long re-emergence status wise to where it is today. I don't believe that either of us would have imagined that to be the case back in 1966.

What thoughts do you have about the structure of the album?

I don't believe that at the time we had a conscious shape in mind. It didn't start as a love/relationships album, though we did have in mind that it would be different to what had gone before. The opener, "Wouldn't It Be Nice" is very up and happy, whilst the closer "Caroline No" is quite the opposite. The other songs are about love in various forms, with "God Only Knows" being the purest. "I Wasn't Made For These Times" I suppose isn't a love song unless it is about love of self. "You Still Believe In Me" came from a good deal of discussion about how Brian felt about his relationship with Marilyn. He felt bad about not being better in fidelity terms for her, and acknowledged an affection for her sisters and other women. "Sloop John B" was a great sounding record, but I suppose that it represented old sounding Beach Boys. Brian was aware Capitol wanted it on for commercial reasons, and *production-wise* I'm sure he wanted it on. Remember that Brian decided the order of the tracks!

After Pet Sounds *you worked with other good writers, didn't you?*

Later I wrote with John Bahler, who the small print readers will know to be a gifted session singer, writer and arranger. We wrote a lot of jingles together, but some songs too. Some of these were used for The Partridge Family, with John often being one of the main voices. I also wrote with Roger Nichols, who was beginning to write with the talented Paul Williams. We both wrote for A&M publishing and spent a good deal of time together. Much of what was written at that later sixties time is now having a second wind with the incredible interest, especially in Japan and Europe, in what is now called soft or sunshine rock.

When you returned to work with Brian again in the nineties for the "Everything I Need" song (Recorded by The Wilsons and Jeff Foskett), what were the differences in the relationship?

The relationship was less collaborative. Brian seemed more inclined to record a demo of a song he'd written and then give me a tape of it to take home and work on. Then I'd come back with the lyric. There was far less back and forth. But that may have been a result of the fact that, by now, Brian knows what I can do. When we worked together in 1966, I was an unknown quantity to him.

In all, we've probably written five or six songs in the last few years. One was called "Rock 'n' Roll Express". He wrote another about his wife Melinda that I did lyrics for. Then, of course, there was "This Isn't Love" which is one that I really like a lot. It found its way into the sound track of the Flintstone's movie sequel called "The Flintstones: Viva Rock Vegas" which, of course, starred Mark Addy from your side of the pond. It was a thrill for me to meet him on the set of the Flintstones movie because we had already become aware of him over here from his wonderful performance in "The Full Monty".

What did you think about the "Pet Sounds Sessions" box set? Did the album stand up to such scrutiny?

Well, I think the correct answer to that is a qualified "Yes". Qualified because you have to remember that the box set was quite expensive. And everyone buying it must have known that there would be an almost microscopic examination of every aspect of the album. So, if you were interested in it, and if you were willing to put out that kind of money to buy it, then I think you would have been the kind of fan who would not only appreciate that kind of scrutiny, but would have been disap-

pointed had it not been there. For the average record buyer, though, it was probably a little much. I, of course, loved it. But then, where this album is concerned, I
can hardly be described as the average record buyer!

What are your thoughts about the Pet Sounds *live experience?*

I thought it was extraordinary. There's now an album recorded at a live performance. I haven't heard it yet. But I'm anxious to. I would never have believed it
would be possible to recreate the sound of the album with such accuracy on stage.
Especially with what are really a lot fewer musicians than were used to record the
album originally.

All of which speaks very highly – and I mean it too! – for the quality and ver-
satility of the musicians in Brian's band. Starting with the Wondermints, and
including everyone else – Jeff Foskett key among them. They are simply a remarkable gathering of musical talents. And I'm not really sure any other mix could have
really pulled it off. One of the key attributes of this particular group of people is
that they all, genuinely, love this music and love and respect Brian and his talent.

*At one stage you said that you wished you had come to England in 1966 to expe-
rience the way our country* did *take to* Pet Sounds *commercially and artistically.
Why do you think there was a difference in the two markets at that, and at subsequent, stages?*

Very hard to say. I don't really know. It could have something to do, I suppose,
with the fact that the California Beach Life fantasy would have been even more
appealing to those living in England. That is, at least, to those who are of the opinion that sunny skies, sand and surf are the only things that really matter in life.

Frankly, I love a lot about England. After all, I was born there. But you can't
say that bright, sunny days and warm, tropical nights are your long suit. So maybe
that had something to do with it. Although it has to be said that *Pet Sounds* didn't
really have anything to do with that fantasy, did it?

Anything you would have done differently??

Yes. I'd have been born Paul McCartney.

No, seriously. I DO still wish I'd gone to London when that album was at its
peak. But that's water under the bridge, as they say. And in the trips I've made
since, I've been treated wonderfully well by all the *Pet Sounds* fans. I really can't
complain. I think it's dangerous – to say nothing of futile – to speculate about
"what might have been". Because if you could in fact change one little incident in
your life, you can't possibly know what the repercussions of that change might
have been. I'll take what I got. And consider myself damn lucky for the way things
have turned out.

Van Dyke Parks
by Bill Holdship

This piece was originally written in the mid-nineties for Mojo *magazine, but was never used. In it Bill Holdship, whilst giving some space for the then current* Orange Crate Art *album, wisely keeps the bigger picture in mind and manages to extract some fascinating retrospective views of the* Smile *project and the working relationship Van Dyke had with Brian.*

Van Dyke Parks looks almost nothing like the old photos most rock fans recall from the *Smile* era. The man responsible for the lyrics that Mike Love always referred to as "acid alliteration" has gone completely grey, which actually makes him look somewhat older than his former songwriting partner.

Dressed in a blue polo shirt with "Ry Cooder" on the pocket and khaki trousers, Parks is warm but reflective, often letting his eyes a-gaze into the distance outside the picture window as he sits in an elegant living room, to discuss his past and present with Brian Wilson. Parks is currently collaborating on a new Broadway musical, but a more pressing project at the moment is *Orange Crate Art*, an album of his songs featuring Brian Wilson's vocals. 'I wanted his voice on;[the title track] because I wanted a Southern California signature," he recalls. Executive producer (and former Warner Bros. president) Lenny Waronker and Parks both requested Brian's presence on the track, which was also spotlighted in the Don Was documentary. "We were both so smitten with his performance that we asked him to continue until he lost interest. And he hasn't lost interest yet!

"The only real association I had with Brian, was during the recording of the *Smile* record. Then I saw him intermittently, but we weren't in the same loop, you might say. During the *Holland* record, when he was in California during that recording, I saw him just enough to generate one tune, which was "Sail On Sailor." We started that tune, and at one time, I was a 50% author, the title being mine. And it developed ... I think there may have been 10 people involved, I'm not sure how many people circled around the effort. Ultimately, (it) reduced my involvement in the song to 10%, which I think is a scant representation of my actual participation. But it's all too common in the business that people find argument with their participation in any effort. I would say that my participation on "Sail On Sailor" is greater than it appears to the publisher, but a lot of people apparently have the same opinion! Nevertheless, I had the tape of that song, the only tape of the song at the time when *Holland* had been refused by Warner Bros. I have the tape which saved that album's production and continued the Beach Boys' professional life at Warner Bros. for another term. I don't know how much of an aesthetic contribution I had in the song, because that was a period, of course, I hear that ... if you can remember it, you weren't there. But I do know that I made a pivotal contribution, because I have the only copy. But that's the sum and substance of the relationship I had with Brian between *Smile* and the present.

"But, to me, Brian is no different [today]. Brian has always been reticent, and hard to read, and I would say a social misanthrope. But he has gifts of greater interest to me, and they were the very things that drew me to him. In a central way, Brian's vocal abilities are undiminished. I don't know what he could do in range (then) that he isn't doing now. He can negotiate from a great C and even a B, arguably a B, to a high E, which is three octaves and some; this is a phenomenal range. An incredible voice. And he is undeniably a brilliant musician with undiminished musical abilities. I don't know the complexities of Brian's social or emotional difficulties, but at the time that I worked for him, he was very famous and everyone wanted to be involved with him. He, of course, represented a bunch of power, and still does, to me. I was surprised and pleased to find that I had the access to him that I did when we began *Orange Crate Art*. I think Brian looks at this as kind of an intermission-an active intermission, because we've been working very hard, intermittently, for two years now. He's had other jobs, and I certainly have, and we're happy to see each other. This has been a relief for both of us.

How does he feel about Capitol's alleged plans for a *Smile* boxset?

"I have no feelings about it, one way or another. I feel pretty neutral about it. My interest is in the occupation of music, not the interpretation of the value of my occupation in music, which is of zero interest to me. That serves somebody else's vanity, it has had no effect on my pocketbook or my opportunities. It doesn't matter to me how things are viewed. When you consider the span of years-30+ years-if there was ever an appropriateness to that work, in some completion, it would've been 30 years ago. It's incomplete, and that fact that it would be carried forward without Brian's control and enthusiastic endorsement, means it's meaningless. That's my belief. I think it's an invasion of privacy, and an attempt to perhaps rationalise what was basically an irrational situation. I think it was irrational that the project was aborted, which maybe comes from a sense of disappointment...

"What does amaze me about it is that there's any commercial gain in publicising that effort any further. Because the project was... I was victimised by the project, I believe, and I'm certain that Brian was. I just think it opens old wounds and does nothing to further anybody's creative process. It doesn't encourage me, and I don't think it encourages Brian, so I don't see what's in it except maybe to fill the coffers of a record company that has a commercial gain in a marginalised or niche industry of re-releases and retroactive marketing. I hold partly responsible for the lack of success of that project at the time, but there were major money problems with the company then too. It was all a tremendous, horrific shock to Brian. I think it was a major part of why that project lost its torque, and I think had a lot to do with Brian's caution about [future] social endeavour. It's too bad that it came from a company that's been otherwise as capable as Capitol. It's too bad. But in short, I think it's a bad idea. If I thought that it were beautiful music and deserving of commercialisation, I would feel differently. Then I would say 'The hell with the artist!' If some public illumination could be offered, but I don't think there's any illumination to be offered."

As far as the possibility of a Beach Boys reunion is concerned, "I think it's a very good thing to have a group, just as long as there's no coercion in it. As long as it does nothing to discourage the autonomy of any member of the group, that seems to me a fine thing. I think it's been shown that Brian has done his most outstanding work when his autonomy was encouraged as a creator. It may be that that has changed, I don't know. In the present project I'm doing with Brian, he has offered no music of his own. But I think that that is, in part, because he's just wanted to serve my interests. The general nature of his involvement with me, as I know mine with him, has always been a sense of reciprocation and fair play. So, he may be wanting to give me enough rope to hang myself, I don't know! I can't figure that out! But I would suggest that the Beach Boys – as an institution Brian has spent time and money and blood, sweat and tears in creating – he should benefit from. I think he's in a win-win situation, I really do. If it gives him too much to do, that would be a different problem.

"It's so hard for me to know any of these people (involved in Brian's various projects) because I'm not really in the loop. I'm like the 10 blind men with the elephant ... I just don't know exactly how many men were around that elephant, but there are a lot of people that have always gravitated to Brian from entirely different spheres or different experiences with him. They've all converged on the same magnet, which is this California sound and the man who made it. My viewpoint of what Brian should be doing might be entirely different from, say, what Mike Love believes the Beach Boys should be doing. Maybe Mike Love believes it's time for the Beach Boys to come up with the archetypal ecology song. Or maybe Mike Love wants to get rid of a few ground squirrels to build another base. I don't know. I have no idea of how to read what those interests are. I've always felt that I was perhaps a little too liberal a spirit for what it is that the Beach Boys do. I think I was probably Brian's left-wing operation, more experimental. But I think the pragmatism in Brian often says 'Do the right-wing, and keep them both flying.' I think he has a lot of social irons in the fire, a lot of social representation in this, in what he does. And I think maybe enough time has passed for him to get back with the group. I don't understand what the recent lawsuit (Ed. – When Mike Love sued Brian for writing royalties) was all about. I was stunned by its outcome, and I was shocked by it. And equally shocked that Brian would find himself able to work with Mike Love in a group after what I would think of as an antagonistic situation. Which boils down to the general hyphenate, 'Fuck-or-fight' That was a terrible thing to inflict on Brian. I know that because I was working with him at the time. Like I say, I'm surprised by the result, and more so if he were back in the group. But I think that they should be encouraged to do it. Because if they can do that, if they can bring peace to our times with such a thing, all power to them. It mystifies me.

"We'll see what happens. I'm not a betting man, so I wouldn't know what the odds are for its relevance. I'm less interested in music, I find, than I am in muddling through life. The larger life. I don't know what the music will mean to me because I've never believed that talent, in and of itself, meant anything. I mean, just knowing that brains can build a bomb! Attitude seems to matter a great deal to me, maybe more so than it does to other people. If the music comes out and it cuts the right attitude or takes the right posture, then I'll like it. So, I hope that their music is more than just handsome; I hope it's successful, and successful at winning hearts and, in a way, to convince people that the Beach Boys have a relevance to these times. My daughter listens to them, so maybe this is a trans-generational continuum that deserves to be applauded and encouraged. So, that's what I'd like to do."

How does he recall the reported animosity that supposedly existed between him and Love during the recording of *Smile*?

"Honestly, I didn't see much of Mike Love, and when he first indicated that he was dissatisfied with my words, I could understand that. I think the words were in a way unfinished, and, like everything else, to me it's like – the product of an abortion. It's not something to be studied. Because it's not a pretty picture; it's an ugly thing. I do think it's unfair that the words should have been analysed so dismissively as they were. I think that that was wrong to do because, in fact, what I was trying to do was pursue Brian's vision. And all I know was that I never changed a syllable of his in his melodies. That's sovereign. Melody is what comes from God. Melodies are feelings; words are thoughts. For example, "Heroes and Villains," everyone of those syllables was met with an article of thought in the lyrics. So I believed in the sanctity of his melodic balance and purpose, and I never intruded on that. And I think I was doing a good job. It's understandable to me that Mike Love didn't like them. They were more sophisticated than he was capable of doing himself, and I can see – now that I look back on it – how he might have had some animosity toward me because, in fact, I took his job – the job that he wanted so desperately. I don't think he meant any real malice toward me. I think I was just the guy who came to dinner and he wanted to make sure I was gone by bedtime. That's how I look at it. "As a matter of fact I went up (north) to play synthesiser on that last Beach Boys record – the one that met with less public favour and curiosity. The most recent one that was done up in Monterey with Terry Melcher and without Brian [*Summer in Paradise*]. I flew up there in a one-engine plane, which I'd never wanted to repeat, but I had the plane up there, so I had to fly back in it! When I was up there, I met Mike Love, and for the first time in 30 years, he was able to ask me directly, once again, what do those words mean? "Over and over the crow flies, uncover the cornfield." And I was able to tell him, again, "I don't know!" I have no idea what those words mean. But I don't think it's an ugly picture. I think it's a pretty picture. And it may be I was thinking about Vincent Van Gogh, or perhaps some impression of an idealised agrarian environment, of some great American prairie, turned into some farmland ... I don't know what I had in mind. Maybe I didn't have anything in mind. I was simply trying to carry on Brian's thought processes. I don't remember. I do know that when I was up in Monterey, Mike Love asked me if he could hitch a ride back with me. He offered to split the plane fare. We landed, and I never heard from him again. But he got a free ticket to ride! So, you might say, in a way, Mike Love owes me one!" He laughs.

"I do think that Brian having to live up to his genius for years has been a real bad thing. I think that's made him more skittish. And I think that's part of the sympathy I have for him. I think it's been ruinous because part of him always wants to be "Joe Average." So, you go from "high cholesterol" to "glacial clarity," you know. And you get both of those things in one recording session. It's a tough thing to reconcile.

"But, it's been so long that I can't remember what happened [during the *Smile* sessions], but it's my impression that Brian didn't really know what to do, so we perhaps got into conversations and perhaps we had one common enemy. That can do a lot in bonding social enterprise – finding a common enemy – and at that time, it would have been the British Invasion. I know at that time, there was a tremendously anti-American sentiment. And that's not something I shared. For example, I can remember the emotions, the dander, that I raised with the title "Surf's Up." To take all those droit, gauche – all those so dreadfully out-of-place sentiments of patriotism, or pride, and a sense of place that was so declasse and so out of fashion at the time – when everyone else was affecting a British accent. Everybody wanted to sound like John Lennon, and there was only one person I thought should sound like John Lennon, and that was John Lennon. And he sounded, at times, a lot like Elvis Presley or other American people. But Lennon was so totally individual that you could understand when they were people who were swept away by the British Invasion. That wasn't something I was prepared to do, and I knew when I met Brian Wilson that I was the only person that could encourage him to be himself. I think Brian then was pushed to an act of great courage – to develop the definition of what a song could do – and I think he pursued it. And, risking all, I think he was overwhelmed by the self-interests of the other fellows in the group, who were ... uh, almost irrelevant to this vision he had of the American Dream. I think I was part and parcel of what it was. And I was abetting him in that effort. So, I think they shot the messenger, but at least they didn't lose the message. And the message has been packaged so successfully, in every retrospective media blitz on the 60's that has come to light recently. For example, in *Forrest Gump*, you see all of these efforts to recapture the courage, almost like virtual reality, to show the actual peril of the time, and the character that it forged in people. Because there is no equivalent today. It seems to me it has been done successfully in other areas. But *Smile* has lost its pleasantry. It's gone. The opportunity is gone. I think it's a cynical effort to try to repackage it. And I just don't get it!

"But I protest too much; I'm not in this business for the money. And it certainly hasn't been what sustained me. It's been the honour of doing the music. And so I'm very protective about that subtle force – that still, small voice that says, "Be right [about things]. Don't be President!" And that's what I'm thinking about when I want to answer questions about whether we should be listening to *Smile* now.

"But it has been wonderful to work with Brian. I've got arguably my last record contract at Warner Bros., and I wanted to go out as I had come in – as a beneficiary of Brian Wilson's California sound. And I wanted to show that spirit – on what may be my last recorded album – we'll see what fate holds for me after this, but this looks like the end of the trail in a way. So I wanted to put first things first. Put the people first. I had a debt unpaid here, and I have tried to make good on it, and I think it's been a very happy moment for both of us. Brian has always felt to me very much like ... well, he suggested everything about the idealised California existence. The one that I still want to confirm. And so now I have a record that is a confirmational experience – in a very intimate or on a very personal level, and – at the same time, it might invite others to re-examine their distractions and about the vulgarities of our age. I think it's a consolation prize, for a Californian.

"What's good, you see, is, that my step isn't as sprightly as it was. Things come harder to me, songwriting does. I'm not as extemporaneous as I used to be. I'm not as proud of my own work; I have less to say, fewer opinions. But I'm content with this situation, because to me we've invigorated an old friendship with new occasion for honour. I could have gone into it with the idea that I was walking with the wounded, but that isn't the impression I have. Because he has a magnificent instrument, and he has lent it to this album project, which has become the focal piece of my effort.

"Ain't that somethin'? I'm still a bit player in the bigger movie!"

Bruce Johnston Interview
by Kingsley Abbott

Bruce has long been acknowledged as the most accessible Beach Boy to members of the fan fraternity, and his intelligent and positive views have always been thought provoking. An Anglophile of the first order, he has been especially supportive of fan activities here, including several guest appearances on the Beach Boys Britain message board, where he has sought to put his views honestly and correctly. Here, in a brand new interview especially for this book, he succinctly describes and justifies the Beach Boys' situation in the new century.

When has been your happiest time with The Beach Boys?

The first year! Without doubt…before I thought about all the politics and when Brian was still in hit records mode. We had no responsibilities, Carl was still a teenager, and it was all so much fun!

When was the most creative time?

For Brian, I think it was up to and including *Smiley Smile* which I consider to be a *very* under-rated album. You don't want to discount all the wonderful music in those hits. Some of the hardcore fans only want to look at the obscure art treasures, but the hits were wonderful. Brian was an incredible vocal arranger.

For the group as a whole, I would have to say *Sunflower*. It was perhaps a short season of real democracy. Though I think I prefer to have a monarch like Brian!

Which recorded songs that you have been involved with as a player or producer do you feel most proud of?

As a singer – everything! With my own stuff, I had my 2¢ worth with "Disney Girls" that I am proud of. Perhaps there could have been more of my material, maybe a lot more, but I would not pressure to take up any of what I saw as Brian's space. I was always optimistic that he would come back. If asked I would have worked on some writing with Brian and Mike. I was disappointed with "Deirdre", where Brian's input was under-whelming…but to be polite I still gave a 50:50 split.

Are you aware of any differences in the way the group has been received over the years in the US, Japan and Europe?

99% of our audiences couldn't care about the hardcore view, and they know a good night when they see one! Certain reactions is what hardcore fans criticise. In the US they always show up…Europe's OK, but even Brian doesn't sell tickets in some places. There will always be a place for the Beach Boys, and 'Hits' albums are always sure things. There is a small amount of fans who will always think differently, but promoters have to at least break even. You know, even our 'lean years' weren't lean…we all have $$$ tucked away! We have our money invested, and The Beach Boys as a concert act keeps going because we *like* what we are doing! Brian, on the other hand, is out on the road now and not really wanting to be. He doesn't need to be doing it, and in a way I'm surprised that he can keep it together...

What motivates you and Mike to keep it all going? Do you not feel creative needs?

I *do* create all the time. I do have projects, and I am satisfied with my songwriting, but that side of it is not through the Beach Boys. We keep going because it's FUN! And it's profitable...it makes a lot of money! I love it! You know, if we did Brian's set we'd probably get shouted down, and probably vice versa. The Beach Boys are not at that stage regarding creativity...I mean, how long do people expect us to stay in the Olympics??? No one ever asks for their money back!

Assuming musical talent, do you think it matters who else is on stage with you and Mike now?

In the best of all possible worlds it would be Al, Carl, Brian and Dennis. You can go to a concert of The Glenn Miller Orchestra and hear 1940s tunes reproduced note for note. All the Beach Boys' material is also note for note...the same arrangements...everything. Perhaps voice wise not in the same timbre, but it's pretty close. The *music* is the star, and that's true for Brian's shows too, where he sits like Bacharach conducting.

As a talented and creative musician, do you not yearn for new material to sit alongside the hits...either on stage or as new recordings?

It would be very difficult to introduce new songs on stage *at this point in our career*. You couldn't really do new Beach Boys songs without original members, so you stick with things people know. People should get over it! Go back and listen to the whole body of work that was made with everybody at their prime. Perhaps soloists can do new material easier, but with us it would be like a 70 year old wearing a 16 year old's bikini! The Beach Boys don't have a problem. We are what we are now, and happy with it. Brian moved on from the group, and effectively *that* Beach Boys died after "Til I Die" and "Surf's Up".

Brian Wilson's star is pretty high again. Do you think he will maintain creativity, or is the current surge of interest just down to the concerts and good marketing?

Here it is relevant to point out that the US and UK viewpoints are very different. Your UK media is much faster, with less diversity. What Brian did in January 2002...well, I would hope that he considers the Royal Festival Hall to be the *highest* point of his career. I really hope that it did it for him. I hope that it was as good as hearing his music on the radio for the first time. It was real for him, a real high point, which is why I was surprised when I heard that he was coming back again so soon. He deserves a Grammy; he should be bigger than John Williams who gets all the Oscar nominations...

What projects or developments can you foresee in the future?

I think on a simple hooky four bar level....maybe some film recording possibilities....I don't particularly want to do more Beach Boy recording. I don't want to undervalue what has gone before.

If you could pick one album and one song from Beach Boys history that you feel would best represent yours and the group's efforts, what would they be?

One album would be *Sunflower*. It was as mature as we could be and still be young. It simply showed off *everyone's* talents, especially Brian's with "This Whole World". Everyone was beyond 100%, and everyone was at their finest for all the right reasons. In a top ten album chart, I'd have *Sunflower* at No 1, nothing at 2-9, and *Pet Sounds* at No 10. For one particular song, I'd have "The Lord's Prayer" which was the finest Beach Boy sound ever made.

Any other reflections on Brian Wilson and The Beach Boys from a new century perspective?

Brian was the only guy that understood when The Beach Boys was over. We caught the brilliance that was the Beach Boys on tape for all time. It's like seeing star light from something that doesn't exist any more. Where is Brian's solo work equal to what he did before?

I was very, very happy at the beginning, and I am now. We're happy and doing well. I *chose* to enjoy what Mike and I are doing now. Mike's always working on lyrics you know. Carl's estate, Brian and Al all get a license fee from what we do. We have recently got a Falcon 2000 private jet for the next five years...

I would LOVE to do a single vocal cameo, perhaps "Disney Girls", on stage with Brian. I'd want it to be in London, and I love for Mike to do one too, but I don't want to change what Mike and I are doing now.

Confidence Lost... and Regained.
The Resurgence of Brian Wilson
by Kingsley Abbott

Brian Wilson's re-emergence since 2000 has exceeded all expectations, and has gathered an incredible amount of positive column inches in the musical and mainstream press. hardcore fans and followers have had all their wildest dreams fulfilled, and still it seems there is more to come. Is this turn of events the best for Brian, or will it yet prove to be another attempt to play off his name as some sceptics have predicted. As a Wilson watcher of forty years standing, I find I now have strong and definite views.

An old British television advert for toothpaste from the sixties ended with a starry halo above a smiling face, accompanied by a single percussive 'ding' denoting the 'Colgate Ring of Confidence'. Everything was alright if you had that special inner confidence, and its subtext played effectively on just how easy it is for self image to be destroyed. Across the pond, as the Beach Boys began their first run of surfin' hits, Brian Wilson appeared relaxed, happy and in total control of his life. He had the confidence of youth, and the abilities to translate aspects of the culture around him into sweetly accessible pop for markets way beyond his native California. He had without doubt hit a groove and was active and successful within it. He was the acknowledged leader of the group, not just as musician-in-chief but also as eldest of the three brothers who formed the core.

To translate the position of someone who was riding a new wave into someone who could generate more and newer waves was a harder task, but it was one that Brian recognised from as early as the second Beach boys album. He was astute enough to realise that there was more happening around him within pop music than the here-today-gone-tomorrow surf and drag craze. A fan of girl group pop, he heard and valued producer Phil Spector's work above all others. As with the rest of us, Brian heard jaw-dropping and ground-breaking sounds emerging from Phil's mini-masterpieces. The previous rules were being churned up and being replaced by a man who was prepared to break all the conventions for uncompromising effect. Brian was awe-struck, and marvelled at the way Spector utilised a comparatively small studio in his own town to build a sound like no other. As well as any growing musical ambition Brian may have been developing, he now had a production style to aspire to, and possibilities growing in his fertile mind as limitless as the images in opposing mirrors. How he coped with the challenge said much of his own family background and his own mental mindset.

Brian had enjoyed average-to-good success through his schooling. Coping fairly well by all accounts with academic areas, it was in sports that he met major challenges. His good height and athletic build led to football and track events, and his father was eager to become the archetypal 'touchline supporter'. Brian had not only the sporting challenges to deal with, but also his father's aspirations to try to live up to. However, Brian's real interests lay elsewhere and the sports life did not sit naturally on what his mother would call his 'gentle soul'. Cousin Mike Love, who all their lives has played 'jock' alpha male to Brian's 'heart on his sleeve' character, was also a constant reminder of a world that he wanted to succeed in but one to which he could not fully commit.

Mike's experience in school, life and relationships was then, and has been since, very different to Brian's. Comparisons in some areas would have found Brian wanting and could have easily dented his youthful confidence, but Brian was smart enough to realise that his route to success lay in developing his own and obvious musical talents.

Any retrospective dissection of the Beach Boys' musical development from 1962 –1966 will read it as the growth of two distinct strands. On the one hand there was the pure pop sensibilities of teen crazes and hedonistic fads that followed a direct line from "Surfin' USA" to "Barbara Ann", and on the other was the adventurous nurturing of a very particular genius that went from "Farmer's Daughter" and "Surfer Girl" thru "Don't Worry Baby" to "Good Vibrations". Brian was central to both strands, but for him one was formulaic whilst the other was his chosen path of progress. The common factor was his increasingly bold use of the studio as a major factor in his productions, an element that he brought straight from his adulation of Spector. Brian was also competitive, a hangover from his school sports world and family upbringing, and once he realised that he had become a major player in pop music this character trait fuelled his fires. Spector became his own personal spectre, causing him to set himself ever higher standards of achievement. Confidence is built upon perceived success, and initially Brian had almost more than he could cope with and, as Marilyn Wilson reflects, the period around "Fun Fun Fun" was probably the happiest for Brian and the group. Brian knew however that there was more to aspire to and set about increasingly achieving more and more adventurous writing and production to raise the group from a teeny fad band to one that could lead a previous un-attained level of pop sophistication. He heard its genesis in Spector's work, and ached to take it further with the Beach Boys.

The songs on the 1964 and 1965 albums achieved some of what Brian aspired to, as he wrote and produced without the strictures of touring. The music that he made in those years are amongst the finest in his canon, and provided more than adequate answer to the new challenges of answering the 'British Invasion' of the US charts. As with all Americans, Brian had been bowled over by the extent of the invasion, but had also realised that the real musical threat came from The Beatles. Mirroring his own development, they had moved from fine individual pop records into development of moods on albums and ideas of 'whole album' production. Indeed it is probable that Brian realised what they were doing almost before they did themselves. Marrying all his growth areas, the stage was set for *Pet Sounds*.

Brian's twelfth album for Capitol was his peak – the pinnacle to which he had been aiming without realising where it would be. Taking production values from Spector and mood from The Beatles, allied to his own developing writing and the Beach Boys' angelic harmonies, he achieved what he desired. It was not even until it was all finished that he realised just how good it was, and that he had really managed to put his whole heart and soul into it. So much so that it was too giant a step for many to adjust to, not least the sales staff at Capitol Records who did not hear the sounds that they best loved: cash registers ringing for quickly and easily digested pop pap. The step forward proved to be too much for some, though The Beatles and much of the pop intelligensia in Britain eagerly embraced it for the gem that it was. Brian himself, living and working in the US, perceived only comparative failure as the first 'Best of' package was rapidly shipped out to fill orders.

With his confidence severely bruised, Brian set to work on what he believed would be his next step: the *Smile* project, which had actually begun during the *Pet Sounds* sessions, continued. "Good Vibrations" emerged after its extensively varied sessions to worldwide acclaim to place Brian right at the top of the mountain, but when you are in that position there is only one way to go...

Seeking what he saw as a yet higher peak, Brian eagerly took "Heroes & Villains" to a local radio station one night for an exclusive. Time had moved on and, with the advent of playlists and the intransigence of the company mindset, Brian's child-like enthusiasm to share his new creation was dashed, and his confidence with it. Though the record was a sizable hit, the *Smile* sessions fell apart as Brian lost his way, and fell deeper into the drugs chasms that had opened around his particular mountain. Sloughs of despair and inactivity took the place of the earlier creative explosions, and Brian was to enter his second twenty-five years a changed, damaged and unconfident man.

Comparing Brian's post-1967 work to his earlier growth is difficult as it is against the background of personal turmoils, drug problems and family upheavals that are dealt with extensively elsewhere. Most important was that, for mant reasons, he had lost the confidence and competitive spark that drove him forward initially. That is not to say that his creative abilities had deserted him, as is so well shown with the early seventies *Spring* album that he co-produced for wife Marilyn and her sister Diana. Here was another 'whole album of good stuff' with a wonderfully gentle mood pervading the whole work. Brian, in some cases producing and engineering whole tracks himself at home, had another work to feel tremendous pride in. Once again he involved himself with the promotion, only to be thwarted by apathy, this time on both sides of the Atlantic, save for a small section of die-hards. It was not a recipe for bringing Brian back, and the ill-fated attempt by The Beach Boys to do just that in 1976 proved to be little more than a cynical marketing exercise.

Brian Wilson had become the man who 'went away for awhile', except his while proved to last from the early seventies until the nineties, despite the release of the 1988 Landy overseen solo album. Despite all the, often deserved, hostile press, it is more than likely that Dr. Landy saved Brian's life, and correctly saw that part of his route to some recovery was through music. Indeed some of that 1988 eponymous album stands up proudly next to earlier work. Brian was back to making music, and even survived probably difficult personal appearances including the surprise guesting at the UK fan convention that September. As time went by it seemed to become evident that Landy was exceeding his brief, and eventually court proceedings were instituted to remove his influence on Brian. However in fans and friends' eyes, Brian was still a damaged man who did not appear to be whole-heartedly involved with any proceedings around him. Through sparse album involvement in the seventies and eighties we had heard a gruff and rasping voice replace the emotional instrument of earlier times, and seen a forbidding demeanour replace the humour and openness. Fans were unsure that they even thought he should try and come back if this is what it meant.

As the nineties rolled in, and with Dr Landy finally out of the picture for good, news began to filter through of Brian's second marriage to Melinda, and of some small scale live work. Through the good offices of his friend Andy Paley, Brian had played a few small live club dates with the material being carefully drawn from his body of work. Reports of the shows varied, with some saying that it was a sad shadow of a figure going awkwardly through the motions once again, whilst others were more optimistic. Generally no hopes were raised very high, as we all knew that Brian had never been a natural 'out-front' perfomer, and, God knows, the baggage that he carried militated against this being any sort of success. However, along with news of the live work came news of fresh writing and record- ing with Andy Paley (Tracks that are well documented in Domenic's Priore's piece in section 3 of this book), and hopes were raised a little. The interviews that appeared during the nineties still suggested an uncomfortable man, but the news of expansion within the ranks by the addition of members of the Wondermints into Brian's band brought some growing positive reviews. The Joe Thomas produced *Imagination* album, which in retrospect was a tangential move from the real route, came amid a blaze of mostly positive publicity. The album was certainly enjoy- able, and Brian's voice seemed brighter and lighter, a fact which at the time was usually put down largely to studio manipulation. The reception of the album and the associated promotional shows led to the firming up of a regular backing band of ten members, and to the *Live At The Roxy* double CD in 2000. Any initial doubts fan had at there being another live trawl through the hits, as might have been expected from The Beach Boys touring band of the time, were quickly dispelled by two key factors: the classy and surprising choice of some of the material, and the quality of the delivery, especially from Brian. Those who knew of them were well aware of the extensive knowledge of the best of Brian's music that was held by Jeff Foskett, Darian Sahanaja and the others. This went some way to explain- ing some of the choices of tracks that fans never believed they would hear Brian attempting live, like "Kiss Me Baby" and "Please Let me Wonder" from the immediate pre-*Pet Sounds* period. Atop it all was the quality of Brian's voice blending with voices that understood every nuance of the harmonies. Even for the most hardcore fans, it took a while to sink in! The live shows had achieved a ren- aissance that few would have thought possible even a few years before.

Throughout this nineties activity, Brian's original group The Beach Boys had been continuing as a live act led by Mike Love and Bruce Johnston after the untimely death of Carl Wilson. For the group, the music was the star, a fact under- lined by the increasingly faceless sidemen who accompanied Mike and Bruce – competent but unknown, leading to suggestions that the group had become a trib- ute act to itself. Doubtlessly, the demand and profitability remained strong, but without a Wilson on stage many turned from the group as a serious creative force. Instead the media and hardcore fan focus returned unmistakably to Brian, who was about to play an absolute ace.

Brian was initially sceptical about the idea of performing *Pet Sounds* live, sim- ply on the basis that he didn't believe that it could effectively be pulled off. Gradually the band convinced him that it was possible, at which time he firmly and enthusiastically took the reins. News reached British shows of the album being performed wonderfully in its entirety, and many fans made the trip to the States to catch the early shows for themselves. Though the early signs for such a major show were not good for Britain, this writer assumed that, should it really do well and catch the public's imagination, it simply could not miss our shores given the history of love for it here. With this is mind, we set about preparing the companion book to this reader, *Pet Sounds – The Greatest Album Of The Twentieth Century*, in anticipation of such a tour. After much on/off news, dates were finally confirmed for London's Royal Festival Hall in January 2002 (along with one each in Scotland and Ireland). Unbelievably three RFH night sold out within days by word of mouth alone, and a fourth was added.

The Royal Festival Hall holds 3,000, and is acoustically a good venue. Its comparative intimacy and fine foyer facilities meant that the atmosphere hours before each show was electric and celebratory before even a single note had been played. Each night the show's sponsor *Mojo* magazine hosted a gathering for the rock media and many music stars, but it was evident that rock's elite would have turned out anyway. Those nights everyone was there as fans taking the opportunity, not only to hear wonderful music, but to give a very personal thanks to a man they quite simply loved. Concerts often attract excitement and deafening enthusiasm, but this was quite something else in the feeling of love that pervaded the whole event. Even the national press, not normally given to such appraisal, was aware of the strength of feeling. Brian's friend David Leaf, accompanying Melinda in the audience each night, stated after the first show that it was the very best show he had ever seen Brian give. For the next three nights it then got even better, with Brian visibly loosening up as he realised the extent of the enthusiasm. Musically the shows were as damn near perfect as possible, with the closing 'love message' of "Love And Mercy" bringing tears to virtually every eye in the house. This time, Brian really was back and London rejoiced.

What effect does such a success have on the artist, or more importantly in this case the man? Artistically, many were surprised when a return tour was announced for June 2002, partly to tie into an appearance on the Queen's Jubilee concert bill. Too soon said some, but when viewed commercially there is no doubting that the demand was there. However there was another element that I had noticed during various interviews with Brian during 2001 and 2002. The earlier conversation, along with other writers I have since spoken to, I found difficult in that Brian answered questions briefly without much expansion. However, as soon as I began an interview immediately prior to the June tour, I was aware of a difference in tone and substance. Like anyone else, I'm sure Brian had his good days and his bad days, a fact no doubt at times exacerbated by his medication, but to my ears this was more than this natural variation. I sensed a lightness, both in his voice and demeanour that heartened me. After the intended questions, we moved on to discussions of health, fitness, TV and holidays during which he even took a trip to the loo! Most significant to me was that during the conversation Brian actually stated that he was a 'genius at music' in relation to the as yet unreleased poetry album he cut with his friend Steve Kalinich in the early seventies (see SK interview in this book). In all interviews I can recall, Brian has previously been self-deprecating of his talents, brushing aside such plaudits, but now it was as if he had finally accepted the mantle. It was the sort of self-belief and positive self image that teachers constantly seek to imbue with children. When speaking to some of the wonderfully friendly band members after one of the June shows, it became evident that they were aware of this as they spoke of how good the January shows had been for

Brian. They mentioned his improving voice, a noticeable tone higher in parts at the June shows, and his vastly improved confidence. The reception at the Royal Festival Hall and the other January shows had formed part of further revitalisation that was a joy to witness. Some would argue that Brian's wounds, both mentally and physically, have run deep, and that consequently very little more could be realistically expected. As a teacher, part of my basic philosophy with children was 'tell them they are wonderful and they will be', and now it seems that something as simple as this could be taking hold of Brian. Is thirty-five years too long to take to regain a 'ring of confidence'? With the right people around him, and a stimulating musical environment, we could yet see him making up for some of the lost time. Never before has the subtext in the words of "You Still Believe In Me" meant so much.

Appendix 1

The Beach Boys Story - Dramatis Personae
by Andrew Doe and Kingsley Abbott

It is hoped that the following list of people will answer some of the "How did they fit into the story?" type of questions...

ALARIAN, Rich	Member of The Survivors with Brian Wilson.
ALEXENBURG, Ron	90s Manager of the band.
ALMER, Tandyn	Lyricist, "Sail on Sailor".
ALTBACH, Ron	Tour / Studio musician, 70s.
ANDERLE, David	Head of Brother Records,1966-67.
ANTHONY, Dean	Author, *The Beach Boys* Glossy photo book.
ASHER, Tony	Lyricist, *Pet Sounds* album.
BACHMAN, Randy	Co-composer, *Keeping the Summer Alive*.
BAKER, Adrian	Tour/Studio musician, 80s/90s.
BARNES, Ken	Author of early book on the Beach Boys.
BAXTER. Jeff	Producer of Carl's *Youngblood*.
BECHER, Curt	Producer of 10 min disco version of "Here Comes The Night in the early 70s.
BENNETT, Scott	90s/00s multi-instrumentalist for Brian, member of Wondermints.
BERNARD, Michael	Programmer for *Brian Wilson*.
BERRY, Jan	Co-composer with Brian Wilson in the 60s.
BENAY, Ben	Session musician, 60s.
BINGENHEIMER, Rodney	Legendary LA scenemaker, DJ, and friend of Brian's.
BLAINE, Hal	Session drummer, 60s & beyond.
BLAKE, Ginger	Member of The Honeys.
BOWLES, Jimmy	Gave Brian Wilson surfing locations for "Surfing USA".
BOWLES, Judy	Early 60s girlfriend of Brian's, subject of "Surfer Girl".
BRITZ, Chuck	Beach Boys studio engineer from 1963-66.
BURCHMAN, Bob	Co-composer of "It's About Time".
CAMPBELL, Glen	Session/ touring musician, 60s.
CAPP, Frank	Session musician, 60s.
CARTER, Ed	Touring/session bassist 1967-95.
CATON, Roy	Session musician, 60s
CAVANAGH, Dwight	Author, *The Smile File*
CHAPLIN, Blondie	Beach Boys member, 70s
CHEMAY, Joe	Studio musician, 70s
CHRISTIAN, Roger	DJ/Lyricist, 60s
COLE, Jerry	Studio musician, 60s.
CUSHING MURRAY, Geoffrey	Co-composer, with Carl and Dennis, *L.A. (Light Album)*.
DAILEY, Jasper	Candid photographer, *Smile* sessions.
D'AMICO, Micky	90s/00s percussionist for Brian, member of Wondermints.
DESPER, Steve	Engineer, 1968-72.

DE LORY, Al	Studio musician, 60s
DOE, Andrew	Co-author, *The Complete Guide to the Music of the Beach Boys*, Omnibus 1997.
DOUGLAS, Steve	Studio musician, 60s.
DRAGON, Daryl	Touring / Studio musician, 70s.
DRAGON, Dennis	Studio drummer, 70s.
DUNBAR, Reggie (aka Murry Wilson)	Co-composer credit on "Breakaway".
DUTCH, Jim	Co-composer *Pacific Ocean Blue*.
ELLIOTT, Brad	Author, *Surf's Up* A History of Beach Boys recordings.
ERLICH, Jesse	Cello on "Good Vibrations".
ESTES, Gene	Studio musician, 60s.
FATAAR, Rikki	Beach Boys member, 70s.
FIGUEROA, Bob	Touring / Studio musician 70s/80s.
FORNATALE, Pete	DJ, journalist and diehard Brian Wilson supporter.
FORTINA, Carl	Studio musician, 60s.
FOSKETT, Jeff	Touring/Studio musician, 80s & Brian's 90s/00s guitarist/vocalist.
GAINES, Steven	Author, *Heroes and Villains*.
GASTWIRT, Joe	Engineer on the band's digital re-masterered compact discs.
GAUDIO, Bob	Producer on "East Meets West".
GELLER, Arnie	Brian Wilson's personal 'gofer', late 60s.
GOLD, Todd	Ghostwriter on Brian Wilson's autobiography *Wouldn't It Be Nice*.
GOLDEN, Bruce	Author, *The Beach Boys and the Southern Californian Pastoral*.
GRANT, Mike	Editor *Beach Boys Stomp* UK fanzine.
GREGORY, Probyn	90s/00s multi-instrumentalist for Brian, member of Wondermints.
GRIFFIN, Gary	Touring/Studio musician, 70s.
GRILLO, Nick	Beach Boys manager 1968-1970
GUDGE, Roy	Co-organiser UK Beach Boys fanzine and annual Beach Boys UK convention.
GUERCIO, Jim	Beach Boys manager 1973-75.
HENN, Rick	Ex-member of the Sunrays, composer "Soulful Ole Man Sunshine".
HINES, Jim	90s/00s drummer for Brian.
HINSCHE, Billy	Touring/Studio musician, 1974-95.
HOROCHEVSKY, Igor	Touring/Studio musician, 1968-72.
HOUSE, Bill	Engineer, 80s.
HULLETT, Tom	Beach Boys manager, 80s.
HUTTON, Danny	Singer and longtime Brian Wilson buddy.
JACKS, Terry	Producer of Beach Boys' version of his own hit, "Seasons In The Sun".
JAKOBSON, Gregg	Co-producer and co-composer on Dennis' *Pacific Ocean Blue*.
JARDINE, Matt	Al's son, and touring / Studio musician with the band, 80s / 90s.
JARDINE, Adam	Al's son, also sang backing vocals on *Keeping the Summer Alive*.
KALINICH, Steve	Lyricist, 60s/70s.
KAYE, Carol	Studio musician, 60s.
KENT, Nick	Controversial celebrity NME journalist, and author of "The Last Beach Movie", collected in *The Dark Stuff*, Penguin 1994.
KENNEDY, Ray	Lyricist on "Sail On Sailor".
KESSELL, Barney	Studio musician, 60s.

KOWALSKI, Mike   Tour drummer, 70s.
KORTHOF, Steve   Mike Love's cousin and 'Gofer' for the band 60s and later.
KNOTT, Joe   Co-composer on "Add Some Music".
LAMM, Karen   Married Dennis Wilson twice in the 70s and
                         co-composer of the Beach Boys track "Baby Blue".
LANDY, Eugene   Brian Wilson's controversial doctor, therapist etc,
                         circa ealy 70s, and again later during the 80s.
LANDY, Evan   Landy's son and Brian Wilson's minder in the 80s .
LAZARUSI, Henry   Beach Boys' manager 1977.
LEAF, David   Author of the excellent *The Beach Boys* and the
                         Californian Myth, journalist and a friend of Brian Wilson's.
LEAF, Earl   Capitol Records employee, 60s (No relation to David above).
LESLIE, Kevin   Employed by Eugene Landy as Brian Wilson's minder, 80s .
LEVINE, Larry   Engineer, 60s .
LEVINE, Steve   Producer *The Beach Boys* album, 80s .
LINNET, Mark   Engineer, 1986-95.
LIPPIN, Ronnie   Brian's co-manager, 90s/00s.
LIZIK, Bob   90s/00s bassist for Brian.
LLOYD, Charles   Touring/ Studio musician, 70s.
LOCKERT, Jim   Engineer, 1967/68.
LOVE, Shawn   Daughter to Mike Love, married Dennis Wilson in the early 80s.
LOVE, Stan   Brian's minder, 1976.
LOVE, Steve   Beach Boys manager, 1975-77, 78-79.
LYNNE, Jeff   Formerly of the Electric Light Orchestra, co-produced
                         "Let It Shine" on the *Brian Wilson* album.
MALLABER, Gary   Studio drummer, 80s.
MANKEY, Earle   Engineer, 70s.
MANSON, Charles   Cult leader in jail for the murder of Sharon Tate and others.
                         Co-composer of "Cease to Exist" which later surfaced as
                         the Beach Boys B-side "Never Learn Not To Love".
MARIE, Sharon   Early 60s Brian Wilson protege.
MARKS, David   Beach Boys member 1962-63.
MAROCCO, Frank   Studio musician, 60s.
MATTHEWS, Scott   Studio drummer, 1980.
McCARTNEY, Paul   Constant devotee of *Pet Sounds*, and Beatle.
McGUINN, Roger   Studio guest musician, 1980s and 90s, and Byrd.
McPARLAND, Stephen   Author, *The Wilson Project*.
MELCHER, Terry   Producer 1986-95, son of Doris Day who formerly worked
                         with The Byrds. Member of duo with Bruce Johnston
                         in the early 60s.
MERTENS, Paul   90s/00s woodwind player for Brian.
MICROS, Mike   Touring / Studio musician, 80s and 90s.
MIGLIORI, Jay   Studio musician, 60s.
MILLS, Taylor   90s/00s vocalist/percussionist for Brian.
MILWARD, John   Author, *The Beach Boys Silver Anniversary*
MORGAN, Alexandra   Lyricist, worked with Brian Wilson in the 80s.
MORGAN, Hite   Produced the band in 1961.
MORGAN, Tommy   Played harmonica on "Help Me Rhonda".
MOFFITT, Steve   Engineer, 70s.
MUNOZ, Carli   Touring/Studio musician, 70s.
NOLAN, Tom   Journalist, *Rolling Stone*.

NORBERG, Bob	Co-composer with Brian Wilson, early 60s.
NOWLEN, Dave	Member of The Survivors, an early Capitol Beach Boys soundalike act, which featured Brian Wilson and three of his friends.
PALEY, Andy	Co-producer and co-composer with Brian Wilson, 80s and 90s.
PAMPLIN, Rushton (Rocky)	Co composer and singer with Spring.
PARKS, Van Dyke	Co-composer *Smile* and composer on *Orange Crate Art*.
PETERS, Jeff	Engineer, 80s.
PEWTER, Jim	DJ/Singer.
PHILLIPS, John	Co-composer of "Kokomo".
POHLMAN, Ray	Studio musician, 60s.
PREISS, Byron	Author, *The Beach Boys Authorised Biography*
PRIORE, Dominic	Author/Compiler of, *Look, Listen, Vibrate, Smile*.
RANDI, Don	Studio musician, 60s.
REAGAN, Ronald and Nancy	Fans with jobs outside the music industry.
REGAN, Russ	Capitol employee, who supposedly gave the Beach Boys their name.
REUM, Peter	US Beach Boys Historian/Archivist.
REYNOLDS, Dick	Arranger of the *Christmas Album*.
RIELEY, Jack	Manager, 1970-73, he introduced ecological issues to the Beach Boys. Rieley also sang lead vocal on "Day in the Life of a Tree" on *Surf's Up*.
RITZ, Lyle	Studio musician, 60s.
ROVELL, Diane	Member of Honeys / Spring.
RUSSELL, Leon	Studio musician, 60s.
SACHEN, Terry	Roadie / lyricist, "I Know There's An Answer".
SAHANAJA, Darian	90s/00s keyboards/vibes player for Brian, member of Wondermints.
SANDLER, David	Co-produced the *Spring* album.
SCHILLING, Jerry	Manager, 80s.
SEIVERS, Jean	Brian's co-manager, 90s/00s.
SIEGAL, Jules	Journalist.
SHARP, Sid	First violin and strings leader on "Fire" music & others.
SMITH SCHILLING, Myrna	Lyricist for Carl.
STAMOS, John	US TV soap star and occasional 80s and 90s part-time Beach Boys member. Stamos also sang lead on "Forever" on the *Summer in Paradise* album.
STEINBERG, Scott	Employed by Eugene Landy as Brian Wilson's minder, 70s.
STRANGE, Billy	Session guitarist, 60s.
STUDER, Jim	Co-composed songs, including the title track, on Mike Love's solo album, *Looking Back With Love*.
TANNER, Paul	Ex-Glenn Miller trombonist who played the theremin-like instrument on "Good Vibrations" and others.
TAYLOR, Derek	Publicist, 1966/7.
TENNILLE, Toni	Touring/Session singer, 1972. Later successful part of hitmaking act, The Captain and Tennille.
TEDESCO, Tommy	Studio musician, 60s.
THEUS, Woodrow	Studio musician, 70s.
TITLEMAN, Russ	Co-producer Brian Wilson.
TOBLER, John	Journalist / Author, *The Beach Boys*.
TORRENCE, Dean	Sang lead on "Barbara Ann", and later designed record

covers for the band in the 70s including *15 Big Ones*. Also of Jan and Dean.

USHER, Gary — Co-composer and Co-producer in the 60s and later on the "Wilson Project", 1986-87.

VAIL, Fred — Promoter and friend of Dennis Wilson.

VENET, Nick — The band's first Capitol producer.

VOSSE, Mike — *Smile* era Beach Boys acolyte.

WARONKER, Lenny — Warners President (ex Sire) and friend of Brian Wilson's.

WAS, Don — Producer of the *I Just Wasn't Made for these Times* film and album, 90s.

WATT, James — US Secretary of the Interior who banned the Beach Boys from a 4th July show.

WHITE, Timothy — Author, of the highly acclaimed *The Nearest Faraway Place – Brian Wilson, The Beach Boys and the Southern California Experience*, of which *Q* magazine recently said "Oh that all rock books aspired to the scope, depth, and sheer vision of this masterly overview of the whole West Coast milieu / ethos."

WHITE JOHNSON, Robert — Lyricist for Carl Wilson, 80s.

WILLIAMS, Carolyn — Brian Wilson nurse and minder, 80s .

WILSON, Audree & Murry — Parents.

WILSON, Carnie & Wendy — Brian Wilson's daughters and musicians.

WILSON, Daria & Delanie — Brian's adopted daughters with Melinda.

WILSON, Marilyn — Brian Wilson's first wife / Member of Honeys / Spring.

WILSON, Melinda — Brian Wilson's second wife.

WINCENTSEN, Edward — Author, *Denny Remembered*.

WINFREY, Gary — Co-composer and friend of Al Jardine.

WOOD, Roy — Brian Wilson fan who played Saxophone on "It's OK" from *15 Big Ones*.

Appendix 2

Beach Boys Top Tens

The Top 10 Beach Boys Albums In The UK

1.   *20 Golden Greats* (1976)
2.   *The Very Best of The Beach Boys* (1983)
3.   *Best Of The Beach Boys* (1966)
4.   *Pet Sounds* (1966)
5.   *Summer Dreams* (1990)
6.   *Best of The Beach Boys, Vol. 2* (1967)
7.   *Summer Days (And Summer Nights)* (1966)
8.   *The Beach Boys' Greatest Hits* (1970)
9.   *20:20* (1969)
10.   *The Beach Boys Today* (1966)

Six of the ten here are compilations, with the massively TV advertised 1976 *Golden Greats* album easily winning. It is likely that *Pet Sounds*, with its continuing critical acclaim, will eventually climb higher up the list.

The Top 10 Beach Boys Singles In The UK

1.   "Good Vibrations" (1966)
2.   "Sloop John B" (1966)
3.   "God Only Knows" (1966)
4.   "Do it Again" (1968)
5.   "Cottonfields" (1970)
6.   "I Get Around" (1964)
7.   "Then I Kissed Her" (1967)
8.   "Barbara Ann" (1966)
9.   "Break Away"(1969)
10.   "Lady Lynda" (1979)

"Good Vibrations" is top of the heap by a long way. Nearly every single is from the 60s – the Capitol years. Saleswise "Wipe Out" from 1987 would have made No. 8 if it had not been a collaboration. Oddly, the group's belated all-time US bestselling single, 1988's "Kokomo", was only a modest UK success, and registers nowhere near the top ten.

The 10 Most Valuable Brian Wilson Records In The USA

Title	Artist	Special Feature/ label / cat no.	Year	Est $ '94
1 Girls on The Beach	Beach Boys	Promo EP / Capitol no cat no	1964	*
2 The Surfer Moon	Bob & Sherri	Blue label 45/Safari 101	1962	1,500
3= Surfin' Safari	Beach Boys	Comp rec. sess EP Capl 2185/6	1962	750
3= The Surfer Moon	Bob & Sherri	White label promo 45/ Safari 101	1962	750
3= Barbie	Kenny & The Cadets	Red and gold vinyl 45/	1962	750
6= Shoot The Curl	Honeys	Picture sleeve 451/Capitol 4952	1963	600
6= Select 'BB Concert'	Beach Boys	EP/Capitol 2754/5	1964	600
6= Spirit of America	Beach Boys	Promo paper sleeve 451	1963	600
9= Excerpts 'BB Party'	Beach Boys	EP/ Capitol 2993/4	1965	600
9= Heroes And Villains	Beach Boys	Discarded Capitol picture sleeve	1967	500

Source Neal Umphred

*No value can be reasonably estimated for this priceless item. There are no known copies in the hands of collectors, although the EP was pressed as a promotional item for the Beach Boys film of the same name.

The Bob and Sherri record features longtime friend Bob Norberg and an unknown female vocalist duetting on an early Wilson composition. Kenny and the Cadets features Brian and brother Carl, performing separately from the Beach Boys. The Honeys, featuring Brian's wife Marilyn, were produced by him.

Appendix 3

"Don't Worry Baby" - A Personal Appreciation by Kingsley Abbott

The recent Top 100 Singles poll in Mojo magazine placed this wonderful song at No. 11. It was the only B side to make the list all on its own, and I also recall that it made the top ten of a similar NME list back in the late seventies. I was especially pleased to see that it has remained popular as it is, and always has been, my favourite individual track. Whilst compiling this book, I happened to ask David Leaf if Brian still held it in the high regard that was always reported to be his view. "Oh yes," came the reply. "He knows it's good."

The song is the perfect marriage of melody, production and full group harmonies. At the time of its release in 1964 I spent what seemed like ages trying to pick up on all the words but they always eluded me. I even tried to locate the sheet music via the Sea Of Tunes name, but never found it. Instead I contented myself with blissfully letting the overall sound wash over me as I sat on our front door step watching the sun set. One night I must have played it about twenty times in a row, and each time the harmonies came back in after the guitar break it seemed to be the most perfect moment ever recorded. It was as if the harmonies were brought ever so slightly higher in the mix at that moment. The feeling that I had then for that marvellous sound has never diminished, and it surely was the song that paved the way for Brian's production masterpiece Pet Sounds.

Appendix 4

A Beach Boys Bibliography

Biographies

The Beach Boys by Byron Preiss. Ballantine, New York 1979.

The Beach Boys And The California Myth by David Leaf. Grosset And Dunlap, New York 1979. 2nd edition Courage Books, 1985.

The Beach Boys in Their Own Words by Nick Wise. Omnibus Press, 1994.

The Beach Boys by John Tobler. Hamlyn, 1977.

Dennis Wilson: The Real Beach Boy by Jon Stebbins, ECW Press, 1999

Denny Remembered by Ed Wincentsen. Vergin Press, 1991.

Dumb Angel: The Life And Music Of Dennis Wilson by Adam Webb, Creation Books 2001

Heroes & Villains by Steven Gaines. Macmillan, 1986.

Silver Anniversary by John Milward. Doubleday & Company, 1985.

The Wilson Project by Stephen J. McParland. PTB Productions, 1992.

Tape #10 by Stephen J. McParland. PTB Productions, 1992.

Wouldn't it Be Nice by Brian Wilson with Todd Gold. Harper Collins, 1991.

The Nearest Faraway Place: Brian Wilson, The Beach Boys and the Southern California Experience by Timothy White. Henry Holt, 1994.

Musicologies

Add Some Music To Your Day: Analyzing And Enjoying The Music Of The Beach Boys edited by Don Cunningham and Jeff Bleiel, Tiny Ripple Books, 2000.

The Beach Boys, A Biography in Words & Music by Ken Barnes. Sire Chappell, 1976.

Brian Wilson & The Beach Boys: How Deep Is The Ocean by Paul Williams, Omnibus Press, 1997.

Dumb Angel Gazette #1 & #3 by Domenic Priore. Surfin' Colours Productions.

Dumb Angel Gazette #2, Look! Listen! Vibrate! Smile! compiled by Domenic Priore. Surfin' Colours Productions, 1988.

Pet Sounds: The Greatest Album Of The Twentieth Century by Kingsley Abbott, Helter Skelter Publishing, 2001.

The Smile File by Dwight Cavanagh. PTB Productions, 1994.

Southern California Pastoral by Bruce Golden. Borgo Press 1991.

Surf's up! The Beach Boys on Record, 1961-1981 by Brad Elliott. Pierian Press, 1982.

The Rainbow Files: Beach Boys on CD by Rene Hulz and Hans Christian Skotte, Forlaget Juvelen, 1995

The Complete Guide to the Music of the Beach Boys by John Tobler and Andrew Doe. Omnibus Press, 1997.

Selected Fanzines

Beach Boys Fun, P.O. Box 84282, Los Angeles, CA 90073, USA. The Official Beach Boys Fan Club.

Beach Boys Stomp, 22 Avondale Road, Wealdstone, Middlesex, HA3 7RE, England.

Beach Boys Australia, P.O. Box 106, North Strathfield, 2137 NSW, Australia.

Beach Boys Britain, (at present a newsletter only), 22 Tealby Close, Gilmorton, Lutterworth, Leicestershire. LE17 5PT

Endless Summer Quarterly, PO Box 470315 Charlotte, NC28247, USA

Appendix 5

Quote Unquote

During the period of assembling this book, and the frequent discussions with the writers that are represented here, I have collected a small but germane set of quotes which are worthy of sharing. Some are very recent, others are from a few years back. They are dated and attributed wherever possible.

"I don't want to talk about The Beach Boys but I do any way." Brian Wilson 1991

"I FEAR The Beach Boys will not find it easy to keep abreast of Brian Wilson's whims. I KNOW Brian Wilson will not find it easy to keep abreast of his whims. I TRUST people will understand." Derek Taylor, 1967

"I was in Dublin and I heard "Good Vibrations". That struck me like a bolt. It finished my folk career!" Max Eastley, ambient musician, 1997.

"I didn't speak to my uncle again after we fired him, but Brian Wilson, as my co-writer, bears responsibility for making it clear I participated in writing those songs." Mike Love, 1993

"The Love law suit has totally freaked Brian out. He really wants him off his back. It's not Brian's fault that Murry stole the publishing. Murry was a total jerk, that's why they sacked him. Now they've sacked Brian! It's unbelievable." Andy Paley, 1993.

"Brian could be involved if he turned up without any partners. We really don't need him commercially. 'Kokomo' sold millions, but artistically we need him more than ever. We're just the guys who take pictures; Brian is our Renoir." Bruce Johnston, 1993.

"It [*Sweet Insanity*] was pathetic. Eugene Landy's lyrics were full of psychological mumbo jumbo. When Wilson brought the tapes in, I thought it was a joke, but it wasn't. It was awful." Howard Klein, Sire Records executive, 1993.

"Now Landy's out of the picture, Brian is writing good stuff. He's happy. Landy and his people put bleepers on everybody connected with Brian. They were like guard dogs." Andy Paley, 1993.

"If I let The Beach Boys back in the studio they're going to snap up my songs like sharks." Brian Wilson, 1993.

"The *Smile* stuff is okay. It shows how crazy we used to be." Brian Wilson, 1993.

"The real greatness of Brian is that he's so spontaneous. All of his best songs, all his greatest moments, have been extremely spontaneous. True creative genius is spontaneous. Rarely does a real genius sit down and plot what he is going to do. It doesn't work that way! Brian wants to be accepted for what he is doing NOW, not for what he DID! Brian never made records for money. He never made records to beat Phil Spector or any other producer for that matter. Brian made records because it was all he could do; all he ever wanted to do. It was straight from his heart and he loved doing it. On the other hand, Mike Love's approach was just the opposite. Mike's very calculated, yet neither one is better or worse or good or bad. They are just two different approaches. However, the altruistic or from the heart approach will allways last the longest." Gary Usher, 1987.

"Music is one of the mediums in the world where you can absolutely involve your-self, emotionally, spiritually and physically. So what I do is get involved." Dennis Wilson, 1977.

"I feel through art...it can be a great deal of help, like Brian in the sixties with what he did and what he can do. I wish he would get off his ass and do it again." Dennis Wilson, 1977.

"When my record [*Pacific Ocean Blue*] was finished, Brian was the first to hear it. In the middle of some tracks he'd say, 'I can't stand this' and walk out of the room. Sometimes he'd laugh. Sometimes he'd cry. I guess he was thinking that he'd seen me grow up as a musician." Dennis Wilson 1977.

"Brian isn't the only genius in the group." Carol Rose, *Rock Magazine* editor, 1977.

"In my opinion, it [*Smile*] makes *Pet Sounds* stink, that's how good it is." Dennis Wilson, 1966.

"There were times when he [Dennis] could only do the logical thing, and that was to beat up Mike Love right on stage! A lot of people would like to have seen this happen; Dennis, in his integrity, made it happen!" Domenic Priore, 1991.

"It's hard to be hip. Sometimes it just hurts your head." Brian Wilson to Bill Holdship, early 90s.

"The thing that you have to understand about Dennis is that Dennis doesn't under-stand." Mike Love, 1968.

"The Beach Boys' show puts itself on. All we have to do is show up. We can do a real turkey of a set and people will come back and say, 'That's the greatest show I've ever seen.'" Carl Wilson, 1981.

"Half of him was a little boy, and the other half was insane." Christine McVie on Dennis Wilson, 80s.

"It was *Pet Sounds* that blew me out of the water. First of all, it was Brian's writing. I love the album so much, I've just bought my kids each a copy of it for their education in life – I figure no one is educated musically 'til they've heard that album". Paul McCartney.

"Their vocal harmonies are unsurpassed...I think Brian was a French horn, Carl was a flute, Al Jardine a trumpet, Dennis a trombone, and Mike Love a baritone sax, before their present incarnation as the Beach Boys." Eric Carmen, 70s.

"Terry Melcher played tambourine on "Here Today". I was playing him the instrumental track from the new box set and he was very rude about the shoddy playing of the tambourine on the track. He asked me "Who is that?" I said "It was you!" Bruce Johnston, 1997

"In the vaults there exists an 8 Track finished master by Charlie Manson that features Carl and Dennis and was produced by them". Bill Scanlon-Murphy, 1997.

"Next year there will be a travelling theatre show called 'Good Vibrations' featuring new arrangements of classic Beach Boys songs as part of a full stage play." Chris White, 1997

"Ha! Ha!" [Loudly]. Brian Wilson, various dates.